Prague

Ph. Gajic/MICHELIN

"Prague is a famous, ancient, kingly seat.
In situation and in state complete,
Rich in abundance of the earth's best treasure,
Proud and high-minded beyond bounds or measure,
In architecture, stately......

From *Taylor's Travels from London to Prague*
(John Taylor ?1578-1653)

Travel Publications

38 Clarendon Road - WATFORD Herts WD SX - U.K.
Tel. (01923) 415 000
www.michelin-travel.com
TheGreenGuide-uk@uk.michelin.com

Manufacture française des pneumatiques Michelin

Société en commandite par actions au capital de 2 000 000 000 de francs
Place des Carmes-Déchaux – 63 Clermont-Ferrand (France)
R.C.S. Clermont-Fd B 855 200 507

© *Michelin et Cie, Propriétaires-Éditeurs 2000*
Dépôt légal mai 2000 – ISBN 2-06-156530-1 – ISSN 0763-1383

No part of this publication may be reproduced in any form
without the prior permission of the publisher.

Printed in the EU 05-00/1/1

Compogravure : Agence LE SANGLIER, Charleville-Mézières
Impression : KAPP-JOMBART-LAHURE, Évreux
Brochure : DIGUET DENY, Breteuil-sur-Iton

Maquette de couverture extérieure : Agence Carré Noir à Paris 17e

THE GREEN GUIDE:
The Spirit of Discovery

The exhilaration of new horizons, the fun of seeing the world, the excitement of discovery: this is what we seek to share with you. To help you make the most of your travel experience, we offer first-hand knowledge and turn a discerning eye on places to visit.

This wealth of information gives you the expertise to plan your own enriching adventure. With THE GREEN GUIDE showing you the way, you can explore new destinations with confidence or rediscover old ones.

Leisure time spent with THE GREEN GUIDE is also a time for refreshing your spirit, enjoying yourself, and taking advantage of our selection of fine restaurants, hotels and other places for relaxing.

So turn the page and open a window on the world. Join THE GREEN GUIDE in the spirit of discovery.

Contents

Maps and plans
Using this guide
Key

Practical information   1

International visitors
Getting around Prague
Basic information
Calendar of Events

Useful addresses   2

Accommodation
Eating out
Cafés and bars
Out and about in Prague:
theatres, music
Shopping

Introduction to Prague   4

The setting
Growth of the city
The look of Prague
Prague, capital
of the Czech Republic
History
Bohemians: Gypsies and Germans
Elements of Architecture
Art and architecture
Intellectual Life
Musical Prague
Cinema
Walks in Prague
Recommended reading   1

Statue on the Svatopluk Čech Bridge

Ph. Gajic/MICHELIN

Ancient doorway

4

xploring Prague 103

ιežský klášter 104 – Belveder 106 – ertramka 107 – Betlémské náměstí 107 Bílkova vila 109 – Břevnovský klášter)9 – Celetná ulice 111 – Muzeum ntonína Dvořáka 112 – Museum ιvního města Prahy 113 – Hradčanské ιměstí 114 – Hradčany 116 – Jiřský ιšter 117 – Josefov 121 – Karlova ce 127 – Karlovo náměstí 130 – ιrlův most 132 – Klementinum 136 – álovská zahrada 137 – Křížovnické ιměstí 138 – Letecké muzeum 139 – ιná 140 – Letohrádek Hvězda 141 – reta 143 – Malá Strana 146 – ιchovo muzeum 157 – Na Příkopě 38 – Národní divadlo 159 – Národní ιzeum 160 – Národní technické ιzeum 161 – Národní třída 163– ιvé město 166 – Nový svět 167 – ιecní dům 168 – Olšanské hřbitovy 'O – Petřín 171 – Muzeum Policie R 173 – Pražský hrad 174 – Rudolfi- m 183 – Muzeum Bedřicha Smetany 34 – Staré město 185 – Staroměstské městí 186 – Státní opera 192 – ιvovské divadlo 192 – Šternberský ιác 193 – Strahovský klášter 195 – . Mikuláše 198 – Sv.Víta 200 – ιja 205 – Uměleckoprůmyslové ιzeum 206 – Ungelt 207 – Václavské městí 209– Valdštejnský palác 212 Veletržní palác 214 – Vinohrady 217 The Vltava 218 – Vyšehrad 220 – ιstaviště 222 – Žižkov 224

Day excursions 227

Brno	231
České Budějovice	234
Český Krumlov	236
Český Šternberk	238
Cheb	242
Františkovy Lázně	239
Hluboká nad Vltavou	240
Hradec Králové	241
Karlovy Vary	244
Hrad Karlštejn	246
Zámek Konopiště	247
Křivoklát	249
Kutná Hora	249
Lednicko-valtický areál	251
Lidice	253
Mariánské Lázně	254
Mělník	256
Nelahozeves	256
Orlík	258
Plzeň	258
Průhonice	260
Slavkov u Brna	260
Tábor	263
Telč	264
Terezín	265
Třeboň	266
Veltrusy	267
Zbraslav	268
Žvíkov	269
Admission times and charges	270
Glossary	279
Index	282

Dials of the Astronomical Clock

Baroque house sign

Maps

MICHELIN MAPS
TO USE WITH THIS GUIDE

Map no.976 Czech Republic ar
Slovak Republic

– a 1:600 000 scale road map w
place name index and a large-sco
plan of the built-up area of Prague.

Map no.987 Germany, Benelu
Austria and Czech Republic

– a 1:1 000 000 scale road me
showing the approaches to Prag
from western Europe.

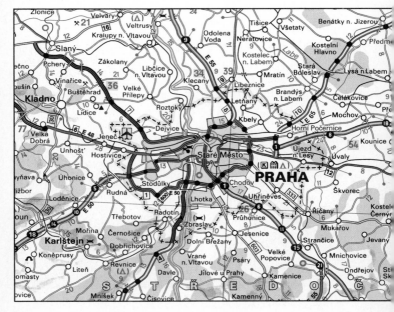

INDEX OF MAPS AND PLANS

...ague – Built-up area	10
...entral Prague – Principal sights	12
...alks in Prague	98
...ay excursions from Prague	228
...olution of Prague	228
...om Czechoslovakia	
...the Czech Republic	228
...rlova ulice	128
...sefov	122
...alá Strana	150
...ažský hrad	150
...aroměstské náměsti	186
...Mikuláše	150
...Víta	150
...clavské náměsti	210
...no	150
...rlovy Vary	150

Plans of buildings

Prague Castle	176
Cathedral of St Vitus	202

Historical maps

Development of Prague	49
Czechoslovakia since 1918	61
The Battle of Austerlitz	262

Town plans

Brno	232
Karlovy Vary	245

Wysocki/EXPLORER

Wenceslas Square

Using this guide

Your Green Guide is a mine of information. It includes:

● **Maps and plans**: At the beginning of the guide there are maps and plans which will help you plan your trip. They include a map of the **built-up area of Prague** showing the city in its context, a map of **Principal sights** highlighting the main attractions of the historic core, a plan of **Walks in Prague**, and a map of **Day Excursions**. In the Introduction there are thematic maps illustrating the city's history and, in the main text, detailed plans of some of Prague's historic districts as well as town plans of Brno and Karlovy Vary.

● **Practical Information**: An array of information about getting to Prague, moving around the city and its surroundings, and using services of all kinds. There is also a list of **festivals** and **public holidays**, a **Czech-English glossary** of everyday words and expressions, as well as a list of **recommended reading** which will enhance your appreciation of this unique city.

● **Useful addresses**: A carefully selected list of places to stay, eat and drink, be entertained, and shop.

● **Introduction**: An in-depth look at Prague, its history, growth and appearance, as well as chapters on art and architecture, intellectual life, film and music.

● **Sights**: The main sights of Prague are described in alphabetical order, using their Czech names, followed by a selection of places which can be reached from the city in the course of a day trip. Further attractions located close to a main sight are described under that heading, giving a comprehensive picture of the city and of some of the many possible excursions from it.

● **Admission times and charges**: The fullest possible details of opening times and charges of the attractions described in the guide (indicated by a clock symbol ⊘ in the text).

● **Index**: To help locate descriptions of places and people.

Your opinion is of interest to us. We greatly appreciate comments and suggestions from our readers. Write to us at the address shown on the inside front cover or at our website: www.michelin-travel.com

Štastnou cestu! (Have a good trip!).

Key

★★★ **Highly recommended**

★★ **Recommended**

★ **Interesting**

Tourism

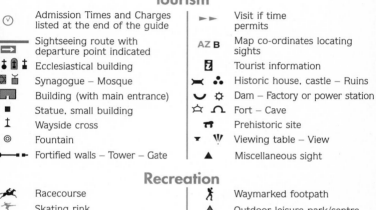

⊘	Admission Times and Charges listed at the end of the guide	►►	Visit if time permits
	Sightseeing route with departure point indicated	AZ B	Map co-ordinates locating sights
	Ecclesiastical building	🖪	Tourist information
	Synagogue – Mosque	⊨ ∴	Historic house, castle – Ruins
	Building (with main entrance)	∪ ☆	Dam – Factory or power station
■	Statue, small building	☆ ∩	Fort – Cave
⊥	Wayside cross	⊓	Prehistoric site
◎	Fountain	▾ ᴡ	Viewing table – View
	Fortified walls – Tower – Gate	▲	Miscellaneous sight

Recreation

	Racecourse	🏃	Waymarked footpath
	Skating rink	◆	Outdoor leisure park/centre
	Outdoor, indoor swimming pool		Theme/Amusement park
ⅅ	Marina, moorings	ᴪ	Wildlife/Safari park, zoo
⊜	Mountain refuge hut	⊛	Gardens, park, arboretum
	Overhead cable-car	⊜	Aviary, bird sanctuary
	Tourist or steam railway		

Additional symbols

	Motorway (unclassified)	⊗ ⊙	Post office – Telephone centre
❶ ❶	Junction: complete, limited	⊠	Covered market
	Pedestrian street	⋅×⋅	Barracks
	Unsuitable for traffic, street subject to restrictions	△	Swing bridge
	Steps – Footpath	∪ ×	Quarry – Mine
	Railway – Coach station	🅱 🅵	Ferry (river and lake crossings)
	Funicular – Rack-railway		Ferry services: Passengers and cars
	Tram – Metro, Underground	⇌	Foot passengers only
ert (R.)…	Main shopping street	③	Access route number common to MICHELIN maps and town plans

Abbreviations and special symbols

H	Town hall (Radnice)	**T**	Theatre (Divadlo)
J	Law courts (Justiční palác)	**U**	University (Universita)
		12	Tramway
M	Museum (Muzeum)		
POL.	Police station (Policie)	🅿	Park and Ride (Záchytná parkoviště)

9

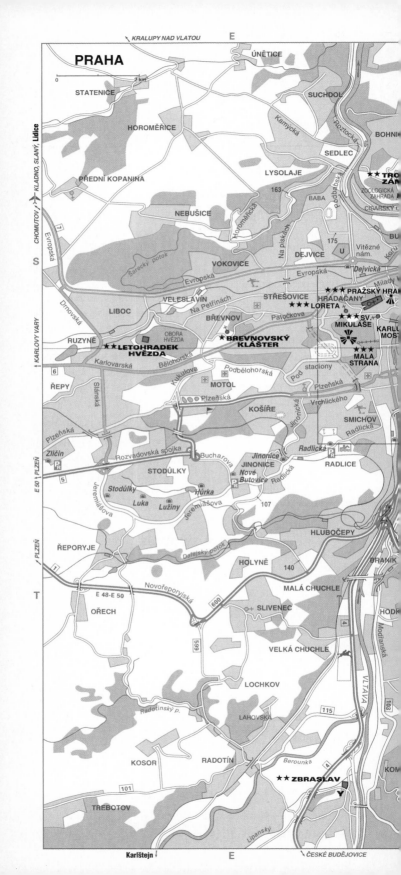

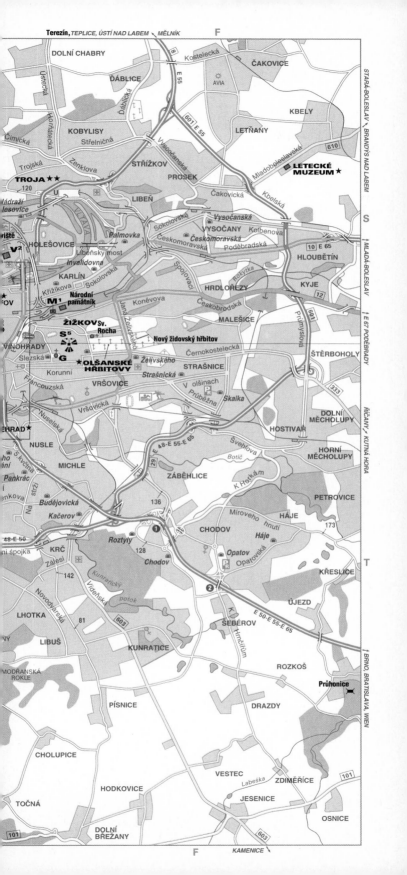

STREET INDEX FOR MAP OF PRAGUE

Street	Page	Grid	No.
Albertov	p.13	CZ	
Anglická	p.13	DY	
Apolinářská	p.13	CDZ	
Arbesovo náměstí	p.12	BY	3
Atletická	p.12	AY	
Badeniho	p.12	BV	
Bartolomějská	p.12	CXY	4
Bělehradská	p.12	DYZ	5
Benátská	p.13	CZ	
Betlémské náměstí	p.13	CX	8
Bieblova	p.12	BZ	
Bílkova	p.13	CX	
Bělohorská	p.10	ET	
Boleslavova	p.13	DZ	
Botič	p.13	CZ	
Bubenečská	p.12	BV	
Bucharova	p.10	ET	
Celetná	p.13	CDX	
Cihelná	p.12	BX	10
Cukrovarnická	p.12	AV	
Čakovická	p.11	FS	
Černínská	p.12	AX	21
Černokostelecká	p.11	FT	
Českobrodská	p.11	FS	
Českomoravská	p.11	FS	
Čiklova	p.13	DZ	
Čimická	p.11	FS	
Dáblická	p.11	FS	
Dejvická	p.12	BV	
Dělostřelecká	p.12	AV	
Dlážděná	p.13	DX	15
Dlabačov	p.12	AX	
Dlouhá	p.13	CX	
Dražického náměstí	p.12	BX	18
Drnovská	p.10	ES	
Drtinova	p.12	BY	
Duškova	p.12	AZ	
Dvořákovo nábřeží	p.13	CX	20
Evropská	p.10	ES	
Francouzská	p.13	DX	22
Francouzská	p.11	FT	
Generála Píky	p.12	AV	
Haštalské náměstí	p.13	CX	27
Havířská	p.13	CX	29
Havlíčkova	p.13	DX	31
Heřmanova	p.12	DV	34
Holečkova	p.12	ABYZ	
Hořejší nábřeží	p.12	BZ	
Horňátecká	p.11	FS	
Horoměřická	p.10	ES	
Horská	p.13	CZ	
Hradčanské náměstí	p.12	AX	37
Hrnčířům	p.11	FT	
Husitská	p.13	DX	38
Husova	p.13	CX	40
Hybernská	p.13	DX	
Italská	p.13	DY	
Chotkova	p.12	BV	43
Jana Želivského	p.11	FST	
Jana Masaryka	p.13	DZ	
Janáčkovo nábřeží	p.12	BY	
Jaromírova	p.13	DZ	
Ječná	p.13	CDY	
Jelení	p.12	AV	
Jeremenkova	p.11	FT	
Jeremiášova	p.10	ET	
Jižní spojka	p.11	FT	
Jindřišská	p.13	DX	46
Jinonická	p.10	ET	
Jiráskovo náměstí	p.13	CY	47
Jugoslávská	p.13	DY	49
Jugoslávských partyzánů	p.12	AV	50
Jungmannova	p.13	CY	
Jungmannovo náměstí	p.13	CX	51
K Horkám	p.11	FT	
K vodojemu	p.12	AZ	
Kamenická	p.12	DV	
Kamýcká	p.10	ES	
Kanovnická	p.12	AX	53
Kaprova	p.13	CX	55
Karlovarská	p.10	ET	
Karlovo náměstí	p.13	CY	
Karmelitská	p.12	BX	
Kartouzská	p.12	BY	
Kateřinská	p.13	CDY	58
Kbelská	p.11	FS	
Ke Štvanici	p.13	DX	61
Ke Karlovu	p.13	DYZ	
Keplerova	p.12	AX	
Klárov	p.12	BX	63
Klimentská	p.13	DX	66
Košarkovo nábřeží	p.13	CX	
Kolbenova	p.11	FS	
Koněvova	p.11	FS	
Korunní	p.13	DY	69
Korunní	p.11	FT	
Korunovační	p.11	ES	
Kostelecká	p.11	FS	
Kostelní	p.13	DV	
Koubkova	p.13	DZ	
Kováků	p.12	BZ	
Kozí	p.13	CX	
Krokova	p.13	CDZ	
Křesomyslova	p.13	DZ	
Křižíkova	p.11	FS	
Křižovnická	p.13	CX	
Křižovnické náměstí	p.13	CX	
Křížová	p.12	BZ	
Kukulova	p.10	ET	
Lazarská	p.13	CY	
Legerova	p.13	DYZ	
Letenská	p.12	BX	
Letenský tunel	p.13	CV	
Libušina	p.13	CZ	
Libušská	p.11	FT	
Lidická	p.12	BZ	
Lipová	p.13	CY	
Loretánská	p.12	AX	
Loretánské náměstí	p.12	AX	
Lublaňská	p.13	DZ	
Malé náměstí	p.13	CX	
Malostranské náměstí	p.12	BX	
Maltézské náměstí	p.12	BX	
Mariánské hradby	p.12	BV	
Mariánské náměstí	p.13	CX	
Masarykovo nábřeží	p.13	CY	
Matoušova	p.12	BY	
Mezibranská	p.13	DY	
Míšeňská	p.12	BX	
Milady Horákové	p.12	ABCV	
Mírového hnutí	p.11	FT	
Mladoboleslavská	p.11	FS	
Mošnova	p.12	AY	
Modřanská	p.10	ET	
Mostecká	p.12	BX	
Mozartova	p.12	ABZ	
Myslbekov	p.12	AX	
Myslíkova	p.13	CY	
Na Bělidle	p.12	BZ	
Na Březince	p.12	ABZ	
Na Florenci	p.13	DX	
Na Františku	p.13	CX	
Na Hřebenkách	p.12	AY	
Na Kampě	p.12	BX	
Na Moráni	p.13	CY	
Na Neklance	p.12	BZ	
Na Pankráci	p.13	DZ	
Na Perštýně	p.13	CY	1
Na pískách	p.10	ES	
Na Pláni	p.12	AZ	
Na Příkopě	p.13	CDX	
Na Poříčí	p.13	DX	
Na Popelce	p.12	AZ	
Na strži	p.11	FT	
Na Supli	p.13	CZ	
Na Václavce	p.12	AZ	
Na valech	p.12	BV	
Na Věnečku	p.12	AZ	
Na Zatlance	p.12	BZ	
nábřeží Edvarda Beneše	p.13	CV	
nábřeží Kpt. Jaroše	p.13	DV	
nábřeží Ludvíka Svobody	p.13	DV	
Nad štolou	p.13	CV	1
Nad Santoškou	p.12	ABZ	
Nádraží	p.12	BZ	
náměstí 4. října	p.13	BY	1
náměstí Jana Palacha	p.13	CX	1
náměstí Kinských	p.12	BY	
náměstí Maxima Gorkého	p.13	DX	1
náměstí Republiky	p.13	CX	1
Náprstkova	p.13	CX	1
Národní	p.13	CY	
Nekázanka	p.13	DX	1
Neklanova	p.13	CZ	
Nerudova	p.12	BX	
Novodvorská	p.11	FT	
Novořeporyjská	p.10	ET	
Novoveská	p.10	ET	1
Nový Svět	p.12	AX	
Nuselská	p.11	FT	
Nuselský most	p.13	DZ	
Oldřichova	p.13	DZ	
Opletalova	p.13	DXY	
Ostrovní	p.13	CY	
Ostrovského	p.12	ABZ	
Ovocný trh	p.13	CX	1
Panská	p.13	DX	
Pařížská	p.13	CX	
Parléřova	p.12	AX	
Patočkova	p.12	AX	
Patočkova	p.10	ES	
Perlová	p.13	CX	1
Peroutkova	p.12	AZ	
Petřínská	p.12	BY	
Petrská	p.13	DX	1
Pevnostní	p.12	AV	
Platnéřská	p.13	CX	1
Plavecká	p.13	CZ	
Plzeňská	p.12	ABZ	
Pod hradbami	p.12	AV	
Pod kesnerkou	p.12	BZ	
Pod Stadiony	p.12	AY	
Pod Stadiony	p.10	ET	
Podbabská	p.10	ES	

dbělohorská	p.10	ET	
děbradská	p.11	FS	
dolské nábřeží	p.13	CZ	
hořelec	p.12	AX	
má	p.12	AZ	
litických věznů	p.13	DY	119
vltavská	p.12	FS	120
okopská	p.12	BX	122
běžná	p.11	FT	
myslová	p.11	FST	
šínovo nábřeží	p.13	CYZ	124
dlická	p.12	ABZ	
sslova	p.13	CY	126
voluční	p.13	DX	
stocká	p.11	ES	
zvadovská spojka	p.10	ET	
munská	p.13	DY	
žová	p.13	DX	
šavého	p.11	FT	128
bná	p.13	DX	
tířská	p.13	CX	
snovka	p.13	DX	129
ntoška	p.12	BZ	
ifertova	p.13	DX	131
kaninova	p.13	DZ	
anská	p.10	ET	
avojova	p.13	CDZ	
zská	p.13	DY	133
inná	p.12	AV	
netanovo nábřeží	p.13	CXY	
ěmovní	p.12	BX	134
kolovská	p.11	FS	
kolská	p.13	DYZ	135
ukenická	p.13	DX	
álená	p.13	CY	
ojovací	p.11	FS	
ořilovská	p.11	FT	136
ahovská	p.12	AX	
akonická	p.12	BZ	
řešovická	p.12	AX	141
elničná	p.11	FS	
udničkova	p.13	CZ	
atovítská	p.12	AV	
obodova	p.13	CZ	
ornosti	p.12	BZ	
rmířská	p.12	AY	
nidkeho	p.11	FT	
anělská	p.13	DY	
aroměstské náměstí	p.13	CX	
efánikova	p.12	BY	
špánská	p.13	DY	138
epařská	p.10	ET	140
urova	p.11	FT	142
édská	p.12	AY	
ehlova	p.11	FT	
oorská	p.13	DZ	
šnov	p.13	DX	143
šnovský tunel	p.13	DV	
máššká	p.12	BX	146
tiště	p.12	BX	147
ojícká	p.13	CZ	
Trojská	p.11	FS	
Truhlářská	p.13	DX	
Turistická	p.12	AY	148
Tynská	p.13	CX	149
U Šalamounky	p.12	AZ	
U Blaženky	p.12	AZ	
U Bruských Kasáren	p.12	BX	150
U Brusnice	p.12	AVX	
U Kasáren	p.12	AX	152
U lužického semináře	p.12	BX	154
U Malvazinky	p.12	AZ	
U Mrázovky	p.12	AZ	
U nemocnice	p.13	CY	
U Nikolajky	p.12	AZ	
U Prašného mostu	p.12	BX	
U Santošky	p.12	BZ	
Uhelný trh	p.13	CX	156
Újezd	p.12	BXY	
Ústecká	p.11	FS	
Úvoz	p.12	AX	
V botanice	p.12	BY	158
V celnici	P.13	DX	161
V Olšinach	p.11	FT	
V Sáreckém údolí	p.10	ES	163
Václavkova	p.12	AV	165
Václavské náměstí	p.13	CDY	
Valdštejnská	p.12	BX	168
Valdštejnské náměstí	p.12	BX	169
Vaničkova	p.12	AY	
Ve Smečkách	p.13	DY	
Veletržní	p.11	FS	
Velkopřevorské náměstí	p.12	BX	170
Vídeňská	p.11	FT	
Vinohradská	p.13	DY	
Vltavská	p.12	BZ	
Vítězná	p.12	BY	
Vítězné náměstí	p.10	ES	
Vlašská	p.12	BX	
Vnislavova	p.13	CZ	171
Vodičkova	p.13	CY	
Vršovická	p.11	FT	
Vratislavova	p.13	CZ	
Vrchlického	p.12	AZ	
Vyšehradská	p.13	CZ	
Vysočanská	p.11	FS	
Výstavní	p.11	FT	173
Wilsonova	p.13	DXY	
Xaveriova	p.12	AZ	
Záhřebská	p.13	DZ	
Zálesi	p.11	FT	
Zapova	p.12	AY	
Zborovská	p.12	BY	174
Zelená	p.10	ES	175
Zenklova	p.11	FS	
Zlatnická	p.13	DX	176
Železná	p.13	CX	178
Žitná	p.13	CY	
5. května	p.13	DZ	
17.listopadu	p.13	CX	180
28.řjna	p.13	CX	

SIGHTS ON MAP OF PRAGUE

(M)=see Museums   (T)=see Theatres

Anežský klášter	p.13	CX
Arcibiskupský palác	p.12	AX A
Armádní muzeum (M)		
Bertramka (Mozart Museum) (M)		
Betlémská kaple	p.13	CX B
Bílkova vila	p.12	BV
Bludiště	p.12	AX
Břevnovský klášter	p.10	ES
Cihelná brána	p.13	CZ
Clam-Gallasovský palác	p.13	CX C
Čechův most	p.13	CV
Černínský palác	p.12	AX
Dětský ostrov	p.12	BY
Divadlo na Vinohradech (T)		
Dům Diamant	p.13	CY D
Dům U černé Matky boží	p.13	CX E
Muzeum Antonína Dvořáka		
(Vila Amerika) (M)		
Faustův dům	p.13	CY
Františkánská zahrada	p.13	CY
Hanavský pavilón	p.13	CV
Hlávkův most	p.13	DV
Hotel Evropa	p.13	DY F
Hotel Meran	p.13	DY F
Hradčany	p.12	AX
Chotkovy sady	p.12	BV
Chrám Nejsvětějšího Srdce Páně	p.11	FS G
Jižní zahrady	p.12	BX K¹
Jiřský klášter	p.12	BV
Jiráskův most	p.13	CY
Josefov	p.12	CX
Jubilejní synagoga	p.13	DX
Kampa	p.12	BY
Karlova	p.13	CX
Karlovo náměstí	p.13	CY
Karlův most	p.12	BCX
Karolinum	p.13	CX
Klementinum	p.13	CX
Kongresové centrum	p.13	DZ
Královská Jízdárna	p.12	BX
Královská zahrada	p.12	BX
Královský letohrádek	p.12	BV
Lanová dráha	p.12	BY
Legio Banka	p.13	DX
Leopoldova brána	p.13	CZ
Letecké muzeum (M)		
Letenský zámeček	p.13	DV
Letná	p.13	CV
Letohrádek Hvězda	p.10	ES
Loreta	p.12	AX
Malá Strana	p.12	ABX
Mánesův most	p.13	CX
Martinický palác	p.12	AX K²
Matky Boží před Týnem	p.13	CX L¹
Míčovna	p.12	BX
Městská knihovna	p.13	CX L³
Palác Goltz-Kinských	p.13	CX P¹
Palác Lucerna	p.13	CDY P²
Palác Michnů	p.12	BX P³
Palackého most	p.13	CY
Panny Marie a Sv Karla Velikého	p.13	DZ
Panny Marie pod řetězem	p.12	BX P⁴
Panny Marie Sněžné	p.13	CY Q¹
Panny Marie ustavičné	p.12	BX Q²
Panny Marie Vítězné	p.12	BX
Pařížská třída	p.13	CX
Petřín	p.12	BX
Poštovní muzeum (M)		
Pomník Jana Husa	p.13	CX Q³
Prašná brána	p.13	DX
Pražský hrad	p.12	BX
Praha-Expo 58	p.13	DV
Riegrovy sady	p.13	DY
Rotunda Sv. Martina	p.13	CZ
Rozhledna	p.12	BX
Rudolfinum	p.13	CX
Schönbornský palác	p.12	BX Q⁴
Schwarzenberský palác	p.12	AX R¹
Slovanský ostrov	p.13	CY
Staré Město	p.13	CX
Staroměstská radnice	p.13	CX R²
Staroměstské náměstí	p.13	CX
Staronová synagoga	p.13	CX
Starý židovský hřbitov	p.13	CX R³
Starý královský palác	p.12	BX
Státní opera	p.13	DY
Stavovské divadlo (T)		
Strahovský klášter	p.12	AX
Sv. Bartoloměje	p.13	CX
Sv. Cyrila a Metoděje	p.13	CY
Sv. Františka	p.13	CX R⁴
Sv. Havla	p.13	CX S¹
Sv. Ignace	p.13	CY
Sv. Jakuba	p.13	CY
Sv. Jana	p.12	BY
Sv. Jana na skalce	p.13	CZ
Sv. Jana Nepomuckého	p.12	AX S²
Sv. Jiljí	p.13	CX S³
Sv. Josefa	p.12	BX
Sv. Josefa	p.13	DX
Sv. Klimenta	p.13	DX
Sv. Kříž	p.13	DX
Sv. Ludmily	p.13	DY
Sv. Michala	p.12	BY
Sv. Mikuláše	p.13	CX
Sv. Mikuláše	p.12	BX
Sv. Petra a Pavla	p.13	CZ
Sv. Rocha	p.11	FS
Sv. Tomáše	p.12	BX
Sv. Václava	p.13	DY
Sv. Vavřince	p.12	AX
Sv. Víta	p.12	BX
Sv. Voršily	p.13	CY S⁴
Štefánikova hvězdárna	p.12	BY
Šternberský palác	p.12	AX
Švermův most	p.13	DV
Táborská brána	p.13	CZ
Televizní vysílač	p.11	FS S⁵

Museums

Armádní muzeum	p.11	FS M¹
Bertramka (Mozart Museum)	p.12	AZ
Letecké muzeum	p.11	FS
Muzeum Antonína		
Dvořáka (Vila Amerika)	p.13	DY
Muzeum Bedřicha Smetany	p.13	CX M²
Muzeum hlavního města Prahy	p.13	DX M³
Muzeum Policie	p.13	DZ
Náprstkovo muzeum	p.13	CX M⁴
Národní muzeum	p.13	DY
Národní technické muzeum	p.13	CV
Poštovní muzeum	p.13	DV M⁵
Uměleckoprůmyslové muzeum	p.13	CX M⁶

Náprstkovo muzeum (M)		
Národní divadlo (T)		
Národní muzeum (M)		
Národní památník	p.11	FS
Národní technické muzeum (M)		
Nostický palác	p.12	BX N¹
Nová radnice	p.13	CV H
Nové Město	p.13	CY
Novoměstská radnice	p.13	CY
Nový židovský hřbitov	p.11	FS
Obecní dům	p.13	DX N²
Olšanské hřbitovy	p.11	FS
Ostrov Štvanice	p.13	DV
Palác Adria	p.13	CY N³

Theatres

Divadlo na Vinohradech	p.13	DY T¹
Národní divadlo	p.13	CY T²
Stavovské divadlo	p.13	CX T³

Toskánský palác	p.12	AX V¹
Trója	p.11	FS
Trojský zámek	p.10	ES
Týnský dvůr	p.13	CX
Uměleckoprůmyslové muzeum (M)		
Václavské náměstí	p.13	CDY
Valdštejnský palác	p.12	BX
Veletržní palác	p.11	FS V²
Vila Kinských	p.12	BY
Vinohrady	p.13	DY
Vojanovy sady	p.12	BX
Vrtbovská zahrada	p.12	BX
Vyšehrad	p.13	CZ
Vyšehradský hřbitov	p.13	CZ
Výstaviště	p.11	FS
Výtoň	p.13	CZ
Zbraslav	p.13	ET
Zpívající fontána	p.12	BV Z¹
Žižkov	p.11	FS
Živnostenská banka	p.13	DX Z²

World
Heritage List

In 1972, The United Nations Educational, Scientific and Cultural Organization (UNESCO) adopted a Convention for the preservation of cultural and natural sites. To date, more than 150 States Parties have signed this international agreement, which has listed over 500 sites "of outstanding universal value" on the World Heritage List. Each year, a committee of representatives from 21 countries, assisted by technical organizations (ICOMOS - International Council on Monuments and Sites; IUCN - International Union for Conservation of Nature and Natural Resources; ICCROM - International Centre for the Study of the Preservation and Restoration of Cultural Property, the Rome Centre), evaluates the proposals for new sites to be included on the list, which grows longer as new nominations are accepted and more countries sign the Convention. To be considered, a site must be nominated by the country in which it is located.

The protected **cultural heritage** sites may be monuments (buildings, sculptures, archeological structures etc) with unique historical, artistic or scientific features; groups of buildings (such as religious communities, ancient cities); or sites (human settlements, examples of exceptional landscapes, cultural landscapes) which are the combined works of man and nature of exceptional beauty. **Natural heritage** sites may be a testimony to the stages of the earth's geological history or to the development of human cultures and creative genius or represent significant ongoing ecological processes, contain superlative natural phenomena or provide a habitat for threatened species.

Signatories of the Convention pledge to cooperate to preserve and protect these sites around the world as a common heritage to be shared by all humanity, and contribute to the **World Heritage Fund.** The Fund serves to carry out studies, plan conservation measures, train local specialists, supply equipment for the protection of a park or the restoration of a monument etc.

Some of the most well-known places which the World Heritage Committee has inscribed include: Australia's Great Barrier Reef (1981), the Canadian Rocky Mountain Parks (1984), The Great Wall of China (1987), the Statue of Liberty (1984), the Kremlin (1990), Mont-Saint-Michel and its Bay (France - 1979), Durham Castle and Cathedral (1986).

**In the Czech Republic,
UNESCO World Heritage Sites include:**

Český Krumlov;

Kutná Hora;

Lednicko-valtický areál;

Poutní kostel sv. Jana Nepomuckého;

na Zelené hoře;

Praha;

Telč.

Baroque house sign

Practical
information

Ph. Gajic/MICHELIN

International visitors

Planning a trip

Seasons – This part of Central Europe has a partly continental, partly oceanic climat[e] and weather patterns are rather unpredictable. Winters tend to be cold, summe[rs] warm and sometimes wet with thundery outbreaks. Because of its location in a basi[n] Prague tends to suffer temperature inversions which trap polluted air and prevent i[ts] dispersal. In the past the main culprit was the smoke emitted by countless heatin[g] plants fuelled by soft brown coal. Many of these have now been replaced by muc[h] cleaner gas heating systems, but the beneficial effect has been cancelled out by th[e] increase in emissions from cars and other vehicles.

The best time to come is in spring and early summer when days are longer but n[ot] yet oppressively hot. Likewise, autumn too can be a good time to visit. Prague [is] crowded, frequently overcrowded, with visitors at most times of the year, but esp[e]cially so in summer. Despite the cold and the short days, a winter break in the ci[ty] can be enjoyable, especially if any snowfall has not yet acquired a sooty covering. Mo[st] attractions remain open and there are fewer tourists.

Outside the capital, the climate is generally similar, though the air is likely to b[e] fresher. In summer, Southern Moravia normally has a distinctly warmer feel tha[n] Prague, while the uplands which define the country's borders are cooler and wette[r.] Provincial attractions like castles and museums tend to close in autumn and not reope[n] until Easter or after.

Documents – For citizens of most European countries, the USA and Canada, a fu[ll] passport valid for at least three months from the date of entry is all that is require[d] to visit the Czech Republic. Nationals of other countries should confirm with Czec[h] embassies or consulates, Czech Centres or [C]SA airline offices whether a visa is require[d] and whether it should be obtained in advance or at a border crossing.

Tourist Information – The Czech Tourist Authority has a number of offices in foreig[n] countries:

United Kingdom – Czech Tourist Authority, Czech Centre, 95 Great Portland Stree[t,] London W1N 5RA. ☎ 0171 291 99 20

United States – Czech Tourist Authority, 1109-1111 Madison Avenue, New Yor[k,] NY 10028. ☎ 212 288 0830

Canada – Czech Tourist Authority, PO Box 198, Exchange Tower, 2 First Canadia[n] Place, Toronto, Ontario M5X 1A6.

Japan – Czech Tourist Authority, Yoshino Bldg, 301, 3-9-17, Kita Aoyama, Minato-k[u,] Tokyo 107. ☎ 3 3409 74 14.

Czech and Slovak Tourist Centre – An independent tour operator with specialist knowledge. 1[6] Frognal Parade, Finchley Road, London NW3 5HG, ☎ 0171 794 3263/3264 [or] 0800 026 7943; website: www.czech-slovak-tourist.co.uk;email: cztc@ctzc.demon.co.u[k]

Currency and Customs – There is no limit on the import and export of foreign cu[r]rency. The Czech crown (Kč) is freely convertible, though the import and export [of] very large amounts should be declared. Most items intended for your personal us[e] during your stay are not subject to duty, but maximum limits apply to the followin[g:]

Tobacco: 200 cigarettes or tobacco equivalent
Alcohol: spirits 1 litre; wine 2 litres
Perfume: 50g

There are no limits on the export of goods, except for antiques and works of art cla[s]sified as items of national heritage. Customs offices will advise.

Travelling to the Czech Republic

By air – Prague's modernised airport is at Ruzyně some 20km west of the city centr[e.] Served by many international airlines, it has direct daily flights to London (BA, Czec[h] Airlines – ČSA – and British Midland) and important European cities, as well as Ne[w] York (ČSA). The nearest airport to Brno and southern Moravia is Vienna.

Connections between Ruzyně and the city centre are by taxi *(see below)* or airpo[rt] bus (stopping at Dejvická Metro station and downtown at Náměstí Republiky (Republ[ic] Square). The cheapest but slowest link is by normal city bus to Dejvická Metro.

By rail – Prague is linked to all neighbouring countries by rail, with direct services t[o] Berlin and Hamburg, Frankfurt and Dortmund, Vienna, Munich, and Paris. The quicke[st] route (c24 hours) from London is by Eurostar to Brussels, changing there and in Cologn[e.] Most international trains call at Prague's main station Hlavní nádraží, but some stop a[t] the suburban stations at Holešovice station and Smíchov, both with Metro stations.

By coach – Several companies operate a London-Prague coach service, among the[m] Kingscourt Express, 15 Balham High Road, London SW12 9AJ, ☎ 0181 673 7500[.] The journey lasts around 18 hr, with refreshment stops only. The Prague terminal [is] close to the Florenc long-distance coach station, with its own Metro station.

Prague main railway station

y car – Main roads radiate from Prague to all neighbouring countries. Although as
ㅑt there is no uninterrupted connection to the western European motorway system,
ㅑarly all the distance between Prague and the German border at Rozvadov/Waidhaus
 now covered by motorway. From London it is about 1 250km to Prague via the
ㅑhannel ports. The quickest route is via Dover-Ostend, while the driving distance can
ㅑe shortened considerably by using the overnight car ferry from Harwich to Hamburg
ㅑbout 660km via Berlin).

 you intend using motorways and dual carriageway roads in the Czech Republic (as
ㅑu will need to do) you must buy a **sticker** (vignette) at the border crossing and display
 on the car windscreen.

ㅑl types of fuel are readily available in the Czech Republic.

Getting around Prague

ㅑrague has an integrated transportation system based on Metro, tram and bus and
ㅑrving the whole of the city. Tickets are cheap and the efficiency and reliability of
ㅑe system make the use of a car redundant, within the city at least.

Metro – The clean, swift, safe and mostly underground Metro links a number of sub-
ㅑrban stations with the city centre. Trains run every few minutes, more frequently
ㅑuring the rush hour. There are three lines, identified by colour. **Line A** (green) runs
ㅑom **Dejvická** station, where it connects with airport buses, to **Skalka**. **Line B** (yellow)
ㅑns from **Zličín** to **Černý Most**, intersecting with Line A at the busy **Můstek** station at
ㅑe foot of Wenceslas Square. **Line C** (red) runs from **Nádraží Holešovice** (with its main
ㅑe railway station) to **Háje**, intersecting with Line A at **Muzeum** station at the top of
ㅑenceslas Square and with Line B at **Florenc** with its long-distance coach station. Metro
ㅑations are identified above ground by the x symbol. Most of the station platforms
ㅑe deep underground and are reached by long runs of escalators. The direction of
ㅑavel is indicated by the terminus station. A recorded announcement warns when the
ㅑain doors are about to close and then identifies the next stop.

ㅑart from the city centre stations noted above, stations often used by visitors include:
ㅑe A: **Staroměstská** (Old Town), **Malostranská**, (Malá Strana – interchange with 🚋 22).

ㅑe B: **Náměstí Republiky** (Republic Square), for the **Obecní dům** and **Masarykovo nádraží**
ㅑasaryk Station); **Národní třída** (National Avenue); **Karlovo náměstí** (Charles Square); **Smí-**
ㅑovské nádraží (Smíchov main line railway station)

ㅑe C: **Hlavní nádraží** (Main Railway Station); **Vyšehrad**.

ㅑam – The tramway network complements the Metro lines to link city centre and
ㅑburbs. Some services are only operated in the rush hour and there is a skeleton
ㅑrvice at night (identified by different numbers in blue). Each tram stop is named,
ㅑd the routes serving it are identified by enamel numbers. Most services run at a
ㅑequency of between 10 and 20 min. A timetable at each stop gives details. Routes
ㅑ particular interest to visitors include:

ㅑ 17: **Výtoň** (for Vyšehrad) – **Národní divadlo** (National Theatre) – **Staroměstská** (Old
ㅑwn) – **Veletržní** (for Veletržní palác Gallery of Modern Art) – **Výstaviště** (Exhibition Park)

Tram in Malá Strana Square

🚋 22: **Karlovo náměstí** – **Národní třída** – **Malostranské náměstí** *(Malá Strana Square)* – **Mal**
stranská (Metro connection) – **Pražský hrad** *(Castle)* – **Pohořelec** *(for Strahov Monastery)*

Bus – Bus routes are designed to serve the suburbs and few penetrate the city centre
They are useful for reaching outlying attractions such as the Collection of Asian A
at Zbraslav or the Aviation Museum at Kbely.

Lanovka/Funicular – Part of the city transport system, this is the cable railway linkin
Malá Strana with Petřín Hill.

Tickets – Most regular local users of city transport have a monthly or quarterly pass.
you intend making several trips a day by public transport it may be worth while buyin
a pass for 24 hr, 3, 5, or 15 days. Otherwise tickets are available singly.
The normal ticket is valid for 60 min (90 min at night and weekends) from the time
validation. Within that time span you can change as many times as you like from one mod
of transport to another. A cheaper ticket is also available; this doesn't allow you to chang
(except on the Metro, where you can nevertheless only travel for up to four stops) and
only valid for 15 min. Tickets can be bought at some Metro stations, newsagents, an
hotels, or from ticket machines (no change given). They MUST be validated befo
beginning your journey by inserting them in one of the cancelling machines provided fe
that purpose at the entrance to Metro stations and inside trams and buses. Ensure whe
you remove your ticket from the machine that it has the time printed on it and have th
ticket ready to show to the plain-clothes inspectors who patrol the system. Your foreig
ness is no defence against the on-the-spot fir
they are entitled to levy.

All types of public transport have designate
seats for invalids and pregnant women, and it
normal for the young or fit to give up the
places to the elderly or frail. There is no smo
ing on public transport.

Information – The Transport Department has i
formation centres at Muzeum station, Holešovi
station, Jungmannovo náměstí (Jungman
Square) and Palackého náměstí (Palacký Square
and information (in English and German) can
obtained from ☎ 24 98 42 50, 29 46 82 an
80 67 90. An excellent system map can be boug
at the information centres.

Taxi

Despite city regulations specifying rates per kil
metre, use of taximeters and so on, overchar
ing is rife and hiring from a cab rank is inadv
able. It's best to telephone a reputable firm su
as AAA (☎ 1080).Your hotel will help. Othe
wise check with the driver what the rate will
and ask for a receipt.

Public transport ticket

Driving in Prague and the Czech Republic

If your stay is limited to Prague, the excellence of the public transport system means that there is little point in hiring a car or bringing your own and many places outside the city can be reached by public transport or tour bus.

In addition, driving conditions in the city are difficult, with dense traffic, a limited number of parking spaces, and competition with trams.

But if you wish to travel extensively beyond Prague a car can be very useful and some excursions can really only be undertaken with your own transport.

Documents – The driving licences of most countries are recognised in the Czech Republic, but if in doubt an International Driving Licence is easily obtained through motoring organisations. You should have proof of ownership of your vehicle and you must be insured. Most British motor insurance policies only provide third party cover and for full cover you will need a Green Card. Use of motorways and similar roads requires you to display a special sticker *(see above)*.

Car hire – Most of the well-known international car hire firms have offices in Prague. Local firms are likely to be cheaper and just as reliable. Hire of car with a chauffeur may be an interesting alternative to a coach trip.

Highway code – Traffic regulations and driving conditions are similar to those in other continental European countries, but note that alcohol tolerance is ZERO. Safety belts must be worn and children under 12 may not sit in a front seat. Accidents involving injury or serious damage must be reported to the police. A red warning triangle, spare light bulbs and a first aid kit must be carried.

Speed limits for private cars:
50kph in built-up areas (indicated by the sign showing the name of the town of village)
90kph outside town
130kph on motorways

Trams have their own traffic signals, so do not move off at a crossing simply because a tram has done so. If there is no central reservation at a tram stop, traffic must halt and allow passengers to cross to and from the pavement.

Parking in Prague is very limited and parking outside an indicated area or overstaying will almost certainly attract a fine or a clamp. Both in Prague and elsewhere it's best to park at a guarded car park rather than leave your car on the street, especially at night.

The road network in the Czech Republic is generally good, though single-carriageway main roads can be congested. Driving behaviour is sometimes erratic. Rush hour traffic in and around Prague is heavy, and there is an additional rush hour as much of the population leaves town for their country cottages on Friday afternoon/evening and returns late on Sunday. In rural areas there may be very little traffic at all.

Michelin map 976 Czech Republic and Slovak Republic covers the whole of the country at a scale of 1:600 000. An excellent large-scale (1:100 000) road atlas is the **Autoatlas Česká Republika** published by Geodézie ČS (Freytag & Berndt).

Useful telephone numbers:
Police: 158
Breakdown service: 154
Central Car and Motor Club: 0/123
Bohemia Assistance Car Club: 0/124

Getting around the Czech Republic by public transport

Rail – The country has a very dense rail network and all towns and many smaller places can be reached by train. Most main lines are electrified while other routes are served by diesel railcars and railbuses. Express trains (rychlík) are reasonably fast, while other trains (osobní vlak) can be extremely slow. Fares are rising but still very low in comparison with the European average. Train is not usually the best option for the excursions from Prague described in this book, though Pilsen is well served and Karlštejn can be easily reached by suburban electric train from Smíchovské nádraží (Smíchov station).

Rail information (in English and German) is available from ☏ 24 22 42 00 and 461 40 30. Full timetable information is displayed at main stations; the easiest timetables to read are those summarising arrival and departure information (white and yellow panels respectively).

Bus – The network of bus routes in the Czech Republic has an even better network than the rail system; in principle every town of whatever size can be reached by bus. The express services linking Prague and other large towns are usually faster and cheaper than the train. Most are run by the former state company (ČSAD, but other operators run services on some of the more popular routes. A trip by long-distance service bus to destinations such as Carlsbad or Brno would be a much less expensive option than a guided tour though the bus itself may be less luxurious. The main long-distance bus station in Prague is at Florenc (with its own Metro station).

Tickets for both rail and bus can be obtained from travel agents, the largest of which is the centrally-located former state tourist agency, Čedok, Na příkopě 18, New Town, ☏ 2419 7111.

Basic information

Tourist information

PIS Pražská informační služba **(Prague Information Service)** – This is the city's official tourist information service, which draws on a constantly updated data base to off[...] comprehensive information on everything likely to be of interest to visitors includi[...] accommodation, attractions, cultural events and guided tours.

PIS publish Cultural Events, a monthly English-language bulletin giving details of the current events (exhibitions, concerts, theatre, film etc) likely to appeal to non-Cze[...] speakers. It is a digest of the far thicker *Přehled kulturních pořadů v Praze* (Summa[...] of the cultural programme in Prague) which has listings of virtually everything ha[...] pening in the metropolis that month, from Sunday afternoon brass band concerts [...] dancing classes and evening lectures.

The PIS's **main information centre** is conveniently located in the entrance to the **Old To[...] Hall,** Staroměstské náměstí (Old Town Square), ☎ 24 48 20 18, and there are other [...] fices at Na příkopě 20, New Town, in the hall of the Main Railway Station, and *(se[...] sonally)* on the ground floor of the tower at the Malá Strana end of Charles Bridge[...] Tourist information centres exist in most provincial towns, identified by the 🄸 logo. T[...] service provided is variable; information on local attractions is always available but he[...] with accommodation may be limited.

Ph. Gajic/MICHELIN

Old Town Hall branch of P.I.S:
Prague Information Service

The Prague Post – This [...] a well-established Engl[...] (or rather American) la[...] guage broadsheet wee[...] newspaper aimed mai[...] at the large expatria[...] community in Prague a[...] the Czech Republic. [...] well as general and bu[...] ness news, it has listin[...] of current cultural even[...] restaurant, café and p[...] reviews, and (in seaso[...] supplements with visit[...] information.

Guided tours – Vario[...] operators offer coa[...] tours of Prague and to [...] tractions outside the ci[...] Since much of the histo[...] centre is only accessib[...] to pedestrians a city to[...] by coach is of limited [...] terest, though it can he[...] in general orientatio[...] The most popular excu[...] sions outside the city a[...] to Karlštejn Castl[...] Konopiště Castle, the fo[...] mer ghetto at Terezín a[...] Karlovy Vary (Carlsba[...] There is intensive adve[...] tising of these tours [...] parts of Prague fr[...] quented by tourists and[...] hotels.

A **walking tour** is probably a better introduction to Prague itself. These are organised [...] the Prague Information Service, using approved multilingual guides who have the rig[...] to wear a badge with the city coat of arms. There are also walks with themes (loca[...] of the Velvet Revolution, pubs etc) run by Prague Walks, Václavské náměstí 60, Ne[...] Town, ☎ 61 21 46 03.

A **river trip** reveals Prague from an unusual perspective. As well as a basic trip lasti[...] about an hour, there are dining, musical and evening cruises. Far less expensive a[...] just as interesting is the regular service *(summer only)* between the city centre a[...] Troja (for the Zoo and Troja Palace) which takes 75 min. Another summer servi[...] takes trippers upstream to the dam and recreational area at Slapy. There are two ma[...] operators: EVD/Evropská vodní doprava close to Čechův most (Čech Bridge) at t[...] northern end of the Old Town (☎ 23 10 208/23 11 915) and PPS, Pražská paroplaveb[...] společnost on the quayside between Palackého most (Palacký Bridge) and Jirásk[...] most (Jirásek Bridge). Rašínovo nábřeží, New Town, ☎ 29 38 09/29 83 09.

Pleasure boat on the Vltava

Services

Banks and money – The unit of currency in the Czech Republic is the Czech crown (koruna česká - Kč), now fully convertible with other currencies. The crown is divided into 100 virtually worthless hellers (haléř). Hellers come in denominations of 10, 20, and 50, crowns in denominations of 1, 2, 5, 10, 20 and 50 and there are 20, 50, 100, 200, 500, 1000 and 5000 crown notes. In very approximate terms, £1.00 = Kč55, US$1 = Kč35.

Banks are generally open 8am-5pm Monday to Friday with a more limited service on Saturday. There are fewer cash dispensers than in western Europe or North America but they normally accept conventional cash cards.

Money can be changed at hotels, travel agencies, bureau de change and banks. There are numerous bureaux de change in convenient locations in Prague. Their exchange rates are likely to be less favourable than those of a bank, but their hours of opening are longer.

Credit cards are becoming more widely accepted, but it is always sensible to carry some cash.

Post – Post offices are generally open 8am to 5pm Mondays to Fridays and on Saturday mornings. The main post office in Prague, with a wide range of facilities, is at Jindřišská 14, New Town, and there is a 24-hour post office at Masarykovo nádraží (Masaryk Station). Stamps can usually be purchased wherever postcards are on sale or at your hotel.

Telephone – Most telephone boxes only accept phone cards, which are available in denominations ranging from Kč50 to Kč150 from post offices and newsagents. Many boxes have instructions in several foreign languages. International calls are expensive, as are all calls made from hotels, which normally add a surcharge of several times the cost of the call. The charge card which charges calls to your personal account can be used in the Czech Republic.

To make an international call dial the international code 00 followed by the country code (44 for the United Kingdom) followed by the area code (minus the figure 0) followed by the subscriber's number.

Dial 0139 for information on international telephone services, 0149 for directory information, and 0132 for an English-speaking international operator (French 0131, German 0133). A free map is published by Czech Telecom showing the location of telephone boxes in central Prague.

Medical services and health – There are no special health risks involved in visiting the Czech Republic, though it is possible that low air quality in Prague may make life temporarily unpleasant for people with respiratory problems. The water supply is safe, though Prague water is somewhat unappetising.

Pharmacies are often able to give advice as well as dispensing drugs. 24-hour pharmacies exist in most towns and there are several in Prague, the most central being at Belgická 37, New Town ☎ 24237207/258189.

Health care is generally of a reasonable standard. Citizens of the United Kingdom are entitled to free emergency treatment, but it is sensible to take out medical travel insurance before leaving as this may entitle you to a choice of treatment and make repatriation straightforward in an emergency.

Emergency first aid for foreigners and emergency dental treatment: Palackého 5, Ne
Town, ☎ 24949181.
A number of clinics in Prague specialise in medical care for foreigners. Among them ar
American Medical Center, Janovského 48, Prague 7, ☎ 807756 (with dental clinic
Canadian Medical Centre, Veleslavínská 30/1, Prague 6, ☎ 3165519;
Na Homolce department for foreigners, Roentgenova 2, Prague 5, ☎ 52922144.

Time – The Czech Republic observes Central European Time, one hour ahead of Gree
wich Mean Time and 7 hr ahead of US Standard Time. Clocks go forward 1 hr betwee
March and late September.

Media – Hotel television sets are normally tuned in to a number of foreign satelli
or cable stations, with German or Austrian stations in the majority.

Foreign newspapers are sold from city centre kiosks. British newspapers genera
arrive the day after publication, except for the European edition of The Guardian whi
is printed in Germany and is on sale the same day.

Personal security – Crime has increased in the decade following the demise of tl
Communist police state, but has still to reach the level of most western capitals, ar
the normal precautions are all that is necessary. Beware of pickpockets, who opera
in areas frequented by tourists, like Wenceslas Square and Charles Bridge. Mal
stranská Metro and Tram 22 have also been favourite target areas. Avoid involveme
with anyone offering to change money; it is illegal, and may be the cover for tl
appearance of a pseudo-policeman who will attempt to relieve you of your passpc
and other valuables.

Emergency telephone numbers:
National Police: 158
City Police in Prague: 156
Ambulance: 155
Fire brigade: 150
Lost property office in Prague: Karolíny Světlé 5, Old Town, ☎ 24235085
The 24-hour police post at Jungmannovo náměstí 9 near the foot of Wenceslas Squa
specialises in helping foreign visitors and normally has multilingual officers on duty

Electricity – Generally 220 volts alternating current.

Opening hours – Most shops open from 8am or 9am to 6pm on working days ar
1pm or 2pm on Saturdays, possibly with a break at lunchtime. Many shops in are
frequented by tourist open late in the evenings and at weekends.
Visitor attractions have variable opening hours, but with rare exceptions (like tl
National Museum in Prague) all close on Mondays. They may also close on public hc
idays. Many provincial attractions close from the end of September to Easter or late
In a hangover from the Communist era, some establishments seem to be run mc
for the convenience of staff than of visitors, closing for long lunch hours and early
the afternoon. Many historic houses and castles can only be visited in the course
a guided tour, which may or may not be at a convenient time. It's worth checking
advance whether you will be able to visit a particular place at the time you wish.

Public holidays

1 January	New Year's Day
Easter Monday	
1 May	Labour Day
8 May	Liberation Day
5 July	St Cyril and St Methodius
6 July	Anniversary of the martyrdom of Jan Hus/ (John Huss)
28 October	Independence Day
24 December	Christmas Eve
25-26 December	Christmas Holiday

Calendar of events

January

Prague . . . . New Year street celebrations.

Easter

Prague . . . . Girls and young women are chased by boys and men who ceremoniously "beat'" them with willow rods and spray them with water or perfume, receiving painted Easter eggs for their pains.

Whit Sunday

Southern Moravian . . . "Kings Ride" procession.
villages

2 May-3 June

Prague . . . . Prague Spring. An international musical event of the first importance, with performances of music, opera and ballet.

May

Prague . . . . Prague Writers' Festival   normally with participation of writers from the English-speaking world.

Late June-early July

Prague . . . . Dance Prague International festival of dance.

July

Karlovy Vary . . . . Karlovy Vary International Film Festival. The major event of its kind in the Czech Republic.

Mid-September

Prague . . . . Prague Autumn International Music Festival. International classical music festival second only in importance to Prague Spring.

October

Prague . . . . Prague Festival of 20C Music.

October

Prague . . . . International Jazz Festival.

December

Czech Republic. . . . . . Christmas Fairs.

St Nicholas, accompanied by a devil and an angel, roams the streets on the eve of his saint's day (5 December), rewarding good children with sweets and frightening the naughty.

Live carp for Christmas Eve dinner are sold from tanks in the streets. Churches have elaborate cribs.

Christmas market in Old Town Square

Useful
addresses

Accommodation

After years of being in acutely short supply, accommodation in Prague now roughly in balance with demand. Choosing a hotel or other lodgin either in or close to the city centre makes most sense, since most of t suburbs are singularly lacking in charm. The accommodation detailed belc will allow you to visit most of the city's major sights on foot. Hotels in t historic centre of the city (Old Town, Malá Strana, around Wenceslas Squar are expensive however, with few double rooms available at much less th Kč 3 500 per night. Private accommodation in a house or more likely a f can be an appealing alternative, costing around Kč 800 per person per nigl possibly more if breakfast is provided. An apartment will cost arou Kč 1 200. When offered private accommodation, check its location careful closeness to a Metro station will bring you to the centre in minutes where a journey involving changing from bus to tram to Metro can take conside ably longer.

There is a good range of hostels for young travellers.

You are strongly recommended to reserve rooms well in advance.

Private accomodation

Čedok: *Na příkopě 18, Prague 1 (New Town) –* ☎ *24 19 71 11 – Open Monc to Friday 9am to 6pm, Saturday 9am to noon.* The former State Tourist Off is still the country's biggest travel organisation and has staff fluent in Engl and other foreign languages.

AVE: *Wilsonova 8, Prague 2 (New Town, in the main railway station)* ☎ *24 22.35 21 – Open daily 6am to 11pm.*

This agency has a special service for people arriving at the last minute.

Private accommodation in Prague and in other parts of the Czech Republic c also be booked in advance from the United Kingdom:

Czech In Holidays: *48 The Avenue, Chiswick, London W4 1HR –* ☎ *0181 747 96ʒ*

Czechbook Agency: *Jopes Mill, Trebrownbridge, near Liskeard, Cornwall PL14 3PX* ☎ *01503 240 629.*

Budget Accommodation

Pension U Lilie – *Liliová 15 –* ☎ *22 22 11 02 – 8 doubles with own facilities frc Kč 1 300 to Kč 2 200.*

In a medieval setting almost facing the entrance to the Klementinum and or a short distance from Charles Bridge, this pension is tucked away at the e of a little passageway. The rooms face on to an internal courtyard where brea fast is taken in fine weather. There is an adjoining restaurant. Higl recommended.

Pension Avalon – *Havelská 15, Prague 1 (Old Town) –* ☎ *26 36 43 – (first floc 6 doubles on first floor with own facilities From Kč 1 000 to Kč 1 500 accord to season,* ☎ *26 71 96 for second and third floor rooms from Kč 550 p person.*

Plainly furnished but perfectly decent, these two pensions occupy the upr floors of an old and characterful building facing Havelská Street, the scene the city's most colourful street market.

Pension U Medvídků – *Na Perštýně 7, Prague 1 (Old Town) –* ☎ *24 21 19 1€ 7 double rooms with shared bath and toilet, Kč 1 600. 10 superior rooms w own bath and toilet Kč 3 000. (Breakfast included).*

Close to the National Theatre, this is an attractively renovated old building abc the famous beer hall of the same name.

Especially Recommended

Adria – *Václavské náměstí 26, Prague 1 (New Town) –* ☎ *21 08 11 11 – Sing from around Kč 5 000, doubles from around Kč 6 000.*

This family-owned and thoroughly renovated Baroque building at the lower e of Wenceslas Square offers every comfort, impeccable service, and insta access to the heart of the city. Rooms at the rear overlook the greenery of t restored Franciscans' Garden.

Betlém Club – *Betlémské náměstí 9, Prague 1 (Old Town) –* ☎ *22 22 15 74 2C comfortable rooms from Kč 1 900 to Kč 2 600 single, Kč 3 500 double.*

Price, location and comfort combine to make this hotel one of the city's mc attractive options. A carefully restored old building, only a short walk frc Charles Bridge, it stands on the same square in the Old Town where John Hι preached in the Bethlehem Chapel. Public spaces are decorated with medieval weaponry, while the spacious bedrooms have a more modern finish. A lift takes you down to breakfast in the ancient stone-built cellars.

loister Inn Hotel – *Bartolomějská 9, Prague 1 (Old Town)* – ☎ *232 77 00* – *25 rooms (70 planned) Single Kč 2 700, double Kč 3 400, with extra bed Kč 3 900.*

Creaking parquet floors, long corridors and an air of serenity which is hardly surprising when you realise that this hotel, just a short distance from the National Theatre, is in fact an old convent.

krále Jiřího – *Liliová 10, Prague 1* – ☎ *24 24 87 97/24 22 20 13* – *11 cosy rooms single Kč 1 650, double Kč 2 850, extra bed Kč 1 000. Two apartments, double Kč 3 300, triple Kč 4 200. (Breakfast included).*

Bearing the name of the 15C Hussite King, George of Poděbrady, this medieval building stands on Liliová Street in the heart of the Old Town, where according to legend you might at any moment bump into one of the Knights Templar carrying his head under his arm.

ampa Hotel – *Všehrdova 16, Prague 1 (Malá Strana)*; – ☎ *57 32 05 08/57 32 04 04 reservations 71 75 19 41/71 75 02 75* – *83 rooms* – *Prices vary according to season. Single between Kč 2 000 and Kč 2 640, double between Kč 3 150 and Kč 4 260.*

In a secluded side street close to Kampa Island in romantic Malá Strana, this comfortable hotel is ideal for a restful stay and in addition has an excellent restaurant.

Something special

esidence Nosticova – *Nosticova 1, Prague 1 (Malá Strana)* – ☎ *57 31 25 16/ 7 31 25 16* – *10 apartments @ Kč 6 120. (extra beds can be provided).*

A stay in this impeccably restored 17C Malá Strana house tucked away behind the French Embassy is likely to be an unforgettable experience. Furnished with antiques, the rooms combine contemporary comfort and a full range of facilities with the patina of times past. Some of them look out over tranquil gardens.

esidence Domus Henrici – *Loretánská 11, Prague 1 (Hradčany)* – ☎ *2051 13 09* – *doubles from Kč 4 200 to Kč 5 600.*

High up above the city and almost opposite the castle gates, this charming establishment has spacious rooms on different levels with fabulous views over Petřín Hill.

krále Karla – *Úvoz 4, Prague 1 (Hradřany)* – ☎ *53 88 05.* – *16 doubles at Kč 6 100, suites at Kč 6 700.*

A stay at the charming King Charles is a right royal treat. This exclusive hotel just below the castle and almost opposite the gardens of Malá Strana has comfortable and characterful rooms with exposed beams, fireplaces, well-chosen furniture and stained glass, plus an equally appealing vaulted restaurant.

or younger travellers

nsion Unitas – *Bartolomějská 9, Prague 1 (Old Town)* – ☎ *232 77 00* – *32 basic rooms with shared facilities* – *Singles Kč 1 020, doubles Kč 1 200, triples Kč 1 650, quadruples Kč 2 000.*

In the same building as the Cloister Inn, the Unitas was once the police station where political suspects were interrogated. You sleep in the cells where dissidents like President Havel once languished.

aveller's Hostel – *Dlouhá 33, Prague 1 (Old Town)* – ☎ *231 1318/231 1234* – *20 beds in doubles, triples and dormitories with shared facilities. From Kč 450 er person (winter) to Kč 500 (summer), dormitory accommodation Kč 350. Breakfast included).*

Centrally located and extremely good value, this large building in the Old Town has several floors converted into hostel accommodation. Plain but clean and cheerful, it's very popular with young Americans. Bonuses include the existence next door of one of Prague's trendiest hang-outs, the Roxy, with frequent rock concerts, a café with Moorish decor, and an office which arranges bookings in other hostels including one in the charming southern Bohemian town of Česk umlov.

stel Sokol – *Újezd 40/450 Prague 1 (Malá Strana)* – ☎ *57 00 73 97* – *98 beds dormitories. Kč 220 per person per night.*

This old palace converted into a school has light and airy dormitories overlooking the gardens of Malá Strana.

CAMP SITES

Císařská louka – *Císařská louka 599, Prague 5 (Smíchov)* – ☎ 545064
36 "bungalows" (chalets) Kč 480 for two people, caravans Kč 160, tents
90 - 130, motorhomes Kč 210, Kč 95 per person and Kč 90 per car. The "Imp
rial Meadows" are on an island in the Vltava, just opposite Vyšehrad, with acce
from the left bank of the river (Smíchov). A ferry every 30 min links the islan
with Smíchovské nádraží Metro Station (Line B). Terrace restaurant.

Sunny Camp – *Smíchovská 1989, Prague 5 (Stodůlky)* – ☎ 652 37 74. – *Carava*
Kč 150, tents Kč 10, motorhomes Kč 200, Kč 90 per person, Kč 100 per ca
Double rooms also available with shared facilities, Kč 780. In a distant suburb b
conveniently located only a step from Luka Metros station (Line B).

Džbán – *Nad lávkou 599, Prague 6 (Vokovice)* – ☎ 36 90 06 – *Rooms for*
(Kč 310 per peson) – 4 person chalets (Kč 900) – caravans (Kč 120), ter
(Kč 90) and motorhomes (Kč 180) – Kč 90 per person and Kč 90 per car.
the western suburbs on the way to the airport but with quite good access
the centre by tram and Metros and close to the attractive Šárka Valley with
lake and recreational facilities.

Eating out

Thankfully, Prague's restaurants are more of a bargain than the city's hote
especially if you stick to the traditional, rather heavy Czech cuisine. Avoid t
unseasoned or mayonnaise-drenched salads, and ask for duck and goose, po
and cabbage, fried cheese, goulash, knuckle of pork, or the Czech Christm
speciality, carp in breadcrumbs. You will not be able to avoid the ubiquito
dumpling, the item most missed by exiles, though rarely will a restaura
example come up to the standard set at home by Mother.

Desserts tend to be limited to pancakes with lashings of cream, fruit, jam
chocolate.

Czech wines, most of them from Moravia, are quite acceptable, and certain
preferable to over-priced foreign wines. Older vintages, so-called "archiv
wines, may or may not be worth the money. Remember you are in the land
beer, and make sure your tasting takes in brews other than Pilsner and Budva
excellent though they are.

In cheaper restaurants and in pubs it is normal to share a table if the esta
lishment is crowded (but ask first). In the pub, signal your desire for beer
placing a beer mat in front of you on the table.

Some establishments levy not only a cover charge but also make you pay f
items like bread and the little tit-bits offered at the start of the meal which yo
thought were complementary. On the other hand, big spenders may
rewarded with an unexpected glass of *slivovice* (plum brandy).

Dobrou chut! Enjoy your meal!

Cuisine in Czech

Restaurant: restaurace
Wine restaurant: vinárna
Pub: hospoda
Café: kavárna
Menu: jídelní lístek
Duck: kachna
Goose: husa
Roast pork with cabbage and dumplings: vepřová pečeně se zelím, knedlíky
Roast beef in cream sauce: svíčková na smetaně
Pork escalope in breadcrumbs: smažený vepřový řízek
Fried cheese: smažený srzý
Carp in breadcrumbs: smažený kapr
Pancakes: palačinky
Beer: pivo
Wine: víno
Water: voda
Tea: čaj
Coffee: káva

Budget restaurants

Havelská koruna – *Havelská 21, Prague 1 (Old Town)* – ☏ 24239331
Open Monday to Friday 7am to 6pm, Saturday and Sunday 9am to 5pm. Main courses around Kč 50.

A new, attractively decorated buffet-type restaurant, ideal for quick and inexpensive eating, half-way between Wenceslas Square and Old Town Square in the Havelská marketplace. All the traditional

Old restaurant sign

Czech dishes, plus salads, cakes and even decent coffee, a fairly rare phenomenon in Prague.

Konvikt – *Bartolomějská 11, Prague 1 (Old Town)* – ☏ 24231971 – *Open Monday to Saturday 10am to midnight, Sunday 11am to 11pm. Standard Czech main courses from Kč 70 to Kč 150.*

This cheerful albeit rather smoky establishment is a favourite with beer drinkers. The back room is rather more secluded. Fried cheese is a good buy here.

U Dvou koček – *Uhelný trh 10, Prague 1 (Old Town)* – ☏ 24229982 – *Open daily 11am to 11pm – Main courses around Kč 100.*

The hoppy aroma is almost overwhelming as you enter this rustic tavern in the Old Town's Coal Market with its vaulted ceilings and dark brown furniture. The somewhat indifferent service in the "Two Cats" is soon forgiven when the Moravian accordionist starts up around 7pm every evening. Typical Czech food. Reservation recommended.

Pizzeria Roma Due – *Liliová 18, Prague 1 (Old Town)* – *no phone* – *Open 24hrs. First-rate pizzas from Kč 100 to Kč 150.*

This picturesque pizzeria just off the Royal Way between Old Town Square and Charles Bridge has bare brick walls adorned with musical instruments and the like and is ideal for stilling that empty feeling that can come on in the small hours.

Café Louvre — *Národní 20, Prague 1 (New Town)* – ☏ 297223 – *Open 8am to 11pm. – Salads, cakes, ready meals or carp Jewish-style for Kč 100.*

This spacious café occupies the first floor of an Art Nouveau building on the street leading to the National Theatre. Done out in slightly strange pastel colours and with impressive chandeliers it still has something of the atmosphere of a 1920s tea dance. At the back there's a billiard hall, open noon to 8pm.

U Bílé kuželky – *Míšenská 12, Prague 1 (Malá Strana)* – ☏ 533096 – *Open noon to 10pm. Main courses around Kč 100.*

Hidden away down a winding lane in Malá Strana, close to Charles Bridge, is the "White Skittle", serving unpretentious food in a rustic setting, duck, pork, cabbage...

Highly recommended

U Provaznice – *Provaznická 3, Prague 1 (Old Town)* – ☏ 24232528 – *Open daily 11am to midnight – Main courses around Kč 100.*

Appetising goulash fumes emanate from the "Ropemaker's" just behind the entrance to Můstek Metrounderground station at the foot of Wenceslas Square. Inside, the welcoming interior has *trompe-l'œil* wall-paintings which go well with the stone walls and the other decor. A series of little rooms provide intimate dining spaces. Service is prompt, the music pleasing, and the food nicely spiced.

Restaurant of the Hotel Evropa – (check name) *Václavské náměstí 25, Prague 1 (New Town)* – ☏ 24228117 – *Main courses from Kč 300 upwards.*

A time-capsule awaits you beyond the majestic revolving doors of the Grand Hotel Evropa - a perfectly preserved restaurant from the end of the 19C, with a profusion of caryatids, mahogany, wrought iron, stained glass and luxuriant stucco.

The Hôtel Evropa

Radegast – *Templová, Prague 1 (Old Town)* – ☎ 2328237 – *Open 11am – 12.30am Generous main courses around Kč 150.*
A short step from Old Town Square but well off the tourist trail, this pub wi
its basic furniture and service is a good place to sample copious quantities
well-crafted Czech cuisine. Hearty and well-fed locals still dominate the pla
both in terms of number and noise. A good choice is the succulent half a duc
enough to satisfy the most Gargantuan of appetites.

Blatnička – *Michalská 6-8, Prague 1 (Old Town)* – ☎ 24233612 – *Open da
11am to 11pm – Main courses around Kč 75.*
In the labyrinth of streets between Old Town Square and Bethlehem Squar
this quiet little restaurant is a favourite with locals for a family Sunday lunc
Traditional dishes and good value. Try their "Velvet" beer for a smooth exp
rience.

Rybářský klub – *U Sovových mlýnů (Malá Strana)* – ☎ 530223 – *Open no
to 10.30pm – Main courses Kč 150 upwards.*
A good excuse for a riverside stroll through the greenery of Malá Strana, t
"Fishermen's Club" occupies a little house on the bank of the Vltava in Kam
Park. Eel, pike, perch from the great fishponds of southern Bohemia are pr
pared to perfection by the owner himself. Definitely the place to try that Cze
classic, carp, either smoked or fried in breadcrumbs.

U Prince – *Staroměstské náměstí 29, Prague 1 (Old Town)* – ☎ 24213404
Open daily 10am to 1am – Main courses around Kč 300.
This restaurant has an unbeatable position almost opposite the Astronomi
Clock in Old Town Square. Inevitably, both the outside terrace and the attra
tive, vaulted interior are full of your fellow-tourists, but the menu has a numb
of original offerings, including "liver and leg of duck a la Prince".

Novoměstský pivovar – *Vodičkova 20, Prague 1 (New Town)* – ☎ 22232448
Open daily 11.30am to 10.30pm. – Dish of the day Kč 100.
Is it a pub? Is it a restaurant? Who cares? Locals don't, and come here
number, thronging the vaulted rooms which are decorated with vivid wall-pain
ings. This being the "New Town Brewery", you can eat alongside gleamin
beer-vats. Prompt and efficient service. A good mixture of Praguers and vi
tors. Try the knuckle of ham at Kč 160.

V Zátiší – *Liliová 1, Prague 1 (Old Town)* – ☎ 24220627 – *Open noon to 3p
5.30 pm to 11pm. – Main courses from around Kč 400.*
A hushed, candlelit setting, solicitous service, and a carefully chosen range
Czech and international dishes maintain the reputation of "Still Life" just c
Bethlehem Square.

Something special

Bellevue – *Smetanovo nábřeží 18, Prague 1 (Old Town)* – ☎ 22220465 – *Op
Monday to Saturday noon to 3pm and 5.30pm to 11pm. – Main courses fro
around Kč 700.*
The owners of this restaurant have pioneered fine food at several locations
Prague, of which this is perhaps the most stunning – a dining room with b
windows looking across the Vltava and Charles Bridge to Malá Strana and t
Castle. The sumptuous champagne Sunday brunch draws in prosperous Pr
guers and the expat elite.

Iffy Palác Club – *Valdštejnská 14, Prague 1 (Malá Strana)* – ☎ *57 32 05 70* – *Open daily 10.30am to 10pm. – Main courses around Kč 400.*

One of Prague's unique eating experiences. This is a real palace, now the home of the Conservatory of Music, which may provide an accompaniment as you climb the splendid staircase and enter a spacious dining room with a ceiling as high as a cathedral's and an opulent decor which more than matches the food. Summer dining on the terrace facing the newly restored Baroque gardens below the castle.

Flambée – *Husova 5, Prague 1 (Old Town)* – ☎ *24 24 85 12* – *Open 11.30am to 1am – Main courses around Kč 900.*

One of the best Czech restaurants in town, housed in intimate vaulted cellars dating from the 13C. Smooth service and imaginative cuisine which justifies the relatively high prices. Exceptional wine list.

modré kachničky – *Nebovidská 6, Prague 1 (Malá Strana)* – ☎ *57 32 03 08* – *Open daily noon to 3.30pm and 6.30pm to 11.30pm – Main courses around Kč 400.*

The "Blue Duckling" hides itself away in a Malá Strana side street. There's space for a few tables in the three rooms tastefully stuffed with antiques and other items assembled by the Czech proprietor. Solicitous service and excellent food, including local specialities; the duck a l'orange is not to be missed.

zar Méditerranée – *Nerudova 40, Prague 1 (Malá Strana)* – ☎ *90 05 45 10* – *Open daily noon to 10pm. – Main courses from Kč 200 to Kč 400.*

This labyrinthine establishment just below the Castle brings a ray of southern sunshine into a city whose skies are sometimes grey. If you're lucky you may be greeted with a glass of sangria, an appetiser for the Mediterranean goodies to follow, served with panache to a musical accompaniment. Just the place to escape the Central European winter, while in summer you can climb endless-seeming steps and enjoy the surprise of a terrace garden overlooking the red rooftops of Malá Strana.

bozízek – *Petřínské sady 411, Prague 1 (Malá Strana)* – ☎ *53 79 05 – Open daily 11am to 11pm. – Main courses from around Kč200.*

Perched up among the orchard trees near the top of Petřín Hill, the "Little Tiger" has the best view in Prague, especially as the twilight dims and the lights come on all over the city. Though not outstanding, the food will not disappoint either.

Cafes and bars

Not to be missed

Obecní dům (Municipal House) – *Náměstí Republiky 5, Prague 1 (Old Town* – ☎ 22 00 27 63 – *Open daily 7.30am to 11pm.*
The lavishly restored Municipal House is THE place to take a break from sight seeing. A pianist plays amid the ornate <u>Art Nouveau</u> decor of the ground flo café, while the basement beer hall accompanies local specialities with excelle

The cafe of the Obecní dům

Pilsner and an evening folklore show on Fridays and Saturdays. Upstairs aga there's splendidly old-fashioned ballroom dancing to a live orchestra eve Wednesday and Saturday evening. Café terrace in summer.

Classic cafes of Prague

Slavia – *Smetanovo nábřeží 2, Prague 1 (Old Town)* – ☎ 24 22 09 57 – *Op Monday to Friday 8am to midnight, Saturday and Sunday 9am to midnight.*
Recently reopened after extensive renovation, this wonderful café in Secessi style was once the haunt of intellectuals, artists and their hangers-on. The t windows facing the Vltava give a superb view of the castle.

Evropa – *Václavské náměstí 25, Prague 1 (New Town)* – ☎ 24 22 81 17 – *Op daily 7am to midnight.*
The Grand Hotel Evropa's café has a stunningly decorated Art Nouveau inter though after admiring it you may prefer, in summer at least, to people wat from the terrace facing the crowds promenading up and down Wenceslas Squar

Rudolfinum – *Alšovo nábřeží 12, Prague 1 (Old Town)* – ☎ 24 89 33 17 – *Op Tuesday to Sunday 10am to 6pm.*
In the grandiose home of the Prague Philharmonic Orchestra, this is an exce tionally spacious and comfortable café with armchairs, sofas and low tables useful stopping place in this part of the Old Town.

Café Milena – *Staroměstské náměstí 22, Prague 1 (Old Town)* – ☎ 21 63 26 02 *Open daily 9am to 11pm.*
Its first floor view of the Astronomical Clock and the Old Town Square mea that the stylish Milena, named after Kafka's lover, is permanently crowded.

Café Savoy – *Vítězná 5, Prague 5 (Smíchov) 9am to midnight.*
A large, splendidly restored café close to the Malá Strana end of the most Le (Bridge of the Legions), with music to soothe away the cares of footso tourists.

Malostranská kavárna – *Malostranské náměstí 5/28, Prague 1 (Malá Strana)* – *Op daily 9am to 11pm.*
A timeless Central European establishment with newspapers to read when y tire of the view of Malá Strana Square. Ideal place to gather your forces befo storming the castle.

A pair of post-1989 literary cafes

The Globe Bookstore and Coffeehouse – *Janovského 14, Prague 7 (Holešovice) Open daily 10am to midnight.*

The long-established focal point of North American expat life, with coffee and snacks to match as well as new and second hand books and regular literary events. In the inner-city suburb of Holešovice, close to the Veletržní palác modern art collection and not far from the Technical Museum and the Výstaviště (Exhibition Park).

Knihomola – *Mánesova 79, Prague 2 (Vinohrady) Open Monday to Thursday 10am to 11pm, Friday and Saturday 10am to midnight, Sunday 11am to 8pm.*

Not far from Jiřího z Poděbrad Metro station and Plečnik's Church of the Sacred Heart, the "Bookworm" is perhaps a Right Bank equivalent of the Globe, with a well-stocked bookshop upstairs and a literary-flavoured basement café beneath.

Traditional pubs

sv.Tomaše - *Letenská 12, Prague 1 (Malá Strana)* – ☎ *536776* – *Open daily 11.30am to midnight.*

The monks from St Thomas' founded a brewery here in 1358. Nowadays the pub's dark beer is brought from the Branik brewery just outside Prague and consumed in ancient vaulted rooms along with traditional meals. Regular evening entertainment with traditional song and dance.

Fleků – *Křemencová 9/11, Prague 1 (New Town)* – ☎ *24915118* – *Open daily 9am to 11pm.*

Tourists from all over the world gather in number at this famous many-roomed pub founded in 1459, drinking in its atmosphere as well as its delicious dark beer, chased down perhaps by a glass of Becherovka or slivovice. In the evening there's traditional music in the Biergarten and a folklore performance inside.

Medvídků – *Na Perštýně 7, Prague 1 (Old Town)* – ☎ *24220930* – *Open Monday to Saturday 11.30am to 11pm and Sunday 11.30am to 10pm.*

Hearty meals accompany the draught Budvar beer served in this establishment founded in the 15C and patronised by locals and visitors alike.

Kalicha – *Na bojišti 12, Prague 2 (New Town)* – ☎ *290701* – *Open daily 11am to 11pm.*

Immortalised by Jaroslav Hašek's Good Soldier Švejk, who got himself arrested here for incautious remarks made at the expense of Emperor Franz Josef, the "Chalice" has been doing a roaring trade ever. The Velkopopovice beer of those days has been replaced by Radegast, but there's no shortage of Švejkiana and other souvenirs, as well as dishes named after characters in the novel.

zlatého tygra – *Husova 17, Prague 1 (Old Town)* – ☎ *24229020* – *Open daily 3pm to 11pm.* Unless escorted here by a regular (like President Clinton was by President Havel), you may find there's no room to spare at the Golden Tiger, one of the last strongholds of serious local drinkers appreciative of the Pilsner drawn at exactly the right temperature from ancient cellars.

Other pubs and bars

Irish Pub O'Brien – *Janovského 36, Prague 7 (Holešovice)* – ☎ *667126557* – *Open daily noon to 1am.*

Irish pub in turn-of-the-century style, a favourite rendezvous of the city's Anglophone community. Guinness every day and live music at weekends.

U Fleků

In the Novoměstský pivovar (New Town Brewery)

Blatouch – *Vězeňská 6, Prague 1 (Old Town) – ☎ 23 28 643 – Monday to Frida*
11am to midnight, Saturday 2pm to 1am, Sunday 2pm to midnight.
Busy little bar popular with the stylish young.

U Vinařů – *Hellichová 4, Prague 1 (Malá Strana) – ☎ 573 125 19.*
The chic and comfortable furnishings of the "Vintner" make a pleasant settin
in which to sample a wide range of wines from the vineyards of the Czec
Republic.

Cybeteria Internet Café – *Štěpánská 18, Prague 1 (New Town) – ☎ 2223 0707*
Open Monday to Friday 10am to 10pm, Saturday noon to 6pm
(http://www.cybeterai.cz).
Internet café with several screens frequented by local webmeisters; refresh
ments available.

John Bull Pub – *Senovážná 8, Prague 1 (New Town) – ☎ 269 2 55 – Ope*
Monday to Friday 8am to 2am, Saturday and Sunday 11am to 2am.
Even after prolonged exposure to the sublime products of Czech brewerie
some expats retain their inexplicable taste for bitter, available in this almo
completely convincing simulacrum of a British pub. The experience comes con
plete with big screen transmission of all those sporting events which migl
otherwise be missed.

James Joyce – *Liliová 10, Prague 1 (Old Town) – ☎ 2424 8793 – Open da*
10.30am to 1am.
Another anglophone hang-out, with Guinness on tap in a bar built from ma
erials rescued from a demolition site in Belfast plus all the TV sport you cou.
wish for.

Molly Malone's – *U obecního dvora 4, Prague 1 (Old Town) – ☎ 534 793 – Ope*
daily noon to 1am.
An Irish atmosphere of near-total authenticity, with an open fire, rickety furn
ture, and various Irish brews as well as the ubiquitous Guinness.

Television Tower – *Mahlerovy sady 1, Prague 3 (Žižkov) – Open daily 11am t*
11pm. The bar of the TV tower in suburban Žižkov is perhaps the most spe
tacular vantage point for an overall view of the city.

Out and about in Prague

Theatres

The city's numerous theatres offer a varied choice of opera, ballet, and plays as well as that Prague speciality, the Black Theatre.

Tickets can be obtained on the door, but it's usually simpler to book through a ticket agency (which will charge a commission):

BTI Bohemia Ticket International – *Na Příkopě 16, Prague 1 (New Town) – ☎ 2421 50 31 – (Internet: www.csad.cz.bti; e-mail: btiinter@login.cz) – Open Monday to Friday 9am to 6pm, Saturday 9am to 4pm, Sunday 10am to 3pm.*

Ticketpro – *Salvatorská 10, Old Town – ☎ 2481 40 20 – Fax 2481 40 21 (Internet: http://www.ticketpro.cz; e-mail: vystupenky@ticketpro.cz) – Open Monday to Friday 8am to 6pm.*

Sedok *Na příkopě 18, New Town ☎ 2419 76 42/2422 36 85.*

Národní divadlo/National Theatre – *Národní 2, Prague 1 – ☎ 2490 14 48 (information in English).*

This magnificent neo-Renaissance building is the country's most important theatre, with prestigious performances of drama, opera and ballet.

Stavovské divadlo/Estates Theatre – *Ovocný trh 1, Prague 1 (Old Town) – ☎ 2421 50 01.*

The scene of the premiere of Mozart's Don Giovanni in 1787 is still one of the leading establishments of Czech theatre and opera.

Laterna Magika – *Národní 4, Prague 1 (New Town) – ☎ 2491 41 29. Booking office open Monday to Friday 10am to 8pm, Saturday and Sunday 3pm to 8pm.* Spectacular fusion of traditional theatre with contemporary audio-visual effects.

National Marionette Theatre – *Žatecká 1, Prague 1 (Old Town) – ☎ 232 34 29.* Marionette theatre for children and adults with performances every evening at 8pm. Classic performances of Mozart's Don Giovanni with large-scale marionettes in traditional costume.

National Marionette Theatre – *Novotného lávka 1, Prague 1 (Old Town).* A celebration of the Beatles, inspired by the film Yellow Submarine, using an array of techniques (Black Theatre, shadow play, back projection, music and dance as well as marionettes). An amazing experience!

Black Theatre

Originating in Prague, Black Theatre combines mime, pantomime, dance, music and lighting effects, together with black-clad actors invisible against a black background.

Ta Fantastika – *Karlova 8, Prague 1 (Old Town) – ☎ 2422 90 78.* Performances based on themes from fairy tales.

Opera in miniature

R. Holzbachova, P. Bériet

Jiří Srnec Theatre (Lucerna) – *Štěpánská 61, Prague 1 (New Town)* – ☎ 2421200
Box office open Monday to Friday 9am to 4pm. Performances at 8.30pm.

Jiří Srnec Magic Theatre of Prague – *Celetná 17, Prague 1 (Old Town)* – ☎ 5792183;
9004 9434 – Box office open Monday to Friday 9am to 4pm – Performance
at 8.30pm. (check title)

The two Jiří Srnec theatres stage performances by what is one of the fines
Black Theatre companies, using ultra-violet light to bring objects into life to th
accompaniment of music and startling sound effects.

Divadlo image – *Pařížská 4, Prague 1 (Old Town)* – ☎ 2329191 – Performance
begin at 8.00pm.

Traditional Black Theatre techniques together with pantomime and contempo
rary dance.

All Colours Theatre – *Rytířská 31, Prague 1 (Old Town)* – ☎ 2161 0173 – Bc
office open daily 10am to 10pm – Performances at 8.30pm.

Music

Classical music

It's almost impossible to resist being drawn into the musical life of Prague a
some point during your stay. Venues include not only the city's great concer
halls, but gardens (Wallenstein Garden, the Castle's Ramparts Garden)
churches (St Thomas', St James', St Ursula's...) and many other places
including interiors not normally accessible to the public such as the Kle
mentinum's Hall of Mirrors.

Státní opera Praha/State Opera – *Wilsonova 4, Prague 2 (New Town)* – ☎ 2422989
*(information), 2422 78.32 (bookings) – Box office open Monday to Frida
10am to 5pm, Saturday and Sunday 10am to noon and 1pm to 5pm.*

Close to the city's main station, this fine building completed in 1888 has a pro
gramme consisting mostly of opera and ballet.

Hudební divadlo v Karlíně – *Křižíkova 10, Prague 8 (Karlín)* – ☎ 2186 8149 Bc

Concert in the Klementinum

office open 10am t
1pm and 2pm to 6pm.
This neo-Baroque builc
ing of 1891 has a reper
toire consisting almos
entirely of operettas an
musicals.

Rudolfinum – *Náměstí Jar*
Palacha 2, Prague 1 (Ol
Town) – ☎ 2489 3111
Box office open Monda
to Friday 10am to noo
and 1pm to 6pm.

The Rudolfinum'
Dvořák Hall is the hom
of the orchestra, cham
ber ensemble an
soloists of the Pragu
Philharmonic.

Obecní dům (Municipa
House) – *Náměstí Repub*
liky 5, Prague 1 (Ol
Town) – ☎ 2200210
– Box office open Monda
to Friday 10am to 6pr
(concerts at 7.30pm).

The Smetana Hal
of the Municipal Hous
is the home of th
Prague Symphony Or
chestra.

Klub Lávka – *Novotného lávka 1, Prague 1 (Old Town)* – ☎ 2421 4797.
Atmospheric concerts based on Mozart's most popular works played by mus
cians in period costume.

Jazz

Agharta Jazz Centrum – *Krakovská 5, Prague 2 (New Town)* – ☎ 2221 1275
Monday to Friday from 5pm to 1am, Saturday and Sunday 7pm to 1am.

R. Holzbachova, P. Bénet

Jazz in the Reduta

One of Prague's best jazz locales, patronised by a mixture of Czech and foreign fans. Sessions daily from 9pm onwards.

Reduta Jazz Club – *Národní 20, Prague 1 (New Town)* – ☎ *24 91 22 46* – *Daily from 9pm.*
Possibly the city's best known jazz club. It was here that Bill Clinton played saxophone, accompanied by President Václav Havel on drums.

Jazz Club "U staré paní" – *Michalská 9, Prague 1 (Old Town)* – ☎ *26 49 20* – *Bar open 7pm to midnight Monday to Saturday* – *Performances from 9pm.*
Jazz excellence in one of the Old Town's medieval cellars.

Jazz Club Železná – *Železná 16, Prague 1 (Old Town)* – ☎ *24 23 96 97* – *Open 3pm to midnight.*
Jazz alternating with world music.

U Malého Glena – *Karmelitská 23, Prague 1 (Malá Strana)* – ☎ *53 58 11 15* – *Open daily 10am to midnight.*
One of Prague's trendiest locales. The ground floor restaurant is popular with tourists, but the real action takes place in the basement, where a mixture of visitors and locals enjoy both jazz and latino sounds.

Rock

Radost FX – *Bělehradská 120, Prague 2 (New Town)* – ☎ *24 25 47 76* – *Open daily 11.30am to 5am.*
Live concerts at 9pm, followed by international DJs. Techno, house, transe, drum'n bass, mixed and trendy clientele. Gallery café and vegetarian restaurant.

Lucerna Music Bar – *Vodičkova 36, Prague 1 (New Town)* – ☎ *24 21 71 08* – *Café open daily 11am to 5pm, club from 8pm to 3am, concerts from 9pm.*
Vast basement venue below the Lucerna complex built by Václav Havel's grandfather in the early years of the 20C.

Rock Café – *Národní 20, Prague 1 (New Town)* – ☎ *24 91 44 16* – *Open Monday to Friday 10am to 3am, Saturday and Sunday 8pm to 3am, concerts at 9pm and dancing from 12.30am to 3am.*
With its metallic decor, the Rock Café only really comes to life once its youthful clientele gets going.

Cabarets

Bohemian Party (Hotel Ariston) – *Seifertova 65, Prague 3 (Žižkov)* – ☎ *22 78 01 99* – Box office ☎ *21 08 52 76* – *Show at 9pm followed by dancing from 10.45pm.*
The only show of its kind in Prague, the Bohemian Party draws on Czech traditions in dance, cabaret, Black Theatre and folklore, concluding with audience participation on the dance floor. Tickets available for dining plus show or for show only.

Folklore

Czech (and especially Moravian) folklore is very rich and varied. One of the best places to enjoy it is in the auditorium of the Městská knihovna (City Library) in Mariánské náměstí, which runs a folklore season all through the summer, with first-rate groups from all over the country as well as from Slovakia and abroad.

Divadlo Na Klárově – *Nábřeží E Beneše 3, Prague 3 (Klárov)* – ☎ 53 98 37.
Traditional Czech song and dance by some of the country's finest performers. Music, song and dance from the country's rich heritage of folklore, presented by some of the country's finest performers.

Moravian musicians in Old Town Square

U Marčanů – *Veleslavínská 14, Prague 6 (Veleslavín)* – ☎ 36 79 10.
A wine bar where the produce of the country's vineyards can be enjoyed to the accompaniment of traditional song and dance. Favoured by tour groups.

Shopping

early all the shops likely to be of interest to visitors to Prague are concen-
rated in the city centre, particularly in pedestrianised streets like Celetná, Na
říkopě, Melantrichova, Kaprova and Nerudova. Popular buys include Bohemian
lass, porcelain, craft goods such as wooden toys, marionettes, dolls in tradi-
onal costume, or painted Easter eggs. Craft goods and other souvenirs are
lso sold from the numerous stalls set up all the year round in Staroměstské
áměstí (Old Town Square) and on Karlův most (Charles Bridge).

lass, porcelain and Bohemian garnets – there are numerous shops selling
hese superb local products as well as factory outlets elsewhere in the country.

ranát-Gold – *Dlouhá 30, Prague 1 (Old Town)* – ☎ *23 15 61 2.*
endants, rings, bracelets and necklaces fashioned from garnets at the famous
stablishment at Turnov in northeastern Bohemia.

klo Bohemia – *Na Příkopě 17, Prague 1 (Old Town)* – ☎ *24 21 05 74 - Open
Monday to Saturday 9am to 7pm and Sunday 1pm to 6pm.*
ine hand-blown glass (24% lead oxide) from the factory at Světlá nad Sázavou.

ana Bohemia – *Staroměstské náměstí 16, Prague 1 (Old Town)* – ☎ *24 23 70 22.*
his shop is notable for the restored frescoes on its main façade as well as for
s range of glass and porcelain.

ohemia Crystal – *Celetná 5 and Pařížská 12, Prague 1 (Old Town)* – *Open daily
am to 7pm.*
xceptionally wide range of handmade glass.

Czech crystal on display

R. Holzbachova, P. Bénet

eletná Crystal – *Celetná 15, Prague 1 (Old Town)* – *Open daily 10am to 8pm.*
wo floors of handmade glass, garnets and porcelain.

Moser – *Na Příkopě 12, Prague 1 (New Town)* – ☎ *24 21 12 93* – *Open Monday
o Friday 9am to 8pm, Saturday and Sunday 10am to 6pm.*
spectacular array of Bohemian crystal as well as fine porcelain from the
actory founded in Carlsbad in 1857.

Wooden toys, marionettes

ohádka – *Celetná 32, Prague 1 (Old Town)* – *Open daily 9am to 8pm.*
wonderful selection of marionettes and objects made of wood displayed in a
heerful and colourful interior.

antasia Kubénova – *Rytířská 19, Prague 1 (Old Town)* – ☎ *26 41 30* – *Open daily
0am to 6pm.*
mall shop with handmade marionettes of unique design.

eská lidová řemesla – *Melantrchova 17, Prague 1 (Old Town)* – ☎ *21 63 24 11.*
n array of handcrafted wooden items, ideal souvenirs.

Bookshops

Books in languages other than Czech have long been a staple of the Pragu[e] scene, and most outlets have a reasonable selection of picture books, novels [in] translation and other items. Illustrated books and old prints can often be foun[d] at bargain prices in the many second-hand and antiquarian bookshops. One o[r] two places catering for the expatriate literary culture have generated cafes wit[h] a congenial atmosphere *(see Cafes and Bars)*.

Anagram – *Týn 4, Prague 1 (Old Town) – ☎ 24895737 – Open Monday t[o] Saturday 9.30am to 7pm, Sunday 10am to 6pm.*
American bookstore attractively located in the medieval Týn Court.

Antikvariát Galerie Můstek – *28 října 13, Prague 1 (Old Town) – ☎ 268058[ ] Open Monday to Friday 10am to 1pm and 2pm to 6pm, Saturday 10am to 1pm*
Fine quality antiquarian books, prints, maps and printed ephemera in a base[-] ment bookstore not far from the lower end of Wenceslas Square.

Antikvariát Karel Křenek – *Celetná 31, Prague 1 (Old Town) – ☎ 2329919 – Ope[n] Monday to Friday 10am to 6pm, Saturday 10am to 2pm.*
A long-established antikvariát with a studious atmosphere and a good selectio[n] of prints as well as old books.

Big Ben Bookshop – *Malá Štupartská 5, Prague 1 (Old Town) – ☎ 2318021 Open Monday to Friday 9am to 7pm, Saturday and Sunday 10am to 6pm.*
Most of the relevant English-language publications can be found in this friendl[y] bookshop.

Jan Kanzelsberger – *Václavské náměstí 42, Prague 1 (New Town) – Open Monda[y] to Saturday 8am to 7pm, Sunday 9am to 7pm.*
One of the largest stocks of new books in town.

U Černí Matky Boží *Celetná 34, Prague 1 (Old Town) – ☎ 24211275 – Ope[n] Monday to Friday 9am to 7pm, Sunday 10am to 7pm.*
The ground floor and basement of the Cubist Black Madonna building ar[e] devoted to new books and maps, with a fine selection of coffee-table items.

Antiques

Antique shops are scattered throughout the city, but the widest selection o[f] good quality pieces at mainstream prices is at the following address.

Dorotheum – *Ovocný trh 2, Prague 1 (Old Town) – ☎ 24222001.*
Right by the Estates Theatre is this branch of the famous Vienna institutio[n] offering items for sale on commission.

Department Stores

With offerings comparable to their equivalents in western Europe, Prague['s] major department stores are all to be found in the city centre. Most incorpo[-] rate a supermarket-style grocery.

Tesco – *Národní 26, Prague 1 (New Town) – Open Monday to Friday 8am to 8pm[,] Saturday 9am to 6pm, Sunday 10am to 6pm. Supermarket open 1 hr earlier.*
One of the showpieces of the Communist era when it had the impeccabl[e] Socialist name of Maj (May), this multi-storey store was then run by K-Ma[rt] before being taken over by the British firm of Tesco.

Krone – *Václavské náměstí 21, Prague 1 (New Town) – Open Monday to Frida[y] 9am to 8pm, Saturday 9am to 7pm, Sunday 9am to 6pm, bakery and super[-] market 1 hr earlier.*
This German store incorporates a well-stocked Julius Meinl supermarket.

Kotva – *Náměstí Republiky 8, Prague 1 (Old Town) – Open Monday to Frida[y] 9am to 8pm, Saturday 9am to 6pm and Sunday 10am to 6pm.*
This Scandinavian-styled store from the 1970s has what is probably the mos[t] complete range of goods and services in town, mostly at very reasonable prices[.] Good choice of glass and porcelain on the second floor.

Bílá Labut' – *Na Poříčí 23, Prague 1 (New Town) – Open Monday to Friday 8a[m] to 7pm, Saturday 8am to 6pm.*
The "White Swan" has faded somewhat since it was opened in the 1930s as [a] fine example of Functionalist architecture. There's another branch at the top o[f] Wenceslas Square.

Baťa *Václavské náměstí 6, Prague 1 (New Town) – Open Monday to Friday 9a[m] to 8pm, Saturday and Sunday 10am to 6pm.*
Functionalist architecture which has kept its cachet, the flagship store of th[e] world-renowned Bata company has shoes for all sorts in its five-storey buildin[g] on Wenceslas Square.

Food

Prague now has a range of supermarket groceries *(see above)* and delicatessen[s] *(lahůdky)* are spread around the city. Shopping for fresh fruit and vegetable[s] is probably best done at the open-air markets in Havelská in the Old Tow[n] *(Monday to Friday 7.30am to 6pm, Saturday and Sunday 8.30am to 6pm)* an[d] by Národní třída Metro station *(daily 7.30am to 7pm)*. The Havelská marke[t] also has a wide range of other products, many of them suitable as souvenirs[.]

Country Life – *Melantrichova 15, Prague 1 (Old Town) – Open Monday to Thursday 8am to 7pm, Friday 8am to 6pm, Sunday 11am to 6pm.*
A pioneer in bringing vegetarian ideas to meat-obsessed Czechs, Country Life is both a well-stocked store and a buffet.

Dům lahůdek – *Malé náměstí 3, Prague 1 (Old Town) – Open Monday to Saturday 9.30am to 7.30pm, Sunday 10am to 6pm.*
The elaborately decorated building which once housed the Rott family's famous ironmongery is now the city's most appetising delicatessen, with fine products offered on several floors. There's tea, coffee, confectionery, chocolate, cheese, sausage and all kinds of specialities, including a good range of Czech and foreign wines. First floor café with a view over Malé náměstí (Little Square).

Fruits de France – *Jindřišská 9, Prague 1 (New Town) – Open Monday to Friday 9.30am to 6.30pm (early closing Thursday), 9.30am to 1pm Saturday.*
French delicacies of all kinds at French -or more than French- prices.

Shopping arcades (pasáž)

Darex obchodní dům - *Václavské náměstí 11, Prague 1 (New Town) – Open Monday to Friday 10am to 8pm, Saturday 10am to 6pm, Sunday noon to 6pm.*
Boutiques, perfume, and other fashion shops.

Lucerna pasáž – *Štěpánská 61, Vodičkova 36, Prague 1 (New Town) – Open Monday to Friday 9am to 6pm.* Classic 1930s arcade set back from Wenceslas Square.

Černá růže – *Na Příkopě 12, Prague 1 – Open Monday to Friday 9am to 8pm, Saturday 9am to 7pm, Sunday 11am to 7pm.*
Restored 1930s arcade gradually filling up with fashion and specialist shops.

R. Holzbachova, P. Bénet

Marionettes on sale everywhere

Castle and river at night

Introduction
to Prague

Introduction to Prague

THE SETTING

Close to the geographical centre of Bohemia, the site of Prague brings together several of the country's characteristic landscapes: to the south, a steep-sided valley, from which the River Vltava emerges, its appearance on the scene marked by the Vyšehrad cliff, its northward course subsequently deflected by a rock spur extending from the limestone plateau to the west; on the left bank of the river, enough flat and well drained land for settlements to grow up in the protection of the stronghold which almost inevitably, was to be built atop the rock spur, defended by nearly sheer cliffs to the south and a deep ravine to the north; on the right bank of the river, a more extensive area of flat land, which, though prone to flooding, offered space for a sizeable town, which could eventually be extended over the gently rising land to east and south. Linking all these elements was the river, which despite its wayward nature could first be forded and later bridged. The Vltava also put the site of the future capital city in touch with the resources of the south of the country and beyond (timber, salt) and with the products of the fertile plain of the Elbe not far to the north. In all it was a site not only "predestined for urban settlement" (Christian Norberg-Schultz) but one of great beauty and variety, which a thousand years of subsequent building has for the most part only enhanced.

GROWTH OF THE CITY

The earliest nucleus

The attractions of the site of Prague were known to prehistoric people, then, at the time of the Great Migrations, to Slav tribes, considerable numbers of whom lived in fortified compounds scattered over much of the area of today's city. In the 9C a stronghold incorporating the country's first Christian church was built by the Pře myslid Prince Bořivoj at **Levý Hradec (Left Bank Castle)**, some distance downstream. This marked the consolidation of Přemyslid rule in Central Bohemia, but it was not long before the princely seat was moved a more suitable site, the rocky promontory which became known as **Hradčany**. Here, sometime before 890, within the earthen rampart of an elongated settlement of timber buildings, Bořivoj founded a second stone church whose foundations can still be seen today.

Castle and townships

In the 10C as the power of the Přemyslids increased, Hradčany acquired more stone buildings including a round church, the predecessor of St Vitus' Cathedral, and the country's first Benedictine monastery, dedicated to St George. At a point where a number of roadways crossed below the castle rock a trading settlement flourished, sending a scatter of ribbon development southwards along the route much later called Karmelitská (Carmelites Street). On the far bank of the river, three roads fanned out from the fording place, all attracting their share of wayside buildings: one ran north-eastwards past a Jewish settlement towards Poříčí, where a township of German merchants was established in the mid 11C; another ran towards where the Powder Tower now stands and onward to eastern Bohemia, while the third followed the river southward towards the Vyšehrad rock, which for a while served as an alternative stronghold to Hradčany.

By the 10C the Vltava was spanned by the first **bridge**, built of timber.

The Staré Město (Old Town) and Malá Strana

The development of the right bank settlements proceeded apace. By the 11C a **market place** – the forerunner of **Staroměstské náměstí (Old Town Square)** – was functioning in central position along the road eastwards and next to it the **Týnský dvůr (Týn Court)** and church had been established as an enclave of foreign merchants. Destroyed by floods the timber bridge was replaced around 1170 a short distance upstream by a ston structure, the **Juditin most (Judith Bridge)**, and the street pattern adjusted accordingly with the forerunner of today's Karlová (Charles Street) linking bridgehead and market place. With plenty of room to expand, the Staré Mesto continued to flourish; around 1230 it was granted its royal charter as a town and by the the middle of the century it had been ringed with a splendid system of defensive **walls** and **towers**. The problem of flooding which had plagued the citizens for so long was solved by the drastic expedient of raising the ground level by two to three metres; many a vaulted cellar in existence today is in fact the original ground floor of a Romanesque house.

By the 13C, the city's considerable Jewish population, previously scattered, had gathered in the ghetto in the heart of the Old Town.

As a counterweight to the burgeoning Old Town, King Otakar II redeveloped the left bank settlement, giving it a regular street pattern and an imported population of industrious German burghers and craftsmen. This was the **Menšíměsto pražské (Lesser or Town of Prague)**, later to be known as **Malá Strana** (variously translated as Lesser or Minor Town/Quarter, Kleinseite in German).

Gothic expansion

In the mid 14C the face of Prague was transformed by Emperor Charles IV, giving it an imprint which has lasted to the present day. The great Gothic **Sv. Vít, Cathedral of St Vitus** rose above the Hradčany skyline, a splendid new **bridge** was thrown across the Vltava, the first **university** in Central Europe was founded in the Old Town, while beyond an extensive new district was laid out around three great market places, one for cattle, one for horses, one for corn; this was the **Nové Město, New Town**, spacious enough within its walls to accommodate the city's growth well into the modern age. The defences were continued on the Malá Strana side of the river, built as much to relieve misery and unemployment as for protection, and consequently called the **Hladová zed', "Hunger Wall"** which still encloses the Petřín Hill. Capital of the Holy Roman Empire, Prague was one of the biggest, as well as most beautiful cities in Europe, with a population variously estimated between 30 000 and 100 000.

Renaissance and Baroque residences

Fine urban residences like the House of the Lords of Kunštát and Poděbrady had existed in medieval times, but it was in the 16C and especially in the 17C and 18C that the urban **palace** became an important, sometimes dominant element in the city scene. Close to the Castle on the Hradčany height, the Schwarzenberg Palace of 1563 typified the architectural exuberance of the Bohemian Renaissance, while the great complex of buildings arranged around a formal garden built in the 1620s by Generalissimo Wallenstein at the foot of the Hradčany height marked the transition from Renaissance to Baroque. The extreme of Baroque ostentation was exemplified by the Černín Palace, begun in 1669, its colossal facade 135 metres long. More typical were the countless minor residences lining the streets of the Old Town and particularly of Malá Strana. Many looked on to secret inner courtyards, but where space permitted others extended their architecture outwards, terracing the steep slopes of Hradčany and Petřín and embellishing them with statuary and fountains to form some of the Baroque era's most delightful **gardens**.

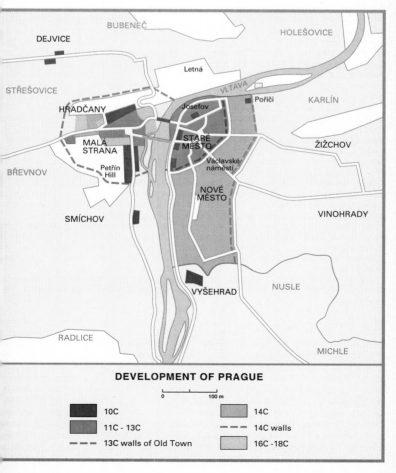

DEVELOPMENT OF PRAGUE

0   100 m

10C	14C
11C - 13C	14C walls
13C walls of Old Town	16C -18C

Prague in 1750

Prague's growth during this period was minimal, indeed the city had lost populatic through emigration and the effects of the Thirty Years War; the total may have sur as low as 25 000, though it recovered rapidly in the 18C, reaching 78 000 in 178 The built-up area remained within the historic boundaries, though Emperor Charle walls were mostly replaced by an elaborate system of Baroque ramparts.

Towards a capital for the Czech nation

As Czech consciousness and self-confidence grew with the National Awakening of th 19C, so Prague roused herself from centuries of slumber. The population expande rapidly as new industries recruited their workforce from the Czech countryside, an working class and middle class **suburbs** like **Smíchov**, **Žižkov** and **Vinohrady** spread beyon the redundant walls. By the end of the century the built-up area numbered some ha a million inhabitants. Railways somehow overcame the complicated contours of th hinterland and arrived at the city gates, in 1845 at what is now Masaryk Station, late at Smíchov and the present Main Station. From about the middle of the century co certed efforts were made to beautify and sanitise the city and provide it with th architectural accoutrements of an incipient capital. Prague had turned her back o the river; now the Old and New Town **embankments** were laid out as promenades an became a setting for fashionable blocks of flats and institutional buildings. For a lor time the only crossing, Charles Bridge was joined by an array of other **bridges**, in 184 and 1868 by a pair of chain bridges, now demolished, in 1876 by the Palacký Bridç Palackého, and just after the turn of the 20C by two particularly lavish structures, th **Most legií** (**Bridge of the Legionaries** – 1901) and the **Čechův most** (**Svatopluk Čech Bridge** 1908). Embodying the burgeoning hopes of national revival, great buildings we placed in prominent locations: the **Národní muzeum** (**National Museum** – 1890) at the to of Wenceslas Square, the **Národní divadlo** (**National Theatre** – 1883) and the **Rudolfinu** (1884) on the riverside, and the **Obecní dům** (**Municipal House** – 1911) next to th medieval Powder Tower at the boundary between Old and New Towns. At every poin monuments and memorials, foremost among them the statue of St Wenceslas reminded Czechs of their history and identity.

While Malá Strana and Hradčany languished in picturesque forgetfulness, the crun bling **Josefov**, **Jewish Town**, was subjected to the ruthless process known as *asanace*; i warren of slums was demolished and replaced by apartment blocks lining broad ne thoroughfares like Pařížská (Boulevard de Paris) linking the riverside with the hea of the Old Town.

The first electric tram ran in 1891 and by the beginning of the 20C the whole ci was knitted together by the tramways which still form a vital part of today's int grated transport system.

The modern city

Declared the capital of the new state of Czechoslovakia founded in 1918, interw Prague took on an increasingly metropolitan character, its population reaching thre quarters of a million in the 1920s. Already flowering in the years before the Fir World War with fine buildings like the Black Madonna House, a progressive arch tecture marked the townscape with an array of Functionalist structures like th **Veletržní palác (Trade Fair Palace)** and modern villa quarters like Baba and Barrando Garden suburbs on the English model were laid out in Dejvice and Hanspaulk Cinemas, theatres, dance halls and nightclubs flourished in the network of arcad (*pasáž* in Czech) centred on Wenceslas Square, whose night-time glamour was ill minated in new-fangled neon. By the end of the 1930s the city's populatic reached the million mark.

ccupation and wartime brought misery and privation, but relatively little physical amage, though bombing devastated some industrial areas and liberation in 1945 saw e destruction of the much of Old Town Square. In the early years of the Commust regime, Prague's needs took second place to those of the provinces and available sources were allocated above all to housing. Low-rise suburbs came first, then comete new "towns" built on the Soviet model from factory-built concrete panels. The ohemian plateau around Prague is now occupied by these monotonous high-rise tates, some of them linked to the centre by the Metro, also Soviet-style and built om 1965 onwards. The road system has failed to keep up with what is one of the ghest rates of vehicle ownership in Europe, though the notorious *magistrála* xpressway running along the edge of the New Town sucks in traffic from all over entral Bohemia. Cars are Praguers' favourite means of escape from their cramped rroundings to the countryside, where many families have a weekend cottage.

HE LOOK OF PRAGUE

o introduction could fail to mention the description of the city as "*Stověžatá Praha*", undred-towered" or "hundred-spired Prague", and the skyline is indeed punctured / an uncountable number of towers and turrets, spires and spikes, domes, belfries, polas and pinnacles. This heavenward rush from roof of church and palace is reinrced by an array of gables, often of extraordinary exuberance in their design. At the me time the city is firmly anchored to the ground. Belying the modernity of many building is a deep **cellar**, of Gothic or even Romanesque date, while splendid arched **cades** help link façades with each other and with street and square.

e importance of a fine façade has been recognised throughout much of the city's story. Most historic buildings put on a fine show for the passing public, with muslar **atlantes** straining to support massive portals, **statues** gracing niches, attics and lustrades, rough stonework concealed beneath smooth stucco or **sgraffito** *(see panel)*. e predominant colour is a rich ochre (one reason for the epithet "Golden Prague"), mplemented by a range of subtle pastels. Paint was in short supply during Comunist times; the prevailing greyness of that era is now fast waning, though some of e garish hues now appearing have no place here.

eyond the street façades is a semi-private world of courtyards, some with galleries *avlač* in Czech), often linked together by doors and passageways, making it possible roam across parts of the city without ever emerging into the public domain. The early)C fashion for the *pasáž*, has only served to increase this network of interior spaces.

The city seen from the tower of St Nicholas'

R. Holzbachova, P. Bénet

PRAGUE, CAPITAL OF THE CZECH REPUBLIC

With a population of about 1.2 million, Prague is far and away the largest city in t
Czech Republic. Traditionally referred to in Czech as *Matka měst* (Mother of Cities) or
Latin as *Praga caput regni* (Prague, head of the kingdom), the city was deprived of
capital status when the Hapsburgs moved their court to Vienna in the early 17C, b
regained it with the proclamation of the new republic of Czechoslovakia in 1918. W
the Nazi occupation in 1939 a further downgrading took place and the city was hum
atingly referred to as "the fourth city of the Third Reich", destined for event
Germanisation. Revival came in 1945, and there was no question that Prague should r
continue as capital when Czech and Slovak Republics went their separate ways in 199
Historically, Prague did not exist as a single unit but was made up of four indepe
dent towns. These still form distinctive districts today, though they have long sir
been amalgamated to form the city of Prague, now known officially as Prague I.

Hradčany is the Castle quarter, consisting of the **hrad** (Castle) itself and its depende
township, virtually unchanged since it stopped growing in the early 18C. Below i
the left bank of the Vltava is **Malá Strana**. With little space to expand, this too has har
altered since its streets were lined with Baroque palaces and town houses in the 1
and 18C. Across Charles Bridge on the far bank of the river is **Staré město** (the Old Tow
embedded within it the former ghetto of **Josefov** (the **Jewish Town**). Always with a co
mercial and trading ethos, the Old Town retains much of its historic character.
boundary with the **Nové město** (New Town) is formed by the semicircle of boulevar
which run along the line of its medieval fortifications. The newness of the New To'
dates back to its foundation in the 14C; it has renewed itself several times since, a
its central square, **Václavské náměstí** (Wenceslas Square), named after the countr
favourite patron saint, is the place where the pulse of city life beats most strongly tod
Given World Heritage status by UNESCO in 1992, this historic core of Prague has o
a small proportion of the city's resident population – about 55 000 – but draws
more than 200 000 people daily to their workplaces in shops, offices, institutio
hotels and restaurants. It is of course the part of the city which is of most interest
visitors, millions of whom come to Prague every year.

Beyond the core and some 10 times its size and population is the so-called **inner c**
densely built up in the 19C and early 20C, and characterised by apartment bloc
interspersed with workshops, institutions and factories, as well as a number of visi'
attractions like the Bertramka, the suburban villa where Mozart completed the sco
of *Don Giovanni*. The Bertramka is in **Smíchov**, on the left bank of the Vltava, but t
most characteristic boroughs of this inner city are right bank **Vinohrady** (Prague II) a
Žižkov-Karlín (Prague III).

Further removed still is the **outer city**, covering twice the area of the historic core a
the inner city combined and with a population of around 500 000, most living
"*paneláks*", the high-rise flats grouped in vast estates with inspiring names like Seve
město (North Town) or Jihozápadní město (Southwest Town). As in many cit
Prague's western suburbs are the most sought after, and Prague VI extending towa
Ruzyně airport has its share of attractive villa quarters, especially in the Dejvice ar
Greater Prague's boundaries stretch out still further into the Bohemian countrysi
taking in smaller communities up to 20km from the centre.

The house signs

A Prague speciality is the house sign. Complementing the two numbers most
buildings have (red for the district, blue for the street) there may be a colourful
plaster panel illustrating the house's name; there's a glorious concentration of
them on Malá Strana's Nerudova (Neruda Street), but they are to be found in
all the city's historic quarters. The names of streets and squares are shown by
means of attractive enamelled signs designed in Secession style; as well as the
street, they give the name and number of the district.

Ph. Gajic/MICHELIN

Street sign and house numbers

History

Origins

attered traces show that the Bohemian basin was occupied by human beings more than lf a million years ago. Much later, around the end of the 6th millenium BC, Neolithic rmers, migrants from southeastern Europe, settled here. But the area only enrs recorded history with the Roman advnce northwards which brought them to contact with its **Celtic inhabitants**. ese Celts were given the name **Boii** by e Romans, and their country called **iohaemum**, from which the English rms **Bohemian** and **Bohemia** are derived. embers of La Tene culture, the Boii em to have been close to forming a cognisable state, but subject to presre from less advanced Germanic tribes the north, were dispersed in the 1C BC d finally subjugated by the Germanic **ircomans** who moved into Bohemia af- being defeated by the Roman general usus in 9BC.

the 4C and 5C AD, Bohemia seems have been little affected by the earst phases of the **Great Migrations**, but e 6C saw the arrival in the area of the st **Slavs**.

AKG Paris

Princess Libuše

620-659	The Slavs form a kingdom under **Samo**, a Gallo-Roman merchant, and conduct military campaigns against the Avars and the Franks. Following the death of Samo there is no trace of a Slav kingdom in Bohemia for a century and a half.
768-814	The reign of Frankish ruler **Charlemagne**, who revives the title of "Roman Emperor" and in the course of several campaigns exacts tribute from Bohemia.
9C-10C	Emergence of the Slavonic **"Great Moravian Empire"** comprising much of the area of present-day Bohemia, Moravia and Slovakia.
863	The missionaries **Cyril** and **Methodius** are sent from Byzantium to convert the Slavs of Great Moravia.
Late 9C	The ruler of the Czechs, Prince (or Duke) Bořivoj builds the stronghold at Levý Hradec downstream from Prague, then moves his capital to Hradčany. He was a member of the Přemyslid dynasty which was to rule Bohemia for centuries.

"A city whose glory shall reach unto the stars"

An inspiring story about the origin both of Prague and of the Přemyslids was told by the 11C chronicler Cosmas. After Čech, the "Father of the Nation", had led his followers into a "land flowing with milk and honey", a subsequent ruler divided his domain among his three daughters. One of them was **Princess Libuše**, who made her home on the high rock above the Vltava at Vyšehrad. One day, gazing across the river towards the Petřín heights, she fell into a trance, in which the vision of a great city was revealed to her "whose glory shall reach unto the stars". Libuše allied feminine intuition to masculine muscle by marrying a son of the soil, a ploughman called **Přemysl**, and together they founded the city of Prague at a place where the stone sill (Czech *práh*) of a house had been set in place.

The Making of a Medieval State

hatever the truth of Cosmas' tale, the dynasty which bore the name of ploughman emysl ruled for centuries over Prague, its surroundings, and later over much of Central rope. The state they created was often at odds with its Germanic neighbours, but ally became part of the Holy Roman Empire. The ruler of Bohemia became one of e seven Electors, the powerful group who met to decide who should be Emperor.

929 (possibly 935)	Christian Prince **Václav (Wenceslas)** is assassinated by his pagan broth Boleslav. Interpretations of the meaning of this act of fratricide va Wenceslas had been brought up as a Christian by his grandmoth **Ludmila**, who was herself assassinated by her pagan daughter D homíra. Was his murder an attempt to set back the spread of Chr tianity? Or was he killed because of his attempts to cement an allian with his German neighbours? The most likely explanation is that death was the result of factional rivalries in the Přemyslid court. Nevertheless, the cult of Wenceslas soon began. Together with grandmother he was canonised, to become the first **patron saints** Bohemia, sanctifying the Přemyslid dynasty and assuring the cou try an honourable place in Christian Europe.
965	Prague is described by the Jewish merchant **Ibrahim Ibn Jakub** as city that through trade is the richest of all" and Bohemia as "t best of the northern lands and the richest in food".
973	The Saxon Thietmar is appointed the first Bishop of Prague. bishopric is subordinate to the archbishopric of Mainz.
983	Prague's second bishop Vojtěch **(Adalbert)** is a Slav, a member of t powerful eastern Bohemian Slavník clan who are the Přemyslic only real rivals. In 993 he was responsible for the foundation of t country's first male monastery at Břevnov. After dying a marty death in East Prussia in 997 Vojtěch was canonised in 999 and years later his relics were brought back to be buried in Hradčan
1032	**Prokop** (or Procopius) founds the monastery of Sázava, devoted the Slavonic rite. He is canonised in 1204 and together wi Vojtěch, Ludmila and Wenceslas forms the quartet of patron sair of Bohemia.
1085	Vratislav I, "King of Bohemia and Poland", moves the royal re dence from Hradčany to Vyšehrad.
1140-1173	Reign of Vladislav II. Under his rule, numerous monasteries a founded, including Premonstratensian **Strahov**. In Malá Strana t Knights of St John Jerusalem build their splendid commande with its church of Our Lady Beneath the Chain. A fine stone **bric** across the Vltava is constructed on the orders of Vladislav's que and subsequently called the Juditin most (Judith Bridge) after h
1212	The **"Golden Bull of Sicily"**, a formal declaration by the Emperor givi Otakar I and his successors the title of King of Bohemia as well the high office of Elector, one of the confraternity of seven w have the right to choose the Emperor.
1233	**Princess Agnes**, daughter of Otakar I, founds a hospital on the riv bank in the Old Town. It is run by lay brothers who later become Order of the Knights of the Cross with the Red Star, the only mon tic order to be founded in Prague. Agnes becames abbess of t adjoining monastery, later named after her. She is canonised in 198
1253-1278	Reign of **King Otakar II**, the King of Gold and Iron" He exten Bohemian rule over Austria and the lands to the south as far the Adriatic and is even considered as a potential Emperor. Aft a campaign in Prussia the city now called Kaliningrad is found and named Königsberg (Kingstown) after him. However, he rous opposition, both at home and abroad, and in 1278 at the Bat of Dürnkrut on the Austrian-Moravian border he is defeated a killed by Rudolf of Hapsburg. During his reign and well into t following century Bohemia enjoys a period of prosperity a Prague emerges as one of the great cities of Europe, a centre courtly literature and Gothic architecture (St Agnes' Convent, O New Synagogue). The chronicle attributed to Dalimil helps est blish the written form of the Czech language.
1306	The assassination of Wenceslas III marks the end of the Přemys dynasty.

Luxembourg splendour

1310	**John of Luxembourg**, son of the future Emperor Henry VII, marries t Přemyslid Princess Eliška and is elected King of Bohemia. Somethi of an absentee monarch, his kingdom interests him mainly as a sour of revenue for foreign adventures, though he succeeded in expandi it to include parts of Silesia and Lusatia as well as the Egerland, t region around present-day Cheb. His son Wenceslas is born in Prag but receives his education in France and is known as Charles.

King John became an almost legendary figure in Bohemian history when, already the victim of blindness, he fights and died in the French army at the Battle of Crécy in 1346.

1338 King John grants the burghers of the Old Town permission to build a town hall.

1344 The status of Prague is enhanced when it is made the seat of an archbishop. No longer subordinate to Mainz, the new archbishop officiates with King John and his son Charles at the laying of the foundation stone of the new Gothic Cathedral of St Vitus.

1346 Known as **Charles IV**, King John's son is elected as both Emperor and King of Bohemia. Prague thus becomes the **"capital" of the Holy Roman Empire**, and, in 1348, the seat of the first university in Central Europe, the **Collegium Carolinum**.

Charles founds and fortifies the great extension to the city known as the Nové Město (New Town), builds churches and monasteries, rebuilds the fortress at Vyšehrad, and replaces the destroyed Judith Bridge by a splendid new Gothic bridge (which is only named **Karlův most (Charles Bridge)**

Charles IV

in 1870). To give employment to workmen faced with starvation he orders the building of the Hladová zeď' **"Hunger Wall"** on Petřín Hill, while to the south of Prague he builds a great castle at Karlštejn as a shrine for the crown jewels and for the holy relics of which he is an assiduous collector.

Multilingual, a master of French, German, Latin and Italian, Charles takes pains to promote the language of the land of his birth, and Czech enjoys a high status during his reign.

1378 Charles is succeeded by his son Wenceslas IV, a weak ruler who allows barons and bishops to dominate his kingdom while the common people suffer the worst of feudal conditions. Plague rages through Prague in 1380. Made into scapegoats for misfortune and despised as the "king's valets", the Jews suffer numerous pogroms, in one of which the ghetto is destroyed.

Gold and silver, dollars and coal

Exploitation of Bohemia's exceptional mineral wealth starts early, particularly around Stříbro (meaning "silver" in Czech) in western Bohemia and Jihlava in the Czech-Moravian Uplands. Then comes the turn of **Kutná Hora**, whose almost incredibly rich silver ores precipitate a massive migration of miners from Germany from 1275 onwards, a phenomenon which has been compared to the 19C Alaskan gold rush. The power and prestige of the later Přemyslid kingdom is to a large extent based on Kutná Hora silver. King Wenceslas II promulgates a mining code in 1300 and orders the minting of "Prague groschen", a coin which becomes legal tender over much of Europe. In 1517 the aristocratic Schlick family become the owners of the rich seams at **Jáchymov (Joachimsthal)** in the Ore Mountains of northern Bohemia and proceed to mint the coins which later became known as "Thalers" (from which the name "dollar" is derived). In the 19C Silesian hard coal became the foundation of the great industrial region around Ostrava. In the 20C the soft brown coal or lignite of northern Bohemia powers the industrialisation of Communist Czechoslovakia, while the uranium of Jachymov fuels Soviet nuclear projects as well as providing unpleasant employment for political prisoners.

Hussite troubles

1414	Radical preacher **Jan Hus** (John Huss) is summoned to the Council of Constance to answer charges of heresy, and despite a promise of safe conduct is burnt at the stake on 6 July 1415.

John Huss burnt at the stake

1419	Hussite demonstrators storm the New Town Hall and throw Catholic councillors from the windows. This first "Prague **defenestration**" marks the start of the **Hussite Revolution**.
April 1420	The Hussites proclaim the Four Prague Articles: communion for the laity in both kinds (in Latin *sub utraque specie*, hence the te Utraquist); asceticism for the clergy; freedom of speech for pre chers; and punishment of mortal sins. Malá Strana is sacked a Vyšehrad destroyed in the course of fighting. Radical Hussit leave Prague and found the town of **Tábor**.
July 1420	In the first of five crusades, the army of Emperor Sigismund defeated on Prague's Vítkov Hill by the Hussite forces led by t southern Bohemian squire Jan Žižka.
1434	A split between the moderate **Utraquists** and the extremist **Tábori** leads to the **Battle of Lipany** at which the latter are routed.
1436	The *Compact* of Basle, a compromise between **Utraquists** and **Cat lics**. Peace returns to a land ravaged by war, impoverished by t flight of many of its German citizens, but with an aristocracy en ched at the expense of the Church.
1458	The nobleman **Jiří z Poděbrad (George of Poděbrady)** is elected **King Bohemia**. Known as the "Hussite king", he strives to maintain ha mony between the different religious parties and even promot a pan-European alliance which some have seen as a forerunner the European Union or even the United Nations.

The Hapsburgs arrive

Between 1471 and 1526 Bohemia is ruled by the Polish **Jagellion** dynasty, who alle the **Estates**, the assembly representing the nobility and the royal towns, to increa their power and influence. When the last Jagellion king, Louis II, is killed in 15. fighting the Turks at the Battle of Mohács in Hungary, the Estates insist on their rig to elect their country's ruler. From a long list of candidates they choose **Ferdinand I Hapsburg**, seeing the Hapsburgs as the only dynasty capable of halting the Turki advance on Central Europe. But Ferdinand is less interested in respecting the tra tional rights and privileges of a largely Protestant Bohemia than in consolidating a centralising Hapsburg power and in restoring the Catholic Church to its former p eminence.

1547	A revolt of the Estates is suppressed and the royal cities, includi the four towns of Prague, are humiliatingly stripped of their p rogatives. Ferdinand I moves his seat to Vienna, leaving his s **Ferdinand of Tyrol** in Prague as Governor. A lover of the arts, t Ferdinand builds the Mannerist Letohrádek Hvězda, **Star Cas** west of Prague and introduces the Bohemian nobility to the cour life-style of the Renaissance.
1556	Ferdinand I becomes Holy Roman Emperor. The Jesuits are in ted to Prague, where in 1562 they establish the **Klementinum** opposition to the Utraquist-inclined old university, the Carolinu Their influence spreads throughout the country.

1575	Crowned king in 1562, Maximilian II approves the "Bohemian Confession" giving protection to Protestants, though this is later withdrawn.
1576-1611	Reign of Emperor **Rudolf II**, a passionate collector and patron of the arts and sciences. Prague witnesses the restoration of churches and the construction of aristocratic palaces in Hradčany and Malá Strana, as noble families from various parts of the Hapsburg Empire move to what is once more an imperial capital. Catholic influence increases.
1609	Together with the moderate Catholics supported by **Matthias**, Rudolf's brother and rival to the throne, the Protestant party forces Rudolf to sign the **Letter of Majesty** guaranteeing freedom of worship.
1611	Work begins on the Lutherans' Trinity Church, Prague's first Baroque place of worship, later renamed Our Lady of Victories when it is given to the Spanish Carmelites. In an attempt to discipline the Estates and ward off his brother Matthias' claims to the throne, Rudolf ill-advisedly calls on his adventurer nephew, Archduke Leopold, to invade Prague with an army of mercenaries from Passau in Bavaria. But the "Passau Army" is chased out of the city and Rudolf forced to abdicate the crown of Bohemia. Matthias is crowned king. Still with the title of Emperor, but ill and alone, Rudolf dies in Hradčany in January 1612.

...e Thirty Years War

...iginating in complex religious and dynastic conflicts, this terrible war began and
...ded in Prague and much of it was fought over the territory of Bohemia, leaving the
...d devastated, depopulated and purged of its Protestants.

AKG Paris

The Second Defenestration of Prague

23 May 1618	The second Prague **defenestration** and the **Rebellion of the Estates**. Inflamed by the Emperor's support of re-Catholicisation, representatives of the Estates storm the castle and throw the Imperial Governors Slavata and Martinic, plus their secretary, into the moat. A provisional government of 30 Directors is formed and an army recruited under the command of Count Thurn and Count Mansfeld.
1619	Made king in 1619, Ferdinand II of Hapsburg is deposed by the Estates and replaced by **Frederick of the Palatinate**. Together with his queen, **Elisabeth Stuart**, the **"Winter King"** enters Prague with great pomp.
8 Nov 1620	**Battle of the White Mountain** *(Bílá Hora)* to the west of Prague in which the Estates army is routed by the Imperial forces. The "Winter King" flees the city. The White Mountain will come to be known as Czech history's blackest day, marking the beginning of the period known as the **Temno** or Time of Darkness.

21 June 1621	The execution on Old Town Square of 27 leaders of the Estat[es] Rebellion, among them several Catholics. The property of those p[ar]ticipating in the uprising is confiscated and sold at knock-down pri[ce] to noble families, both Bohemian and foreign, who had remain[ed] loyal to the Imperial cause. Among them are Germans, Spaniards, [Ita]lians, Flemings and Croats.
1627-1628	Bohemia is given a new constitution, effectively transferring Cze[ch] sovereignty to Vienna, while German acquires the same official s[ta]tus as Czech. Re-Catholicisation is ruthlessly implemented by Ar[ch]bishop Harrach. Protestants are given the choice – **conversion** [to] **Catholicism** or exile; some 150 000 choose exile, among them t[he] great humanist Comenius.
1631-1632	Prague occupied by a Saxon army. Some exiles return, only to m[eet] with hostility and incomprehension.
1648	Following their previous attempts in 1639 and 1645, the **Swe[des]** occupy part of Prague, plundering the treasures of Malá Stra[na] and the castle. But they are foiled in their attempt to cross t[he] river by the heroic efforts of students and the Jewish commun[ity] who barricade the Old Town end of the bridge. A **Marian column** is erected in Old Town Square to mark the def[eat] of the Protestant forces. But the city has lost many of its inha[bi]tants and half its houses are empty.

Darkness or Baroque brilliance?

The period which begins with the defeat at White Mountain is also an age in which t[he] face of Prague is immeasurably brightened by the splendours of Baroque art and arc[hi]tecture.

1653	Prague University is merged with the Jesuit Klementinum. T[he] Jesuits control education at all levels. Later, the Jesuit cens[or] **Antonín Koniáš** promulgates his own *"Index of Prohibited or Dan[ge]rous and Suspicious Books"* and boasts of burning more th[an] 30 000 volumes during his career.
1683	The statue of Canon **Jan Nepomucký (John of Nepomuk)**, martyred [in] 1393, is put in place on Prague's bridge. In 1729 he is canonis[ed] with much ceremony and his cult promoted with the intention [of] effacing John Hus from popular memory.

Ph. Gajic/MICHELIN

The murder of St John Nepomuk

1740-1780	Reign of **Empress Maria-Theresa**
1741	During the War of the Austrian Succession (1740-8) Prague [is] occupied by Bavarian and French forces. Supported by the ma[jo]rity of the Bohemian Estates, the Duke of Bavaria is crowned Ki[ng] of Bohemia but in 1742 the city is retaken by an Austrian ar[my] under the command of Prince Lobkowicz.

1744	Prague is occupied by the Prussians and Frederick the Great gains much of the province of Silesia.
1757	Prague suffers another, harsher, Prussian occupation in the course of the Seven Years War.
1780	The prototypical "enlightened despot" Emperor Joseph II implements his policy of centralisation, refusing to have himself crowned in Prague and promoting German as the official language of the Empire. He had previously ordered the dissolution of many monasteries and banished the Jesuits. He promotes education and does away with many of the oppressive laws burdening the Jewish community, though all Jews are required to take a German name.

he nation awakes

e reforms promoted by Maria Theresa and Joseph encourage trade and industry d the development of a Czech middle class. The Czech language is codified and ived, Czech history rediscovered, and the idea of a Czech nation with ancient rights d a bright future takes hold.

1805	The French under **Napoleon Bonaparte** win a great victory over the Russians and Austrians at the **Battle of Austerlitz (Slavkov)** in Moravia. In contrast to the devastation it suffered during the Thirty Years War, Bohemia remains relatively unscathed by the Napoleonic Wars.
1818	Foundation of the National Museum.
1836	Coronation of Ferdinand V as King of Bohemia. He is the last Hapsburg to be crowned in Prague. Adolph Fischer notes that the city has 67 churches and 99 towers, thereby meriting the name of "hundred-towered Prague" *(stověžatá Praha)*.
1848	The **Year of Revolutions**. Vienna and Budapest rebel against the Metternich regime. A **Pan-Slav Congress** is held in Prague at which František Palacký develops the idea of Austria as a bulwark against German nationalism ("Austro-Slavism"). An uprising of radicals, students and workers is rapidly put down by General Windischgrätz. **Emperor Franz Josef** takes the throne in Vienna, but despite promises is never crowned in Prague. The high hopes of the reformers and rebels of 1848 are disappointed as a reactionary regime is established in Vienna. The only concrete improvement is the emancipation of the peasantry.
1866	Prussian armies enter Bohemia and crush the Austrian forces at **Sadová** near **Hradec Králové (Königgrätz)**. By the Treaty of Prague the Austrian Empire is excluded from the affairs of a Germany now dominated by Prussia.
1868	The foundation stone of the **Národní divadlo** (National Theatre) is laid. Unlike the National Museum whose purpose was to display the riches of a Bohemia both German and Czech, this is one of a series of great national institutions whose ethos is predominantly Czech, intended to consolidate the gains of the National Revival. Crowds demonstrate against the *Ausgleich*, the Austro-Hungarian Compromise of 1867 which creates the Dual Monarchy and gives Hungary complete control over her internal affairs. This is in painful contrast to the situation in the Czech and other Slav lands of the Empire.
1871	The offer of **"Fundamental Articles"**, intended to give Czechs a measure of Home Rule and parity in representation with their German fellow-countrymen, is withdrawn after German and Hungarian protests.
1882	The nationalist gymnastic association known as **Sokol** (Falcon) meets in Prague for the first time.
1891	A great **Jubilee Exhibition** is held in Prague to commemorate the first exhibition of its kind a century earlier. Boycotted by German exhibitors, it nevertheless attracts nearly 2.5 million visitors.

he birth of Czechoslovakia

ech hopes for a kind of federalised Austria in which their national aspirations could realised change during the First World War to demands for outright independence association with their Slovak cousins. The collapse of Austria-Hungary in 1918 ows these demands to be met. The new state of Czechoslovakia inherits most of e old Empire's industry, but its prosperity and its democratic regime fail to save it m Nazi Germany, which exploits Czech-German antagonisms to bring about its mise.

1914	Outbreak of the First World War. Early Russian successes unlea a wave of Pan-Slav enthusiasm which is crushed by the Austr authorities.
1915	The 15th Prague Infantry Regiment desert en masse to the R sians. During the the war tens of thousands of Czech and Slov **legionnaires** fight on the Allied side in France and Italy as well Russia. In exile, **Tomáš Garrigue Masaryk** and **Edvard Beneš** promote t idea of an independent Czechoslovakia to the Allies.
1916	The death of Emperor Franz Josef elicits genuine sorrow amo his Czech subjects, but the growth of extreme German natio lism turns the populace against the regime.
28 Oct 1918	Proclamation of the Czechoslovak Republic in Prague's Obe dům (Municipal House). A mob tears down the Marian column the Old Town Square as a symbol of Hapsburg rule.
21 Dec 1918	Masaryk returns to Prague in triumph. Choosing a motor-c rather than the state carriage, the President-Liberator is driv from station to castle accompanied by legionnaires, Sokol me bers, and women in traditional costume.
1920s	Prague is the capital of the new state, a kind of multi-ethnic Hap burg Empire in miniature, with several important minorities, which the Bohemian Germans – now calling themselves Sude Germans – outnumber the Slovaks (3.1 million as against 1.9 m lion. Despite being a parliamentary democracy of an almost mo kind and despite Masaryk's undoubted wisdom and fairness, Cze nationalism is the ruling ideology; the Hussite period is idealis and the "injustice of 1620" is reversed by confiscation of the gr landed estates formed at that time. Foreign policy depends French guarantees of the new frontiers and on the Little Enter an alliance with the other states formed from the ruins of t Hapsburg Empire, Romania and Yugoslavia.
1930s	**The Great Depression** hits the **Sudetenland** particularly hard, aggra ting tensions between Czechs and Germans. Having served f terms as President, Masaryk retires in 1935 and is succeeded his Foreign Minister and long-term collaborator, **Edvard Ber** Though ostensibly demanding only a degree of autonomy, t nationalist *Sudetendeutsche Partei, Sudeten German Party*, Konrad Henlein becomes a Trojan horse for a Nazi Germany int on destroying Czechoslovakia.
29 Sept 1938	The **Munich Agreement** signed by Britain, France, Germany and It forces Czechoslovakia to cede the Sudetenland to Germany, le ving the country an economically impotent and strategically fenceless rump. Rather than urging his fellow-countrymen to fig Beneš resigns and goes into exile a second time, along with te of thousands of others.

Czechoslovak legionaries escort Masaryk into Prague

CZECHOSLOVAKIA SINCE 1918

▢ Czechoslovakia 1918 - 1938	▢ Czechoslovakia 1945 - 1993
▨ Occupied by Hungary 1938 - 1945	▢ Czech Republic 1994
▨ Protectorate of Bohemia-Moravia 1939 - 1945	----- Others frontiers

The "Protectorate of Bohemia-Moravia"

Hitler orders Slovakia to secede from what is left of Czechoslovakia, and Prague is occupied on 15 March 1939 by the Wehrmacht. Modelled on the French colonial regime in Tunisia, the "Protectorate of Bohemia-Moravia" is proclaimed, with **Konstantin von Neurath** as Reichsprotektor. The Czechs are promised the opportunity to develop their national life but in reality the Nazis intend to Germanise the country by immigration and expulsion of "racially unsuitable elements". In the meantime a stick and carrot policy is followed, with persecution of intellectuals on the one hand and extra rations for workers prepared to labour in the armaments industry on the other.

17 Nov 1940	After the death of a student in the course of a demonstration, German police raid student hostels and deport 1 200 young men to concentration camps. All Czech institutions of higher learning are closed down.
24 Nov 1941	The fortress town of **Terezín (Theresienstadt)** is turned into a ghetto for Jews before they are transported to the death camps. Of the roughly 118 000 Jews living in the Czech lands in 1939, some 78 000 will perish.
1942	A wave of terror, which includes the destruction of the village of **Lidice**, follows the assassination of acting Reichsprotektor **Reinhard Heydrich** by parachutists sent from Britain. The parachutists are cornered in the crypt of Prague's Orthodox Cathedral and die there after desperate resistance.
May 1945	**The Prague Uprising**. Several days before the arrival of the Red Army the citizens of Prague rise against the occupying Germans, temporarily aided by the Vlasov Army composed of renegade Russians in German uniform. Already in possession of western Bohemia, US forces are not permitted to intervene. Some 1 691 Czechs are killed in the Uprising, out of a total of about 360 000 Czechs and Slovaks who have died in the course of the war as a whole.

Darkness falls again

1945-1948	Czechoslovakia is re-established in its prewar frontiers, though the far eastern province of Sub-Carpathian Ukraine is annexed by the Soviet Union. President once more, Beneš relies less on the western Allies and more on the USSR and the **Czechoslovak Communist Party** (KSČ), which forms the largest group in parliament and provides the prime minister, **Klement Gottwald**. Wholesale nationalisation takes place, collaborators are expropriated, and 2.7 million Germans are deported. Communist control is extended over police and people's militia.
25 Feb 1948	The **Communist coup d'etat**. Non-Communist ministers resign, hoping that Beneš will dissolve the government and order new elections, which are certain to return a smaller number of Communists. Massive demonstrations in Wenceslas Square and Old Town Square and the threat of bloodshed shake the elderly and frail Beneš who allows a Communist government to be formed.

10 March 1948	**Defenestration** of popular Foreign Minister **Jan Masaryk**, son of th[e] former President, and the only remaining independent member [of] the government. An emigration comparable to that of 1938 tak[es] place.
1952	Having overseen numerous political purges, Party Secretary **Rud[olf] Slánský** is himself arrested and together with 13 other high-rankin[g] Communists as leaders of "the Zionist international conspiracy[".] After a **show trial** on Soviet lines, 11 of the accused are sentence[d] to death. Thousands of others suffer persecution of various kind[s] including forced labour in uranium mines.
Early 1960s	A mild form of de-Stalinisation takes place, despite resistance fro[m] unimaginative leaders like Antonín Novotný, and victims of th[e] show trials are rehabilitated.
1968	The **Prague Spring**. On 5 January, the Slovak **Alexander Dubč[ek]** becomes First Secretary of the Ksč and strives to introduce **"Soc[ia]lism with a human face"**. Public support is overwhelming, but on 2[1] August half a million Warsaw Pact troops invade Czechoslovaki[a]. Dubček and other members of the government are flown to Mo[s]cow in chains and forced to concede a halt to reform. Anoth[er] massive emigration takes place.
16 Jan 1969	In protest against the invasion and its consequences, the stude[nt] **Jan Palach** sets fire to himself by the Wenceslas statue. His funer[al] is attended by half a million people.
17 April 1969	Dubček is replaced by a fellow-Slovak, Gustáv Husák, himself [a] victim of the show-trials of the 1950s. He presides over **"norma[li]sation"**, in which the Communist Party is purged of all tho[se] connected with the 1968 reforms and citizens are guaranteed [a] quiet life and a modicum of consumer goods in return for no[n] involvement in politics.
1977	A group of intellectuals signs **Charta 77** demanding that the gover[n]ment respect its own laws.
1987	Visit of Soviet President Gorbatchev, whose policy of *perestroï[ka]* terrifies Czechoslovak apparatchiks.

Dubček and Havel in 1989

Velvet Revolution
and birth of the Czech Republic

Jan 1989	Demonstrations marking the anniversary of the death of **Jan Palach**.
17 Nov 1989	Mass demonstration marking the anniversary of the anti-Nazi student rebellion of 1939. The police react viciously and the **Velvet Revolution** begins, with opposition coordinated by the Civic Forum (Občanské Fórum) led by dissident playwright **Václav Havel**.
29 Dec 1989	Havel is elected President of Czechoslovakia.
1990s	Withdrawal of the 75 000 Soviet troops stationed in the country since 1968. The process of **restitution** begins to return nationalised and confiscated property to its former owners. Another process, **"lustration"**, intended to unmask murky pasts, sometimes declines into wild accusations of cooperation with the secret police. Yet another process, **privatisation**, leads to the export of much of the country's wealth by unscrupulous operators, many of them former Communists with good contacts and access to industrial and financial information.
1992	Unable to resolve their differences within the framework of a single state, Czech Prime Minister Klaus and Slovak Prime Minister Mečiar decide to divide the country. **The Czech Republic** is proclaimed on 1 January 1993, its President Václav Havel.
1999	Along with Hungary and Poland, the Czech Republic becomes a member of NATO and expects to be among the first wave of post-Communist countries to join the European Union early in the new millenium.

e chapters in the Introduction on Art and Architecture, Intellectual Life and Music
ve an overview of Prague culture as it has developed over the centuries. Reading
em before you begin your visit will place buildings and works of art in their context
d greatly increase your appreciation and enjoyment.

Bohemians

BOHEMIANS

The name Boii given by the Romans to the Celtic inhabitants of what is now the Czec Republic persisted (as Bohemian in English, Böhm in German) for centuries as a wa of describing the country's inhabitants of whatever ethnic origin. Nowadays the Czec Republic is an ethnically homogenous country, with the Slavs who form the va majority of its population describing themselves as Czechs. The most numerous co temporary minority are the Gypsies, while in the past Jews *(see p. 121)* and Germa made up a significant proportion of the population.

GYPSIES

Of North Indian origin, the Gypsies arrived in what is now the Czech Republic som time in the 13C. and have led an often precarious existence on the edge of socie ever since. Many prefer to describe themselves as *rom* (pl. *roma*) meaning simp human being. Their existence on the margins of society has been a precarious on During the German Occupation the Czech Gypsies were treated in much the same wa as Jews, losing all but a few hundred of their number. Two concentration camps we set up, one at **Lety** in southern Bohemia, the site of which is now, controversially, pig farm.

After the Second World War and the expulsion of the country's German inhabitant the Czechoslovak government's attempts to resettle the empty border distric involved the movement there of many Gypsies from **Slovakia.** Despite the unfamili surroundings, and despite the breaking up and dispersal of many traditional extende families, these new Czechs played an essential part in repopulating the borderland an their labour was indispensable in reviving its economy. Communist policy aimed assimilation, but was often applied half-heartedly and with limited success. But wi the demise of Communism, many of the unskilled labouring jobs on which Gypsi depended simply disappeared. Their plight was not eased when Czechoslovakia spl and the government of the new Czech Republic, in the face of international criticis made it difficult for them to obtain Czech citizenship, putting undue emphasis o foreign (including Slovak) origin, criminal records and command of Czech. Widesprea discrimination persists among the population at large, with numerous instances skinhead attacks and social segregation; furious controversy was aroused when the was a proposal to build a high wall to separate Gypsy and "white" housing in th industrial city of Ústí nad Labem.

Small wonder that there is a strong temptation for Gypsies to seek refuge elsewher in 1997 many were seduced by TV programmes showing an idealised picture of li in Britain and Canada into attempting to emigrate to those countries. But there a positive developments as well. The President has maintained a steadfast defen against prejudice. A Gypsy deputy sits in Parliament and there is a Gypsy newsread on TV. And in the 1998 elections the extremist Republican Party, which had bas much of its appeal on anti-Gypsy sentiment, lost all its seats.

Gypsies live in most parts of the Czech Republic; in Prague they are concentrated the industrial suburbs of Smíchov and Žižkov.

GERMANS

The often productive, often fraught relationship between the Germanic and Slav inha itants of Bohemia effectively came to an end after the Second World War, with th **expulsion** of virtually the whole of the German population of Bohemia and Moravia.

Rulers, churchmen, burghers and miners – In the Middle Ages, western cultur influences from whatever part of Europe were naturally transmitted to the Czechs v the neighbouring, German-speaking lands. Czech rulers married German princesses a matter of course and the earliest monasteries were staffed with monks fro Germany. When Prague became a bishopric in 973 it was subordinate to the arc bishopric of Mainz. Courtly ways had a Germanic tinge, and it was fashionable Germanise the name of a family or a residence.

Even more important were the changes that occurred during the great Europe-wi expansion of the High Middle Ages, when the growing rural population migrated ou wards from the existing settled areas to found new villages, clear forests, dra marshlands and push the boundary of cultivable land high into the uplands. In centr parts of Bohemia, this 12C-13C work of reclamation and colonisation was carried o by Czech peasants, but in the thinly populated and densely forested **borderlands** th new population was mostly drawn from the adjacent German lands like Austri Bavaria and Saxony. At the same time, the Přemyslid kings were attempting strengthen the Czech state by establishing **towns**, which they populated with Germ burghers and craftsmen and which were governed by municipal laws modelled on th German pattern. When metal ores began to be mined in earnest in places like **Kut Hora**, the skilled workforce was largely drawn from Germany.

rmans and Czechs in Prague – In **Prague**, a community of Germans had existed in
 Poříčí area since the mid 11C, while the **Týn Court** or **Ungelt** behind the Old Town
uare served as an enclave for foreign, mostly German merchants, who worshipped
the Týn Church. Much of the Old Town had a Germanic character, with streets of
e patrician houses radiating from the Square, while Czechs tended to live further
st, around what is now Betlémské náměstí (Bethlehem Square). Tensions existed
ween the two communities, but with nothing like the ferocity that was to develop
ater, more nationalistic times. When in 1409 King Wenceslas IV gave special priv-
ges to the students and professors of the "Bohemian Nation" at the university, some
hough not all – of their German-speaking colleagues departed in a huff to places
learning on the far side of the frontier, despite the term Bohemian applying to any
tive inhabitant of the country.
er the Hussite Wars of the early 15C German influences waned; not only in Prague
t in many towns the numbers of Czech burghers increased and the reins of munic-
l government were taken over by Czechs. For a while a Bohemian symbiosis seemed
hold, with less importance attached to ethnic origin than to religious confession.
e noblemen who stormed Prague Castle in 1618 to defenestrate the Catholic Im-
ial Governors were more aware of their Protestantism and their desire to preserve
ir aristocratic privileges against Imperial encroachment than of the language they
oke. After the defeat of the rebellious Estates at the Battle of the White Mountain
1620, those executed on Old Town Square included several German-speakers.

e spread of Germanisation – But the White Mountain and its aftermath did mark
urning point in the relative status of Czech and German in Bohemia. In the forced
igration of Protestants, the country lost many of its natural leaders. Much of their

fiscated property was dis-
buted amongst a new aris-
racy, drawn from those who
d helped restore Imperial
l Catholic fortunes. This new
ng class came from all over
rope (with names like
warzenberg and Buquoy),
 beholden to a court which
d withdrawn to Vienna, were
on Germanised. For two cen-
ies and more, polite and ed-
ated life was carried on in
rman, with Czech being re-
ded as the speech of the
ver orders. Mozart would
e been surprised on his vis-
 to Prague if he had not
ard German spoken all
und him. Even the Czech in-
ectuals who pioneered the
ional Revival at the begin-
g of the 19C were educated
German and, to begin with
least, found it easier to ex-
ss themselves in that lan-
age.

Bohemian Germans

**and its retreat from
gue** – During the course of
 19C, the Czechs and Ger-
ns of Bohemia and Prague found themselves in increasingly antagonistic camps.
ticularly in Prague, Germans resented the loss of their supremacy, as the city filled
 with Czech speakers drawn from the surrounding countryside and as an increas-
ly confident Czech middle class began to take over the city's governance. Though
peror Franz Josef could remark in 1868 with satisfaction that "Prague has a thor-
hly German appearance", by 1882 the last German councillors resigned en masse
en the council decided that henceforth all street signs would be in Czech only. In
 same year the university founded by Emperor Charles IV in 1348 split into sep-
te Czech and German institutions.
 the turn of the century the German community amounted to only a fraction of the
's total population; most were business people, civil servants, students and other
mbers of the middle class.
h the founding of the independent state of Czechoslovakia in 1918 the Germans of
gue felt even less welcome, while their increasingly nationalistic fellow-countrymen
what had come to be called the **Sudetenland**, after failing to secede from the new
ublic, only accepted their new situation with great unwillingness. Efforts to build
ges between the two communities faltered with the onset of the Great Depression
he end of the 1920s, which hit the German inhabitants of the borderland particu-

larly hard, and left its population open to siren voices from a Germany transformed
Hitler into his Third Reich. German Prague had a final flowering as refugees fr
Nazism like Thomas Mann settled here, however briefly. When the 1938 Mur
settlement gave Hitler the Sudetenland, the euphoria of most Bohemian Germ
obscured the plight of others forced to flee, like Socialists, Communists and Jews.

Occupation and expulsion – Occupied by the Nazis from 1938-45, longer than
other country except Austria, and brutally treated, the Czechs were in no mood
forgive Bohemian Germans their enthusiastic acceptance of Nazism and the threa
posed to the very existence of the Czech nation. Plans conceived by the governm
in exile to expel the German population were confirmed by the Allies. Between
end of the war and 1947 some 2.7 million were transferred to Germany, at the s
often in chaotic and cruel conditions, later in a more organised way. A minority v
could prove that they had resisted Nazism were allowed to stay, though with no rig
as a community. The country lacked the human resources to fully repopulate the ab
doned Sudetenland; though towns like Karlovy Vary/Carlsbad soon came back to
hundreds of settlements simply disappeared, decayed, destroyed or absorbed into
encroaching forest. The expulsion was carried out by the postwar, democratic Be
government, not by the Communists, and consequently Czechs consider the expel
to have no right to compensation. The issue remains problematic.

Czech or German?

In the 1920s, the leader of the Czech Social Democratic Party was a Mr Němec (meaning German in Czech), while the German Social De-
mocrats were led by a Dr Czech. Centuries of
intermarriage left something like a fifth of all
Czechs with a German name and a similar proportion of Bohemian Germans with a Czech one,
belying the rigid ethnic divisions which have
plagued the relations of the two communities in
modern times.

Elements of architecture

Romanesque

Rotunda of the Holy Cross – Old Town

Dating from the early 12C, this is the oldest of Prague's three remaining circular churches.

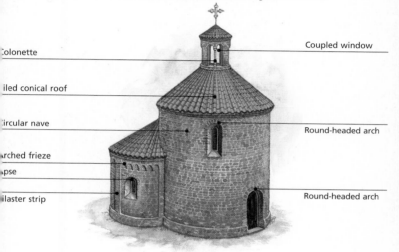

Colonette

Tiled conical roof

Circular nave

Arched frieze

Apse

Pilaster strip

Coupled window

Round-headed arch

Round-headed arch

Gothic

St Vitus' Cathedral (begun c 1344) – Hradčany

The chancel, begun by Matthew of Arras in 1344 and after his death in 1352 brought to a triumphant conclusion by Peter Parler, reveals both French and English influence.

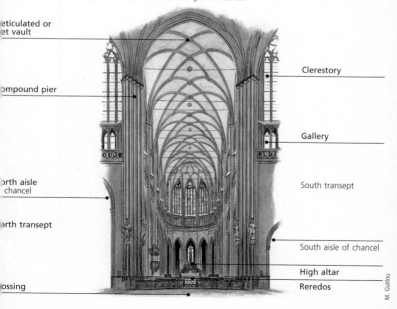

Reticulated or net vault

Compound pier

North aisle of chancel

North transept

Crossing

Clerestory

Gallery

South transept

South aisle of chancel

High altar

Reredos

M. Guillou

...ce Architecture

Schwarzenberg Palace (1545-63) – Hradčany

...g the finest of the city's Renaissance palaces. Its bold, Italianate forms were much imitated during the
...n Renaissance revival style in the late 19C.

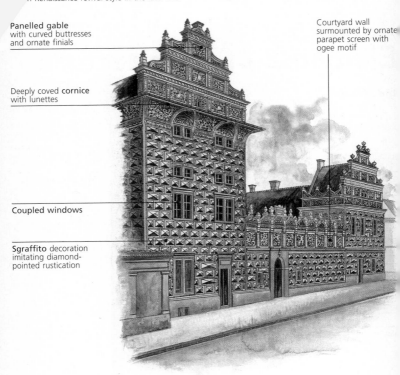

Panelled gable
with curved buttresses
and ornate finials

Courtyard wall
surmounted by ornate
parapet screen with
ogee motif

Deeply coved **cornice**
with lunettes

Coupled windows

Sgraffito decoration
imitating diamond-
pointed rustication

Baroque Architecture

St Nicholas' Church (from 1702) – Malá Strana

The sober articulation of the church's southern flank contrasts with the dynamic counterpoint of convex ar
concave forms of the west front.

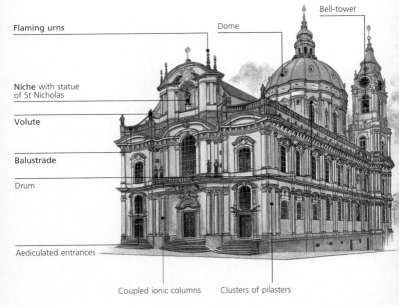

Flaming urns

Dome

Bell-tower

Niche with statue
of St Nicholas

Volute

Balustrade

Drum

Aediculated entrances

Coupled ionic columns   Clusters of pilasters

St Nicholas' Church, interior (from 1703)

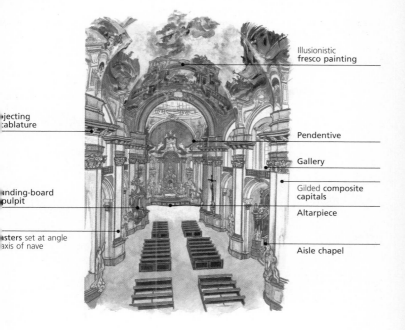

Illusionistic fresco painting

jecting ablature

Pendentive

Gallery

nding-board pulpit

Gilded composite capitals

Altarpiece

sters set at angle axis of nave

Aisle chapel

Portal of Clam-Gallas Palace (1713-19) – Old Town

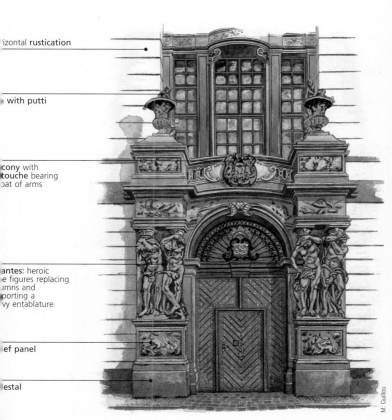

rizontal rustication

with putti

cony with touche bearing at of arms

antes: heroic figures replacing umns and porting a vy entablature

ef panel

estal

M. Guillou

Baroque Garden Design

Ledebour and Small Pallfy Gardens (late 17C, remodelled late 18C)

A number of Prague's Renaissance, Baroque and Rococo gardens were laid out on steep slopes previous terraced for vines or orchard trees.

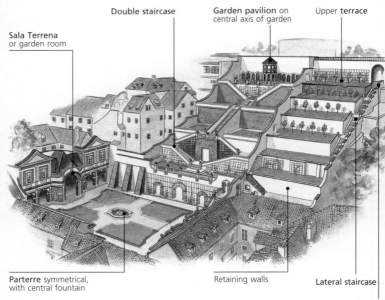

Double staircase

Garden pavilion on central axis of garden

Upper terrace

Sala Terrena or garden room

Parterre symmetrical, with central fountain

Retaining walls

Lateral staircase

Boundary w

Medieval Military Architecture

Karlštejn Castle (begun 1348)

Though with most of the elements of a military fortress, Karlštejn was conceived mainly as a shrine repository for sacred relics and a place of retreat for Emperor Charles IV.

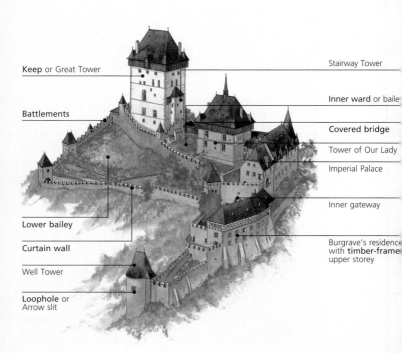

Keep or Great Tower

Stairway Tower

Inner ward or baile

Battlements

Covered bridge

Tower of Our Lady

Imperial Palace

Inner gateway

Lower bailey

Curtain wall

Burgrave's residence with timber-frame upper storey

Well Tower

Loophole or Arrow slit

eo-historical Architecture

National Museum (1891) – New Town

e museum is one of a number of monumental edifices built in the late 19C which use Renaissance or roque forms to proclaim their civic or national importance.

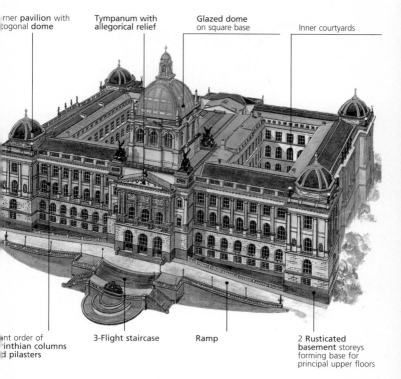

rner pavilion with togonal **dome**

Tympanum with allegorical relief

Glazed dome on square base

Inner courtyards

nt order of rinthian columns d pilasters

3-Flight staircase

Ramp

2 **Rusticated basement** storeys forming base for principal upper floors

cession or Art Nouveau Architecture

Municipal House (1909-12) – Old Town

e most ambitious and sumptuously decorated of all Prague's buildings in Secession style, the Municipal use (Obecní dům) was also the last, as architects turned away from this highly ornamental style.

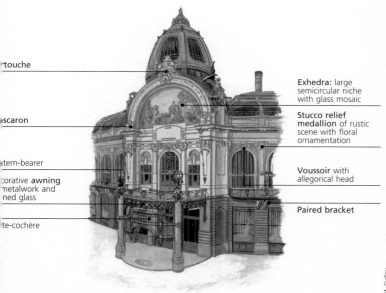

touche

scaron

tern-bearer

corative awning metalwork and ned glass

te-cochère

Exhedra: large semicircular niche with glass mosaic

Stucco relief medallion of rustic scene with floral ornamentation

Voussoir with allegorical head

Paired bracket

M. Guillou

Modern Architecture

Bank of the Legions (now Czech Trade Bank – 1921-23) – New Town

A late offspring of the uniquely Czech Cubist movement in architecture, this is a fine example of the sh
lived National or Rondo-Cubist style, in which typically Slavonic rounded forms and the national colours w
employed to striking effect.

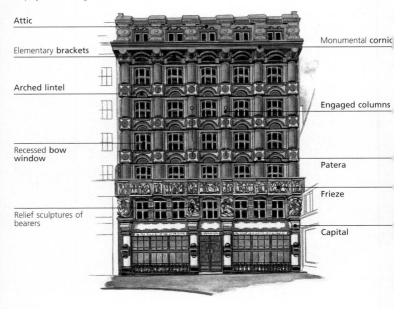

Attic

Monumental cornic

Elementary **brackets**

Arched lintel

Engaged columns

Recessed **bow
window**

Patera

Frieze

Relief sculptures of
bearers

Capital

Bata Shoe Store (1927-9) – New Town

A purpose-built Functionalist structure on a key city centre site which abandons all attempts at conventio
ornamentation and instead exploits new materials like reinforced concrete and plate glass. A sense of orde
completion is given by the stepped recession at the top of the building and by the doubling of mulli
between narrower panes of glass. Curtain wall acts as a weatherproof skin but not as a structural supp
to the floors.

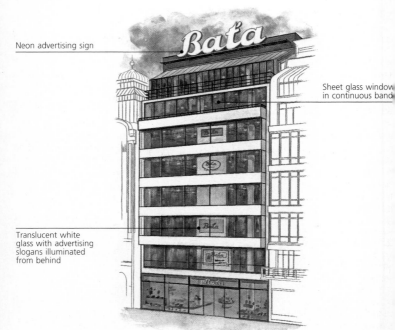

Neon advertising sign

Sheet glass window
in continuous band

Translucent white
glass with advertising
slogans illuminated
from behind

LOSSARY OF ART AND ARCHITECTURAL TERMS
SED IN THE GUIDE

lée: avenue of clipped trees in a formal garden

tarpiece: ornamental structure placed above and behind an altar, frequently used as setting for a religious picture or carving

nbulatory: link between the side aisles at the eastern end of a church to allow circu-tion around the sanctuary

se: semicircular east end of a church, behind the main altar

cade: row of small arches, usually raised on columns or pilasters

lante: figure of a man used as a supporting or decorative column

ial chapel: chapel sited at the eastern end of a church on the building's main east-est axis

iley: area between the outer walls of a castle and its central buildings

rrel-vault: vault in the form of a continuous arch

rtizan: small overhanging turret with lookout holes and defensive loops

lvedere: park or garden structure built to enhance appreciation of a viewpoint

acket: piece of projecting stone or timber supporting a beam or cornice

attice: temporary projecting wooden gallery or parapet used during sieges

pital: enlarged uppermost part of the shaft of a column

ancel: part of the church reserved for the clergy and choir containing the high altar

apter-house: room in a monastery where the chapter of canons or nuns congregate

rnice: continuous moulded projection at the top of a wall (or other feature)

ur d'honneur (French): formal entrance courtyard, usually with flanking wings and reen wall and gates

rtain wall: length of wall or rampart between two towers or bastions

twater: V-shaped projection on the upstream side of a bridge pier designed to protect e structure from damage by debris

gaged column: a column attached to or merging with a wall

liated scroll: sculpted spiral ornamentation, decorated predominantly with stylised liage motifs

zebo: small ornamental structure commanding a view

achicolation: overhanging gallery or parapet with floor openings through which boiling or missiles could be dropped on assailants

arian column: column topped by statue of Virgin Mary, usually in prominent public place

erlon: solid part of a battlemented parapet between two embrasures

t vaulting: vaulting with ribs forming lozenge-shaped panels

jee: a curve bending one way then the other

atory: chapel for private prayer

sáž (Czech): shopping arcade

vlač (Czech): courtyard housing with access galleries

aster: rectangular pier projecting slightly from wall

nnacle: tall, thin terminal feature atop a buttress

ague column: elaborately decorated Baroque column erected to celebrate deliverance om plague

iel: bay window cantilevered out from a wall

suary: storehouse for human bones, often arranged in decorative patterns

rterre: level space in garden laid out in formal patterns

tto (plural: putti - Italian): chubby naked cherub

od screen: carved screen in a church separating the chancel from the nave

istication: stonework treated to give effect of ruggedness and strength

la terrena (Italian): room giving on to garden (usually of Baroque palace)

raffito: technique in which part of an upper layer of plaster decoration is scraped off expose the contrasting layer beneath, creating a pattern or figure

de aisle: aisle running alongside each side of the nave of a church

andrel: triangular space between an arch and its surround

ar (or stellar) vault: vault with ribs arranged in star-like pattern

ele: upright stone slab, often used as a grave marker

epped (or crow-stepped) gable: triangular upper part of a wall supporting the two slopes the roof and which has stepped sides

ucco: plaster used to form decorative features

ibune: raised platform at one end of a church, reserved for the seat of the bishop high-ranking church dignitaries

iforium: middle storey in the wall of a church above the side aisles and below the erestorey, usually treated as an arcaded passageway

iptych: painting or sculpture composed of three hinged panels which can be folded back

ompe-l'œil: painting technique giving the illusion of three-dimensional reality

plute: a spiral scroll which is the distinctive feature of an Ionic capital, also used in onsoles and brackets

Art and architecture

The Prague-born poet Rainer Maria Rilke called Prague "an epic poem of architecture", and the city's location at a crossroads of European culture has left it with extraordinarily rich and varied legacy not only of building but of all forms of art. In some periods Prague and Bohemia have been at the forefront of artistic development. In others international trends have been adapted to local circumstances, while periods of provincial isolation and stagnation have had the incidental effect of perpetuating or preserving the achievements of previous eras. In the 14C, Charles made Prague the capital of the Holy Roman Empire, stimulating a glorious flowering of Gothic creativity in painting, sculpture, architecture and even engineering and town planning, a phase brought to an abrupt halt by the Hussite troubles of the early 15. In the late 16C and early 17C eccentric Emperor Rudolph II brought artists, alchemists and adventurers from all over Europe to his court, making it a glittering centre of Mannerist culture. The 1620 Battle of the White Mountain may have been a political disaster for the Bohemian nation, but the Counter-Reformation brought with it a wave of Late Renaissance and especially Baroque artistic production barely equalled elsewhere in Europe. Quieter times followed, but as national consciousness grew in the 19C, Czech pride expressed itself in monumental public building in historicist style, followed by an effusion of Art Nouveau art and architecture which made the city one of the centres of the Central European Secession style. Cubism flourished too, including a uniquely Czech Cubist contribution to architecture. Then, with the establishment of an independent Czechoslovakia, Prague became one of the focal points of Modernist endeavour in all spheres of art, though it is only since the fall of Communism that the Czech heritage of for example Functionalist architecture or Surrealist painting has begun to enjoy the wide appreciation it deserves.

Romanesque architecture

Prague has few examples of the architecture of the pre-Romanesque and Romanesque periods, though there is documentary evidence that the early city was built of limestone and that it "prospered from commerce like no other town". By the 12C each distinct quarter of the city had its little Romanesque church and fine town houses were built. Little remains of the churches apart from a trio of Romanesque rotundas, though the vaulted cellars of many a later dwelling, particularly around Staroměstské náměstí (Old Town Square) and Malé náměstí (Little Square), date from this period, and represent the former ground floor level, adjusted in the 13C to lessen the risk of flooding. The finest example of early building of this kind can be seen in the rib-vaulted rooms of the Romanesque palace in the Old Town known as the **Dům pánů z Kunštátu Poděbrad** (House of the Lords of Kunštát and Poděbrad). On the castle heights, there are substantial remains of some of the interiors of the original royal palace but the outstanding monument of the period is the **Bazilika sv. Jiří** (St George's Basilica), completed around 920, an austere masterpiece of Romanesque building, though much of the present structure dates from mid-12C reconstruction.

Ph. Gajic/MICHELIN

The Romanesque in Prague: St George's Basilica

Gothic art

The Prague of Emperor Charles IV

During the reign of Charles (1346-78), and to a lesser extent that of his son, Wenceslas IV (1378-1419), Prague and Bohemia reached a level of artistic achievement seldom equalled since. At the heart of the Holy Roman Empire, the city became a cultural centre of the first importance, its skyline pierced by numerous towers and spires. A splendid Gothic cathedral rose over the castle hill and the River Vltava was crossed by a boldly engineered bridge more than 500m long, later named Karlův most (Charles Bridge) after the ruler who had ordered its construction.

e Gothic style had arrived in Prague in the 1230s, probably from Burgundy, and
e of the very first structures to be in the new style was the **Anežský klášter** (St Agnes'
nvent) in the Old Town. A few decades later work began on its near neighbour,
e **Staronová synagoga** (Old-New Synagogue), one of the oldest and best-preserved of
kind in Europe, with superbly carved corbels in its vaulted interior and with the
brick gables typical of the final, Flamboyant phase of Gothic design.

arles IV was determined to make Prague the greatest city in Central Europe and
cond only to Rome as a centre of Christianity, and conducted his architectural pro-
ts in the framework of a far-sighted urban plan which allowed the town to expand
an orderly way while retaining its aesthetic unity. The old Romanesque stronghold
the castle hill was replaced by an imposing and lavishly decorated Gothic royal res-
ence. In 1344 Prague became the seat of an archbishop. The Romanesque basilica
St Vitus was demolished and in its place Charles ordered the construction of a spa-
us new **cathedral**. Its first architect was **Matthew of Arras**, who planned a structure
ong the lines of the great cathedrals of his native land, though by the time of his
ath only the majority of the east end had been completed. His successor **Petr Parléř**
eter Parler) continued the work, adding between 1375 and 1385 the 21 famous
rved busts which grace the triforium and which are among the first examples of
alistic portraiture in this medium. Of superb quality, they depict as well as members
the royal family people involved in the building of the cathedral, including Parler
mself. In 1348, the first university in Central Europe began its work in the Old Town,
yond the walls of which a vast urban extension began to take shape. With broad
reets linking its trio of market places, this **Nové Město** (New Town) covered an area
veral times the size of the original city, and was perhaps the most ambitious town-
anning project ever undertaken in medieval times.

inting

e painting of the period was characterised by the conflict between idealism and nat-
alism, though in the second half of the 14C both art and thought moved towards a
owing realism. This trend was quite distinct from the medieval conception of reality
rceived as a scene of miracles concealing mysterious forces, and represented a move-
ent away from the fantastic towards naturalism and abstraction. Mysticism, sorcery
d the cult of relics all developed simultaneously, and a desire for profound religious
perience influenced all the art of the 14C. As a result, depictions of the Martyrdom
d Death of Christ, the suffering of the Virgin Mary and the torments of the saints
ere rendered realistically.

alian influences were strong, particularly as far as iconographical motifs and composi-
nal elements are concerned. Bohemian artists strove to attain a more harmonious re-
tionship between line and colour, while at the same time discovering the full potential
colour. The **Master of the Vyšší Brod Altarpiece** drew much of his inspiration from Italian
otifs, notably in the harmonious colouring of some of his faces, in direct contrast to

e traditional Bohemian use of
tense, mottled colour. Even
e bold modelling of faces and
ands and the treatment of
ace were characteristically
alian, the first signs of a move
wards naturalism.

epictions of the Madonna en-
yed great vogue, many of
em having an enchantingly
oetic quality, like the
adonna of Kladsko.

ter about 1360 the Italian in-
uence diminished as Bo-
emian art began to assert its
wn values and identity, draw-
g inspiration from its own
aditions and by its choice of
bject. The typically Bo-
emian love of varied colour-
g was joined by a preoccu-
ation with intense facial
xpression, the tight organisa-
on of groups of figures and
mplexity of composition. In
ddition, there was an attempt
fuse the art of southern Eur-
pe with that of the north. In
e *Death of the Virgin of*
osatky, for example, the rep-
sentation of hands and facial
xpressions was evidence of an
terest in observation typical
northern Gothic art.

The Resurrection by the Master
of the Třeboň Altarpiece

One of the most appealing and individual painters of the period was **Master Theodoric,** ▪
sponsible for the superb series of panel portraits commissioned by Charles IV for the He
Cross Chapel of Karlštejn Castle. His substantial figures with their lively and express▪
faces have a humanity which goes far beyond the traditional idealism of Gothic art, thou▪
their gentle modelling through the play of light and shade is characteristically Bohemia▪
Towards the end of the 14C Bohemian painting gradually abandoned realism of expre▪
sion and reverted to a poetic idealism inspired by a desire for greater spirituali▪
Nevertheless, investigation continued into ways of representing space and perspectiv▪
wonderfully illustrated in the landscape and architectural backgrounds painted by the la▪
of the trio of great Bohemian Gothic painters, the **Master of the Třeboň Altarpiece**.
Wenceslas IV (1378-1419) attempted to continue the work of his father, but his effo▪
were frustrated by the religious crisis which marks the end of the 14C and beginning ▪
the 15C. The movement initiated by Jan Hus (John Huss) to return religion to Christi▪
fundamentals and the subsequent period of violence and conflict known as the Huss▪
Wars had varied effects on the arts. Building came to a stop and there was much destru
tion. Only the choir was completed of the great Church of Our Lady of the Snows, intend▪
by Charles IV to dominate the New Town. But book illumination continued, especially ▪
bibles, with lavish decoration and expressive miniatures. With the end of the Hussite tro▪
bles there was a recovery, and the prosperous period between 1450 and 1550 was t▪
golden age of Bohemian towns and cities, during which the arts were patronised by t▪
emerging middle class as well as by the royal court. A final flowering of the Gothic st▪
is seen in such exuberant creations as the Royal Oratory in St Vitus' Cathedral, the wo▪
of **Benedikt Ried**, architect for the castle, who was also responsible for the fantasti▪
swirling **vaulting** of the **Vladislavský sál** (Vladislav Hall).

Rudolph II and the School of Prague

Moving to Prague in 1583 from a Vienna threatened by the Turkish advance throu▪
southeastern Europe, Hapsburg Emperor Rudolph II set up a court whose patronage ▪
the arts and sciences equalled that of his predecessor Charles IV, though its spirit cou▪
not have been more different. It was said that Rudolph made the city a "second Pa▪
nassus", and the Emperor was not infrequently depicted as Hercules, protector of the ar▪

Architecture

Though Rudolph himself was more interested in painting and sculpture than architectur▪
the buildings of what had been an essentially Gothic city had already began to be infl▪
enced by the new ideas of the Renaissance. The transition is dramatically visible in t▪
Vladislav Hall, where Ried's Late Gothic vaulting and pinnacled buttresses contrast wi▪
walls pierced by generously dimensioned rectangular windows which are entirely Rena▪
sance in conception. As early as 1535, work had begun on the **Královský letohrádek** (Roy▪
Summer Palace) or Belvedere; the arcades running around the elegant and harmonio▪
little building recall the architecture of northern Italy. Elsewhere in the city, the aristo▪
racy adopted Renaissance ideas with enthusiasm when building or rebuilding their tov▪
mansions and palaces. Many a tall and narrow Gothic façade, particularly in Malá Strar▪
was decorated with motifs in Renaissance style without necessarily changing the structu▪
of the building behind. Gradually a typical Bohemian Renaissance style emerged, chara▪
terised by tall gables with bold volutes, deep cornices, and bold sgraffito decoration ar▪
exemplified most perfectly by the great **Schwarzenberský palác** (Schwarzenberg Palace) bu▪
between 1555 and 1576 close to the western entrance of the castle.

Royal Summer Palace

School of Prague

Rudolph II by Arcimboldo

As Rudolph established his court in Prague and word of his munificence spread, painters and sculptors flocked to the city from all over Europe, enjoying the status conferred on them by an Emperor who regarded them as artists and not just as craftsmen. Some were admitted into Rudolph's innermost circle and even, like the painter Hans von Aachen (1552-1615), given diplomatic responsibilities. The city became a great centre of artistic production in the Late Mannerist style, characterised by the elongated, distorted yet graceful forms evident in such works as the *Triumph of Wisdom* by **Bartolomaeus Spranger** (1546-1611).

The Emperor's exercised a determining influence in the formation of the School of Prague. He acquired a rich array of paintings by the great Italian masters like Veronese, Parmigiano, Tintoretto, Da Vinci as well as by northern European artists like Breughel and Dürer, whose Feast of the Rose Garlands was transported with great effort across the Alps from Venice. When unable to obtain original works, Rudolph ordered copies; Joseph Heintz the Elder for example made a number of copies of paintings by Titian.

By 1590 the School of Prague was firmly established, at its core the painters Van Aachen, Spranger, Heintz, the sculptor **Adrien de Vries** (†1626), and the Milanese **Guseppe Arcimboldo** (1527-93), famous for his extraordinary "composite heads", portraits made up of fantastic combinations of fruit, flowers, vegetables and other materials, and often involving visual puns on the character or profession of the subject. Art was also made to serve a propaganda role; mythology and allegory were used to promote the Emperor's prestige, with numerous portraits and other paintings showing Rudolph dominating both the political and the natural worlds in the guise of a god or hero of myth. In a famous picture by Arcimboldo, the fruits and flowers from which his portrait is built up are far from being frivolous but symbolise the perennial nature of Hapsburg rule as well as the peace and prosperity of his reign. By contrast, the portraits of the Emperor by Van Aachen are more realistic but less convincing in a symbolic sense. This painter also uses witty or playful touches to express shades of meaning which are sometimes so subtle as to be beyond interpretation. His treatment of mythological and allegorical subjects is intended to entertain as well as to convey the moral and spiritual lessons which were once the province of religious painting, a genre little in vogue at Rudolph's court. Landscape, still-life and animal painting flourished, however, not least because of the Emperor's passion for natural history. He seems to have had a special fondness for **Roelant Savery**'s (1576-1639) alpine landscapes, with their dramatic scenery and mysterious atmosphere.

Rudolph's abdication and death marked the end of the School of Prague and the dispersal of its many talented protagonists to other patrons throughout Europe. The 3000 or so works of art that the obsessive Emperor had amassed were dispersed in their turn, stolen, looted or sold, and only a handful of them remain in Prague today.

Baroque Prague

The arrival of the Baroque in Prague was delayed by the persistence of the Mannerist style which had flourished during Rudolph II's reign and its early development occurred in the unpromising context of the aftermath of the Battle of the White of 1620 and the successive campaigns of the Thirty Years War.

Indissolubly associated with the enforced re-Catholicisation of the country, the Baroque style found little favour at first, but gradually won acceptance, reviving dormant local traditions and fusing them with the new, mainly Italian ideas. As palaces, churches and monasteries were built or rebuilt, the city began to be transformed, parts of it almost taking on the appearance of a stage set, full of dramatic and audacious touches. As in the past, many of the artists, designers and craftsmen came from abroad, from Germany, the Low Countries, France, as well as from Lombardy and the Ticino. Once the dynamic forms and the expressive qualities of Italian Baroque architecture had taken hold in Bohemia, they were further transformed.

By 1700 Bohemian Baroque had established its own strong personality, and durin the following two decades the country enjoyed one of the most glorious periods i its artistic history. By the end of the century, as Rococo was giving way to the Cla sical Revival, the face of Prague had acquired the charm which makes it s celebrated today.

Architecture

Perhaps the most important Early Baroque building in Prague is **Sv. Salvator** (St Saviour Church), part of the Klementinum and modelled on the Jesuits' Gesú Church in Rom Begun in 1578 in Renaissance style, its originally sober west front was subsequent remodelled to make it one of the most lavish of Baroque façades. Another strikir structure of this early phase is the monumental **Matyášova brána** (Matthias Gate) of 161 at the western end of the castle, a bold design once attributed to Vincenzo Scamoz but almost certainly the work of Giovanni Filippi. Between 1624 and 1630 the wa lord Albrecht von Wallenstein employed Italian designers to create a great palace a the foot of the castle hill. Still very much in the spirit of the Renaissance, the **Valdštejns palác** (Wallenstein Palace) nevertheless looks forward to the Baroque; its great Sala Te rena is outstanding, as are the ceiling paintings showing the general as Mars, the Go of War or the garden sculpture by Adrian de Vries. On an even more monumental sca is the vast **Černínský palác** (Czernin Palace) in Hradčany, built by Francesco Caratti be tween 1669 and 1677, its harmonious appearance assured by the colossal order e engaged columns rising through three floors to the cornice. The forceful modelling o the main façade with its play of light and shadow is characteristic and can be seen i buildings all over the city. In a rustic location just outside Prague is the **Trojský zám** (Troja Palace), a very different kind of palace. It was built between 1679 and 169 by the Burgundian **Jean-Baptiste Mathey** (c 1630-c 1695), who also designed Sv.Františk (St Francis' Church) on Křižovnické náměstí (Knights of the Cross Square). At Troj Mathey moved away from Italian traditions, drawing instead on the French model o a central block flanked by symmetrical wings and pavilions. Also on the French mode the palace and its large garden form a harmonious whole, the parterres and allées o the latter being integrated with the building by means of a balustraded terrace and magnificent double stairway with lavish statuary. **Landscape design** was as important i the heart of the city as in the suburban countryside of Troja; in Malá Strana, palac grounds were laid out in the form of exquisite terraced gardens, forming an almos continuous band of verdure beneath the castle and on the lower slopes of Petřín Hi By the end of the 17C the Baroque triumph was complete. From about 1710 onward inspired by the buildings of Borromini and Guarini, church architecture in Prague too on an almost fantastic look, with undulating walls and a proliferation of detail exen plifying a radically new conception of space and understanding of theatrical effect. Th defining building of this phase is the monumental **Sv. Mikuláš** (St Nicholas' Church) dom inating Malostranské náměstí (Malá Strana Square), one of the great Baroque churche of Central Europe. Worked on by both **Christoph Dientzenhofer** (1655-1722) and his so **Kilian Ignaz Dientzenhofer** (1689-1751), it has a convex/concave façade of exceptional vi tuosity and a lavishly decorated interior beneath a 74m-high dome. The Dientzenhofe were responsible for numerous other buildings in Prague, but the finest works by the highly original contemporary, **JB Santini-Aichl** (1677-1723) are outside the cit

St James' Church

mmissioned to restore or re-
ild monastery churches
en victim to warfare or ne-
ect, Santini turned to med-
al models for inspiration,
oducing a strange and com-
lling synthesis of the Gothic
d Baroque which has no par-
el elsewhere in places like
llec near Kutná Hora and,
en more spectacularly, at the
bey church at **Kladruby** in
stern Bohemia.

ulpture

no other city in Europe does
ulpture play a more public
e than in Prague, where the
wnscape is marvellously en-
hed by the Baroque statuary
church façades, palace por-
s, and above all by the trans-
rmation of the Charles Bridge
o a processional way by the
stematic placing of sculpture.
e first Baroque sculptor of
portance was **Johann Georg**
dl (c 1620-80), who, like his
inter counterpart Karel
réta, is considered to be the
under of the realistic tradi-
n in Bohemian art. Working

Baroque Beauty by M.B.Braun

R. Holzbachova, P. Bénet

limewood as well as in stone, Bendl combined restrained modelling with a sense of
roque drama derived from Roman models. His successors, most of whom provided
atuary for Charles Bridge, were also influenced by the Baroque sculpture of Rome,
apting it to the more sombre light of Central Europe and to the traditional mater-
s of Bohemian sculpture, in particular coarse-grained sandstone. Foremost among
em were **Matthias Bernard Braun** (1684-1738) and **Ferdinand Maxmilián Brokoff** (1688-
731). Brokoff learnt his skills from his father Johann (1652-1718), who had come
Prague from his native Slovakia, and their workshop provided more than half the
atues for Charles Bridge. The son's work is distinguished from the father's by its vig-
ous expressiveness and confident handling of form, seen not only on the bridge stat-
s but also in the atlantes of the Morzinský palác (Morzin Palace) and the Mitrovice
mb in Sv. Jakub (St James' Church). Sometimes called the Bohemian Bernini,
B Braun was at least the younger Brokoff's equal in conveying intense emotion, most
amatically in the bridge statue of St Luitgard.
e Baroque tradition in sculpture continued into the middle of the 18C, albeit with
ninished vigour, and then, as in the rest of Europe, was succeeded by the lyricism
d gracefulness of the Rococo. Serenity and refinement replaced drama and
namism, and there was a greater interest in the decorative arts than in large-scale,
blic work.

inting

e most celebrated artist of the Bohemian Baroque was **Karel Škréta** (1610-74).
om a Protestant family which fled the country after the 1620 Battle of the White
ountain, he trained in Italy before converting to Catholicism and returning to his
tive country, where he became known above all for epic altarpieces painted for
e now dominant Roman Catholic Church. His work is remarkable for its realism,
rticularly in his portraits, which show a deep psychological insight. Another
nvert to Catholicism was **Michael Willmann** (1630-1706), who also served his
lopted church with great devotion, painting numerous altarpieces which alternate
ld realism with a contemplative spirituality. Much of the work of his stepson Jan
ška (c 1650-1712) has similar qualities, though his smaller paintings anticipate
e spirit of the Rococo.
Protestant who did not convert and consequently lived most of his life abroad was
e intriguing figure of **Jan Kupecký** (1667-1740), whose appealing portraits show
eat psychological insight. But the leading painter of the High Baroque of the early
8C was **Peter Brandl** (1686-1735), a native of Prague. Basing his work on direct obser-
tion, he used vivid colour and bold chiaroscuro to achieve dramatic, yet realistic
fects in both religious works and portraiture. His *Self-portrait* in the Jiřský klášter
t George's Convent) National Gallery collection is outstanding, as are a number of
ter portraits which he painted using his fingers rather than brushes.

Following the triumphant decoration of Troja's Great Hall with illusionistic frescoes the Godyn brothers from Flanders, **fresco painting** enjoyed a great vogue in Prague, most successful and prolific exponent being **Václav Vavřinec Reiner** (1689-1743), nev theless there are fine works too by Franz Xavier Palko (1724-67) and Johann Luk Kracker (1717-79). Though the great Viennese fresco painter **Franz Anton Maulbert** (1724-96) carried out only one commission in Prague, the ceiling of the **Philosoph** **Hall** at **Strahovský klášter** (Strahov Monastery), it ranks as one of his finest works.

The move in painting away from the grand themes and expansive treatment Baroque to the more intimate concerns of Rococo is delightfully illustrated in the ma tiny genre scenes of court and country life painted by **Norbert Grund** (1717-67).

The Nineteenth Century

By the end of the 18C, artistic activity was at its nadir in a Prague which had su into provincial lethargy. The enthusiasm for the ideas of the Enlightenment of rule like Emperor Joseph II had put an end to the patronage of the Church, while t Bohemian aristocracy had gravitated towards the court in Vienna. But a new for was in the making – Czech nationalism, which was to prove as influential a patron any in the country's history.

The first efforts to revive a national culture were made by enlightened, German-spea ing aristocrats like Count Sternberg, who towards the end of the 18C had helped fou the Patriotic Association of Friends of Art, a body whose art collections later form the core of the National Gallery. In 1818, together with Count Kolowrat, another pu lic-spirited member of the Sternberg family was inspired by ideals of *Landespatr tismus* (a Bohemian patriotism embracing both the German and Czech traditions of t country) to establish the National Museum. But by the middle of the century the ti of purely Czech nationalism was flowing so strongly that *Landespatriotismus* was d

funct; from now on archite ture, painting, sculpture a the decorative arts would en lessly proclaim the revival the Czechs as a nation, a many of Prague's monumer of the period are suffused wi a sometimes overbearing n tionalistic spirit.

Architecture

Neo-Classical architecture left rel tively few traces on the tow scape of Prague, though th **Stavovské divadlo** (Estates Th atre), opened in 1783, dom nates the Ovocný trh (Fru Market) in the Old Town ar the **U Hybernů** (Hibernian Church) of 1811 is a fine b isolated example of the Empi style. The great public edific of the Czech National Reviv which were built from th 1860s onwards were mostly a grandiloquent neo-Renai sance style. The first was th **Národní divadlo** (National Th atre), begun in 1868. Designe by **Josef Zítek** (1832-1909) ar rebuilt by **Josef Schultz** (184 1917), after it had burne

Exuberant architecture of the Czech Renaissance revival

Ph. Gajic/MICHELIN

down shortly before completion, it was lavishly decorated inside and out by the lead ing artists of the day who were henceforth known as the "**National Theatre Generation** They included the sculptors Bohuslav Schnirch, Josef Myslbek and Anton Wagner ar the painters Mikoláš Aleš, Václav Brožík, Vojtěch Hynais and František Ženíšek. Schul went on to provide the collections of the National Museum with an equally prestigiou home in similar style; the **Národní muzeum** at the top of Wenceslas Square was complete in 1890 and the National Theatre generation was again involved in providing it wit allegorical and symbolic decoration glorifying the Czech nation and its homeland.

This monumental neo-Renaissance style continued to be used for public building albeit on a smaller scale and perhaps with less conviction in structures such a Schultz's Uměleckoprůmyslové muzeum (Decorative Arts Museum) of 1900. Nation ally minded business too favoured the style, as demonstrated by Osvald Polivka palatial **Živnostenská banka** (Czech Trading Bank) of 1896. The specifically Czech versio of Renaissance architecture was revived, and its picturesque medley of stepped gable oriel windows and colourful sgraffito used to cheerful effect in buildings such as th Wiehlův dům (Wiehl Building) of 1895-6 in Wenceslas Square.

19C genre painting *The Egg Market* by L Marold

the meantime, a Bohemian version of the **Gothic Revival** had run its course, its prin-
pal exponent being **Josef Mocker** (1835-99). His restoration of countless medieval
uildings has been criticised for its excessive zeal, but is now seen in its own right as
n authentic contribution to the country's architectural heritage. Certainly Prague's
nage is almost inconceivable without the tall chisel roofs Mocker gave to the Prašná
rána (Powder Tower) and the Charles Bridge towers, and the Karlštejn Castle he
ecreated from near-ruin is one of the great symbols of the country. And for many
ears Mocker was the architect for the cathedral, bringing the work begun by Matthew
f Arras and Peter Parler close to completion.

ainting and sculpture

he dominant figure in Czech painting in the mid 19C was **Josef Mánes** (1820-71),
ember of a famous artistic dynasty. His fascination with his country, its past and its
eople, is expressed in a varied output ranging from portraiture to landscape. He was
so responsible for what is one of the city's most prominently displayed works of art,
ne gilded calendar disc showing sentimentalised cameos of the labours of the year
hich form part of the Orloj (Astronomical Clock) in Old Town Square (the version
ow on show is a copy). Mánes' equal in portraiture was Karel Purkyně (1834-68),
ho, like Josef Návrátil (1798-1865) was also a distinguished still-life painter. The
ational Revival encouraged the production of large-scale pictures glorifying the
ation's sometimes mythologised past; the foremost history painter of this kind was
clav Brožík (1851-1901), responsible for such immense canvases as *The Condemna-
on of Master John Huss* of 1883. **Mikoláš Aleš** (1852-1913) was capable of similarly
ic depictions of history, though he is more famous for his prolific book illustration;
s devotion to the country's traditions and its folklore led him to be celebrated as
he most Czech of all our artists". **Jakub Schikaneder** (1855-1924) began his career
ith realistic narrative paintings and rustic scenes, but by the end of the century was
ainting mysterious but wonderfully harmonious townscapes suffused with twilight
elancholy.

hemian sculpture continued to languish in the early 19C. The most important figures
ere the brothers Josef (1804-53) and Emanuel Max (1810-1901), but their stiffly
rved, academic figures on Charles Bridge belong to the German, rather than
hemian tradition, and have none of the vitality of their Baroque counterparts. Far
ore lively is their masterpiece, the Monument to Field Marshal Radecky of 1858,
owing the great soldier carried aloft by eight of his men; its glorification of Haps-
rg military success made it unacceptable after Czechoslovak independence in 1918,
d it was removed from its position in Malostranské náměstí (Malá Strana Square)
d is now on show in the Lapidarium. Late-19C sculpture was almost completely dom-
ated by the figure of **Josef Václav Myslbek** (1848-1922), one of the National Theatre
eneration. His figures of Slavonic heroes on Vyšehrad are full of the fervour of the
ational Revival, and Myslbek was the only possible choice when the decision was
1887 to erect the Wenceslas Square monument to the country's patron saint. But
e **statue of St Wenceslas** on his stallion, which occupied the sculptor right up until his
ath and went through successive transformations, puts aside Romantic expressive-
ss in favour of a Classical and calm statement of chivalric honour and dignity.

81

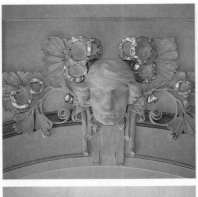

82

the last decade of the 19C, Czech artists, designers and architects were tiring of e endless recycling of historical forms, and seized with alacrity on the new possiities of the movement known in Britain and France as Art Nouveau, and in Vienna d Budapest as well as in Prague, as **Secession** (Secese in Czech). With its love of wing lines and asymmetrical and organic forms, Secession design soon lent itself to rely decorative effects, though its original protagonists thought of it in far more dical terms as an integrating force for all the arts. The streets of the rapidly panding Prague of the time are lined with apartment blocks featuring rich Art uveau ornamentation, particularly in stucco, but also in mosaic, ceramic and metwork. Key buildings include the Grand Hotel Evropa of 1903-5, the main railway ation of 1909, the U Nováků Casino of 1904 with its brilliant mosaic by Jan Preisler, d above all the **Obecní dům** (Municipal House). Completed in 1912 by the architects vald Polívka and Antonín Balšánek, this prestigious structure, like the National eatre, also incorporated the work of many of the most prominent artists of the ne. Among them was **Alfons Mucha** (1860-1939), who spent most of his early career Paris and is known internationally for his ornate theatre posters. In Prague, to which returned in 1910, he is seen as a patriotic artist who remained faithful to the ideals Art Nouveau, and was responsible not only for an epic cycle of paintings depicting e rise of the Slav peoples, but also for stained glass for the newly completed nave St Vitus' Cathedral as well as the design of banknotes and postage stamps. Equally rsatile was **Max Švabinský** (1873-1962), whose early work was much influenced by ench Symbolism and who also designed colourful stained glass for the cathedral as ell as mosaics for the Národní památník (National Memorial) on Žižkov Hill.

e tradition of monumental public sculpture was continued by a pupil of Myslbek, nislav Sucharda (1866-1916), notably in the **monument to František Palacký** of 1912, in ich he left the contained forms of his master far behind in a sculptural grouping ose dynamic movement exceeds even that of its Baroque antecedents. Another ominent sculpture is the unconventional **monument to John Huss** in Old Town Square, e work of **Ladislav Jan Šaloun** (1880-1946), entirely in the spirit of Prague Secession ugh much influenced by Rodin's Burghers of Calais. However, the least convennal and most original sculptor of the period was **František Bílek** (1872-1941), who is also an outstanding graphic artist. His deeply spiritual vision drew on many pects of contemporary thought as well as on the Christian heritage and Eastern relin, and he was one of the few European artists to succeed in expressing the ideas Symbolism in sculpture. His greatest legacy is perhaps his symbol-laden villa, which designed himself. Another figure standing somewhat apart from the mainstream is **Jan Zrzavý** (1890-1977), a "painter of the inner vision", whose pictures, whimal yet profound, sometimes recall the work of Paul Klee.

odernism

the end of the first decade of the 20C, the Secession was effectively over, though ists like Mucha continued to work happily in the style. More avant-garde spirits comned to form **Osma** – the Group of Eight. Among them were **Bohumil Kubišta** (1884-1918) d **Emil Filla** (1882-1963), both devoted to the role of colour in expressing spiritual vals. In his Paris studio, equally convinced of the central role of colour, **František Kupka** 371-1957) moved from more or less representational paintings inspired by Symbol n to a growing abstraction which attempted to parallel the effects of music. After a ng delay, he is now recognised as one of the great pioneers of 20C abstract art.

e ideas and techniques of French Cubism were thusiastically taken up in Prague, one of the first ech Cubist paintings being the happily named bišta's *Smoker*. And at the same time as archi tural Art Nouveau was moving away from or mental excess to the more sober and structural proach exemplified by the Mozarteum of 1913 Jan Kotěra (1871-1923), a uniquely **Czech Cub architectural movement** developed. There are few ernational parallels to the **Dům U Černé Matky boží** ack Madonna House) completed by **Josef Gočár** 880-1945) in 1912 or the **Vyšehrad villas and flats Josef Chochol** (1880-1956). Though the eaking-down and rearrangement of plane faces was more feasible in painting and ulpture than in building, these and other hitects succeeded in creating wonder ly facetted, sometimes almost dia ntine forms of great originality and ting appeal. Their work was oed in the decorative arts, ch furniture and ceram s designed in the ist style.

Cubist sculpture by Otto Gutfreund

Narodní Galerie v Praze

A committed Cubist in his early works, perhaps the greatest Czech sculptor of the 2ᵗ was **Otto Gutfreund** (1889-1927), with expressive bronzes like his *Anxiety* of 1911 or ᵗ even more tormented *Don Quixote* of the same year. But by the end of the First Wo war Gutfreund had abandoned Cubism in favour of **Civilism** or **Objective Realism**, an affe tionate celebration of ordinary life with "a new sculpture for a new country". Typical this are the delightful little coloured wood figures of everyday scenes of work such *Trade* and *Industry* of 1923, or the charmingly posed trio of mother, father and ch in *Family* of 1925. Together with **Jan Štursa** (1880-1925), Gutfreund was commission to design the sculptural decoration for Josef Gočár's **Legiobanka** (Bank of the Legion their work, Štursa's in the form of monumental consoles, Gutfreund's in the shape a frieze extending along the whole width of the façade, celebrates the prowess of t Czechoslovak legionaries who fought on the Allied side in the First World War.
A number of Gutfreund and Štursa's contemporaries, among them Karel Dvoř (1893-1950), worked in a similar style, and their figures depicting ordinary folk work or play adorn many a city building of the period.

Rondocubism

The Legiobanka itself was completed in 1923, and was a product of a second arc tectural style unique to Bohemia, **Rondocubism**, whose lifespan was as short as that architectural Cubism. Intended to incorporate specifically Slav values, it featured ᵗ national colours of red and white as well as massive cylindrical, circular and segment shapes echoing the forms of simple timber construction. An even more monumen Rondocubist structure than the Bank of the Legions was the fortress-like **Palác Ad** (Adria Palace) of 1925, the work of Pavel Janák and Josef Zasche, but Rondocub buildings are rare; the style was attacked by the younger generation of architects superficial, decorative, and unnecessarily nationalistic, and it soon gave way approaches based on cool appraisal of a building's functions and the exciting pote tial of modern materials like steel, concrete and glass.

Functionalism

Inter-war Czechoslovakia was a democratic, progressive and prosperous state, certai in comparison with its neighbours, and Functionalism in architecture perfectly suit the national mood. Prague has many buildings from this early, heroic phase of Mode architecture, among them the great **Veletržní palác** (Trade Fair Palace) designed by Jo Fuchs and Oldřich Tyl which so impressed Le Corbusier in the year of its completi in 1928. Its magnificently spacious interior is still admired for its purity of expressi and perfection of its proportions. Other landmark buildings of this period include ᵗ **Baťa store** of 1929 on Wenceslas Square as well as the group of structures built for ᵗ **General Pensions Institute** on what is now Náměstí Winstona Churchilla (Winston Churcl Square) in suburban Žižkov on the edge of the city centre. Clad in ceramic tiles to res the steam and smoke from the nearby main railway station, it consists of wings of ͻ ferent heights; its long horizontal bands of windows became a feature of office buildin for several decades. Estates of Functionalist houses sprang up in outlying areas, mͻ famously at the **Baba Villa Colony** on a splendid hilltop site in the north of the city. F lowing the example of the Werkbund show-house exhibition in Stuttgart in 1927, mͻ than 30 houses were constructed between 1928 and 1940 by many of the leadi architects of the day. Though their stucco has peeled, these boxy houses with th large rectangular windows, generous balconies and freely flowing interior spaces s embody the domestic ideals of the progressive architecture of the time. In 1931, suburban Střešovice, the Moravian-born but Vienna-based architect **Adolf Loos**, kno for his dictum "Ornament is Crime", built a large villa for the Müller family wh exhibits a similar concept of interior space, the "Raumplan". Further Modernist vi were built around the great **Barrandov** film studios high above the Vltava to the so of the city centre, as well as a glamorous panoramic restaurant and night-club wit lighthouse-like tower which, as the **Barrandovy Terasy**, became the in place to see and seen in Prague. But perhaps the most ambitiously conceived house of the period a one of the finest examples of what came to be known as the International style in arc tecture is the **Vila Tugendhat** in provincial Brno, an iconic structure designed by ᵗ German architect **Mies van der Rohe** in 1930.

Standing aside from Functionalist enthusiasm and instead drawing his inspiration fr Classical architecture and the historical context within which his work was to be was the Slovene architect **Josip Plečnik** (1872-1957). Between 1920 and 1934 Pleč painstakingly adapted the castle's courtyards, interiors and gardens to their conte porary role, but his greatest single achievement is his extraordinary church in ᵗ suburb of Vinohrady, the **chrám Nejsvětějšího Sdrce Páně** (Church of the Most Sacred He of Our Lord).

Devětsil and Surrealism

Some of the architects who pioneered Functionalism were associated with the **Devě** group of artists presided over by the poet, theoretician, collage artist and public **Karel Teige** (1900-51). In love with modernity and experimentation of all kinds a basing its operations on the famous Café Arco, the group recruited members fr ll the artistic disciplines including poetry and even gave honorary membership to uch emblematic figures of the contemporary world as Charlie Chaplin and Harold loyd. Members like **Toyen** (the name chosen by Marie Čermínová) (1902-80) and ndřich Štyrský (1899-1942) attempted to create "visual poetry", developing a method of seeing the world in such a way that it becomes a poem". Devětsil had defiantly leftist orientation, though several of its members were eventually expelled om the Czechoslovak Communist Party for their "incorrigibly petty bourgeois" anings.

he group dominated progressive artistic production throughout the 1920s, and even fter its demise in 1931 several of its members like Teige, Toyen and Štyrský con- nued to play leading roles in the **Surrealist Group** which succeeded it, and which staged s first exhibition in 1935 in the brilliant white Functionalist Mánes Building of 1928. he French Surrealist, André Breton, was much taken with Prague when invited here y the Group, declaring it "the magical metropolis of old Europe". The leading painter f Czech Surrealism was **Josef Šíma** (1881-1971), who depicted mythical landscapes opulated by floating torsos, crystals, and cosmic eggs. Surrealist sculptors included adislav Zívr (1909-80), but perhaps the most original artist of the 1930s was **Zdeněk** ešánek (1896-1965), who was fascinated by the potential of kinetic art and electric ghting; his light-kinetic fountain at the Paris World Exhibition of 1937 won much cclaim, but other projects for providing Prague with large-scale public sculpture of is kind failed to reach fruition.

rt under Nazism and Communism

ith the imposition of the Nazi Protectorate of Bohemia-Moravia in 1939, progres- ve artistic activity came to an end, at least as far as its public role in national life as concerned, and the visual arts languished during the long decades of Communist le. Nevertheless, painters and others came together in 1942 to form **Group 42**, and e grim cityscapes of artists like František Hudeček (1909-90), Jan Smetana (b 1918) d Kamil Lhoták reflect the desolation of the years of occupation.

fter the *coup d'état* of 1948, the Communists tried to turn talent to their own ends. surprising number of artists continued to flourish under the new regime, especially their work had the appropriate patriotic and "popular" flavour. Many were rewarded ith the title of "National Artist". The aged Max Švabinský played a similar role to that f Mucha in the First Republic, producing portraits of Party heroes and designs for osters and postage stamps to order. No artist could have been more folksy than **Josef** da (1887-1957), made famous by his woodcuts illustrating Jaroslav Hašek's novel he *Good Soldier Švejk*; his stock scenes of village life and rustic characters were end- ssly recycled. Another much-loved illustrator, Adolf Zábranský (b 1909), worked on 35m-long sgraffito panel, now removed, of the 1945 Liberation for the garden of e Ledebour Palace featuring sturdy girls in peasant dress greeting soldiers of the Red rmy. Other commissions had n even more unhappy out- ome. In the 1920s, as an Ob- ctive Realist, the sculptor akar Švec (1892-1955) had eated a minor masterpiece in e shape of his speeding *otorcyclist*, but was driven to icide when commissioned to eate the monstrous Stalin emorial on Letná Plain. The jective Realism of the inter- ar period could be seen as a nd of predecessor of the **So- list Realism** favoured in the oviet bloc, but most of the inting and sculpture pro- ced under this banner seems eless and empty of content. cialist Realist architecture joyed a brief vogue in the 50s, but has left behind only e structure in unashamedly alinist style, the "wedding- ke" skyscraper of the **Hotel In- national** (now the Holiday). Most architecture of the mmunist period was carried t in a modified version of nctionalism, though in the 70s a new kind of monu- entalism made itself felt in

Stalinist skyscraper: the Hotel International

the shape of domineering buildings like the Koospol building on the road to the ai
port, the Czech Parliament uncomfortably close to the National Museum, and th
fortress-like Palace of Culture at Vyšehrad. Functionalism's nemesis came with the ou
ward extension of Prague in the form of "settlements", vast and impersonal housir
estates assembled from factory built concrete panels on the Soviet model.

Following the fall of Communism in 1989, no specifically Czech architectural style h.
emerged, the most-discussed structure of the 1990s being the **Taneční dům** (Dancir
Building) by American architect Frank Gehry, prominently positioned on the Vlta
Embankment.

Intellectual life

In modern times intellectuals have played a decisive role first in defining and then
leading the Czech nation. But long before this, Prague was a centre of advance
thought, whose influence frequently reached far beyond the boundaries of Bohemi

Medieval radicalism

In the Middle Ages, as part of the medieval Holy Roman Empire, and sometimes i
capital, Prague was in touch with intellectual currents streaming to and from all par
of Europe. Its university, the first such institution north of the Alps and west of Par
was founded in 1348 by the great Emperor Charles IV, whose upbringing and mer
bership of the Luxembourg dynasty made him as familiar with France and Italy as wi
Central Europe. One of the university's brightest students was **John Huss** (Jan Hu
(c 1372-1415), who was awarded his Master's degree in 1396. For years there h.
been theological ferment in Prague, with preachers like **Waldhauser** and **Milič** rejectir
the worldliness of the church, their message reinforced by the heretical writings
the Englishman John Wyclif. Initially no rebel, Huss' resolve to "live in the truth
Jesus Christ" inevitably brought him into conflict with the ecclesiastical establishmer
His excommunication, trial at Constance and subsequent burning at the stake in 14
made him a figure of European stature, a Reformer before the Reformation and,
the Czech lands and beyond, the inspiration for decades of destructive religio
struggle, the Hussite Wars.

Jewish learning

The development of Christian thought in Prague was paralleled by the activities
scholars from the Jewish community. There had been a flowering of such sche
arship in the 13C, when learned Jews, among them **Isaac ben Moses** who had studi
in Paris, the Rhineland and Regensburg, worked on additions to the inherit
Talmud commentaries while **Abraham ben Azriel** assembled a great compendium
Jewish knowledge entitled *The Spice Garden*. At the same time as John Huss w
propagating his radical ideas, **Jom tov Lipmann-Mühlhausen** was investigating met
physical questions of faith and free will. A century later, a group of Prague schola
began issuing the first texts in Hebrew to be published north of the Alps. But
was the late 16C that saw a Golden Age in Jewish learning and culture, its defini
figure the great **Rabbi Judah Loew ben Bezalel** (c 1520-1609). Widely believed to
the creator of the monstrous Golem *(See p. 126)*, Rabbi Loew was in fact a scho
of the first rank, industriously attempting to reconcile Renaissance ideas wi
Jewish tradition and ritual.

A cultivated court

It seems that the wisdom of Rabbi Loew aroused the interest of Emperor Rud
II, enough for the eccentric ruler to summon him from ghetto to royal palace
least once. The Emperor's interests were certainly wide-ranging, and during I
reign (1576-1611) the court at Prague was not only a centre of high culture b
of serious learning, though mingling with philosophers, physicians and serio
astronomers, were astrologers, alchemists, and outright charlatans. Attempts
Rudolf's retinue to unravel the occult secrets of the universe or transmute ba
metal into gold have contributed to the legend of "Magic Prague", and there
many an entertaining tale told about the activities of the tin-nosed Dani
astronomer **Tycho Brahe** (1546-1601), the English scholar **John Dee** (b 1527) or
colleague, the confidence trickster Edward Kelley. But valuable work was done to
Tycho made precise observations of the movement of celestial bodies which
colleague, **Johannes Kepler** (1571-1630) developed further, opening the way
Newton's later investigations.

arkness falls

ne enforced exodus of Protestants from Bohemia after the Battle of the White Moun-
in in 1620, the status of Prague as a mere provincial town, the rigorous enforcement
the Counter-Reformation, all ushered in the period which Czech historiography has
rmed the **Temno** or Time of Darkness, from which the nation was only to emerge
ith the National Revival of the 19C. One great loss was that of the Moravian humanist
n Amos Komenský (1592-1670). Universally known as **Comenius**, the exiled Komenský
ught refuge in Poland, England, Sweden, Hungary and Holland, where he was hailed
r his "pansophy", a system of beliefs aimed at unifying all Christendom, as well as
r his extraordinarily progressive theories on education, many of which had to await
e 20C for implementation.

National Revival

ith the triumph of the Counter-Reformation and the supremacy of the German lan-
uage, a specifically Czech culture virtually disappeared during the two centuries of
e *Temno*, and it was left to the lower orders of society to keep the language alive.
us preserved, the language was rediscovered by intellectuals of the National Revival
the beginning of the 19C. In the first years of the century **Josef Dobrovský** (1753-
329) published a *History of Czech Language and Literature* and a two-volume *Czech-
erman Dictionary*, while **Josef Jungmann**
773-1847) proved the power and
chness of Czech by translating into it
assic works from English and German
well as working tirelessly on his great
zech-German Dictionary, the five vol-
nes of which were borne reverently at
e head of his funeral procession in
347. That these and similar efforts
ere not merely academic was proved
the historian **František Palacký** (1796-
376), whose six-volume *History of the
zech Nation in Bohemia and Moravia
ok 46 years to write and whose ac-
unt of the Hussite Wars re-estab-
hed the figure of John Huss firmly in
e minds of his fellow-countrymen; in
e revolutionary year of 1848 Palack
minded the world that Bohemia and
e Czechs were not merely an ap-
ndage to a basically Germanic Central
rope, first by refusing to attend the
ankfurt Parliament of the German
npire, then by holding a Slavonic Con-
ess in Prague itself. His most famous
iom about the Czechs proved
ophetic: "Before Austria was, we
ere, and when Austria no longer is,
e shall be!"

Franz Kafka

lacký's *History* was a national one,
tended to restore to the Czechs a
nse of their identity through a revitalised consciousness of their long, and sometimes
orious past. In the course of the 19C Prague became an overwhelmingly Czech city,
e undisputed centre of an increasingly confident nation whose cultural autonomy was
mly established and which also looked forward to some form of political autonomy
thin the Austro-Hungarian Empire. Czech life in city and countryside was celebrated
writers like **Jan Neruda** (1834-91) *(Tales of Malá Strana)* and **Božena Němcová** (1820-
) *(Babička* or *Granny)*, and there was also a final flowering of Prague German, par-
ularly German-Jewish culture. **Franz Kafka's** (1883-1924) name is indissolubly linked
th his native city, but he was only one the many writers who drew sustenance from
rn-of-the-century Prague and the intensity of its urban life. As much as in Vienna, it
is here that archetypal café society thrived, Czech intellectuals and their hangers-on
vouring the Union (fondly called the *Unionka*), the German-speakers the Arco. The lat-
were famously satirised by the acerbic **Karl Kraus** (1874-1936), owner-editor of the
erary journal *Die Fackel* (The Torch), in the sadly untranslatable line *"Es werfelt und
odet und kafkat und kischt"*. This links Kafka
th poet, dramatist and novelist Franz Werfel
390-1945) (who later married Gustav Mahler's
dow and spent his last days in Hollywood), **Max**
d (1884-1968) (who saved Kafka's work from
struction) and **Egon Erwin Kisch** (1885-1948)
e "raging reporter"(who survived many vicissi-
des to return to Prague after the Second World
ar and become a Communist city councillor).

Kafka's signature

T.G.M.

In the hubbub of the turn-of-the-century city, the quiet voice of **Tomáš Masaryk** (185 1937) could sometimes be heard. Son of a Slovak coachman and a German-speakin Moravian mother, as Professor of Philosophy and Sociology at Prague's Czech Ur versity, Masaryk was a determined opponent of everything irrational, fightin anti-Semitism, nationalism, and clericalism, and earning himself much unpopularity the process. An elected member of the Austrian Parliament, he hoped for Czech se government within the Empire, but with the changed circumstances brought abo by the First World War came to see that there was no alternative to outright ind pendence. First and foremost a philosopher, and no longer a young man, he becan the driving force behind the movement to unite Czechs and Slovaks, raising an arr from émigrés and deserters to fight on the Allied side and returning to Prague triumph in 1918 to become the first President of Czechoslovakia, fondly referred always as T.G.M.

Masaryk was the friend of the brothers **Josef** and **Karel Čapek** (1890-1938), the latt internationally known for his dramas *R.U.R.* (standing for *Rossum's Univers Robots*, which introduced the word *robot* into the English language) and *T Makropoulos Secret* Often presided over by Masaryk, the influential politico-litera circle known as "The Castle" met regularly at the Čapeks' villa in Vinohrady, settin the intellectual tone of this first, democratic republic of Czechoslovakia, and pr moting the values of liberalism and tolerance which became increasingly redunda during the totalitarian 1930s. Karel Čapek died of a broken heart in 1938 when t Munich settlement tore his country apart, while Josef perished in the Bergen-Bels concentration camp.

Leftward moves

In the inter-war period many thinkers had embraced Communism, looking to the litt known Soviet Union for inspiration. During the Occupation, leftward and pro-Russi leanings were intensified by the perceived betrayal of Munich and by the heroic res tance put up by the Red Army to the German assault. Little intellectual resistance w put up to the Communist coup d'état of February 1948 and what there was so crushed. Many members of the intelligentsia found rewarding post as cultural app ratchiks of one kind or another. **Vítěslav Nezval** (1900-58), the leading figure in t innovative poetry of the 1920s and 30s, indulged in shameless Stalin-worship a became head of the nationalised film industry, while the writer **Zdeněk Nejedlý** (187 1962), promoted in old age to Minister of Education and National Enlightenme laboured tirelessly to validate the regime by emphasising its roots in the natior history, particularly with Hussitism.

Dissidence

By the early 1960s Czechoslovak Communism was in crisis, failing economically a politically, and dealing heavy-handedly with attempts at cultural revival. Within t Communist Party intellectuals agitated for fundamental change, their efforts culr nating in the Prague Spring of 1968 which won the support of the whole nation a represented the last chance for Communism to reform itself. The "normalisatio which followed the Warsaw Pact invasion of August 1968 excluded all those capat of independent thought from any part in the running of the country. Dismissed fro universities and other institutes, poets, dramatists, economists and philosophers fou themselves cleaning windows or stoking boilers, their writings published, if at all, *samizdat* form.

When not in jail or being harassed by security police, the playwright **Václav Ha** (b 1936) rolled barrels in a provincial brewery. Acclaimed for his early 1960s absu dist comedies like *The Garden Party* which poked fun at bureaucracy, Hav continued to write in the 1970s, though works like the so-called *Vaněk Trilo (Audience, Private View and Protest)* could only be performed privately or abroa In 1977, together with the philosopher Jan Patočka and former Foreign Minist Zdeněk Mlynář, Havel founded **Charta 77**. Despite the very real risk of imprisonme some 1 800 people eventually signed the Charta, which called on the governme unsuccessfully, to respect its own laws and uphold human rights. With little intere in politics as such, Havel concerned himself with the moral basis of action and sa the moral individual, rather than any dogma, as the foundation of society. Alo with his fellow-dissidents, he gave the Velvet Revolution of late 1989 a voice; elect President at the end of that momentous year, and re-elected twice since, Havel h stood by the values which sustained him throughout his dissident years and h done all in his power to reconnect his country to the humanist traditions upheld his philosopher predecessor, Masaryk.

Musical Prague

"The conservatory of Europe"

his is how the Englishman Charles Burnley described Bohemia in 1772, and roughout their history, the Czech people have indeed displayed an innate taste for usic, which they love to listen to and above all to play: "Co Čech, to muzikant", or Scratch a Czech and find a musician", as the saying goes.

people of song – In the Middle Ages, it was partly through song that Czechs came establish their identity. They celebrated it with a *Kyrie*, the famous *Hospodine, miluj ny*, and a hymn to St Wenceslas came to serve as their national anthem. Grerian chant was developed at the Chapter of Vyšehrad and the *Book of Canticles* of George's Abbey, on the Hradčany, is well-renowned.

e Hussite belief in the simple values of early Christianity led them to disapprove of lyphony in music, and they discouraged the use of organs in church music. They couraged congregational music and hymn singing, in Czech – which had previously en forbidden in church music – rather than Latin. Together with folk music, this shion for choral music was a foundation for the singing societies which became such feature of Czech music in subsequent centuries.

hen Emperor Sigismund tried to reconquer Prague in 1420, the song *Povstaň, ovstaň, veliké město pražské* (Rise, rise, great city of Prague) was written, and before ch battle, the Hussites intoned *Ktož jú boží bojovníci* (You who are soldiers of God). ediscovered in the 19C, this canticle became a musical symbol for the struggle of e Czech nation to rescue what had been lost under Austrian rule.

nder the protection of the Church and aristocracy – In the 16C, and especially in the iroque era, both the aristocracy and the Church promoted musical education, often lping country folk with talent to break out of serfdom into a musical career. The Jesuits, e Piaristes and the Minorites bestowed the titles of **"magister musicae"**, on such people **Černohorský**. Some fine private orchestras, or **"kapela"**, were established and took their ace in the palaces of Prague's nobility. Alongside this scholarly music, **popular songs**, used r religious processions, enjoyed a renaissance. The Jesuits reclaimed the old airs by moving from the lyries any heretical elements, and **Father Stayer**, a native of Prague, prered an extensive book of songs which ran into six editions between 1683 and 1764.

ssociations and institutions – Thanks to this musical culture, which calls to mind saying of the time **"every Czech is born with a violin under their pillow"**, the music of the IC became a powerful instrument of the Czech National Revival. Thus, it was in the estigious State Theatre, which gave a triumphal welcome to Mozart in 1787, that e Czech national anthem, the air *Kde domov můj* (Where is my country?), taken om an opera by **František Škroup**, resounded for the first time. Above all, several soci- ies were created to enlist and help the country's musicians. The **Society of Performers**

Building of the Hlahol Choral Society

collected funds for ageing musicians and for the orphans of musicians. The **Prague Co[**
servatory, the first in Europe, was founded in 1811 and produced fine musicians, li[**
the violinist Josef Slavik and the singer Henrietta Sontag. Public concerts were orga[
ised to show off the talents of young musicians. Concerts on Slavonic Island (the[
called Sophia Island) attracted foreign composers such as **Berlioz** as well as **Liszt**, wh[
wrote a monumental work called *The Bohemians and their Music*.

In the second half of the century, the musical societies, in which Czechs and Germa[
had mingled, disappeared and the two cultures drifted apart. The Prague societ[
Hlahlol, created in 1861, was directed by **Smetana**, with the motto "Through song,
the heart, through the heart, to the Nation". The idea was born of a national instit[
tion where Czech composers and musicians could perform, and in 1868 the foundatio[
stone of the **National Theatre** was laid. In the same spirit, from the end of the 18C t[
today, numerous scholars have endeavoured to collect the **popular songs** and **traditio[
dances** which were the inspiration for the works of **Smetana** and **Dvořák**, as well as **Janáče[**

A city shaped by music

A favourable urban setting – Bells ring out from Prague's "hundred towers", amor[
them ancient **carillons**, like the one at the **Loreta**, built by Petr Naumann in 1694. Sin[
the Middle Ages, **trumpet players** have accompanied the city's festivals from many [
tower, especially in Baroque times; in 1891, Dvořák composed fanfares for them o[
the occasion of the country's Jubilee Exhibition. Today, the fanfare for the cast[
guards keeps the tradition alive. On a more sombre note, Dalibor's Tower on Hradča[
recalls the legendary role of the violin in helping Czechs through troubled times.

In the midst of the towers runs the broad Vlatva. Its murmuring sound and the noi[
of its mills, as on Kampa Island, have inspired many a piece of music. As early [
1715, musical processions were organised on the river in honour of Jan Nepomuc[
(John of Nepomuk), thrown into the river from the Charles Bridge. Zach, Jacob an[
Brixi composed a **"musica navalis"**, mainly for wind instruments, performed, througho[
the century, from boats drifting downstream.

The churches of Prague have always provided wonderful music. The **Church of the Knigh[**
of the Cross with the Red Star was famous for its **"sepolkras"**, oratorios given during Le[
and sung by two choirs from the galleries opposite the church. The music at Strah[
Abbey, aroused the enthusiasm of Mozart at the time of his visit in 1787, while t[
music of St James' Church attracted Černohorský. In his early years Dvořák earned[
modest living playing a church organ an Janáček composed for this instrument.

Some of the **old house signs** have musical connotations, such as the three violins at 210/1[
Nerudova Street, home to three generations of violin-makers between 1667 and 174[
including the celebrated Tomas Edlinger. The old town square offers a more bloo[
trace of bygone music, in the form of a memorial to the composer **Kryštof Harant z Polž[**
executed among the other leaders of the Estates Rebellion on 21 June 1621.

Concert halls and opera houses – Prague is also famous for its concert halls a[
opera houses. The **V Kotcích Theatre** opened its doors in 1737 and organised the fir[
performance of a comic opera in Prague, *La Serva Padrona* (The Maid as Mistress) [
Pergolesi. **Gluck** staged his operas here. In 1781 Count **Nostitz**, started the building [
a theatre which would put on three operas a week. Although its director, **Štepánek**, mac[
every effort to show Czechs works, eventually the theatre became exclusively Germa[
in character. The Czechs then set up a stage at the **Provisional Theatre**, which gradua[
became integrated into the National Theatre. Inaugurated in 1881, the latter was [
become their great temple of Czech music. To compete with the Czechs, the Germa[
built the **New German Theatre** in 1888 (the present-day State Opera). Although the tw[
publics usually ignored each other completely, Mahler, welcomed by the Germans, w[
not rejected by the Czechs. After 1918, the New German Theatre opened itself to th[
Czechs and its head, Zemlínský, introduced recent foreign works. The **Vinohrady Theat[**
built in 1904-7, competed with the National Theatre with its opera performance.

A number of concert halls were built in the course of the 19C. On **Slavonic Island**, a fir[
hall was constructed in 1837, and the **Rudolfinum** opened its doors in 1884. The **Konvi[**
or the **Platýz**, near the church of St Martin-in-the-Walls, provided a setting for co[
certs and other musical entertainment. In the Communist period attendance at [
concert or the opera provided a way of meeting at a time when public gatherin[
were forbidden; musical life took on political overtones.

Finally, Prague is a city of music festivals. The best-known is the **Prague Spring Festiv[**
created in 1946. This international festival of music, including a competition for pe[
formers, opens on 12 May, the anniversary of the death of Smetana, with [
performance of *Má vlast*. In September, around St Wenceslas' Day (28 September[
there is the Prague Autumn Festival. In October and in November the Jewish festiv[
of music, Musica Judaica, takes place.

An array of composers

Prague has always had an ambiguous relationship with composers, allowing som[
natives to depart, at the same time attracting numerous foreigners. This enriched th[
city's musical life as early as the Middle Ages, when a variety of musicians, Germa[
French, Slovene, Italian, came to serve the Court.

The glories of the Baroque

The glories of the Baroque – The 18C is the Golden age of Czech music and the Baroque period provides further examples of this characteristic cultural interaction, with many Czech musicians making a name for themselves elsewhere in Europe. **Jan Dismas Zelenka** (1679-1745) was a double-bass player, employed for 35 years at the court of Dresden. In 1723 while in the services of the elector of Saxony he arranged a performance in Prague of his allegorical piece *Sub olea pacis et palma virtutis (Under the boughs of peace and the palm of virtue)* for the coronation of Charles VI. **Bohuslav Matěj Černohorský** (1684-1742),

Winged and gilded drummer from, St Thomas' Church

the other great composer of the era, has the misfortune of losing the greater part of his work in a fire at the church of St James, of which he was organist and of the work of the man the Italians called *"Il Padre Boemo"* – only 15 pieces remain. In Italy, **Josef Mysliveček** (1737-81) also attracted a title, that of *"Il Divino Boemo"* (the Divine Bohemian), indicating how much his operas were appreciated. **Johann Stamitz** (1717-57), the violinist, worked mainly in Mannheim and was the father of sonata in its modern form. **Jiří Benda** (1722-95) spent 28 years in Berlin and later Smetana was based in Sweden and Dvořák in the United States of America.

Two leaders of the Cathedral Orchestra were particularly distinguished. **František Xaver Brixi** (1732-71) took up his post at the age of 17 and left more than 500 compositions, mainly oratorios of the Passion and several solemn masses. The second, **Jan Antonín Koželuh** (1738-1814), influenced the Prague Opera through his works in the italian style, such as *Alessandro nella India* (1760) and *Demmofoonte* (1772), which successfully brought the Nostitz Theatre back to life.

Two illustrious 18C visitors – No-one aroused the passion of Praguers more than **Wolfgang Amadeus Mozart** (1756-91). In 1782 and 1786, *The Abduction from the Seraglio* and *The Marriage of Figaro* triumphed at the **Nostitz Theatre**. As reports from the time reveal, the whole city was seized by "Figaromania". The climax was the premier of *Don Giovanni* on 29 October 1787, which Mozart had completed at the **Bertramka**, the house of his friends, the Czech composer **František Xaver Dušek** and his wife Josefa (1753-1824), an accomplished singer. The production of Mozart's *La Clemenza dit Tito* in 1802 marks the end of the era of Italian opera in Prague. From now on, German *singspiel* and the opera sung in Czech prevailed.

Ludwig van Beethoven (1770-1827) stayed in Prague on two occasions, in 1796 and 1798, as is commemorated by the plaque on the house at 285 Lázeňská Street. Invited by Countess Josefina Clary, herself a musician, Beethoven gave some private concerts and composed the *Sonatina and theme with variations for harpsichord and mandolin*. His music was played for the general public at the State Theatre, under the direction of **Carl Maria von Weber**, the German composer, who was director of the German Opera House in Prague (founded in 1807) between 1813 and 1816.

Towards a national music – The transition between the "Bohemian classicism" of the 18C and the great masters of the National Revival is made by **Václav Jan Tomášek** (1770-1850). Personal composer to Count Buquoy, he wrote mainly for piano and contributed to the development of Czech Romanticism. **Jan Václav Hugo Voříšek** (1791-1825), one of the founders of the National Museum, is a figure of prime importance in the National Revival. He composed little, but some of his chamber music as well as his *Symphony in D Major* achieved a degree of fame.

The person who most embodied the National Revival was **Bedřich Smetana** (1824-84). After having taken part in the 1848 uprising, he wanted to help the Czech nation to be reborn through his music, and in the same year, with the help of

Infant musicians

Liszt he founded the Nation[al] School in Prague, which soo[n] became a very fashionab[le] school of music. Smetana[‘s] works are permeated with folk lore, and his works convey [a] strong patriotism, as is the ca[se] in his cycle of six symphonic p[o]ems, *My Country*, two of whic[h] *Vltava* and *From the Fields an[d] Groves of Bohemia*, are ofte[n] performed separately, and als[o] in his operas such as *Libuše* [and] *Dalibor*. His love for Bohem[ia] didn't prevent Smetana fro[m] being well-received abroad, no[t]ably in Sweden.

This blend of patriotic passio[n] and openness to foreign infl[u]ence is also found in **Anton[ín] Dvořák** (1841-1904), who b[e]came the key inspirational figu[re] for Czech music after the dea[th] of Smetana. He did not have t[he] early exposure to classical mus[ic] that Smetana had had, and h[is] roots were even more firmly [in] Czech peasant culture (Smetan[a] had grown up speaking on[ly] German), being nourished b[y] traditional Slavonic music, n[ot] only Bohemian but also fro[m]

Bedřich Smetana

other regions such as the Ukraine and Poland. However, though this made him potentia[lly] a more credible focus for nationalism than Smetana, Dvořák was in fact more influence[d] by the world of international music. He left a varied body of work, from symphonies [to] chamber music, not to mention choral pieces and a few operas.

Continuity and innovation in the 20C – **Dvořák** directed a class in composition at th[e] Prague Conservatory and from this emerged **Vítězslav Novák** (1870-1949), who was al[so] influenced by the popular songs of Moravia and Slovakia, and **Josef Suk** (1874-1935[,] **Josef Bohuslav Foerster** (1859-1951) and **Otakar Ostrčil** (1879-1935), who developed [a] new symphonic style, modernised the Czech National School. This then received th[e] creative inspiration of the Moravian **Leoš Janáček** (1854-1928). Having completed h[is] training as an organist and composer abroad, Janáček returned to live and work [in] Brno. His works, with new harmonies and colourful instrumentation, were appreciate[d] in Prague, and the *"Cunning Little vixen"* of the opera has its statue in the Petřín Ga[r]dens. After him, **Bohuslav Martinů** (1890-1959), a pupil of Suk, mixed Moravian folk lore, jazz and the neo-Classicism of Albert Roussel, who was his teacher in Paris. A[s] well as some symphonic poems, he wrote music for the cinema and for television.

A professor of composition at the Prague Conservatory between 1923 and 1953, **Ale[š] Hába** researched the use of micro-intervals, his life-long study of which was triggered b[y] his acquaintance with Czech and Slovak folksong, which both use modified scales.

During the Stalinist era, musical creativity was curbed, and even experimental compose[rs] like Haba produced more orthodox music such as his *Wallachian Symphony* (1952).

Some freedom returned in the 1960s, and then again in the 1980s, when something [of] the emotive and fervent nationalist spirit of Smetana and the 19C returned to Czec[h] popular music.

Klementinum cherub

Cinema

e convoluted history of Czechoslovakia in the 20C is reflected in its cinema. While
e great studios at Barrandov provided film-makers with some of the world's most
-to-date facilities in the 1930s, Nazi occupation and Communism forced creative
rits into conformity or exile. But paradoxically, it was the slight easing of Commu-
t censorship which resulted in the most glorious period in Czech cinema; in the
w Wave of the 1960s films were produced which ever since have been seen as
aracteristically Czech in their understated humour and wry observation of human
ilty.

The early screen

echs' first exposure to cinematography came in 1896 when the citizens of
rlsbad were treated to moving pictures and Edison's Kinetoscope was demon-
ated in Prague. By the 1920s some 20 feature films were being made every
ar and the Czechs' favourite star, the long-legged Anny Ondráková became
own as Anny Ondra when she was tempted away by Alfred Hitchcock to make
ackmail. At the same time the artistic avant-gardists of Devětsil, who had elected
arlie Chaplin an honorary member of their group, were experimenting with the
etic and surrealistic possibilities of the new medium of cinema. With the arrival
sound the cinema took off in popularity, and evening crowds filled Prague's
ndred-plus movie houses, among them the ornate auditorium of the Lucerna
mplex built by Václav Havel's grandfather. In 1933 the future president's uncle,
loš, together with the architect Max Urban, developed what were probably the
st advanced film studios in Europe at Barrandov just outside Prague, and over
e years the name Barrandov became synonymous with the Czechoslovak film
ustry.

e 1930s were the era of matinée idols like Oldřich Nový (Kristián, 1939) and of
mour queens like the Slovak Hedwig Kiesler, later known as Hedy Lamarr
xtase, 1933) and Lida Baarová, who achieved notoriety as the mistress of Josef
ebbels.

e genial satirists Jiří Voskovec and Jan Werich, already famous for their sur-
alistic satire shows at the Liberated Theatre, transferred their act with great
ccess to the screen in Svět patří nám (The World Belongs to Us) (1937).
novative documentary films included a lyrical evocation of the traditional life
the Slovak peasantry in Karel Plicka's Zem spieva (The Song of the Earth)
935).

ring the Occupation Barrandov was taken over by the Nazis who improved its
eady superb facilities and used it to turn out more than 100 lavishly produced
t forgettable films. After the war Barrandov was nationalised and was soon
apted to the requirements of Socialist Realism, with films glorifying industrial pro-
ction and exaggerating out of all proportion the role of the country's Communists
the wartime Resistance, as in Němá barikáda (Silent Barricade) by Otakar Vávra
949). The long-lived Vávra (1911) was the great survivor of the Czech cinema,
hnically brilliant, choosing and adapting his themes to the spirit of the times and
o playing a leading role in Prague's famous school of film FAMU, founded in 1945
eck), where he won the respect of the young generation who would initiate the
novations of the 1960s.

Animation

Czech animation made its debut on the international stage in 1946 when Jiří
Trnka (1912-69) won the Grand Prix du dessin animé for his Zvířátka a Petrovští
(Little Animals and Brigands). Trnka became the grand old man of animation
with dozens of enchanting films in which he drew on the country's rich traditions of fairy tale and legend as well as on the work of artists and illustrators
like Josef Lada; in 1955 he based his marionette film The Good Soldier Švejk
on Lada's classic illustrations to Hašek's immortal novel. Trnka helped establish
a superlative standard of animation whose vitality can still be discerned in the
high quality of some Czech TV's productions for children. In the 1980s and
1990s the public became familiar with the surrealistic vision of Jan Švankmajer
(1934-), who used puppets, objets trouvés, modelling clay, skeletons and junk
to create the disturbing and sometimes frightening world of Alice (1988), Faust
(1994) or Konec stalinismu v Čechách (The Last Days of Stalinism in
Bohemia – 1990).

Scene from *A Blonde in Love* by Forman

The New Wave and after

Alternating between their customary repression and outbreaks of mild liberalism, t
Czechoslovak censors of the 1960s permitted the making and sometimes the screeni
of a remarkable wave of films, the work of young directors like Miloš Forman *(Lá:
jedné plavovlásky – A Blonde in Love – 1966, Hoří, má panenko – The Firemen's I
– 1967)*, Ivan Passer *(Intimate Lighting – 1965)*, Jan Němec *(Démanty noci – L
monds of the Night – 1965)*, Jiří Menzel *(Ostře sledované vlaky – Closely Obser
Trains – 1966)*, or Věra Chytilová *(Sedmikrásky – Daisies – 1966)*. Socialist herc
were left far behind in these films, which connected with other currents in Czech li
like irony, irreverence, and a sense of the absurd, and brought the country's cine
to the attention of the world. Such independence could not survive the crushing
the Prague Spring in 1968 and the "normalisation" that followed. Conformity
silence ruled, and much talent left the country, though not all achieved the inter
tional success of Forman, who carried his characteristic vision forward in *Taking*
(1972) and *One Flew over the Cuckoos Nest* (1979). At home Vávra completed
monumental trilogy *Dny zrady/Days of Treachery, Sokolovo* and *Osvobození Pra
(The Liberation of Prague)* dealing in a rather wooden way with Czechoslovak hist
from the time of Munich to the end of the Second World War.

After 1989 the state subsidies which had supported film-making dropped away, pai
to be replaced by foreign interest in exploiting the resources of Barrandov and t
expertise of well-trained technicians in making international blockbusters. There I
been no new New Wave, though films of quality continue to be made like the ri
drama *Kráva (The Cow)* (1995) by veteran director Karel Kachyňa or *Mandrage*
(1997) by Wictor Grodecki, a sombre tale of Prague street boys. International succ
was achieved by Jan Svěrák in *Kolja* (1996) in which Czech/Russian relations a
played out in the sentimental story of a middle-aged man forced to adopt a small b

Remember – there is more than one kind of Michelin star:
  – some refer to architectural monuments and museums
  – others refer to groups of buildings or to details

A selection of house signs

Walks in Prague

PRAGUE IN A DAY

This whole day walk introduces you to Prague's four historic districts, shows you th
city from a number of classic viewpoints, and takes you past – if not inside! - many
the principal sights. It's a long walk, on hard surfaces, but there's no need to do it
a hurry and there are plenty of places to take a break *(see Useful addresses p. 29)*

The walk begins with a ride on the (for visitors) extremely useful Tram no 22. Yo
can catch this at a number of stops in the city centre, including e ramp to the entran
to **Strahovský klášter★** (Strahov Abbey), across the monastery courtyard and out throug
the doorway at the far end. Turn right to the symbolic vineyard with its wonderf
panorama over the orchards of Petřín Hill, Hradčany and the city as a whole. Retur
to the monastery courtyard, go down the tunnel into Pohořelec Square, turn righ
along Loretánská (Loretto Street) and left into Loretánské náměstí (Loretto Squar
to admire the **Černínský palác★** (Černín Palace) and the **Loreta/Loretto Shrine★★★**, wher
if your timing is right, you will hear its famous carillon.
Return to Loretánská and continue towards **Hradčanské náměstí★★** (Hradčany Squar
whose palaces include the **Schwarzenberský palác★**, the home of the Military Museun
and the **Šternberský palác★★**, which houses the National Gallery's European art colle
tion. Leaving these for a later visit, watch the changing of the castle guard if you a
here on the hour *(the main ceremony is a midday)*, go through the castle gates an
into the Second Courtyard. Buy a ticket in the foyer of the Chapel of the Holy Roc
for the Starý královský palác (Old Royal Palace), then continue to the Third Cour
yard. Peep into the **chram sv. Víta★★★** (St Vitus' Cathedral) with its 20C stained gla
and array of monuments, then go across the courtyard to the **Old Royal Palace★★**, wit
its magnificent Vladislav Hall and the Louis Wing which was the scene of Prague
Second Defenestration.
Emerge from the palace and after admiring the east end of the cathedral and th
façade of **Jiřský klášter★★** (St George's Convent), go downhill and turn left towards **Zla
ulička★★** (Golden Lane). Leave the castle at its eastern end, and, if it is summer, ent
the castle's **south garden★★** *(Out of season go down Staré zámecké schody (Old Cast
Steps) and turn right into Valdštejnská (Wallenstein Street)*, and go down t
Valdštejnská through the **Baroque gardens★★** of the palaces beneath the castle.

Malostranské náměstí★ (Malá Strana Square) with its choice of restaurants, pubs an
cafes is a good place to have a midday break and take a look at the façade
sv. Mikuláš★★★ (St Nicholas' Church). Or you could have a picnic among the trees
Kampa Island and enjoy the view of the Old Town on the far side of the River Vltav
Whatever you choose to do, make your way to the little square of Na kampě at
northern end of **Kampa Island** and go up the steps on to **Karlův most★★★** (Charles Bridge
On the far side of the bridge, turn right through the pedestrian tunnel and walk alon
the embankment with its superb views across the river to Hradčany. Turn left at th
Národní divadlo★★ (National Theatre) along **Národní třída★** (National Avenue), then le
down Na Perštýně to **Betlémské náměstí** (Bethlehem Square) with its chapel where Joh
Huss preached, then on along Husova (Huss Street) to rejoin the main stream
tourists moving along **Karlova★★** (Charles Street) between Charles Bridge an
Staroměstské náměstí★★★ (Old Town Square).
There are plenty of opportunities to take a break on and around the square, thoug
the energetic might want to climb the tower of the Old Town Hall for the panoran
over the Old Town. The **Josefov★★★** (Jewish Quarter) just to the north should be save
for another day, though you might just want to look at the outside of the **Starono
synagoga★★★** (Old-New Synagogue).

Once refreshed, go down the passageway to the left of the Týn Church and into th
Ungelt or **Týn Court★**, turning right as you leave past the façade of **sv. Jakuba★** (St Jame
Church). The passageway ahead of you leads into **Celetná Street★**, where you turn le
towards the venerable **Prašná brána★** (Powder Tower) and the glittering Art Nouvea
Obecní dům★★★ (Municipal House), whose café may induce you to pause yet again.
The final lap of the walk takes you through the commercial heart of the city, fir
along **Na příkopě★** (Moat Street) and then into **Václavské náměstí★★★** (Wenceslas Squar
itself. Conclude the walk at the **Wenceslas statue★★** or on the steps of the **Národ
muzeum★** (National Musuem) with its splendid view down the whole length of th
Square.

A SELECTION OF DAY WALKS

*For convenience, all these walks are assumed to start from the "Golden Cross", th
busy meeting point of Wenceslas Square and the semicircle of boulevards marking th
boundary of the Old and New Towns. Some walks involve use of public transport, fo
which you must have a validated ticket.*

radčany – The Castle Quarter

ke the Metro *(Line A, green, direction Dejvická)* from Můstek station two stops to alostranská station, change to Tram no 22. and get off at Pohořelec for **Strahovský šter★** (Strahov Abbey). After looking at Strahov's fabulous libraries, go down to the mbolic vineyard just below the monastery for the panorama over the city. Loretánská pretto Street) descends towards the **Loreta/Loretto Shrine★★★** and the **Černínský palác★** ernín Palace). Černínská (Černín Lane) leads north into the charming little street own as Nový Svět (New World), which in turn, via Kanovnická, leads into **Hradčanské něstí★★** (Hradčany Square) with its grand palaces including the **Šternbersky palác★★** cernberg Palace) with the National Gallery's collection of European art and the warzenberský palác★** with the Military Museum.

yond the blue-uniformed guardsmen are the treasures of the **Hrad★★★** (Castle) and ám sv.Víta★★★** (St Vitus' Cathedral). You should make sure you see at least the inside the **Starý královský palác★★** (Old Royal Palace) and the minuscule dwellings of **Zlatá ka★★** (Golden Lane) as well as the **south gardens★★** of the castle *(in season)*.

e quickest way to return to the Golden Cross is down Staré zámecké schody (Old stle Steps) to Malostranská Metro station, but there are any number of other pos- ilities; in season, the terraces of the **Baroque gardens★★** below the Castle descend to dštejnská (Wallenstein Street) which leads in one direction to the Metro, in the her to **Malostranské náměstí★** (Malá Strana Square) and the stop for tram no 22 back Národní třída, the nearest stop to the Golden Cross. Malá Strana Square can also reached via Nové zámecké schody (New Castle Steps) or **Nerudova★★** (Neruda eet).

alá Strana

alk to Národní třída tram stop *(it's one stop on the Metro, but quicker on foot)* and ke **Tram nos 6, 9, 22 or 23** across the most Legií (Legionaries Bridge) to the Újezd pp. Go back the way you have just come and turn left into Šeřiková Street, right st the tiny church of **sv. Jana na prádle** (St John at the Wash-house) on to **Kampa Island** th its fine views across the river to the Old Town. Cross one of the footbridges over e Čertovka/Devil's Brook to **Maltézské náměstí★** (Maltese Square), then continue into sy Karmelitská (Carmelite Street). The church of **Panny Marie Vítězné★** (Our Lady of ctories) is on the north side of the street, as is the entrance to the **Vrtbovská zahrada★★** rtba Garden). Turn left up Tržiště (Market Street) and its continuation Vlašská alian Street) with their grand embassy buildings like the **Schönbornský palác** *(USA)* and e **Lobkovický palác★** *(Germany)*. To the right, charming lanes and steps lead up to rudova★★** (Neruda Street) which descends to **Malostranské náměstí★** (Malá Strana uare) with the great Baroque church of **sv. Mikuláš★★★** (St Nicholas).

north out of the Square along narrow Sněmovní (Parliament Street), then right into dštejnská náměstí (Wallenstein Square), dominated by the main facade of the dštejnský palác★★** (Wallenstein Palace). To the left is the entrance to the **Baroque gar- as★★** below the castle. Wallenstein's great palace is now the home of the country's nate, but it is normally possible to walk through the courtyard into its **formal garden★★** therwise walk along Valdštejnská, *through the garden of Malostranská Metro station d back up Letenská)*. Go along Letenská and into the little **riverside park** just upstream om Mánesův most (Mánes Bridge) for an unusual **view** across the water to the Old wn. Return to Malá Strana Square and the tram stop via U lužického semináře and stecká (Bridge Street) or to the city centre via Charles Bridge and the Old Town.

ld Town and Josefov/Jewish Quarter

alk east along **Na příkopě★** to the **Prašná brána★** (Powder Tower) and the **Obecní dům★★★** unicipal House), then west along Celetná Street, turning right through the court- rd of No 17/595 continuing into Malá Štupartská. Opposite **sv. Jakuba★** (St James' urch) turn left into the **Ungelt★** (Týn **Court**) and on into **Staroměstské náměstí★★★** (Old wn Square).

ave the Square by walking north along Pařížská (Boulevard de Paris) and into the efov★★★** (Jewish Quarter) with the **Staronová synagoga★★★** (Old New Synagogue), the arý židovský hřbitov and other memorials from the thousand-year Jewish history of ague. Široká (Broad Street) leads to náměstí Jana Palacha (Jan Palach Square), the **ěmeleckoprůmyslové muzeum★** (Decorative Arts Museum) and the **Rudolfinum★**. Avoid the avy traffic on Křížovnická Street by heading back into the Old Town along Kaprova eet and turning right into Valentinská Street and **Mariánské náměstí** (Marian Square). through the courtyards of the **Klementinum★** and emerge on to **Křížovnické náměstí★★** nights of the Cross Square) at the end of the **Karlův most★★★** (Charles Bridge). Pen- ate the Old Town again via busy **Karlova★** (Charles Street), and turn right along ová Street into **Betlémské náměstí** with its **chapel** made famous by John Huss. Just yond the far end of the square, find the narrow entrance to Jilská Street and turn ht almost at once into even narrower Vejvodova Street which will bring you into chalská and Uhelný trh (Coal Market). From here Rytířská (Knight Street) runs aight towards the **Stavovské divadlo★** (Estates Theatre). Just before you get to the eatre, the short street known as Na můstku brings you back to the Golden Cross.

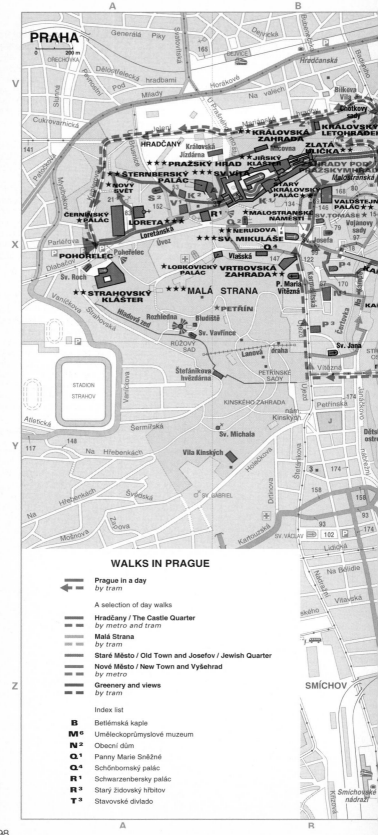

WALKS IN PRAGUE

Prague in a day
by tram

A selection of day walks

Hradčany / The Castle Quarter
by metro and tram

Malá Strana
by tram

Staré Město / Old Town and Josefov / Jewish Quarter

Nové Město / New Town and Vyšehrad
by metro

Greenery and views
by tram

Index list

B	Betlémská kaple
M⁶	Uměleckoprůmyslové muzeum
N²	Obecní dům
Q¹	Panny Marie Sněžné
Q⁴	Schönbornský palác
R¹	Schwarzenbersky palác
R³	Starý židovský hřbitov
T³	Stavovské divlado

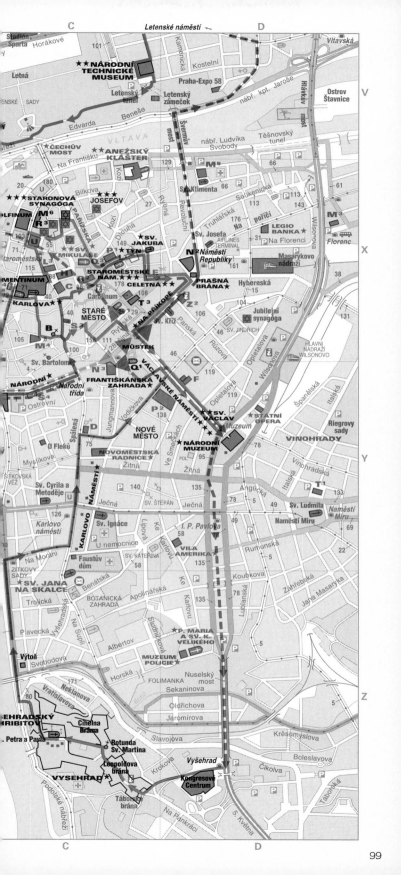

The New Town and Vyšehrad

Head for **Jungmannovo náměstí**, noticing on your left the strange **Cubist street lamp★**. I the statue of Jungmann turn left into the entrance to the **Františkánská zahrada★** (Fra ciscan Gardens), which together with the great Gothic church of **Panny Marie Sněžné** (Our Lady of the Snows), is a reminder that the New Town is not really that new all. The exit from the Gardens leads into one of the early 20C arcades *(pasáže Czech)* which are such a feature of **Václavské náměstí** (Wenceslas Square) and whic enable you to walk undercover much of the way towards the top end of the Squa with the **Wenceslas statue★★** and the **Národní muzeum★** (National Museum).

Take the Metro *(Line C, red, direction Háje)* from **Muzeum** station two stops Vyšehrad station. From the terraces of the monumental Communist-era **Palác kultu** (Palace of Culture) walk westwards along V pevnosti Street through the two gat ways guarding the **Vyšehrad★** rock. Admire the views up and down the river and g into the **Slavín★** (National Cemetery). Steps lead down to the riverside and the sca tering of **Cubist buildings★**. **From the Výtoň tram stop**, Tram no 3 will take you into th park-like **Karlovo náměstí★** (Charles Square) and on to the **Václavské náměstí** stop, th nearest to the Golden Cross.

Greenery and views

Letná Plain to Hradčany – Walk east along Na příkopě to **Náměstí Republiky** tram st and take **Tram no 8** across the river to **Letenské náměstí** (Letná Square) stop. Go dov Ovenecká Street and round the **Národní technické muzeum★** (National Technical Museum to reach the garden restaurant on the edge of **Letná Plain** overlooking the river and th Old Town. Walk west, past the plinth where the Stalin statue stood and past the ex berant little late 19C **Hanavský pavilón** restaurant, all the time enjoying the views. Cro the modern footbridge into **Chotkový sady** (Chotek Gardens) and enter the **Králov zahrada★** (Royal Gardens) by the **Královský letohrádek** or **Belveder★**. Turn left towards th castle on leaving the gardens, but turn right at the entrance and walk through th **Zahrada na baště** (Bastion Garden) into **Hradčanské náměstí★★** (Hradčany Square).

Recommended reading

History and context

We the People, by Timothy Garton Ash, Penguin 1990 – The author witnessed sever of the revolutions of 1989, and was on the balcony with Václav Havel and Alexand Dubček as they addressed the crowds in Wenceslas Square.

Prague in Black and Gold, by Peter Demetz, Penguin 1997 – Glittering survey of c history by a Yale professor who returned to the city of his birth after long exile.

Czechs and Balances, by Benjamin Kuras, Baronet 1996 – A Czech-born playwright livir in Britain takes a light-hearted look at his native country's often heavy burden of histor

Prague in the Shadow of the Swastika, by Callum MacDonald and Jan Kapla Melantrich 1995 – The grim realities of life as lived in Prague at the time of the Na "Protectorate of Bohemia-Moravia".

Praha-Prag-Prague – The Turbulent Century, by Jan Kaplan and Krystyna Nozarzewsk Kěnemann 1997 – A hundred years of city history in sophisticated scrapbook form, i wealth of illustrations drawn from Jan Kaplan's unrivalled collection of Prague ephemer

Magic Prague, by Angelo Maria Ripellino, Picador 1994 – An atmospheric tra through myth, mystery and squalor.

The Coasts of Bohemia, by Derek Sayer, Princeton 1998 – A marvellously research and colourful account of how Czechs set out to create an identity for themselves the 19C and 20C.

Gloria & Miseria – Prague During the Thirty Years War, by Michal Šroněk and Jarosla Hausenblasová, Gallery 1998 – Sumptuous illustrated history of the devastating co flict which began with the Second Defenestration of Prague.

Bohemia in History, Edited by Mikuláš Teich, Cambridge 1998 – Learned essays key periods in Bohemian history by resident experts.

The Masaryks – The Making of Czechoslovakia, by Zbyněk Zeman, Tauris 1976 – 20 Czechoslovak history seen through the lives of the country's founder, President-L erator Tomáš Garrigue Masaryk, and his son, genial Foreign Minister Jan.

Prague Spring – A Report on Czechoslovakia 1968, by Zbyněk Zeman, Penguin 19 – Full account of the events leading up to the Warsaw Pact invasion of August 196

Art and architecture

Kubistická Praha/Cubist Prague 1909-1925, A Guidebook, by Michal Bregant, Len Bydžovská, Vojtěch Lahoda, Zdeněk Lukeš, Karel Srp and Rostislav Švácha, Ode 1995 – Bilingual guide to Prague's unique heritage of Cubist art and architecture.

Rudolf II and Prague – The Court and the City, edited by Eliška Fučiková and othe

Thames & Hudson/Škýra 1997 – A lavishly produced and exhaustive survey of the marvels and mysteries of city and court during the rule of the eccentric and art-obsessed Emperor Rudolf II

Czech Art Deco 1918-1938, various authors, The Municipal House 1998 – The definitive catalogue of a major exhibition held at the Obecní dům/Municipal House covering all aspects of Art Deco from architecture and complete interiors to jewellery, glass, ceramics, clothing and posters.

The Architecture of Prague and Bohemia, by Brian Knox, Faber 1962 – The classic introduction, written at a time when only the deepest commitment to the subject could have borne such marvellous fruit in terms of analysis and frequently poetic judgements.

Prague – A Guide to Twentieth-Century Architecture, by Ivan Margolius, Artemis 1994 – An amazing amount of information packed into a pocket-sized softback, pithily written and adequately illustrated.

Czech Modern Art 1900-1960, The National Gallery in Prague 1995 – A compact introduction to the undeservedly little-known treasures of modern Czech art, based on the collection on display at Prague's Trade Fair Palace.

Genius Loci, Towards a Phenomenology of Architecture, by Christian Norberg-Schultz, Academy 1980 – Chapter 4 "Prague" of this seminal work on the structure and meaning of place celebrates Prague as a unique organism of site, building and history.

Prague – A Guide to the 19th and 20th Centuries, by Jiří Šourek and Zdeněk Lukeš, Artfoto 1997 - Brilliant illustrations and brief captions capture the essence of the city's 19C and 20C architecture

The Architecture of New Prague 1895-1945, by Rostislav Švácha, MIT 1995 – A coffee-table counterpart to Ivan Margolius' volume, with an academically heavy-weight text.

Prague – Eleven Centuries of Architecture: Historical Guide, by Jaroslava Staňková, Jiří Štursa and Svatopluk Voděra, PAV 1992 – Available in a range of languages, this is a very thorough reference work on the development of the city and its architecture from the earliest times to the present, clearly illustrated with analytical sketches.

Literature

The Good Soldier Švejk and His Fortunes in the World War, by Jaroslav Hašek, Penguin 1973, translated by Cecil Parrott – The first complete translation – by the former British ambassador – of the adventures of the ever-willing Good Soldier, the immortal creation of the beer-soaked and anarchic writer who was a co-founder of the satirical political movement "The Party for Moderate Progress within the Bounds of the Law".

Kafka, Love and Courage, the Life of Milena Jesenská, by Mary Hockaday, Deutsch 1995 – Vivid evocation of Bohemian life in early 20C Prague, this is the best account of the extraordinary life of the woman who was the recipient of Kafka's Letters to Milena.

My Merry Mornings, by Ivan Klíma, Readers International 1985 – Having spent part of his childhood in Terezín, Klima published short stories in samizdat after the crushing of the Prague Spring. This collection includes a famous account of selling carp for Christmas dinner

The Unbearable Lightness of Being, by Milan Kundera, Faber 1985 – Kundera's best-known novel, set partly in the Prague Spring, and subsequently filmed with great success.

Traveller's Literary Companion to Eastern and Central Europe, edited by James Naughton, In Print 1995 - Includes introductory essay on Czech literature, author biographies, extracts from literary works and brief literary guide to Prague and the Czech Republic.

Prague Tales, by Jan Neruda, various editions – Short stories by the "Dickens of Malá Strana".

Prague, A Traveler's Literary Companion, by Paul Wilson, *1995* – Extracts from the works of Czechs who took the city as their subject, and an irresistible introduction to further reading.

Others

Jewish Sights of Bohemia and Moravia, by Jiří Fiedler, Sefer 1991 – A brief history of Jewish life and history in the Czech lands, plus a detailed gazetteer of sites.

The Serpent and the Nightingale, by Cecil Parrott, Faber 1977 – Wryly written memoirs by a former British ambassador.

Prague Winter, by Nikolaus Martin, Peter Halban 1990 – Incarcerated in Terezín by the Nazis, the author then fled the country to escape Communist rule.

So Many Heroes, by Alan Levý, 1980 (original title *Rowboat to Prague*) – The journalist author experienced the Prague Spring and Warsaw Pact invasion at first hand and was later expelled from Czechoslovakia. He returned in 1990 and founded the city's English-language newspaper, the Prague Post.

Prague Farewell, by Heda Margolius Kovaly, Gollancz 1988 – Having survived Auschwitz, the author experienced the destruction of her committed Communist husband in the infamous 1952 Slanksy show-trial.

Charles Bridge

Exploring Prague

ANEŽSKÝ Klášter★★

After a process of restoration lasting a whole century, the convent founded
Přemyslid Princess Anežka (Agnes) on the northern edge of the Old Town has becor
a splendid home for the national collection of 19C Czech art. Saved from ruin a
degradation, the complex can once more be appreciated as one of the finest exa
ples of Gothic architecture in the Czech Lands.

HISTORY

The construction of the convent was begun in the 1230s with the building of t
Church of St Francis and the long eastern wing which stretched all the way to t
newly-built riverside ramparts of the Old Town. Responsible for what was the ve
first Gothic structure in the Old Town, its builders were much influenced by conte
porary developments in the Cistercian architecture of Burgundy. They worked first
stone, then in brick. Around the middle of the century the cloister was completed
well as the **Chapel of the Virgin Mary**, beyond which is the elegant presbytery of **St Saviou
Church** of about 1270, architecturally the most striking part of the complex. Its ro
functions are indicated by the capitals with portrait heads of kings and queens, wh
the carved head above the altar is assumed to be a portrait of Agnes herself; a nic
intended for her burial was let into the wall of the Chapel of the Virgin Mary.

Despite periodic flooding by the wayward waters of the Vltava, the convent flourish
throughout the Přemyslid period and into the reign of Emperor Charles IV. But by t
beginning of the 15C its life had stagnated; in 1420 the nuns were turned out by t
Hussites, who melted down the convent's silver plate and set up an arsenal within
walls. In 1556, following the loss to the Jesuits of their establishment near the Char
Bridge (the later Clementinum), the Dominicans took over. Their management of t
property seems to have involved its use as a brewery, timber yard and glass furna
and caused constant complaint. They also subdivided the adjacent convent of t
Minorities into cheap lodgings, giving the area a dubious, low-life reputation whi
persisted for hundreds of years. Though the nuns regained possession after the Bat
of the White Mountain, the institution never really flourished again. The first Prag
convent to be shut down in 1782 under Emperor Joseph II's reforms, it too was pa
titioned up by slum landlords; by the end of the 19C it seemed inevitable that it wo
be demolished in the course of the widespread redevelopment of the Old Town. E

St Agnes

The daughter of King Otakar I and sister of future King Wenceslas I, Agnes was
born in 1211. The upbringing of this independent-minded girl seems to have
nurtured her vocation; a succession of suitors including Emperor Frederick
Hohenstaufen II himself were cast aside in favour of the contemplative life she
had experienced at the early age of three, when she was sent away to the convent at Třebnice in Silesia. In her early 20s, attracted to the teachings of St Francis of Assisi and following the example of her cousin Elizabeth of Thuringia,
Agnes founded a hospital as well as a convent for the Poor Clares, the female
equivalent of the Franciscans. In 1234 she was appointed abbess of the new institution, whose high status was reflected in an ambitious and influential building programme which lasted some 50 years and which marks the introduction
of the new Gothic style into Bohemia.

Deeply committed to the Franciscan ideal of poverty, Agnes engaged in polemic
with the Papacy for more than 20 years, her wish that the rule of St Francis be
substituted for the Benedictine rule being finally granted. Her abstemious life
– she is said to have lived on a diet of raw onions and fruit – did not stop her
using her family connections to place the convent at the very heart of
dynastic life. The country's most precious relics were housed here; in 1249
Wenceslas I was crowned in the conventual Church of St Francis, and only four
years later, buried here, in what was intended to be a prestigious mausoleum
for the Přemyslids.

During her lifetime Agnes had become the object of veneration, which increased
after her death in 1282. But all attempts to have her canonised were fruitless
until the end of the 20th century; in the very last days before the fall of Communism, in November 1989, she was pronounced Svatá Anežka Česká - Saint
Agnes of Bohemia. And just over a year later, in 1991, Cardinal Tomášek gave
this much loved figure from the country's distant past a new role – that of
patron saint of all workers in the gas industry.

Agnes' convent, despite its sorry state, had won a place in the hearts of Praguers, and it was saved from destruction by public protest. An "Association for the Renovation of the Convent of the Blessed Agnes" was founded in 1893; archeological and repair work was carried out sporadically throughout the 20C, until in 1963 the complex was acquired by the National Gallery. A thoroughgoing reconstruction followed, allowing this marvel of early Gothic architecture to be appreciated once again, though inevitably the sheer quantity of new work necessary has meant some loss of "atmosphere".

NATIONAL GALLERY OF CZECH 19C PAINTING

Originally thought of as an appropriate home for the Gothic collections of the National Gallery (now in St George's Convent in Hradčany), the upper floor of the convent has been adapted to offer a very complete survey of the country's 19th century painting. Labelling throughout is in English as well as Czech and introductory panels at the head of the stairs explain the evolution of Czech art during this period.

Visit ⊙ – **Rooms 1-3** are dominated by pictures by the famous Mánes family, Antonín (1784-1843), Václav (1795-1858), Josef (1820-71, and Quido (1828-80). Among the works by **Josef Mánes** is the evocative canvas *Landscape with River Labe, Říp and Surroundings* (1863), the subject of which is the confluence of Bohemia's two great rivers the Vltava and Elbe (Labe) with, rising over the plain in the distance, the distinctive shape of Říp Hill, the eminence from which, in the 6C, "father of the nation" Čech surveyed the lands which were to bear his name. Landscape is a persistent theme throughout the gallery, reflecting artists' discovery of the richness and variety of the Bohemian and Moravian countryside. Another linked theme is that of fascination with the nation's history and a determination to celebrate its more colourful episodes in a truly epic way. Thus Room 5 has a monumental painting by Antonín Lhota Čermák (1812-1905) Přemysl *Otakar II bringing Christianity to the Heathen Prussians* alongside equally ambitious depictions of the *Crucifixion* and the discovery by Columbus of the shores of America. Room 6 has fine still-life paintings and portraits by the distinguished Karel Purkyně(1834-68) as well as pictures by Soběslav Hyppolit Pinkas (1827-1901) and Viktor Barvitius (1854-1902) reflecting in very different ways their life and work in France. Filling the end wall of the convent's east wing is perhaps the ultimate Czech history painting, reproduced countless times in school textbooks and elsewhere. Václav Brožík's (1851-1901) huge oil sketch *The Condemnation of Master John Huss* (1883) brilliantly crystallises his generation's concept of the moment when this national hero faced his accusers. To the left of the scene, the powerful figures of the established Church, in the centre the defiant black-clad radical preacher, in

Jakub Schikaneder, master of the twilight townscape

the far right a pair of his sturdy supporters, in the background perfidious Emper
Sigmund, hiding his face in shadow. No rebel himself, in 1898 Brožík paint
another vast canvas, *Tu felix Austria, nube!* to celebrate Emperor Franz-Jose
Jubilee; its ostensible subject was the betrothal of Hapsburg princess Maria
Ladislav Jagiello but its contemporary message, well understood at the time if n
accepted by all, was that of peaceful cooperation among the peoples of the mul
national Austro-Hungarian Empire. For this fine show of Hapsburg patriotis
Brožík was elevated to the peerage.

The prolific Mikoláš Aleš (1852-1913) equalled the impact of Brožík's histo
paintings with his *Meeting of George of Poděbrady with Matthias Corvinus* (1878
where the "Hussite King" George calmly demonstrates his power over his defeat
Hungarian opponent. Other comparable attempts to bring the national past to dr
matic life include František Ženíšek's (1849-1916) *Oldřich and Božena* showing
fateful encounter between prince and peasant maiden, but perhaps of wider appe
are further studies of the particular beauties of the Czech countryside such as t
Šumava Primeval Forest (1892) by Julius Mařák (1832-99) or *Summer Afterno*
in the Jezera Mountains (1863) by Alois Bubák (1824-70). Bedřich Havrán
(1821-99) devoted 30 years of his life to exploring his native land and renderi
it in meticulous detail, as in his *View of the Castle at Český Krumlov* (1882). T
visual delights of Prague provided an inexhaustible subject for artists like Havráne
but more memorable than his somewhat literal depictions are the lively stre
scenes by Luděk Marold such as The *Egg Market in Prague* (1865-98) or the my
terious urban twilights and snowscapes of **Jakub Schikaneder** (1855-1924),
atmospheric that river fog and gaslight seem to emanate from the very surface
the canvas.

BELVEDER (Královský letohrádek)★★

Royal Summer Palace Hradčany

Tram 22

Heralding the arrival of Italian Renaissance ideas in the heart of Central Europe, t
little summer palace built by Ferdinand I for his Queen Anna finishes off the easte
end of the Royal Gardens with an elegant flourish.

Only later did the name "Belvedere" catch on, but the arcaded pavilion has always e
joyed some of the best views over city and casetle as well as being the prettiest
sights itself. It is often cited as proof of Ferdinand's great love for his consort and
supposed to have been kept secret as a surprise present for her, though its constru
tion lasted several decades and was not completed until after her death. Two prin
pal architects were involved, as well as a host of mostly Italian craftsmen. The init
design was by Paolo de
Stella, who worked here fro
1537 until his death in 155
From 1557 the new castle a
chitect, Bonifaz Wohlmut, w
in charge, his main contrib
tion being the upper floor a
the extraordinary copper ro
in the form of the upturned h
of a boat. The building was fi
ished in 1563.

The palace ☽ – A light a
airy arcade runs all arou
the pavilion. It has delica
columns with Ionic capita
and among the rich relie
on mythological and histo
ical subjects is one showi
Ferdinand offering Anna
gift of figs. Doors and wi
dows show the influence
Serlio's *General Rules*
Architecture, just publish
and immensely influential
spreading the decorati
ideas of the High Rena
sance north of the Alp
Above the arcade,
balustraded balcony givi

Ph. Cajic/MICHELIN

Renaissance fountain by the Belvedere

even wider views is reached from the upper floor which was intended to serve as a ballroom and gallery. On the ground floor were richly furnished rooms, stripped bare by the plundering Swedish soldiery at the end of the Thirty Years War.

The summer palace seems to have served its purpose well as an integral part of the Royal Gardens *(see p. 137)*. It was a favourite place of retreat for Emperor Rudolf II, who allowed his astronomers to use it as an observatory. Under the utilitarian rule of Emperor Joseph II in the late 18C it sank from being a place of courtly pleasure and celestial wonder to serving as an artillery laboratory. Then in the middle of the 19th century over-confident "improvers" altered the interior almost beyond recognition, giving it a two-flight staircase and decorating it with wall-paintings (now removed). A couple of restorations later, the Royal Summer Palace forms part of the castle galleries and makes an attractive setting for temporary exhibitions of various kinds.

BERTRAMKA★

Mozartova 169, Smíchov Underground Anděl or Tram 4, 7, 9, 10 to Bertramka

In the 18C the countryside began immediately outside the walls of Prague, and the city was surrounded by farmsteads, many of them converted into pleasant retreats for the rising middle classes. One of these was the **Bertramka**, where a timber vintner's house among the vineyards of Černý vrch (Black Hill) was transformed at the beginning of the 18C into a charming villa. Given the name of one of its owners, Franz of Bertram, it was bought in 1774 by Mozart's most cherished Prague friends, the Dušeks. **František Dušek** was a successful music teacher, while his wife, Josefa, a former pupil, was an acclaimed singer. They had met Mozart in Salzburg and offered to make him welcome at any time. Mozart first came to Prague in 1787, where, the Dušeks being away, he was the guest of Count Thun and took great delight in the "*figaromania*" which had swept the city; "Nothing is played, sounded, sung, or whistled but... Figaro" he wrote. Later the same year he enjoyed the convivial surroundings of the Bertramka while completing *Don Giovanni (see p. 192)*.

Further visits to the city which had taken Mozart to its heart followed in 1789 and 1791. On his death, a requiem composed by František Antonín Rössler-Rosetti was performed in Malá Strana's Church of St Nicholas, the crowd spilling out into the square.

Mozart's sojurns in Prague inspired Eduard Mörike's novella *Mozart auf der Reise nach Prag (Mozart's Journey to Prague)* and Peter Schaeffer's play *Amadeus*, triumphantly filmed by the Czech director Miloš Forman.

The house and its surroundings retain much of the atmosphere of the late 18C. Mozartians started to make the pilgrimage here as early as the 1870s, when they could sign a visitor's book, but the Bertramka's present lay-out as a museum dates from 1956.

BETLÉMSKÉ Náměstí

BETHLEHEM Square, Old Town
Underground Národní třída

focal point among the labyrinth of streets in the southwestern part of the Old Town, is little square with its cafes and restaurants is named after the rebuilt Betlémská aple (Bethlehem Chapel) which, with its two massive gables, is its dominating feature.

BETLÉMSKÁ KAPLE (Bethlehem Chapel) ⊘

Despite being reconstructed almost from scratch in the middle of the 20C, this simple church radiates the stern spirit of the radical religious tradition embraced by Master John Huss (Jan Hus) and his followers. The building's very plainness seems a reproach to the power, wealth and prestige of a Catholic Church which Huss and others of like mind so wished to reform but which preferred to crush their ideas by force.

In the late 14th century this quarter of the city, in contrast to the wealthier, German-dominated area around Old Town Square, was inhabited almost exclusively by Czechs, open to the reformist ideas propagated by young clerics spirited enough to defy the disapproval of Court and Church. To provide them with a place to preach, an alliance of townsfolk and noblemen was formed, which furnished funds and a site (a former malthouse). Completed in the short space of three years (1391-4), the chapel was a straightforward but spacious structure, intended to accommodate as large an audience as possible for the sermons (delivered not in

Latin but in Czech) which stressed the importance of the word of God, witho
which "we would be like Sodom and Gomorrah". In line with this declaration b
its founders, the walls were later decorated with texts by Huss and his colleagu
Jakoubek ze Stříbra. Huss himself preached here for ten years, living above th
adjacent sacristy from which there was direct access to the pulpit. These quarte
now house a small museum. For more than a century the chapel was one of th
main strongholds of the Hussite Utraquist movement, but after the Battle of th
White Mountain it fell into the hands of those most bitter opponents of the Refo
mation, the Jesuits. In 1786 it was partly demolished, though some of its wa
were later incorporated into new residential buildings.

From the mid 19C onwards, the growing national self-awareness of the Czechs an
the cult of Huss stimulated a desire to rebuild the chapel. Tireless research led
the discovery of the remaining walls and of early plans of the building. But actu
reconstruction only began in 1948 under the Communist regime, which had its ow
reasons for promoting Huss as a people's hero, and was completed in 1952.

John Huss

Born around 1372 in the village of Husinec in southern Bohemia, this clever
son of a farmer soon made his way to Prague, where he studied at the university and, after taking his master's degree, was ordained as a priest. Huss's
way with words helped him play a full part in the controversies plaguing the
church at the time, but was well regarded by his superiors, who appointed
him to the Bethlehem Chapel. Here he came into closer contact with the teachings of the Englishman Wycliff, already condemned at home as a heretic. But
it was the controversy over indulgences which brought Huss to prominence,
when in 1412 he protested in public against the execution of a trio of young
demonstrators who had demonstrated against this corrupt practice. Expelled
from Prague, Hus continued to preach to countryfolk and set out his now
radical beliefs in a series of essays. A Church determined to crush heresy sum-
moned him to appear before a grand council at Constance, where all his attempts to win over his interrogators by his reasonable arguments failed to
save him from a death sentence. On his way to be burned at the stake, Huss
was led past the bonfire where his writings were suffering a similar fate. His
ashes may have been disposed of in the waters of the Rhine, but his name
survived to trouble Church and State for many years to come.

Náprstkovo muzeum (Náprstek Museum of Ethnography) ○ – *Betlémské náměstí*
Founded in 1862 by the industrialist Vojta Náprstek (1826-94), Prague's littl
visited ethnographical museum is devoted to the Native cultures of Australasia an
Oceania and the Americas and makes up in charm and accessibilility what is lac
in comprehensiveness.

The collections are housed in a purpose-built structure beyond the courtyard o
the Náprstek residence. The energetic Vojta Náprstek (the name means "thimble
was a leading light in 19C Prague society and his home was a salon for the city
literary and scientific intelligensia. His interest in industrial progress and innov
tion was stimulated during exile in the United States after his part in the 184
Revolution. On his return he promoted inventions like the refrigerator and th
sewing machine, as well as becoming an enthusiast for female emancipation an
establishing a magnificent library. He was in touch with many Czech travellers an
explorers, whose donations formed the basis of the museum's exhibits, now pa
of the National Museum.

The museum draws on the vast resources of the national collections for tempora
exhibitions (which may only be loosely based on ethnographical themes), while i
main collections are displayed on the **third floor (Australasia and Oceania)** and the **first flo
(Native Cultures of North and South America)**. Exhibits are a mixture of permanent an
temporary displays, with labelling almost entirely in Czech. But many of the objec
on show make their appeal directly, like frightening figures and ritual masks fro
New Guinea and the Solomon Islands, ingenious Inuit implements from the Arcti
or charming figurines and fine ceramics from South America.

Bartolomějská (ulice) (Bartholomew Street) – Almost synonymous with the hea
quarters of the Prague Police which occupies most of the south side of the stree
Bartolomějská can be reached via winding Průchodní, a narrow lane spanned b
arches. In a commanding position at the corner of Bartolomějská with Na Perštýr
is the massive **Police Building**. Completed in 1925 and strongly Cubist in characte
it is decorated with carvings and statuary on the theme of Work, reminders of i
original function as Trade Union Association headquarters. Under Communisn

Bartolomějská was synonymous with the notorious STB (State Security), some of whose cells were installed in the **former convent** on the north side of the street. It was here in his dissident days that Václav Havel was interrogated. After the convent had been restituted to its previous owners, part was made into a hotel and pension, with visitors queueing up to sleep in the cell once occupied by the future president. The convent's little Baroque **Sv. Bartoloměj** (Church of St Bartholomew), makes little impact on the street, but the interior, with murals by VV Reiner, reveals itself as an exquisite and immaculately restored example (1731) of the work of Kl. Dientzenhofer.

Sv. kříže (Chapel of the Holy Cross) – Dating from the early 12C and one of the city's three surviving Romanesque rotundas, the tiny Chapel of the Holy Cross was built by the side of the highway leading from Vyšehrad to the river crossings beneath the castle. Now looking rather forlorn in a setting of much bigger modern buildings, it is nevertheless a fascinating reminder of the city's early history. It has a conical roof capped by a lantern, and within its circular stone wall are fragments of 14C wall paintings. The splendidly appropriate railings are the work of the 19C artist Josef Mánes.

BÍLKOVA Vila
BILEK Villa Hradčany
Mickiewiczova 1 Tram 18 to Chotkovy sady

he Symbolist sculptor František Bílek (1872-1941) designed this extraordinary uilding in 1910 on a prominent corner site in the Hradčany garden suburb both as studio and a home. Restored, it houses numerous examples of his work, but the uilding itself, a total work of art with furniture, fittings and even the heating system esigned by Bílek himself, which makes the strongest impression.

The villa – Curved in plan, the villa is fronted by Egyptian columns representing stalks of corn, while its red-brick walls symbolise the fertile earth. Bílek's original intention was to place his statue of *Moses* in a commanding position in front of the building, but this was replaced by an equally expressive work, *Comenius Bidding Farewell to His Country*. Inside, not only sculpture and graphic works but also the surroundings of everyday life reveal the artist's intense preoccupation with the sacred.

BŘEVNOVSKÝ Klášter★
BŘEVNOV Monastery — Prague VI
Bělohorská ulice, Tram 8, 22

lmost surrounded by the grim apartment blocks of Prague's western suburbs, the enedictine monastery of Břevnov is the oldest in the country, founded more than thousand years ago. Its present appearance is Baroque, the result of an ambi- ous early-18C rebuilding which ranks among the finest work carried out by the ientzenhofer dynasty of architects. Misuse and neglect during the Communist eriod ran parallel with conscientious attempts by archeologists to unravel the nonastery's long history; the dispossessed Benedictines returned in 1990, and the nany treasures of the abbey and its superb church are once more accessible to ne public.

HISTORY

egend has it that the monastery was founded as a result of Prince Boleslav II and ishop Vojtěch (Adalbert) of Prague meeting at a spring after dreaming the same ream. Whatever the truth of the story, the institution's origin can be traced back to ne year 993, when Vojtěch returned from Italy with a band of Benedictine monks. řevnov flourished, becoming an important centre from which Christianity was spread hroughout Bohemia and neighbouring countries, despite Vojtěch's martyrdom at the ands of the heathen Prussians. An imposing Romanesque basilica was built, followed y a Gothic church, but much was destroyed in the early 15C by the Hussites. Glory ays came again in the early 18C, when two energetic abbots employed the Dientzen- ofers to rebuild church and monastery on a grandiose scale. Another high point was eached in the early 20C, when the abbey acquired an enviable reputation as a centre f learning and publishing, activities pursued on a smaller scale in exile in Bavaria uring the Communist period. On the return of the monks in 1990 a backlog of estoration awaited, some of the monastery buildings having served as police archives, thers as a library store.

GROUNDS

Church of St Margaret

R. Holzbachova, P. Bénet

The monastery is approached through a Baroque gateway surmounted by a statue of St Benedict with angels. Substantial outbuildings flank the lime avenue leading towards the church, the granary to the left being particularly impressive. Another gate to the left of the church gives access to the much decayed **gardens**, laid out to designs by Kilian Dientzenhofer and once graced by a superb orangery. The **spring** where Boleslav and Vojtěch allegedly met became an important place of pilgimage and the Baroque **pavilion** built over it has been restored.

★★**Abbey Church** ☉ – Dedicated to St Margaret, the monastery church is a very different building to St Nicholas in Malá Strana but nevertheless one of the Dientzenhofers greatest achievements, grandly proportioned and with masterly use made of all the apparatus of Baroque design. It was built by Christoph Dientzenhofer between 1709-16, though his son Kilian Ignaz may have added some finishing touches. The exterior, topped by huge gables and cornice statues by Jäckel, has a colossal Ionic order. Inside, the lack of aisles creates a single, unified space of great majesty. Side altars consist of paintings by Peter Brandl, in *trompe-l'œil* frames, while the ceiling frescoes by Steinfels show scenes from the abbey's history. The intersecting oval forms of the vaults are carried on pilasters set, for the first time in Prague, at angles to the axis of the nave. Beyond the pulpit is the abbot's glazed oratory. The main altar has statues of St Margaret and angels by Jäckel

Crypt – *Guided tour in conjunction with tour of monastery*. Below the floor of the Baroque church are evocative remains of the far older buildings which precede it by hundreds of years, excavated between 1978-83. There are fragments of the walling of the Gothic church, but most impressive is the semicircular eastern end of the Romanesque crypt with sturdy columns and round-arched openings.

★**Monastic Buildings** ☉ – *Guided tour*. Begun by Christoph Dientzenhofer, the monastic quarters were completed after his retirement and death in 1722 by Kilian Ignaz. Of the buildings arranged around three courtyards, only the eastern block is open to the public. Staircases, and corridors and rooms are splendidly conceived and have paintings, ceiling frescoes and much else of interest. The finest spaces include the **Chinese Lounge**, with light and airy Oriental wall paintings, but the high point is reached in the **Theresian Hall**★★, with its sumptuous decoration by the Asam brothers from Bavaria. Their wonderfully lively ceiling fresco shows how the Blessed Gunther avoided eating meat on Friday by miraculously causing a roast peacock to fly away from the royal table.

The key on page 9 explains the conventional signs used in this guide.

CELETNÁ ulice★

inking the heart of the Old Town to the Powder Tower and the Obecní dům, this usy street forms the first stage of the Royal Way once followed by the coronation rocession on its way to castle and cathedral. Lined with a succession of fine man-ions, many of which conceal Gothic or Romanesque fabric behind or below their nostly Baroque façades, the street owes its name to the pastrycooks who flourished ere in the Middle Ages before being displaced by a more patrician population.

★**Prašná brána (Powder Tower)** ⊘ – One of the city's best known landmarks, the Gothic Powder Tower rises 65 m to the ridge of its distinctive chisel cap. The tower plays an important role in the townscape, helping to turn the corner from Na Příkopě (Moat Street) into náměstí Republiky (Republic Square) as well as standing guard over what was the main approach to Prague from Kutná Hora. Built around 1475 and modelled on Peter Parler's bridge tower of a century before, it replaced one of the original 13 towers forming part of the Old Town's defences and was intended to add to the status of the area around the Royal Palace. But not long after work had begun, King Vladislav II moved his court back to the castle, and although the tower was almost complete it had to await a permanent roof until the 18C. It fell into disrepair and its appearance was not improved when the Prus-sians bombarded it during the siege of 1757. For many years it served as a gunpowder store, and the name given it then has stuck. Between 1875 and 1886 it received the enthusiastic attentions of architect Josef Mocker who gave it its present highly romanticised neo-Gothic appearance. Apart from embellishing the tower with its tall chisel cap and spiky corner turrets, Mocker ornamented the four façades with sculptures of allegorical figures, saints, and Czech rulers.

The long climb to the gallery at the top of the tower is well worth while for the **panorama**★ of the city as well as for its foretaste of the Royal Way, with Celetná ulice far below pointing towards far-off Hradčany. On the second floor, a small exhibition draws on "hundred-towered Prague" to make fascinating comparisons between towers old and new.

Beyond the Powder Tower, Celetná heads westward towards the Old Town Square, passing on the right the Pachtův Palace *(no 31/585)*, rebuilt in Baroque style by Kl Dientzenhofer in the 1740s. Incorporating a short stretch of arcade opposite is the New Mint *(no 36/587)*, where coins were produced until the end of the 19C; two of the atlantes supporting its balcony are in the form of Kutná Hora silver miners. During the revolutionary year 1848 the building served as military HQ, and it was here that a stray rebel bullet killed General Windischgrätz's wife, no doubt contributing to his severity in putting down the revolt.

Standing in surprising harmony among these older buildings at the corner of Celetná and the Fruit Market (Ovocný trh) is the dark orange **Black Madonna House**★ (Dům U černé Matky boží), one of the earliest and perhaps the finest of the city's

The Cubist Black Madonna House by Josef Gočár

Cubist buildings. Built in 1912 as an department store to the design of Josef Goč[á]
it has a modernity which is in almost shocking contrast to the nostalgically dec[o]
rated Obecní dům, completed only months previously. The architect's use of
reinforced concrete frame allowed him to create a richly modelled façade wi[th]
much use of glass, while Cubist detailing (portico, balcony railing, mansa[rd]
windows...) completes the wonderfully bold and satisfying picture. The cag[e]
statue of the Black Madonna herself was rescued from the original Baroq[ue]
building and suspended at the corner of this stunning addition to the early-20th
townscape.

The Black Madonna House makes an eminently suitable setting for a permane[nt]
exhibition of **Czech Cubist Art**, with examples of some of the extraordinary furnitu[re]
paintings, graphic works and ceramics of the epoch, drawn from the collectio[n]
of the Czech Museum of Fine Arts.

Celetná continues westwards, with many an elegant Baroque façade. *no 22/56*
U Supa (The Vulture) has a modern hanging sign but the original lettering in Fren[ch]
and German of "Gindle the jewellers". In the 1930s, by now a Functionalist rath[er]
than a Cubist, Gočár built the very plain shop at *no 15/586* for the Bat'a sh[oe]
firm. Among several grand buildings the grandest is probably the 7-bay Hrz[án]
Palace *(no.12/558)* with atlantes by Brokoff. Entrances and passageways invi[te]
further exploration; the courtyard of *no 17/595* leads through to the next stree[t]
Štupartská, while *no 11/598* has a delightful galleried *pavlač*. *no 8/556*, U čerb[é]
slunce (The Black Sun), has a famous house sign. The last houses on the nor[th]
side of the street lean up against the flank of the Týn Church; the Kafka fam[ily]
lived for a while in *no 3/602*, U tří králů (The Three Kings), and the young Fran[z]
is supposed to have occupied the back bedroom with its secret window looki[ng]
down on to the Christians worshipping below. With a wonderful view over O[ld]
Town Square, the last building in the street U Sixtů (Sixtus House) *(no 2/55[5])*
retains its Romanesque basement.

Muzeum Antonína DVOŘÁKA
VILA AMERIKA★

DVOŘÁK Museum Ke Karlovu 20 Metro I. P. Pavlova

In 1720 Count Jan Václav Michna employed Kilian Ignaz Dientzenhofer to build [a]
summer residence for him in the southern part of the New Town, which at that da[te]
was still quite countryfied, a place of gardens and orchards. Given the name Amerik[a]
after a nearby inn, the villa is a unified Baroque composition of a formal garden wit[h]
sculpture by MB Braun and a central building flanked by twin pavilions. The youn[g]
Dientzenhofer had just returned from 10 years of study abroad, and his charmin[g]
design shows the influence both of France and the Vienna of the great archite[ct]

Lukas Hildebrandt. Sinc[e]
1932 the villa has housed th[e]
museum ⊙ devoted the com[-]
poser **Antonín Dvořák** (184[1]
1904), and during the sea[-]
son there are delightfu[l]
musical evenings which pu[t]
his music in context.

Dvořák led a life of great sim[-]
plicity and regularity, hi[s]
great passions apart from mu[-]
sic being railways and pigeon[-]
fancying. Born in the village [of]
Nelahozeves *(see p. 256)* nort[h]
of Prague, he was destined t[o]
follow in his father's footste[ps]
as a butcher, but instead, en[-]
couraged by his schoolteach[-]
ers, turned to music. Afte[r]
moving to Prague in 1857 h[e]
earned a meagre living as [a]
church organist and as an or[-]
chestral musician, notably a[t]
the Prozatímní divadlo (Prov[i-]
sional National) Theatre. H[e]
drew attention to himself i[n]
1873 with his *Hymnus*, an[d]

Vila Amerika

R. Holzbachova, P. Béhet

s awarded a grant to study in Vienna. Soon afterwards he composed his *Stabat ater*, a poignant piece inspired by the death of his three children. In 1877 the suc- ss of his *Moravian Songs* marked a turning point in his career. In the 1880s Dvořák ured Great Britain several times and received an honorary doctorate from Cambridge iversity (his doctor's robes are on display). He also visited Germany and Russia, in- ting as a patriotic Czech everywhere he went that his name should be spelt with its cents intact (including what for most foreigners is the troublesome *háček* above the r). 1890 he began teaching at the Prague Conservatory, though his courses there were errupted by a three year stay in the United States as Director of the National nservatory in New York. On his death in 1904 he was buried at the National Ceme- y in Vyšehrad.

ich influenced by his contemporary Brahms, Dvořák's extremely varied output was some extent inspired by Negro spirituals but much more by the **folk music** of his tive country and of the other Slavonic peoples. As well as nine symphonies, including e immensely popular *From the New World*, there are the Slavonic Dances written st for piano and then orchestra, numerous chamber works and religious pieces, nong them his *Stabat Mater, Mass, Te Deum* and *Requiem*. Dvořák's operas met th less success.

Muzeum HLAVNÍHO MĚSTA PRAHY★

PRAGUE CITY Museum – Prague 8
Na Poříčí 52 Metro Florenc

e museum collections of the City of Prague are housed in a neo-Renaissance lace built in 1898 on the site of the Poříčí Gate which once guarded the approach the northern end of the New Town. Completed by Antonín Balšánek to a design Antonín Wiehl, the building is one of the trio of museums (National Museum, useum of Decorative Arts) erected in the expansive period towards the end of the C, and like them was designed to impress with the dignity and importance of its ling. Stairs lead up to the central portico, which is surmounted with a tympanum th allegorical reliefs and a statue representing the *Spirit of Prague* by Ladislav loun. The rooms of the permanent exhibition open off the raised ground floor, ile a three-part staircase graced by a circular painted panorama of Prague leads the upper floors.

Langweil's model of Prague

History of Prague exhibition ⏱ – The somewhat time-worn displays tracing the evolution of the city from the prehistoric period to the 17C are slowly being renewed and reinterpreted, with some labelling in English. There is much of interest, from plans showing how the different districts of Prague evolved and how they were finally drawn together into one city, to works of art, models, and artefacts of all kinds. The more recent history of the city is the subject of temporary exhi- bitions on the upper floor, drawn from the museum's vast holdings and often of

exceptional interest. Here too is the original of the great disc showing the labou
of the months and the signs of the zodiac, created by Mikoláš Aleš for the Astr
nomical Clock on the Old Town Hall, but the great attraction is the superb **Langwei
model Prahy** (Langweil's Model of Prague).

★★ **Langweil's Model of Prague** – A humble lithographer, Anton Langweil devoted t
whole of the period between 1826 and 1834 to this extraordinary project, to t
detriment of his large family and his own health, though he cannot possibly ha
been affected by tedium – the meaning of his name in German.
To a scale of 1:148, the card and paper model covers an area of about 20 m² a
shows the Old Town and most of Malá Strana and Hradčany in fascinating deta
It's an invaluable and meticulously accurate portrayal of the city before the ons
of industrialisation. Part of its fascination lies in noting how little has changed co
pared with most great cities, part in being presented with features as they us
to be. In Langweil's model the city still turns its back on the river, whose ban
are occupied by mills, dumps and timber yards; the unrestored Powder Tow
stands next to the Royal Court, the cathedral lacks its nave, and Old Town Squa
has its original shape and the Marian column at its centre.

HRADČANSKÉ Naměsti★★
HRADČANY Square – Hradčany
Tram 22 to Pražský hrad

Once fringed by the humble dwellings of the Hradčany district's medieval inhabitan
Hradčany Square is now a great cobbled esplanade rising beyond the castle's weste
gates, lined by aristocratic palaces and the residences of the cathedral clergy. It p
vides ample room for the swarms of visitors, at their most numerous when t
blue-uniformed soldiers march to and from the Loretanská barracks for the ceremo
of the Changing of the Guard.

★ **Schwarzenberský palác (Schwarzenberg Palace and Military Museum)** – *Hradčans
náměstí 2/185*. This magnificent Renaissance residence dominates the southe
side of the square and is an inescapable part of the Hradčany skyline. The t
wings facing the square are topped by splendid stepped gables and are linked
a fanciful courtyard wall. The east wing has a splendidly curved Italianate corni
with lunettes. The most striking feature, almost dizzying in its effect, is the over
pattern of black and white sgraffito work, with elaborate friezes and panels in
tating bold rustication. The palace was built in the mid-16C by the Italian archite
Agostino Galli for the Castle Burgrave, Count Lobkowicz. It owes its present na
to the Schwarzenberg family, minor gentry from Bavaria who rose to eminence
the 17C thanks to their loyalty to the Emperor and soon ranked among the bigge
landowners in Bohemia. After 1989, one of their number, Prince Karl, return
from exile to head Václav Havel's presidential chancellery.
The palace houses the pre-20C collections of the **Military Museum** ⊙, whose other m
branch is in Žižkov. They include a wealth of weapons, uniforms, medals, ma
models, documents and works of art, enough to convince anyone of the decisive r
of armed conflict in the history of Central Europe. Only a selection of these treasur
can be shown at any one time, but temporary displays are often of exemplary qual
and the splendid spaces of the interior are worth visiting for their own sake.
On a more modest scale altogether but in a superb location overlooking Ke hrad
the steep approach road to the castle, is the Empire-style **Salm Palace** of 1840, or
part of the Schwarzenberg estate and subsequently occupied by the Sw
Embassy.

Arcibiskupský palác (Archbishop's Palace) – *Hradčanské náměstí 16/56*. Balanci
the Schwarzenberg Palace on the opposite side of the square is the equally pr
tigious **residence of the Archbishop of Prague**, the Primate of the Czech lands. It w
extended and given its distinctive Rococo façade in the mid 18C in response to t
overall improvement of the square and the approach to the Castle, though sor
of the earlier work of Jean-Baptiste Mathey, like the portal, was retained. T
decor of the interior *(only rarely opened to the public)*, is even more sumptuo
than the façade; 18C Archbishop Příchovský commissioned superb French tape
tries on exotic themes under the general heading of the New Indies, there a
collections of Vienna and Delft ware, and superb late-medieval busts of St Pe
and St Paul.
Appointed Archbishop in 1946, Mgr Josef Beran was unable to enjoy all this ma
nificence for very long; following the Communist coup in 1948, he was effectiv
imprisoned for 16 years, and although eventually amnestied was never allowed
return to his palace. His successor was Archbishop Tomášek, who maintain
contact with the political opposition and who was largely responsible for the cano
isation of St Agnes, an event which took place only days before the fall
Communism.

★★Šternberský palác (Sternberg Palace/National Gallery of European Art) – *See p. 193* – As the funnel-shaped square widens towards its western end the cobbles divide and the central triangle is laid out as a little park. With its figure of the Virgin Mary, the **plague column** rising against the green background is a late work by Brokoff, begun in 1726. The north side of the square is lined by the former dwellings of the cathedral canons, the south side by a convent incorporating Hradčany's old parish church, St Benedict's.

Toskánský palác (Tuscan Palace) – *Hradčanské náměstí 5/182*. The square is closed at its western end by the monumental palace built around 1690 to designs by Jean-Baptiste Mathey for Count Michael Thun-Hohenstein. Now used by the Ministry of Foreign Affairs, it is an unusually symmetrical composition with twin projecting sections and portals. The balustrade is graced by allegorical statues, the pavement in front by modern stone bollards, and the corner with Loretanská by a fine figure of St Michael.

Martinický palác (Martinic Palace) – *Hradčanské náměstí 8/67*. The northwestern corner of the square is occupied by the Renaissance palace built around 1600 by the Martinic family, one of whose members was one of the Imperial councillors famously defenestrated in 1618. On becoming the headquarters of the city planning department it was rescued from its lamentable state as a much-subdivided lodging-house. The delightful sgraffito patterns are based on Old Testament themes.

Admission times and charges for the sights described are listed at the end of the guide.
Every sight for which there are times and charges is identified by the symbol ⊙ in the Sights section of the guide.

HRADČANY ★★★

Castle District
Tram 22 to Pohořelec

The smallest of Prague's four historical towns, the Castle District spreads westwa
from the castle along the spur of land which drops steeply to Malá Strana on t
south and the Stag Moat to the north. The area's growth and change, never rap
came to an almost complete halt in the 18C and today, freed of all through traf
and with little commercial development, a stroll around Hradčany evokes the dream
provincial (any Prague of more than two centuries ago.

Before the township's foundation in 1321, the area was wooded, traversed by t
roadway running from the royal stronghold past the Strahov monastery and on
western Bohemia and Nuremberg. Roughly occupying the area of today's **Hradčans
náměstí** (Hradčany Square), the settlement attracted those who for one reason
another needed to be as close as possible to the castle. Though a market w
established quite early on, the area never competed with the commercially far mo
vibrant Malá Strana in its more favoured location close to the river crossing. T
district grew only slowly, staying within the medieval walls built by Charles IV a
the later Baroque fortifications, fragments of whose massive brick walls and ba
tions are still in evidence today. The humble folk who were the original inhabitar
were gradually displaced by grander people; one wave of fine building took pla
after the great fire of 1541 which almost completely devastated the area, and mo
mansions and palaces were built or rebuilt by those shrewd or fortunate enou
to find themselves on the winning side after the Battle of the White Mountain
1620 (check).

★★**Strahovský klášter** – See p. 195

Pohořelec – Cobbled and partly arcaded, with its eastward slope drawing visito
downhill towards the castle, this charming square was first laid out in the la
14th century, and although its present appearance is mostly Baroque and Roco
a number of older buildings survive. Pohořelec means "place of fires" and the ar
has been consumed by conflagrations more than once during its long history; t
Hussites burnt it down in 1420, it was devastated by the great fire of 1541 a
suffered much damage during the French occupation in 1742. An 18C Nepom
statue stands in the centre of the square. The main entrance to the Strah
monastery is to the west, via the ramp which rises from the southern side of t
square, but a more exciting approach is through the steep passageway cut throu
house no 8, U zlatého stromu (The Golden Tree).

Úvoz – The Baroque former Hospital of St Elizabeth in the southeastern corner
Pohořelec marks the beginning of this road, which on its way down to Nerudo
and Malá Strana gives wonderful views over the orchards of Petřín Hill and t
city beyond. There are several named houses built into the cliff-like hillside, p
ticularly towards the lower end of the street, among them "The Green Grape
"The Stone Column", the last with sun and moon signs as well (the 18C pain
Kristián Luna lived here), and a big Rococo house, U tří sekyrů (The Three Axe

Loretánské náměstí (Loretto Square) – A square in name only, Loretánské námě
is divided by the great retaining wall which separates the Loretto Shrine from t
Czernin Palace. Crouched to the north, between the charming walled lanes leadi
down to Nový Svět *(see p. 167)* is the modest monastery of the Capuchins,
church left without a tower in accordance with the order's strict rules.

★★★**Loreta (Loretto Shrine)** – See p. 143.

★**Černínský palác (Černín Palace)** – This great mass of masonry was begun in 16
on the orders of Jan Humprecht, Count Černín, who intended it to be the mo
prestigious residence in Prague. Its 150 m long façade is articulated by

---

Jan Masaryk

Son of Czechoslovakia's founder and first president, Jan Masaryk (1886-
1948) was perhaps the most popular politician the country ever produced.
Charming, cosmopolitan, his humour laced with melancholy, he helped keep
alive the spirit of the nation by his broadcasts from Britain during World
War Two. As a non-party Foreign Minister, he was kept on in the cabinet
after the Communist coup in February 1948, a cynical manoeuvre designed
to smooth the transition to a full dictatorship. Controversy still surrounds
the circumstances of his death.

colossal order of 30 engaged columns rising over a ground floor whose bold rustication seems to anticipate Czech Cubism's fascination with angular architectural forms. The overwhelming pretension of the building is matched by the hubris suffered by many of those associated with it.

Černín's fortune came from profits amassed during the Thirty Years War, his taste from his stay in Italy as Ambassador to the Venetian Republic. But his palace proved a bottomless pit, swallowing up the family fortune over several generations. Despite the efforts of the best architects and designers and an army of workmen, the great edifice was never in a really fit state to live in, and Jan Humprecht died long before it was completed. Emperor Leopold I referred to it as "a big barn"; the French mistreated it in 1742, the Prussians in 1757; in despair, the family sold it to the state in 1851. It became a barracks, its beautiful French garden a drill square. Recovery came in the 1930s, when it was carefully restored as the Czechoslovak Ministry of Foreign Affairs, just in time to provide accommodation for the Nazi *Reichsprotektor* and his successor, "Hangman Heydrich". Heydrich was assassinated in

Ph. Gajic/MICHELIN

Martinický Palace: restored Renaissance sgraffito work

1942. In 1948 the body of Jan Masaryk was found in the palace courtyard, the much-loved foreign minister having apparently committed suicide in despair at the Communist take-over of his country.

Loretánská – Widening into what is almost a square and graced by one of the district's extraordinarily elaborate lamp standards, the road down to the castle is dominated by the Italianate **Martinický palác**, the second palace built in Hradčany by the Martinic family. Now the barracks for the castle guardsmen, it faces the Hrzánský palace, modest in height on this side but needing a full five stories to reach (voz far below. The road narrows again before reaching Hradčany Square; on the south side, Radniční schody (Town Hall Steps) drop steeply down towards Malá Strana. On the first landing, the old Hradčany Town Hall is an attractive little Renaissance building, its sgraffitoed facade adorned with the imperial and district coats of arms.

★**Hradčanské náměstí** (Hradčany Square) – See p. 114.

JIŘSKÝ Klášter★★

Bazilika sv.Jiří/Národní galerie: sbírka starého českého umění
St George's Convent

St George's Basilica/National Gallery: Early Bohemian Art, Hradčany
Tram 22 to Pražský hrad

bold, blood-red Baroque façade faces the east end of St Vitus' Cathedral on the r side of the castle's Jiřské náměstí (St George's Square). Behind it is a surprise, Romanesque basilica of sublime austerity, once the church of the adjoining nvent, the very first to be established in the Czech lands. Both church and nvent have been de-consecrated; the former is used for concerts, while the latter now the home of the nation's outstanding collection of medieval, Renaissance d Baroque art.

★**BASILICA** ⊘

Despite much rebuilding and restoration, **St George's Basilica** is the country's finest remaining Romanesque building. Its foundation, by Prince Vratislav I around 920, dates from the early years of Christianity in the Czech lands, its formal consecration to 925, when the remains of the murdered St Ludmila, the grandmother of St Wenceslas and like him one of the patron saints of Bohemia, were deposited here. Most of the present structure dates from the rebuilding which followed a destructive siege in 1142.

The **Early Baroque west front** was added in 1657-80. Statues of Vratislav ar Ludmila stand atop the main pilasters, while obelisks echo the pair of sl **Romanesque towers** in pale limestone which form such an essential part of tl Hradčany skyline. St George and the dragon appear in stucco form in the pe iment of the west front, and again as a lively carving in the tympanum of tl **Early Renaissance portal** added to the south side of the basilica around 1515 I the castle architect Benedikt Ried.

The plain stone walls of the tall and narrow **nave** are carried on massive piers ar columns and are pierced at gallery level by a series of openings, above whi smaller windows admit light. Přemyslid rulers lie buried at the eastern end of tl nave, while the remains of Vratislav I are kept in a fascinating 14C cabinet wi the appearance of a Gothic doll's house.

St George's Convent: Baroque façade and Romanesque towers

The **choir** and semi-circular apse are approached via an elegant Baroque dout staircase; remains of Romanesque and Late Gothic frescoes depict the Holy C and the Coronation of the Virgin. Beneath the choir, the **crypt** is of evocative si plicity, with simple columns and cubic capitals. The Romanesque tympanu installed here shows the Virgin Enthroned flanked by abbesses (copy, original St George's Convent), while a Baroque figure of Vanity shows a female form spectacular decay. To the south of the choir is the **Chapel of St Ludmila**, with a 1« tomb of the saint made by the Parler workshop on the orders of Charles IV. In t southwestern corner of the basilica, the **Chapel of St John Nepomuk** with its illusic istic ceiling painting was added by Ferdinand Maximilian Kaňka in 1722.

★★CONVENT: Sbírka starého českého umění ⊘
(Early Bohemian Art)

St George's founding abbess was **Princess Milada**, the daughter of Prince Bolesla and a niece of St Wenceslas. Educated in a Regensburg convent, Milada return from a sojourn in Rome bearing the Pope's permission to establish what in t year 973 was the first Benedictine convent in Prague. Many of her successc in the office of abbess were princesses of the Přemyslid dynasty; the conve became renowned as a prestigious place of learning for young ladies of not birth, as well as gaining a high reputation as a centre of production of illun nated manuscripts. Successive rebuildings continued into the Baroque peric but in 1782, like many institutions of its kind, the convent fell victim to the wa of closures ordered by Emperor Joseph II, and was subsequently misused as . artillery barracks and as a penitentiary for the priesthood. Restoration w undertaken by the Communist regime, which fortunately failed to implement t idea of turning it into a Museum of the Czechoslovak People. Since 1975 it h formed a fine home for the **National Gallery's** collection of the **Medieval, Renaissar and Baroque art of the Czech lands.**

★★ Medieval Art – Displayed in the basement and on the ground floor of the convent's cloister, and despite the return of a number of works to their original owners as part of the post-Communist restitution process, the superb collection of medieval painting and sculpture recalls the prominent role played by the Czech Lands in artistic development in the later Middle Ages.

The large bronze of *St George and the Dragon*★★ is the original of the statue which graces the castle's Third Courtyard. Dating from around 1373 and the work of German sculptor brothers from far-off Transylvania, its presence in Prague remains a mystery. Even lacking his lance, the elegantly poised George seems certain to slay the

St Vitus by Master Theodoric

rather small dragon, despite the creature gripping him firmly by the foot with its long prehensile snout.

The glory of this section of the gallery consists of the paintings by such masters as the court painter Theodoric and the anonymous artists of the **Vyšší Brod** (Hohenfürth), **Třeboň** (Wittingau) and **Litoměřice** (Leitmeritz) Altarpieces.

Master **Theodoric** (active in the 1350s and 60s), commissioned by Charles IV to cover the walls of the Chapel of the Holy Cross at Karlštejn with saintly portraits, is represented here by a fraction of his output. His unconventional **portraits**★★★, extending outwards to cover their frames, glow with vitality, and his depictions of living persons such as the Emperor himself are considered to be among the very first attempts at individual portraiture. By contrast, the *Vyšehrad Madonna*★ by an unknown master from around 1350 is, despite her radiant beauty, conventional in the extreme, with the static quality of an icon painting. The exquisitely detailed panels of about the same date painted by the **Master of the Vyšší Brod Altarpiece**★ have something of the same quality; they include scenes of the *Annunciation, Nativity and Adoration of the Magi*.

Great individuality is achieved again by the **Master of the Třeboň Altarpiece**★★★, active around 1380. His representations of saints, male and female, have great appeal, but it is his *Agony in the Garden, Entombment and Resurrection* which enchant with their combination of deep religious vision and fascinating human and natural detail. While Christ prays and the disciples are lost in slumber on the Mount of Olives, Judas and the soldiery peer nervously over the fence; as He arises, ethereally, from the Tomb, the waking guards seem caught between disbelief and fear of dereliction of duty.

Fine examples of the so-called "Beautiful Style" which flourished in Central Europe around 1400 include a variant of the *Krumlov Madonna*★, a delicately balanced carving in which the Virgin gently restrains her fretful Infant, and the painting of the lovely *Madonna of St Vitus*. Much later, marking the transition to the Renaissance and notably more realistic, are works like *St Barbara and St Catherine*★ by the **Master of the Litoměřice Altarpiece**★, active in the first years of the 16C.

Among sculptural works removed from their original sites is the great **Tympanum**★ from the North Porch of the Tn Church. Its rich and complex carving was the work of the Parler studio, the figure of Christ Crucified probably by Peter Parler himself.

St Anne's Chapel is the oldest remaining part of the convent; it houses a fine altarpiece of around 1480 as well as the original of the Romanesque tympanum in St George's Basilica.

Renaissance, Mannerist and Baroque Art – Displayed in the spacious first floor galleries of the convent, the paintings and sculpture here offer an excellent overview of art in Bohemia from the 16C to the late 18C.

The fabulous collections assembled by art-loving Emperor Rudolf II at the end of the 16C and beginning of the 17C have long since been dispersed, but the atmosphere of his court is suggested by many of the Mannerist works exhibited here.

They include a muscular *Hercules* by Adriaen de Vries (c 1545-1626). a picture the coyly smiling *SS Wenceslas and Vitus* by Bartolomaeus Spranger (1546-1611) Hans van Aachen's (1551/2-1615) erotically charged *Suicide of Lucretia*, and lan scapes of remote and bosky places by Roland Savery (1576-1631).

The founder of Bohemian Baroque painting, the nobleman Karel Škréta (1610-74) is represented by a number of fine works, including a large-scale portrayal *St Charles Borromeo visiting victims of the plague in Milan*★, and there are pictures by contemporaries Michael Leopold Willmann and Jan Liška. Some of the Hig Baroque sculpture on display is outstanding; among the works by **Ferdinand Maxmili Brokoff** (1688-1731) there is a splendid pair of *Moors*★, while **Matthias Bernard Bra** (1684-1738) is represented by several pieces, including a study for his impa sioned *Vision of St Luitgard*★ on Charles Bridge. Among the many outstandi paintings by **Peter Brandl** (1668-1735) is a wonderful *Self-portrait*★ of around 169 The highly expressive *St Simeon with the Christ Child* of c 1730 is supposed have been painted by Brandl using his fingers instead of brushes. Brandl's equ in portraiture was Jan Kupecký (1667-1740), here represented by his *Portrait the Miniature Painter Karl Bruni*★ and by his *Self at Work and Likeness of his Wi* There are portraits and landscapes and a *Still Life with Skull* by the prolific fres painter Václav Vavřinec Rainer (1689-1743), and numerous tiny studies of Roco gallantry by Norbert Grund (1717-67).

*New **Michelin Green Guides** in English include:*
Amsterdam - Berlin - Bruxelles — Budapest et la Hongrie - Californie - Danema Norvège, Suède, Finlande - Florence et la Toscane - Floride - Guadeloup Martinique - Mexique, Guatemala, Belize — Prague - San Francisco - Sicile - Vien

JOSEFOV★★★

The Jewish Quarter – Old Town
Metro Staroměstská

Close to the heart of the Old Town stands a clutch of synagogues together with a cemetery crammed with toppling tombstones. Charged with mystery and with memories of a thousand years of history, these are but fragments of what was one of the most important Jewish communities in Europe, the focal point of Jewish life in all of Bohemia and Moravia. The Jewish presence in Prague stems from the earliest times; over the centuries the fortunes of the city's Jews varied according to the whims of rulers, the changing moods of the Christian populace, and their own ability to adapt. Periods of prosperity alternated with pogroms and expulsions. Contained for much of its existence within its own walls, the Jewish Quarter survived many misfortunes until, in the late 19C, much of its original population having deserted it, it fell victim to a comprehensive slum clearance programme, *the asanace*. Under Nazi rule, the country's Jews suffered the horrors of the Final Solution, while the Josefov became the repository of looted Jewish property. Its synagogues are now museums, save for the Gothic Old-New Synagogue, built at the same time as nearby St Agnes' Convent, but, unlike its neighbour, still in use for worship after more than seven centuries.

JEWISH PRAGUE

The first substantial account of Prague was written by a Jew, Ibrahim ibn Ya'qub, from Tortosa in Spain. His account, written in Arabic around 895 for the Caliph of Córdoba, describes a city "made richer by commerce than all others". His co-religionists may have had a part in this prosperity, having already settled here in the previous century. The early Jewish settlements were scattered in various locations, but in the 13C they were consolidated within the newly fortified Old Town, where eventually an independent Jewish Town came into being, defined by its own walls and gates, the activities of its population regulated by all kinds of discriminatory legislation. Whereas the Jews had once practised all kinds of crafts and trades, they were now limited to money-lending, an activity forbidden to Christians, and initially scorned by the Jews themselves. Enlightened kings like Otakar II profited from this, protecting the Jews and drawing off wealth from them like "honey from the bees", while less enlightened rulers went along with popular prejudice, doing little to stop the riots and pogroms which cost the lives of Jews throughout the Middle Ages. One of the worst was in 1389, when Easter coincided with Passover; aroused by inflammatory sermons, Christian congregations armed themselves with axe and hatchet "as if they wished to fell a forest" and swarmed through the streets, sacking houses and synagogues and slaughtering over 3 000 Jews. In the early 16C the Christian citizens conspired to expel those they regarded as their competitors in commerce; royal reluctance to relinquish revenue was eventually overcome, and in 1541 Ferdinand I ordered the Jews to leave the kingdom. Much hardship ensued before the order was revoked in 1563, but the period that followed saw a Golden Age, when intellectual life flourished and the community was led by eminent men like scientist and chronicler David Gans (1541-1613), enlightened entrepreneurs like **Marcus Mordecai Maisel** (1528-1601) and scholars such as Judah ben Bezalel, better known as **Rabbi Loew** (c 1520-1609), legendary creator of the **Golem** *(see p. 126)*.

In 1648, Jews helped defend Charles Bridge against the Swedes, their heroism being rewarded by Emperor Ferdinand III who presented them with a flag which is still on display in the Old-New Synagogue. A century later, a very different story... accused in 1744 of collaborating with the invading Prussians, the Jews were ordered out of the city, though they were allowed to return when the drastic impact of their absence on the economy began to be felt.

This last expulsion had been ordered by Empress Maria Theresa; her son, Emperor Joseph II, dealt with the Empire's Jews in a more enlightened way. His Edict of Toleration of 1781 abolished almost all of the ancient measures limiting Jewish participation in social and economic life. Henceforth Jews could dress as they liked, practise virtually any trade, and attend all types of school, though as part of the Emperor's promotion of German as the language of administration, Jews had to choose a German name for themselves. In honour of the Emperor, the ghetto became known as Joseph's Town (Josephstadt or Josefov). By the middle of the 19C Prague's Jews were mostly identified with the city's German-speaking community, now dwindling rapidly. A last glorious flowering of Prague German literature in the early 20C was very much the work of Jewish writers like Franz Kafka, Max Brod, Franz Werfel and Johannes Urzidil.

Kafka had been born in 1883 on the very fringe of the Josefov, but by this time the city council was already planning the *asanace*, the razing of the ghetto's insanitary courtyards, sunless streets, and close-packed dwellings. By now the Jewish own had been abandoned by its more respectable inhabitants for more salubrious quarters in the suburbs, leaving it to poor or fanatically orthodox Jews, and to the Prague underclass. The area became the haunt of low life of the wretchedest kind, an object of fascination for early tourists and an inspiration for writers of horror

Redevelopment duly took place in the first years of the 20C; stinking ... replaced by smart apartment blocks in a variety of styles and crooked ... oy broad streets like Pařížská třída. Only the synagogues, the Jewish Town Hall, ... the cemetery were spared.

Perhaps paradoxically, these central edifices of Jewish life continued to be spared during the brief and brutal period of the German Protectorate of 1939-45. The Nazis return to a more than medieval barbarity encompassed both the destruction of the country's Jewish population and the preservation of what was left of the physical fabric of the ghetto. Sacred objects and other looted treasures were brought here and stored, future props for a planned "Museum of a Vanished Race". Granted a temporary stay of execution, Jewish scholars laboured as cataloguers and classifiers, their devoted work laying the foundation for today's State Jewish Museum whose displays occupy several synagogues and chronicle the country's rich Jewish heritage.

★**Pařížská třída (Paris Avenue)** – Few contrasts could be greater than that between the gloom and mystery of the ghetto and the "turn-of-the-century" stylishness of the shops and apartments on either side of this broad street, laid out in the first years of the 20C between Old Town Square and the Čech Bridge across the Vltava. Designers used neo-Renaissance, neo-Baroque and Secession elements to create a procession of turn-of-the-century architecture without equal in Prague. Façades are enlivened with richly-decorated oriel windows and balconies and patterned with all kinds of elaborate plaster-work, busts, florid female figures, swirling plant-based patterns and even admonitory mottoes, while above the eaves rise extravagant gables, attic windows, towers and turrets.

One of the city's most prestigious addresses ever since its inception, Pařížská is nowadays lined with airline offices and exclusive shops. It was the most ambitious project of the asanace, intended to enhance Prague's metropolitan image and carried out with no regard whatsoever for the ghetto's ancient street pattern. Originally named Mikulášská (St Nicholas Street) because of the presence of St Nicholas Church at its Old Town Square end, it was given its present name – perhaps best translated as Boulevard de Paris – in 1926, less because of its resemblance to a Parisian boulevard than as a tribute to the France which had been instrumental in freeing the Czechs from Austria-Hungary at the end of the First World War.

JOSEFOV

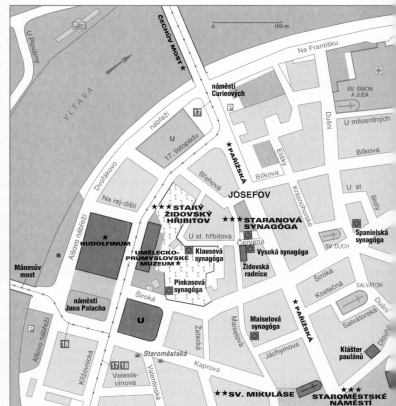

The Jewish Town Hall clock

Židovská radnice (Jewish Town Hall) – *Maiselova 18/250*. This cheerful Rococo building with its tower and famous clock was a mid-18C rebuilding of an edifice first erected in 1580. For a Jewish building to have a tower at all was a great privilege, possibly granted in this case because of Jewish help in the fight against the Swedes. The tower is surmounted by a star of David and carries a conventional timepiece with four faces while the clock framed in the gable below has a dial lettered in Hebrew. In a gesture towards the way in which Hebrew script is read, its hands turn to uncanny effect in an anti-clockwise direction, a surreal phenomenon much relished by the French poet Apollinaire when he came here in 1902.

The predecessor of today's Town Hall was one of several buildings paid for by the Jewish Town's mayor, **Mordecai Maisel**, the richest man in Prague and one of the triumvirate of wise men who oversaw the community's affairs during its golden age at the end of the 16C. As well as giving financial aid to scholars and the poor, Maisel endowed the ghetto with a new synagogue, a hospital, ritual baths and several schools. He maintained good relations with the Bohemian nobility and with Rudolph II, whose wars with the Turks he helped finance, but this failed to stop the Emperor breaking the solemn promise he had given to allow him to dispose of his inheritance as he thought fit; on Maisel's death, Rudolph had his goods confiscated and pursued his heirs through the courts.

Klausová synagoga (Klausa Synagogue) ⊘ – *U starého hřbitova*. Close to the entrance to the cemetery, the late 17C Klausen Synagogue is now part of the State Jewish Museum and houses a fine array of objects illustrating religious life. Among them is a cycle of paintings dating from the 1780s which depict in fascinating detail the activities of the burial society, the charitable organisation which ensured that death, burial and commemoration were conducted with proper ceremony (check).
The synagogue itself replaced a trio of structures (*klausen* in German) dating from Mayor Meisel's time, before which this corner of town had been a notorious red-light district. The building's elaborately stuccoed barrel vault survived a late 19C reconstruction.

Vysoká synagoga (High Synagogue) – *Červená*. This synagogue shares much the same architectural history as the adjacent Town Hall, which it formed part of until the 19C. Once used for displays of the State Jewish Museum, it has now been restituted to the Jewish community and is not open to the public.

★**Staronová synagoga (Old-New Synagogue)** ⊘ – *Červená*. Attracting myth and legend about its origin and about the meaning of its name, the Old-New Synagogue with its high gables and atmospheric interior seems to distil the very essence of Jewish Prague.
This most picturesque of the ghetto's buildings was in fact begun around 1270 and as well as being among the most venerable Gothic edifices in Bohemia is one of the oldest synagogues in which worship still takes place. While its stonework bears the marks of the masons who worked on the nearby convent of St Agnes, legend has it that the stones were carried here from the ruined Temple in Jerusalem

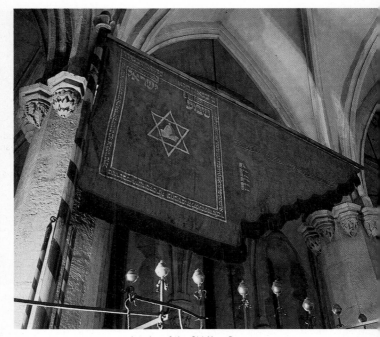

Interior of the Old New Synagogue

and that the synagogue's name comes from the Hebrew *Al tnai* meaning "pro sional" (corrupted to *Alt-Neu* in German), since it will have to be dismantled a returned to Jerusalem at the coming of the Messiah. Other tales tell of the syr gogue being found fully formed when a soothsayer directed the elders of t community to strip away the soil from a mound. A more prosaic explanation of name is that it was originally called the "New" Synagogue when it replaced earlier building, the Old being added when another "new" establishment was bu in the 16C in nearby Široká Street.

Well below present-day pavement height, the synagogue's floor is probably the original ground level of the Old Town before it was raised as a flood pr tection measure. Again, there is an alternative explanation, namely that the le was lowered in order to accommodate the building's tall stepped gable and st it overlooking any nearby Gentile structure – such presumption being strictly fc bidden. Whatever the reason, visitors have to step down, first entering t barrel-vaulted antechamber. The doorway into the synagogue proper has a typ panum with a richly carved relief of a vine, its twelve roots representing t 12 tribes of Israel, its four stems the four rivers of Creation. Beyond is a su prisingly lofty double nave, its vaults supported by hexagonal pillars and giv five ribs instead of the usual four which might be taken to represent the Chr tian cross. The corbels have fine foliage carving, though one, on the south wa has been left plain, a characteristic indication of the synagogue's "provision. status. Around the walls are the original seats, while in the centre, surround by a Gothic grille, is the *almemar* or *bimah*, the rostrum from which the Tho is read. Magnificent chandeliers, dating from the 16C to the 19C hang abov By the east wall stands the shrine containing the Thora. The banner present by the Emperor can also be seen, its central device representing the headge of the defeated Swedes. Eight men would carry it in proud procession on t (fairly rare) occasion of a royal visit to the ghetto. Window slits allowed wom to watch services from a side chamber.

For much of its existence the synagogue served not only as a place of worsh but as a centre for community life and as a law court dispensing the justice the largely self-governing Jewish Town. Its most famous rabbi was Judah Loe ben Bazalel, legendary creator of the Golem, the man of mud whose rema may still be hidden high up in its attics.

Maiselova synagóga (Maisel Synagogue) ⊘ – *Maiselova*. Originally built on a lavi scale in 1592 as a private place of worship by Mayor Meisel, this synagogue w twice damaged by fire and rebuilt, and finally reconstructed in neo-Gothic style 1905. It houses a fascinating collection of silver as well as displays on the evo tion of the Jewish community up to their emancipation in the 18C.

Pinkasova synagóga (Pinkas Synagogue) ⊘ – *Široká*. One of the Jewish Town's oldest synagogues, dating from 1535, the Pinkas Synagogue stands on even earlier foundations, excavations carried out in the 1970s having revealed remains of wells and ritual baths. The building was intended as a private place of worship for Aaron Meshulam Horowitz, a member of one of the ghetto's wealthiest families. Much altered in the mid 19C, it is now a very public place indeed, an inspired memorial to 77 297 Jews from Bohemia and Moravia who perished in the Holocaust. Between 1954 and 1959 their names were individually inscribed on the walls of the synagogue, only to be effaced after the building was closed in 1968. The official reason for closure, water penetration, had some validity, but the frequently anti-Zionist Communist regime found it convenient to delay repair and re opening, and it is only since 1989 that the names have been painstakingly been restored, making the building one of the most moving memorials to the fate of European Jewry.

Starý židovský hřbitov (Old Jewish Cemetery) – *Entrance from U starého hřibitova*. This is one of the strangest of all cities of the dead, a chaos of 12 000 tombstones crammed tightly together within the confines of surrounding buildings and its own high walls. Tall trees reaching up to the light cast a dappled shade on the irregularly undulating surface of what is the oldest burial ground of its kind in Europe, the resting place of great names from ghetto history as well as a host of lesser folk.

The earliest tombstone dates from 1439, when Jews were prohibited from burying their dead beyond the walls of their town, the last from 1787, when an Imperial decree put an end to burial in built-up areas. Between those dates as many as 80 000 bodies may have been interred here, the ground being used again and again until the dead lay as many as twelve deep. A tombstone of 1439, a simple stele, is that of Rabbi Abigdor Karo, a witness to the pogrom of 1389, whose elegaic description of those dreadful days used to be read in every Prague synagogue on the Day of Atonement. Later tombstones become more elaborate. Symbols alluding to the profession or name of the deceased are common, like the hands raised in blessing of the priestly Cohens, the fox of the Fuchs family or the mouse of the Maisels. Baroque tombs carry lengthy inscriptions praising the character and achievements of the deceased. Many visitors make for the tombstone of Rabbi Loew, close to the wall opposite the entrance to the cemetery. His grave attracts many a wishful note, held in place by a pebble, though others receive this honour too. Among other great men buried here are Mayor Meisel, scientist David Gans, and Rabbi David Oppenheim (1664-1736) whose unequalled collection of Hebrew manuscripts was given to Oxford's Bodleian Library.

With the closing of the old cemetery in 1787, the community began to use a new cemetery at Olšany in what is now the suburban borough of Vinohrady *(see p. 217)*.

The Old Jewish Cemetery

Mystery and Magic in the Ghetto: the Rabbi and the Golem

The crooked streets and exotic-seeming inhabitants of Prague's vanished ghetto have spawned an array of legends whose power to intrigue and fascinate is undiminished despite the origin of most of them in relatively recent times.

The most famous of all these stories features the stern figure of **Rabbi Loew** and his **Golem**, the archetypal Frankenstein monster modelled from mud from the banks of the Vltava and set to work for its master. In the best tradition of such creatures, the Golem tires of his servitude and runs amok, but is eventually tamed or destroyed. Rabbi Loew was of course a real person, one of the greatest Jewish scholars ever to live in Prague, though he was not born here and only became Chief Rabbi in his eightieth year. Prague's Golem deserves his capital G because of his intimate association with the city, but golems were around long before the closing years of the 16C. In a Hebrew commentary dating from the late 12C, a Jewish scholar from the Rhineland

describes how a golem may be made by occult means, while closer to Rabbi Loew's time a Christian chronicler reports on the fate of Elijah Baal Shem of Chelmno, crushed to death under a mass of clay when his golem collapsed on him.

Rabbi Loew seems an unlikely figure to be associated with such tales. Born in either Poland or Germany, he became chief rabbi of Moravia where he won respect as an efficient administrator and dispenser of justice. In Prague, where his rabbiniate lasted 10 years until his death, he was known for his strict views on ceremony and education and for his insistence on close study of the Torah and Haggadah. His interest in the occult was a scholarly one, and it may have been this which led to a famous encounter with Rudolf II. One contemporary source describes how the learned rabbi was brought to the castle in secret and conversed with Rudolf who remained concealed behind a curtain, while a later version has him summon-

AKG Paris

Wegener's silent film version of the Golem

ing up the spirits of the Jewish patriarchs for the Emperor's entertainment and enlightenment. Whatever passed between these representatives of "magic Prague" was certainly embroidered later to form part of the exotic tapestry of the Late Renaissance Rudolfine court with its preoccupation with cabbala, alchemy and the supernatural. A persistent legend associated with Rabbi Loew was his use of magic powers to prolong his life. How Death defeated him, hidden in the rose handed to him by an innocent young girl, inspired the splendid statue by L Šaloun on the New Town Hall in Mariánské náměstí *(see p. 137)*.

By the mid 19C the reputation of Rabbi Loew as a worker of miracles had become firmly established and the first golem stories began to appear. There are several versions, but many elements are common. Accompanied by a small retinue, the rabbi proceeds at night to the banks of the river, where a figure of clay is formed and cabbalistic ritual performed. An amulet bearing the unutterable name of God is slipped into the creature's mouth; he comes to life and he becomes the rabbi's faithful servant, carrying out all his tasks without question. On the Sabbath, when no work may be performed, the amulet is removed and the golem becomes inert. Alas! One Friday evening the rabbi, preoccupied by his daughter's illness, forgets; the golem is seized by rage, smashes up his surroundings and lumbers out into the streets of the ghetto, causing chaos and terrifying the inhabitants. The rabbi runs from the synagogue and rips the amulet from the golem's mouth and the monster, pacified, crumbles into clay once more. His remains are shovelled up and placed in the attic of the synagogue, where they remain to this day. Anyone daring to disturb them is likely to be jinxed for the rest of their days.

Perhaps the most memorable of Golem tales is the 1915 novel by **Gustav Meyrink**, but the image most people have of the rabbi's man of mud is the one that dominates **Paul Wegener's** gripping film of 1920, an Expressionist classic of the silent screen. His earthy-textured Golem is a large and cumbersome, serf-like figure, whose demise comes about when a little girl jumps all unsuspecting into his arms – the triumph of innocence over evil. The film's portrayal of Prague – crooked streets pullulating with people, tall-gabled houses set at crazy angles, sinister goings-on in the shadows – gave the world a defining, darkly picturesque image of the city.

Španělská synagóga (Spanish Synagogue) ⊘ – Built in 1868, the Spanish Synagogue was the only relatively modern addition to the ghetto's buildings before the *asanace* began. Its exotic, neo-Moorish style of architecture was much in favour among designers of synagogues at the time. Its opulent interior, with much gilding against a background of dark reds, greens and browns, has been restored and houses displays of great poignancy which illustrate the story of Bohemia's Jewish communities from the end of the 18C onwards.

Other synagogues – As in many Central European cities, Prague's increasingly prosperous Jewish families participated in the move away from the oppressive conditions in the city centre to new suburbs. In the Second World War the synagogues built to serve these new communities lost their congregations. Some of them, like the severe 1930s Functionalist synagogue in Smíchov, were converted into storerooms, while the huge synagogue at Vinohrady, one of the biggest in Europe, was ostentatiously left to burn down by the German-controlled fire brigade following an American bombing raid in early 1945.

Not far from the Josefov, in Jeruzalemská Street in the New Town, is the **Jubilejní synagoga** (Jubilee Synagogue), built in the same neo-Moorish style as the Spanish Synagogue.

KARLOVA★★

CHARLES Street Old Town
Metro Staroměstská

⬛owing a crooked course from Malé náměstí to Charles Bridge, Karlova forms the ⬛ond stage of the **Royal Way** between the Old Town and the castle. Almost traffic-⬛e and trodden daily by thousands of tourists, it threads its way past a variety of ⬛ps occupying the ground floors of some of the city's most venerable buildings. ⬛every turn, other streets and alleyways tempt the visitor to stray ever deeper into ⬛ labyrinthine core of the Old Town.

Malé náměstí (Little Square) – The origins of this attractive, funnel-shaped square go back to the days of the Přemyslid kings, and, as is common in this part of town, some of its buildings have vaulted basements which were once the ground or even the first floor of a Romanesque or Gothic dwelling. The east side of the square is arcaded. Most of the façades are now Baroque in style, but perhaps the most striking is the most recent: *no 3/142* was built as a hardware store for VJ Rott in the late 19C and is boldly painted to designs by Mikuláš Aleš while examples of the owner's wares are featured in the lunettes above the top row of windows. In the Middle Ages the square housed at least two apothecaries, one of them at *no 11/459*, the Richter House. Next door, *no 12/458* has a 14C shop window, the city's oldest, while *no 13*, U zlaté koruny, is the charming Schnöblingova pharmacy and boasts a double eagle as well as the golden crown of its name.

In the centre of the square, the well-head has a wrought iron grille of great delicacy dating from the mid 16C, topped by a gilded Bohemian lion added a little later.

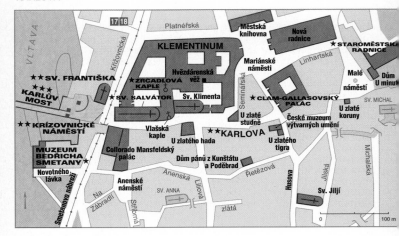

A double bend lined with more fine Baroque and Rococo houses leads into Husov (Huss Street), one of the main arteries of the medieval town, running north pa the Clam-Gallasovský palác (Clam-Gallas Palace) to Mariánské náměstí and sou past Sv.Jiljí (Church of St Giles).

★**Clam-Gallasovský palác (Clam-Gallas Palace)** – *Husova 20/158*. Though it only h a narrow street to dominate rather than the square originally planned, the Baroqu palace built between 1713-9 by Bernhard Fischer von Erlach for Johann Wenze Count Gallas, is the grandest of its kind in the Old Town.

The site had enjoyed high status long before the days of Gallas, an Imperial of cial whose most impressive posting had been to Naples as Viceroy. A nob residence of Romanesque times was succeeded by a Gothic palace built for Ma grave Jan Jindřich, brother of Charles IV which the Kinskys rebuilt in Renaissan style. When Wilhelm Kinsky was murdered along with treacherous General Wa lenstein in 1634 the palace was given by the Emperor to the Gallas family.

Johann Wenzel's choice of architect reflects not only his determination to build home worthy of his position in society but also the decisive influence of the Au trian Baroque on contemporary Bohemian architecture. Von Erlach, already work on Vienna's Karlskirche, thought highly enough of the Clam-Gallas Palace include it in his *Entwurff einer historischen Architektur*, a lavishly engraved con pendium of the world's architecture. He employed Prague's greatest sculpto Bernhard Matthias Braun, to animate the rather severe façade with a variety sculpture, though it is the pairs of Herculean figures striving to support the **tw porticoes** that capture the attention of every passer-by. The interior is one of t finest in the city, with a grand staircase with more statuary by Braun as well frescoes by Carlo Carlone. For many years the palace was a centre of social li with concerts and theatrical performances; it now houses the city archives, tran ferred here when their previous home, the north wing of the Old Town Hall, w destroyed in May 1945, and an occasional concert is still held in one of its sum tuous rooms.

Husova (Huss Street) – Among the Baroque houses along Husova, the twin Rena sance gables of *no.19/229* stand out. This building now houses tempora exhibitions staged by the České muzeum výtvarných umění (Czech Museum of Fi Art), while its neighbour, *no.17/228*, is one of the most famous of all Prague pul U zlatého tygra (The Golden Tiger), its Pilsener beer kept at exactly the right te perature in its ancient cellars. For long a meeting place of hard-drinking locals a literati, the Golden Tiger is not renowned for its hospitality to outsiders, thou an exception was made for an American president once he had been introduc by his Czech counterpart.

Further along on the opposite side of the street, the 14C Sv. Jiljí (Church St Giles) has massive, solidly buttressed towers recalling those of the Malte Church in Malá Strana. The Domincans came here after being made to leave t Klementinum. The interior is a thoroughgoing exercise in "Baroquisation", w frescoes by VV Reiner and an array of fine carving.

Řetězová Street leads westward off Husova. A special sense of Prague's long h tory can be gained at *no 3*, the Dům pánů z Kunštátu a Poděbrad (House of t Lords of Kuntát and Poděbrady). This medieval palace dates from around the ve beginning of the 13C. Added to by the most famous member of this dynasty eastern Bohemian nobles, Jiří (George of Poděbrady – 1420-71), the "Huss

King", it retains its original ground floor, now at basement level, consisting of three rooms with vaults supported on central pillars. Between 1453 and 1458 the palace was the seat of the country's affairs while George was acting as regent during the minority of King Ladislav Posthumous. In 1458 George was unanimously elected king on Ladislav's death, the only monarch of Czech descent to have enjoyed this honour. For this, and because for a while he succeeded in restoring the country to order, he is still revered by Czechs, who also remember his − unsuccessful − attempt to persuade his fellow-princes to set up a kind of European Union to which all potential disputes would be referred. From its junction with Husova, Karlova continues westward, widening out into a space resembling a small square. In contrast to the somewhat blank walls of the Klementinum *(see p. 136)* to the north is the luscious facade of the corner house *no 3/175* ingeniously squeezed in between Karlova and Seminářská. Called U zlaté studně (The Golden Well), the house dates from Renaissance times, but its superb stucco decoration is Baroque, celebrating by its depiction of saints the delivery of the country from the plague. Almost blocking the exit of Karlova opposite is U zlatého hada (The Golden Snake), now a restaurant but once Prague's very first cafe, established in 1713 by an Armenian trader who had begun his career by selling coffee in the street.

The Golden Well House

Ch. Boisvieux

Sv. Klimenta (Church of St Clement) ⊘ − Forming part of the formidable south wall of the Klementinum, this is one of the three places of worship which served this great institution. Now a Greek Catholic church, it was built to the designs of Kilián Ignáz Dientzenhofer in 1711-3 and its interior boasts some of the finest carving and statuary by **Mathias Bernard Braun**.

Vlašská kaple (Italian Chapel) ⊘ − This exquisite little Renaissance chapel seems deliberately placed to direct the stream of pedestrians around the side of the Klementinum. Perfectly oval in plan and built around 1600, it was one of the first centrally planned buildings of its kind north of the Alps and served the city's substantial Italian community of the time.

No 2/189 Colloredo-Mansfeldský palác (Colloredo-Mansfeld Palace) − Marking the meeting point of Karlova with the Smetana Embankment and Knights of the Cross Square, this splendid palace was built for Prince Vincenz Paul Mansfeld-Fondi around 1730 though there are substantial traces at basement level of the previous medieval building on the site. It was in this older building that Frederick of the Palatinate, the Winter King, paused to organise his flight following the disastrous Battle of the White Mountain in 1620. The sumptuous oval ballroom makes a strange setting for the gruesome exhibits of the **Museum of Torture**.

To either side of the magnificent portal by Braun is an arch; the one to the east is glazed, the window of one of the city's most stylish antiquarian bookshops, while the one to the west swallows and disgorges the continuous stream of traffic along the embankment.

Between 1607 and 1612 the adjoining Renaissance building, No 4/188, was the home of Rudolf II's astronomer **Johannes Kepler**. It was here that he had his observatory and here that he wrote some of the works like *Astronomia nova*, *Astronomiae pars optica* that laid the foundations of modern astronomy and optics. Beyond the arcaded courtyard there is access to **Anenské náměstí** (St Anne's Square).

★ **Křížovnické náměstí (Knights of the Cross Square)** − *(see p. 138).*

KARLOVO Náměstí★

CHARLES Square - New Town
Metro Karlovo náměstí

One of the three civic spaces laid out in the mid 14C as focal points in Charles IV
grandiose New Town, the 8.5 ha square now named after the great Emper
was originally called the Cattle Market, though it served other purposes as well. It w
here that citizens gathered to hear Imperial pronouncements, or to view the holy reli
kept in a long since vanished chapel and put on display once a year. For much of
existence the square must have been a scruffy place; ruler-straight Ječná Street wa
reputedly orientated to allow the west winds to blow away the accumulated odou
of the cattle market, to say nothing of those emanating from the building known a
the "Hering Haus" (New Town citizens had a monopoly on sea-fish sales). Converte
into a park in the 19C, the square is now a leafy oasis in the otherwise densely buil
up city centre, with fine trees, lawns, play areas and a wealth of commemorati
statues. Around it stand buildings in a variety of architectural styles ranging fro
medieval to modern.

★**Novoměstká radnice (Town Hall of the New Town)** ⊙ – With its tall tower, the Tow
Hall dominates the northern, narrower flank of Charles Square. Work on it starte
soon after the Emperor had outlined his plan for the New Town in 1348 ar
despite several rebuildings much Gothic work remains in the basement, the vaulte
entrance hall, and parts of the tower. A thorough reconstruction at the beginnir
of the 20C attempted to return the whole building to something like its earli
appearance and the trio of neo-Renaissance gables and the cap on the tower da
from this time.

It was at the Town Hall that Prague's first **defenestration** took place, thus esta
lishing the city's venerable tradition of dealing with political opponents by hurlir
them from a window. Led in procession by their priest, Jan Želivský, a large crov
of Hussites demanded the release of arrested comrades who were being held insi
the Town Hall. When stones were thrown from the upper windows, the m
stormed inside and ejected a dozen aldermen and the mayor on to the lances ar
pikes held in readiness below. Those not killed in this way were bludgeoned
death on the cobblestones.

Some 221 steps lead to the top of the 42 m-high tower which gives a wonderf
panorama★ over the New Town and the city in its setting. On the way up there
a Baroquised Gothic chapel and a view into the Great Hall, with its fragments
murals and massive ceiling beams supported by equally substantial stone corbe

Sv. Ignáce (Church of St Ignatius) ⊙ – This Baroque church and the adjoining colle
running half the length of the square were the New Town headquarters of t
Jesuit Order. Designed by Carlo Lurago in 1665-70 on the model of the Order
places of worship in Rome, the church proclaims the glory of the Order's founde
St Ignatius of Loyala, whose figure appears high up on the gable. Other fine sta
uary adorns the splendid portico and the interior is lavishly decorated.

Faustův dům (Faust House) ⊙ – With a Gothic core, then Renaissance, Baroque ar
later additions, this substantial town mansion on the southwestern corner of t
square has a long history, though its Faustian connections are relatively recent,
creation of the Romantic imagination. It was not in fact Dr Faustus who lived he
but a succession of characters whose activities were enough to inspire the leger
Prince Wenceslas of Troppau, who dabbled in alchemy, then Rudolph II's cou
alchemist Edward Kelley who failed to make gold for his master, and latterly a c
ebrated chemist, Count Mladota of Solipysky. The house is used for art exhibitio

Sv. Jana na Skalce (Church of St John on the Rock) ⊙ – Reached either through
gateway at the corner of the square or via a dramatic double stairway fr
Vyšehradská Street, this small and rarely accessible church is one of the mast
pieces of the Baroque architect **Kilián Ignáz Dientzenhofer**. Built in the 1730s, it is
masterpiece of geometrical sophistication. Beyond the twin towers turned inwa
at an angle, the interior is all convex curves, with a central octagon squeez
between the ovals of vestibule and choir. The convex shapes of the exterior repe
this pattern in reverse, and the dynamic effect is intensified by variously pattern
windows arranged at different heights.

To the west, beyond the deep cutting of Vyšehradská, is the **Emauzy** (Emma
Monastery), one of the religious institutions founded by Charles IV. Also called
Slovanech (Monastery of the Slavonic Monks), it housed Croatian monks from t
Dalmatian coast and was intended to help repair the schism between the Easte
and Western Church. Still awaiting reconstruction, the monsastery has fine fr
coes in its cloister and one of the few additions to a church made unc
Communism, an ingenious and elegant double spire replacing one destroyed in
air raid.

Heroism in the crypt

By late 1941, the Czechoslovak government in exile in Britain had become alarmed by the apparent passivity of the Czech population under Nazi rule. Despite the fears of the local resistance movement that overt action would provoke unacceptable reprisals, the decision was made to send parachutists charged with assassinating **Reichsprotektor Reinhard Heydrich**. "Hangman" Heydrich was duly waylaid as he drove to his office in Hradčany on the morning of 27 May 1942, and died from his wounds a few days later. German fury knew no bounds, culminating on 10 June in the destruction of the village of Lidice and the shooting of all its male inhabitants (*see p. 253*). Meanwhile seven of the parachutists had been given refuge in the crypt of the Church of St Cyril and St Methodius. But they were betrayed by a colleague, driven to despair by the Nazi wave of terror, the "Heydrichiada". Before dawn on 18 June, the area to the west of Charles Square was sealed off, and the church attacked by the Prague SS Guards Battalion. Despite the odds, the parachutists fought back vigorously and the Germans were forced to order the fire brigade to flood the crypt in an attempt to flush them out. Even then the Czechoslovaks managed to buy time by pushing out the hosepipe. But their situation was hopeless. As the waters rose around them, the remaining defenders used their last bullets to shoot themselves.

Sv. Cyrila a Metoděje (Orthodox Cathedral of St Cyril and St Methodius) – Resslova. Originally consecrated for Roman Catholic worship and dedicated to St Charles Borromeo, this fine Baroque church stands in Resslova Street which drops towards the Vltava to the west of Charles Square. It was designed by Pl Bayer and completed by Kilian Ignaz Dientzenhofer in 1736. Closed like so many religious establishments during the reign of Joseph II, it was used as a military storehouse, then as a technical institute. It was rescued from this fate in the 1930s, when it became the cathedral of the Czechoslovak Orthodox Church. In 1942 the building was the scene of violent fighting when the assassins of Heydrich *(see panel)* were cornered in the crypt, which is now the Národní památník obětí Heydrichiády **(National Memorial to the Victims of the Heydrich Terror)** ⊘, with displays on the parachutists' mission and its terrible consequences.

Taneční dům – The "Dancing House" at the junction of Resslova and the Vltava embankment at Rašínovo nábřeží is no ballroom but a striking Postmodern office block. Designed by the Californian architect Frank Gehry and completed in 1996, it has cumbersomely playful towers whose embrace of each other has also led to its being called "Fred and Ginger". The building is crowned by a panoramic restaurant.

Spálená Street – Long before the New Town was thought of, this street formed part of the ancient route connecting the river crossing and the Old Town with Vyšehrad. It acquired its present name "Burnt Street" after many of its houses were destroyed by a great fire in 1506. At the corner with Lazarská, *no 4/82* is the **Dům Diamant** (Diamond House), built as a department store in 1913 in a style combining elements of Secession with a wealth of Cubist details. Some of the meticulously chiselled stonework does indeed have a diamantine quality, particularly around the portal. Provoking great controversy at the time was the way in which the statue of St John Nepomuk belonging to the adjacent Baroque Church of the Holy Trinity was set in an uncompromisingly Cubist frame.

A Tavern

U Fleků – (Křemencova 9/183). Beer had already been brewed in this famous establishment for centuries before it was were taken over by the Flekovský family in the mid 18C. Records go back to around 1430, but it's quite likely that the Czechs' favourite drink was being drunk here even earlier then. Since 1843 the obligatory tipple has been a strong dark beer brewed on the premises and dispensed here and nowhere else. At the turn of the last century U Fleků was tastefully rebuilt in neo-Gothic style with plenty of panelling in the same shade as the beer together with cheery murals and mottoes. The clientele in those days included artists, actors and writers, among them that great connoisseur of pub life, Jaroslav Hašek, author of *The Good Soldier* Švejk. Nowadays U Fleků's mock-medieval halls, leafy beer garden and brass band make it an essential stop on the tourist trail.

KARLŮV Most★★★

This miracle of medieval engineering spanning the Vltava has linked the Old Town with Malá Strana and the castle for six and a half centuries. Guarded by towers at either end, it is a Gothic structure of great finesse as well as strength and durability. In the Baroque period, its embellishment with a glorious avenue of saintly statues turned every crossing of the river into a kind of pilgrimage.

Carts, carriages, and coronation processions have come this way, but the bridge has also been a place of commerce, conflict, trial and punishment, as well as revelry and commemoration. Freed of its vehicular traffic, it now serves as an arena for entertainers and souvenir sellers as well as an incomparable platform for viewing the beauties of the city on either bank of the broad river.

HISTORY

For hundreds of years the great Gothic bridge was unique, so much so that it was simply referred to as "Prague Bridge" or the "Stone Bridge", only being given its present name in 1870. It had ancestors, however. The first was a timber construction, already in use in the 10C, but destroyed by a great flood in 1157. The second bridge was called the Juditin most (Judith Bridge) in honour of King Vladislav's queen, Judith of Thuringia. Completed around 1160 and built soundly in stone on the model of the recently constructed bridge over the Danube at Regensburg, it was a wonder of Romanesque construction, defended by towers at either end. But in 1342 it too fell victim to the Vltava, destroyed by the masses of ice and other debris swept down by the February floodwaters. Soon after, **Charles IV** seized the opportunity to rebuild the river crossing as part of the array of civic improvements intended to make the city a worthy capital of the Holy Roman Empire. The Emperor laid the foundation stone of the new bridge on 13th July 1357, a date chosen for its favourable astrological indications. The building material was sandstone, held in place by mortar mixed with wine and eggs, a technique which gave the work such strength that dynamite had to be used when repairs

were carried out in the late 19C. Supervising construction was **Petr Parléř**, architect of the Gothic cathedral rising over Hradčany. He also designed the Old Town Bridge Tower, intended by Charles to have no equal in the Christian world. Though still unfinished, in 1378 the bridge was complete enough to carry the Emperor's funeral cortege. A few years later, in 1393, it was the scene of the murder of Canon Jan Nepomucký (John of Nepomuk), cast into the river and left to drown, supposedly because of his refusal to reveal the secrets of the Queen's confessional to her jealous husband, Wenceslas IV.

Seasonally battered by floodwater and ice floes, the bridge was severely damaged on several occasions, the worst disaster coming in 1890, when three of its arches were swept away. The bridge witnessed human as well as natural violence; it was the scene of fierce fighting, firstly in Hussite times, then in 1648 at the end of the Thirty Years War, when the Swedish troops who had occupied Malá Strana were held up at the Old Town Bridge Tower by a motley militia of students and Jews led by Jesuits. Exactly 200 years later, in June 1848, another force led by students barricaded the bridge and defied the cannon of General Windischgrätz (a scene dramatically reproduced in the Petřín diorama – *see p. 172*), and barricades appeared again during the Liberation in May 1945.

A wooden calvary had been sited on the bridge at an early date, and at the very beginning of the 16C the knight Bruncvík, a Roland figure symbolising civic freedoms, was added. But it was in the late 17C and early 18C that the appearance of the bridge was transformed by the systematic placing of sculpture. The cult of Nepomuk had begun in 1683 with the installation above one of the central piers of his now familiar statue with its starry halo. Other saintly figures followed, a dozen of them of them from the workshop run first by Jan Brokoff and then by his far more talented son, Ferdinand Maxmilian. Other superb sculptures from this era are by Braun, Jäckel, and Mayer, their life and vigour not equalled by the rather academic figures put up in the 19C following damage by flood and artillery fire. The very last addition, Karel Dvořák's figures of Cyril and Methodius, was made in 1938, on the 20th anniversary of the founding of Czechoslovakia. Much of what is on show today consists of copies, many of the original sculptures having found protection from the elements in the National Lapidarium.

M. Guillou

John of Nepomuk – patron saint of bridges

Canon Jan Nepomucký had to wait 300 years for real fame. Victim of an obscure quarrel between king and archbishop, in 1393 the unfortunate cleric was abducted by a gang of thugs in royal pay, dragged at night-time to the bridge over the Vltava and thrown into the murky waters. For a while his body bobbed on the surface, accompanied by a crown of dancing stars. The legend that he had been killed because of his refusal to betray the secrets of the queen's confessional to her jealous husband came to life again in the 17C. The Counter-Reformation was in full spate, and needed a saint, preferably a Jan, to counter the powerful hold another Jan, Jan Hus (John Huss) still had over the Czech people. The bronze statue of Nepomuk by Brokoff went up on the bridge as early as 1683, but it was only in 1719 that his body was exhumed and his tongue, miraculously, found to be a healthy red colour. Nepomuk's canonisation was celebrated in style 10 years later, with a week-long festival focussed on the bridge. For many years the saint's day was marked by a great procession through the city to the site of his martyrdom. His popularity is also attested to by the innumerable Nepomuk statues which guard bridges throughout Catholic Central Europe.

ACROSS THE BRIDGE
FROM OLD TOWN TO MALÁ STRANA

The bridge's first arch is concealed beneath Křížovnické náměstí (Knights of the Cross Square – *see p. 138*), while its first pier supports the splendid Old Town Bridge Tower. From here fifteen further arches carry the 9.5 m carriageway to the pair of towers marking the approach to Malá Strana. Spanning not just the Vltava but also the northern end of Kampa Island and the Čertovka or Devil's Brook, the 516 m bridge follows not a straight but a subtly S-shaped alignment.

★★ **Staroměstská mostecká věž (Old Town Bridge Tower)** ⊘ – Completed around 1380, the tower guarding the eastern approach to the bridge served many purposes, ceremonial and symbolic as well as defensive. Beneath the chisel roof and the gallery with its spiky corner turrets (all added by the indefatigable 19C restorer **Josef Mocker**), the townward face of the tower has retained its elaborate medieval decoration (though the sculptures are replicas). There are the coats of arms of the lands which formed part of the Bohemian kingdom, and at first floor level, with two arches of the bridge as pedestal, the figure of St Vitus. To his left is King Wenceslas IV, to his right the elderly Emperor Charles IV. Saints Adalbert and Sigismund appear higher up, above a realistically depicted lion. Low life is represented at the base of the archway by the figure of a girl being groped by a lecherous knight.

The archway itself has a vault with rib patterning resembling that of the cathedral. Beyond, the west face of the tower lost its decoration during the 1648 siege.

Sculptural decoration of the Old Town Bridge Tower

Ch. Boisieux

The tower is built on a pier of the bridge; its basement served as a prison, its first floor as a guardroom. The splendid 16C ceiling from the Old Town Hall was installed here by Mocker in the late 19C; beneath it is an original and entertaining exhibition on the **music of tower galleries**. From the gallery at the top of the tower there is a magnificent **vista**★★ along the whole length of the bridge as well as a close-up view of the Old Town's towers.

For a whole decade after the execution in 1621 of the leaders of the Estates rebellion, everyone crossing the bridge had to endure the gruesome sight of several severed heads displayed on spikes atop the tower.

★★**The sculpture** – Though many are masterpieces in their own right, the 30 sculptures and sculptural groups make their greatest impact as a whole, a processional way uniting the historic quarters of the city across the broad river. Despite the later additions, the overwhelming impression is that of the dynamism of the Baroque works, of animated figures seen in succession against the constantly changing city skyline.

Placed on opposite pairs on pedestals at regular intervals, the statuary forms an integral part of the bridge's structure, crowning the massive but elegantly designed piers whose shape is emphasised by the timber cutwaters. Pride of place is taken in the centre of the bridge on the downstream side by the solitary bronze figure of **St John Nepomuk**, placed here in 1683 on the supposed 300th anniversary of his martyrdom. Calm and restrained compared with many of the other sculptures, the Nepomuk statue was the work of several hands; a clay original by the Viennese Matthias Rauchmüller formed the basis for a wooden model by Jan Brokoff, while the cast was made in the Nuremberg workshop of Wolfgang Herold. The five gilded stars of Nepomuk's halo used to be the regular target of souvenir hunters, but less daring visitors content themselves with touching the pedestal panel depicting his martyrdom, a gesture guaranteed to bring good fortune.

In the early years of the 18C several other sculptures from the Brokoff workshop took their place on the bridge, most of them presumed to be by Jan's son, **Ferdinand Maxmilian Brokoff**. Outstanding among them are:

St Francis Xavier *(fifth left from the Old Town Bridge Tower)*; the Jesuit missionary, in the act of baptising a heathen prince, is supported by a quartet of pagan dignitaries. The bible-bearing figure may be that of Brokoff himself.

Saints Vincent and **Procopius** *(10th left from Old Town Bridge Tower)*; while St Vincent revives a corpse, his colleague treads heavily on the Devil. The panels below celebrate the pair's deeds, involving the conversion of improbable numbers of Jews and Turks and the crushing of further devils. At a lower level on the same pier stands the figure of Bruncvík (Roland), the guardian of civil liberties. His unsheathed sword, perhaps prophetically, was renewed just before the outbreak of the Velvet Revolution.

Saints John of Matha and Felix of Valois and **the Blessed Ivan** *(14th left from Old Town Bridge Tower)*; one of the most elaborate and popular of the bridge's sculptures celebrates the work of these saints in succouring Christians who had fallen into infidel hands. Languishing with pitiable expressions in the cave below them are several such victims, guarded with sublime indifference by a splendidly pot-bellied Turk and his cur.

A somewhat different spirit is evident in the nearby figure of **St Luitgard** by **Matthias Bernard Braun** *(12th left from Old Town Bridge Tower)*, perhaps the most striking work of all in this great outdoor gallery and the one which shows the Baroque striving for emotional intensity at its most extreme. In her vision, the blind Luitgard, a Cistercian nun, was allowed by the dying Christ to kiss his wounds; here she clasps his knee while He – improbably – reaches down from the Cross to draw her to him while above the letters INRI flutter in a divine breeze.

Malostranské mostecké věže (Malá Strana Bridge Towers) ⊙ – Framing the dome and bell-tower of St Nicholas' Church between their chisel roofs, the **Malá Strana Bridge Towers** constitute one of the most photographed compositions of this photogenic city. The smaller tower is the older. Built around 1130 as part of the defences of Malá Strana, it was then adapted to guard the approach to the Judith Bridge. It still incorporates Romanesque masonry, but was much altered towards the end of the 16C with a Renaissance gable and other features. A battlemented gateway connects it to the **taller tower**, built around 1464 and obviously inspired by the Old Town Bridge Tower though the statuary intended to adorn it never materialised.

It too offers marvellous **views**★★ from its gallery, while inside is an **exhibition** on **the history of the bridge**.

KLEMENTINUM

CLEMENTINUM – Old Town
Metro Staroměstská

The city's largest building complex after the castle, this great stronghold of the Counter-Reformation extends over more than two hectares close to the Old Town end of Charles Bridge. Now the home of several libraries of national importance, the Clementinum was built in stages by the Jesuits after they had been invited into the country in the mid 16C to lead the struggle to re-Catholicise the predominantly Protestant population. Behind its mostly blank walls are churches, chapels, courtyards and an observatory as well as a series of magnificent Baroque and Rococo interiors, sad few of which are accessible to the general public.

HISTORY

It was only a dozen or so years after the foundation of the Society of Jesus in 154 that several of its members arrived in Prague at the invitation of Emperor Ferdinand They took up residence in the old monastery at the end of Charles Bridge, Dominican occupants being moved to St Agnes' Convent at the northern end of the Old Town. Greeted at first with abuse and stone-throwing, and briefly exiled in 161 the Jesuits nevertheless succeeded in making their college an attractive place for the education of the sons of the nobility, as much through their flair for show and ceremony as for their teaching. But they really came into their own after the Battle of the White Mountain. In 1622 they were put in charge of the Charles University, that previous hot-bed of Hussitism, and from the mid 17C to well into the 18C the Clementinum was the subject of an ambitious building programme, involving the demolition of more than 30 houses and the diversion of several streets, as well as the incorporation of three churches. The best architects were employed, among them Carlo Lurago, Francesco Caratti, Giovanni Orsi, František Kaňka and Kilián Ignaz Dientzenhofer.

After Emperor Joseph II's expulsion of the Jesuits in 1773, the Clementinum continued as a academic institution, as well as housing an important printing press and the Imperial Library, in part based on the contents of confiscated Jesuit libraries throughout Bohemia. In the interwar period the buildings were sensitively converted to house the Národní knihovna (Czech National Library), whose manuscript collections include priceless treasures such as the Vyšehrad Codex of 1085 and the illustrated Velislavova bible of about 1340. There is a also a substantial collection of writings by John Wyclif, the 14C religious reformer, brought here by young Czechs who had studied under him in England; one of them is annotated by John Huss "O Wyclif Wyclif, you will trouble the hearts of many!"

THE BUILDING

Exterior – The most impressive face the Clementinum presents to the outside world is that of its **west wing**, along Křížovnická Street. Built by Caratti in 1653, has colossal pilasters and statues by Cometa of Roman emperors, but its intended effect is marred by the continuous traffic along the narrow street. Between the wing and the Church of St Salvator, a portal gives access to the Clementinum first courtyard. Other entrances are from Karlova Street and Marianské náměst the latter with a fine Baroque facade graced with a bust of Joseph II and symbol of the Arts and Sciences.

Beyond is a series of courtyards. The first, western courtyard is graced with a 184 statue by Josef Max of a youth, in commemoration of the part played by the Clementinum's students in fighting off the Swedish attack on the Old Town in 1648

Access to the National Library is from the second courtyard.

Interior – Among the interiors *(normally only open to authorised readers)* the summer refectory on the ground floor was designed by Lurago. It has a huge Rococo stove, neo-Baroque bookcases, stucco putti and paintings by Tausch, and is now the main reading room. On the upper floor, all with superb decoration, are the Mozart Hall, the **Mathematical Hall** and the **great Library**, the latter designed 1727 by Kaňka and with a superlative collection of geographical and astrological globes running its entire length.

★ **Zrcadlová kaple (Mirror Chapel or Hall)** – Designed by Dientzenhofer in 1724 as private place of worship, this splendid space has **mirrors** integrated with its stucco decoration. It is in regular use for concerts, and is thus one of the Clementinum few accessible interiors.

Hvězdárenská věž (Astronomical Tower) – Begun in 1722 and crowned by a lead figure of Atlas, the tower was used for astronomical and meteorological observations from 1752 onwards. Until well into the 20C, when midday showed on the tower's sundial, a flag was hoisted as a signal for a gun to be fired from the Letná ramparts.

★ **Sv.Salvator (St Saviour's Church)** ⊙ – Together with the Italian Chapel and St Clement's *(see p. 129)*, **St Saviour's** is one of the three churches forming part of the Clementinum. Begun in 1578 in Renaissance style along the lines of the Jesuits' mother church – the Gesú – in Rome, the building was much extended in Baroque style around 1640 by Lurago, given its dome by Caratti in 1649 and its towers by Kaňka in 1714. With its splendid portico added in 1653, and with an array of sculptures from the workshop of Jan Bendl, the church's west front closes the vista from Charles Bridge and makes a fine entrance to the Old Town.

In the richly decorated interior, more statues by Bendl – representing the Apostles – adorn the confessionals. The church is the resting place of one of the most zealous of all Counter-Reformation warriors, the censor Koniáš, a notorious burner of books in the Czech language. Until 1945, St Saviour's served Prague's German Catholics, then became the principal church of the Slovaks resident in Czechoslovakia's capital.

NEARBY

Mariánské náměstí (Marian Square) – The idea of extending Marian Square southwards to give the Clam-Gallas Palace *(see p. 128)* a more spacious setting came to nothing, and the square, once the site of a Romanesque church, retains its modest proportions.

Opposite the entrance to the Clementinum is the Nová radnice (New Town Hall). Built in 1911 by Osvald Polívka to allow the historic town hall in Old Town Square to be used for ceremonial purposes, it is a sombre, symmetrical structure in late Secession style, enlivened by allegorical sculptures. Flanking it are two splendid sandstone figures by Ladislav Šaloun: to the left, the Iron Man, to the right the encounter of **Rabbi Loew** with Death in the form of a rose reached to him by a maiden. The north side of the square is dominated by the Městská knihovna (City Library), a sober exercise in interwar neo-Classicism with Art Deco interiors; it has a spacious gallery which stages temporary exhibitions on a variety of themes.

Attracting more public attention than either of these fine civic edifices is the fountain let into the wall of the Clam-Gallas Palace; its lively female figure representing the Vltava is popularly known as Terezka.

KRÁLOVSKÁ ZAHRADA★★

ROYAL GARDENS – Hradčany
Tram 22 to Královský letohrádek or Pražský hrad

rst laid out in the 1540s , the Royal Gardens and Summer Palace *(see p. 106)* are idence of Ferdinand I's desire to extend court life beyond the medieval confines of e Hrad into the sunlight and spaciousness of the plateau to the north of the Stag oat. Full of horticultural and architectural interest in themselves, the gardens make wonderful introduction to the castle, whose walls and towers are glimpsed between e glorious specimen trees which grow here.

ne gardens flourished under Ferdinand and especially under Rudolph II, when they arboured tender plants like figs, almonds and pineapples and exotic animals like leop- ds, tigers and an orangutan. Parrots were tethered to the trees with golden chains d there was even a dodo. It was here that the first tulips in Europe were grown, om bulbs brought from Constantinople. The gardens underwent frequent alteration a result of war damage and changes in fashion. Originally formal, they were remod- led in the 19C on naturalistic lines.

 Communist times the gardens were the preserve of the government elite, but now rm a popular link between the castle and the Summer Palace.

★ **Belveder (Royal Summer Palace)** – *See p. 106.*

★ **Zpívající fontána (Singing Fountain)** – The formal Renaissance garden with its geometrical layout of paths and parterres bordered by low-cut hedges is a meticulous reconstruction, carried out in the mid 1950s. Forming a perfect setting for the Summer Palace, it has at its centre the famous **"Singing Fountain"**, cast in bronze by the maker of the cathedral's Sigismund Bell and placed here in 1568. Topped by a jaunty little bagpiper, the fountain owes its name to the thrumming sound made by the water falling into its elegant basin.

Míčovna (Ball Game Hall) – Built by Bonifác Wohlmut between 1565-9, this splendid single storey Renaissance pavilion with its sgraffito decoration was intended to give courtiers the opportunity for "vigorous bodily movement". Burnt down during the Prague Uprising of 1945, it was rebuilt in the early years of the Communist regime, which accounts for the sly insertion of a hammer and sickle among the recreated sgraffito work. Nearby is a fine Baroque sculpture of *Night*

Ball-Game Hall sgraffito

from the Braun workshop. Other sculpture in the garden includes a splendid Hercules fountain by Bendl. The Ball-Game Hall is used for presidential receptions as well as for temporary exhibitions.

Close to the western exit to the gardens is the modest **Presidential villa**, and opposite it the site of the Rudolph II's menagerie, the so-called **Lion Court**. The approach across the Stag Moat to the northern entrance to the castle was once a bridge to which Rudolph added a lower storey, enabling him to visit the gardens in private.

KŘIŽOVNICKÉ Náměstí★★

KNIGHTS OF THE CROSS Square – Old Town
Metro Staroměstská

The essence of Prague seems to be concentrated in this small square which links Charles Bridge to the labyrinthine streets of the Old Town and which serves as a kind of vestibule to the glories of Malá Strana and the castle on the far bank of the broad river. The square's sides are defined by two of the city's finest Baroque churches, the approach to the bridge is guarded by the noble Gothic bridge tower, and a focal point is provided by a statue of Emperor Charles IV. The dignity of the square, often described as one of the most beautiful in Europe, is diminished by the role it plays in the city's transport system. Two of Prague's main arteries cross here. From the crooked Royal Way leading through the Old Town emerges a constant stream of visitors heading for the bridge, while barring their way is an equally constant flow of traffic running parallel to the course of the river. A single traffic light mediates, with surprising success, between the throng of pedestrians and the motor vehicles and tramcars which shoot surprisingly from a portal on the south side of the square. One obvious solution, an underpass, is out of the question, since hidden beneath the square is an arch of Charles Bridge, an inviolable monument from the medieval past.

★★**Staroměstská mostecká věž (Old Town Bridge Tower)** – *See p. 134.*

★**Sv. Salvátora (St Saviour's Church)** – *See p. 137.*

★★**Sv. Františka (Church of St Francis)** ☉ – This Baroque church is the ecclesiastical masterpiece of the French architect, Jean-Baptiste Mathey, who built it – assisted by Carlo Lurago – between 1679 and 1689 for the Knights of the Cross with the Red Star, whose monastery it adjoins. The centrally-planned church, the dome of which seems to call to the greater dome of St Nicholas on the far side of the river, rose over the foundations of a much earlier, Gothic, place of worship, erected by the Knights in the middle of the 13C *(see panel)*. The rusticated facade of the church faces south, overlooking the square; with its Doric pilasters, bold pediment, high attic and concave corners, it wears a severe air. The statues of saints in the niches and above the attic were added in the 1720s; the figure of St Vitus atop the "vintner column" at the eastern corner is by Bendl. The dome, more visible in the wider townscape than from the square, has prominent ribs and is carried on a eight-windowed drum the authenticity of whose colouring has been the subject of much controversy. The wonderfully harmonious and well-proportioned interior has statuary by various sculptors and a fine ceiling painting of the *Last Judgement* by VV Reiner.

★Gallery of the Knights of the Cross ⊙ – With the restitution of its property after 1989, the once-banished Order has opened up part of its monastery as a gallery for some of its greatest treasures. The individual buildings making up the monastery complex are of various dates; the medieval structures were redeveloped in early Baroque style in the mid 17C by Carlo Lurago, the wing facing the Vltava has a neo-Classical upper storey, while the main block was rebuilt in Secession style in the first decade of the 20C. As well as a splendid array of liturgical objects, the Gallery has a Gothic altarpiece, a Black Madonna, and a fine selection of Baroque paintings. In addition there is a fascinating, grotto-like **subterranean chapel** with stalactite decoration and an equally fascinating glimpse into Prague's deep past in the shape of foundations of the **Judith Bridge**.

Emperor Charles IV statue – The statue stands on the site of an old toll-booth and guard-house, demolished in 1847 when the square was given its present appearance. It was intended to mark the 500th anniversary of the founding of Prague University by Charles IV in 1348, but its unveiling was delayed by the rev-olutionary events of 1848 in which many students participated. The monument, with its statue of the Emperor holding the University's title deeds and its allegories of the University's four faculties, was finally dedicated in 1851.

The Knights of the Cross with the Red Star

This charitable order of monks can trace its origin to around 1233, when the Franciscans set up their hospice close to the convent established by St Agnes on the northern riverbank of the Old Town. In 1252 they moved to the Old Town end of the Romanesque Judith Bridge, with the right to collect tolls and the duty to keep the bridge in good repair. The Order is the only one of Czech origin still working. In the past its influence extended over much of Central Europe, and for a century and a half from around 1550 its Grand Master was also Archbishop of Prague. The rebuilding of their church at the end of the 17C was intended as a counter-blast to the Clementinum's Church of St Saviour, its Jesuit owners being regarded as relative upstarts. The glory of the Order only wound down slowly; it remained an important centre of cultural production for many years, and its high musical reputation persisted into the 20C. Gluck was organist here, as was **Dvořák**.

LETECKÉ Muzeum★

AVIATION Museum – Kbely

Metro Českomoravská then bus to Letecké muzeum (Direction Kbely)

...oused in hangars of the historic Kbely aerodrome, the national aviation museum has ...e of the largest collections of aircraft in Europe. Despite its relative inaccessibility ...d lack of visitor facilities the museum repays a visit for anyone with even the ...ightest interest in aircraft, and its displays are a reminder of the fascination which ...e study and conquest of the heavens have long had for the inhabitants of this land-...cked country.

...he Kbely field, for many years an air force base, was also Prague's first commercial ...rport, a regular Prague-Strasbourg-Paris service departing from here in October ...920.

Visit ⊙ – Supplemented by aviation memorabilia and an array of anti-aircraft artillery, the 100-plus aeroplanes on display give a comprehensive picture of military and civil flight in this part of Central Europe. Many of the machines, like those from the **Avia** works, reflect the advanced state of Czechoslovak aviation, especially in the interwar period. In the Second World War exiled Czechoslovak pilots manned several RAF squadrons in the Battle of Britain, flying planes like the Supermarine **Spitfire**, while their counterparts on the eastern front fought in Lavochkins and the famous Ilyushin **Sturmovik**. In 1945 the Luftwaffe, driven from most of its airfields in Germany proper by the advancing Allies, made a last stand here, and the museum has not one, but two examples of its pioneering twin-jet fighter, the **Messerschmitt 262**. Cold War rivalries are represented by a fearsome line-up of Soviet-built machines, and there is even an American-built Phantom, as well as a Northrop Tiger, captured in Vietnam.

Several of the museum's aircraft, including a replica of a First World War Nieuport fighter, are airworthy, and are put through their paces at an annual Air Show.

A continuation of the rocky spur on which the castle is built, **Letná Plain** seems to force the Vltava to turn eastwards as the river approaches its bushy and precipitous face. From the parkland on the edge of the plateau there are fine **views** over Prague, particularly over the Old Town. To the north stretches an open area backed by grim apartments and the great **stadium** which is the home of the famous Sparta football team.

The Stalin Statue

Czech enthusiasm for Stalin predated the Communist coup of 1948; proposals for a monument to the Soviet leader were made immediately after the 1945 Liberation, and he was made a freeman of Prague in 1947. In 1949 a competition was organised for a monument on the Letná heights which would join Castle, Vyšehrad and National Memorial on Vítkov Hill in dominating the city skyline. The competition was won by the celebrated sculptor Otakar Švec (1892-1955) with his proposal showing Stalin in Napoleonic pose at the head of two groups of working people, one Soviet, the other Czechoslovak.

Construction of the 30 metre high project lasted from 1952 to 1955, gave work to 23 stonemasons and 600 labourers, and absorbed 7000 m³ of granite. In a gesture recalling the building of the National Theatre, stones from all over the republic were incorporated into the foundations. By the time of the solemn unveiling of the monument on 1 May 1955, Stalin was dead and so was Švec, stress having driven him to suicide. Barely a year later, Krushchev denounced the Stalinist "cult of personality", and by 1961 Stalin's corpse had been removed from its place alongside Lenin in the Red Square mausoleum. Orders came from Moscow to do something about the Prague statue, nicknamed the "Meat Queue" by city wits. After agonising deliberations, the decision was taken to destroy the monument. It took several weeks and hundreds of tons of explosives before the colossus finally crumbled.

The statue has gone, but the network of steps and footpaths of which it was the focus remain. Colonised by skateboarders, the vast plinth now carries a huge metronome, joined for a few weeks in 1996 by a monster inflatable of pop star Michael Jackson, advertising his poignantly named "History" tour.

Stalin surveys Prague

ver the centuries the Letná has been the scene of festivities, demonstrations, and ilitary manoeuvres. **King Otakar II's** coronation celebrations took place here, and it was ere that Emperor Sigismund's army paused before going on to its defeat on Vítkov ill on the far side of the river. In the Communist period the masses were ordered to arade here on May Day, and it was here in 1955 that the massive Stalin statue was rected. The last days of Communism in Bohemia were marked on the Letná when 1 estimated million people assembled here to rattle their key-rings in support of the elvet Revolution.

o the east, the green spaces of the Letná merge with the densely built-up suburb of olešovice, while to the west there is an attractive footbridge link across the ravine viding the Letná from Chotkovy sady (Chotek Gardens) and the Královská zahrada Royal Gardens).

Chotkovy sady (Chotek Gardens) – This little park was laid out in 1830 on the site of an old timber yard by Count Karel Chotek, Governor of Prague between 1826-43. An indefatigable civic "improver", Chotek was responsible for many other parks and open spaces as well as the Vltava embankments and the serpentine road winding up from Malá Strana to these northern heights. To the west the park is dominated by the **Belvedere** *(see p. 106)*, while at its heart is a grotto populated by characters from the works of the neo-Romantic poet Julius Zeyer. Franz Kafka called Chotek's park "the prettiest place in Prague".

Hanavský pavilon (Hanava Pavilion) – Now a restaurant, this delightful little building with its overload of fanciful neo-Baroque detail was originally a show-piece for the Duke of Hanau's ironworks at the Jubilee Exhibition of 1891. Easily dismantled because of its innovative cast-iron structure, it was re-erected here in 1898. Its terrace offers one of the best **panoramas★★** over river and city. Just to the west are the substantial remains of the most formidable section of the Baroque fortifications, Bastion XIX, from which the midday gun was fired until 1918. The palatial villa here, now a government guest house, was built in 1911 by the politician Karel Kramář, who later became independent Czecho-slovakia's first prime minister.

As well as the Hanava Pavilion, the Letná also has the Letenský zámeček (Little Letná Castle), a pleasant 19C building with a restaurant and plenty of outside tables. The superb aluminium and glass Expo '58 restaurant which was the Czechoslovak Pavilion at the **1958 Brussels World Exhibition** is, unfortunately, closed.

LETOHRÁDEK Hvězda★★
STAR Castle or Summer Villa
6km west of Hradčany – Tram 18 to Petřiny

1 1530 **Ferdinand I** laid out a hunting park in woodland once owned by the monks f nearby Břevnov and later enclosed it with a continuous wall, but it was his son, rchduke **Ferdinand of Tyrol** who in 1556 gave the park its most distinctive land-ark, this star-shaped pavilion. A highly cultivated man, the archduke planned this nost unusual structure himself, though he also employed several architects cluding **Bonifaz Wohlmut**; in plan it is a six-pointed star, with an intricate internal yout of rhomboid-shaped rooms and central 12-sided chamber. The appeal of nese unusual spaces is enhanced by their decoration with quite outstanding stucco ork, almost certainly carried out by Italian master craftsmen; it features more nan 300 panels mostly depicting cheerful scenes from Antiquity. Star Castle's riginal, extremely tall cupola has long since been replaced by the present plain oof, but the impact of the building's Renaissance geometry at the focal point of everal avenues remains undiminished.

It was here in 1620 that the victors of the Battle of the White Mountain consoli-dated their forces before moving into the undefended city. The castle and hunting park fell into disuse and were subsequently damaged by manoeuvring armies. A thoroughgoing restoration of the building, regarded as a model of its kind, was carried out 1949-51. The innovative Renaissance architecture of Star Castle might seem an incongruous setting for the **museum** ⊘ of the two of the leading figures of the 19C Czech National Revival, the writer Alois Jirásek (1851-1930) and the painter Mikoláš Aleš (1852-1913), but like many of their contemporaries both were obsessed with Czech history and legend and in particular with the signifi-cance of the great battle of 1620.

Bílá hora (White Mountain) – The White Mountain is no mountain, merely the high point (381 m) of the bleak limestone plateau where the fateful battle was fought on 8 November 1620. Now covered in unlovely suburban housing, it's where Tram no 22 turns after its long climb up from Hradčany. There seem to be few echoes of battle here; the principal monument is the pilgrimage church ▪ Panny Marie Vítĕzné (Our Lady Victorious), consecrated in 1720 in the course ▪ the week-long celebrations marking the hundredth anniversary of the battle. Lil other places of pilgrimage in Bohemia, it secludes itself behind high walls, entere through a highly decorative portal. Chapels stand at the corners of the cloiste while the small central church has ceiling paintings by **V.V. Reiner** and **C.D. Asam**. Th project seems to have been directed by both **Santini** and **K.I. Dientzenhofer**.

The Battle of the White Mountain

After skirmishing with each other across the Bohemian countryside, the Imperial, Catholic army led by Tilly and Buquoy and the forces of the Protestant Bohemian Estates under the command of **Count Thurn** finally joined in battle on the morning of 8 November 1620. More or less equally matched in numerical terms, the armies were mostly composed of mercenaries, French, Spanish and German on the Catholic side, Hungarians, Austrians, Germans, Moravians and Bohemians on the Protestant side. Among the Catholics were future generalissimo **Albrecht von Wallenstein** and future philosopher **René Descartes.** A probing movement against the Hungarians on the Protestant left wing unexpectedly put them to flight, leaving the main force exposed, and despite mounting a vigorous counter-attack, the Estates' army collapsed, streaming back to the city in disarray. The royal guardsmen were cornered around Star Castle and swiftly put to the sword.

Thurn was ready to make a final stand, but, thrown into panic, the ineffectual **"Winter King" Frederick** and his Stuart Queen Elisabeth quit the the city in haste, leaving behind much treasure including an English Order of the Garter. Their flight, with its mile-long wagon train, is amusingly depicted in a splendid wooden relief in the cathedral.

For Catholics, the battle took its place with the defeat of the Turks at the Battle of Lepanto (1571) as a triumph for the Faith, and churches were raised in both Prague and Rome to celebrate the victory. For Bohemia's Protestant nobility, clergy and intellectuals, German as well as Czech, it was a disaster; their leaders were executed, their property confiscated and tens of thousands of them forced into exile. Ever since the National Awakening of the 19C, the defeat at the Battle of the White Mountain has been seen by many Czechs as marking the beginning of centuries of national humiliation, an age of darkness.

LORETA ★★★

here are few contrasts quite so striking in Prague as that between the solemn bulk
the Černín Palace and this cheerful place of pilgrimage facing it across the square.
he of the best times to visit the Baroque complex of the Loretto is when the car-
on has just stopped tinkling from the tall tower and the tourists push into the
urtyard like the pious pilgrim crowds of yesteryear, eager to admire the curiosities
thin, above all the *santa casa*, the replica of the Virgin Mary's house in Nazareth.

ISTORY

he Loretto legend originated in 13C Italy, when angels are supposed to have rescued
ary's humble birthplace from the advance of the infidel, spiriting it through the skies
Dalmatia and thence to a laurel wood in Italy. In fact it was the Angeli family who
ought parts of her dwelling to Loretto ("place of laurels") in 1294, a destination
osen because of its location in the Papal States, which could be relied upon to
otect such precious relics.
he "holy home" soon became the object of a cult, and later the shrine built by Bra-
ante inspired imitations all over Catholic Europe, several dozen of them in Bohemia.
ague's santa casa was the most popular, attracting pilgrims in large numbers. It
as commissioned by Kateřina Benigna, the pious spouse of Count Lobkowicz, and
ilt, probably by Giovanni Battista Orsi, between 1626 and 1631. The holy site was put
the care of the monks of the adjoining monastery, founded in 1600 as the first Capuchin
tablishment in the Czech lands. An arcaded courtyard was added in mid-century,
en in the early 18C another generation of the Lobkovicz family paid the Dientzen-
ofer dynasty of architects to complete the complex by adding an upper storey to the
urtyard, designing the splendid west-facing façade, and building the Church of the
ativity.

EXTERIOR

Its air of festive gaiety in no way diminished by the great retaining wall dividing
the square into upper and lower halves, the Loretto presents a welcoming face to
the world. Presided over by the tall tower of the carillon and profusely adorned
with statuary, the **façade★★** completed by Kilian Ignaz Dientzenhofer in 1721-24
has been compared to an altarpiece. Atop the gables are figures of Mary *(left)* and
the Angel of the Annunciation *(right)*, while along the cornice are ranged statues
of saints, among them, on the right-hand chapel, the inevitable St John Neopmuk.
St Joseph and John the Baptist stand over the portal, which is flanked by stubby
columns carrying St Francis and St Anthony. In front is a superb balustrade populated by putti, who also accompany the stairway rising to the south.
The famous **carillon★** has bells made in Holland in 1694; the tune it rings out every
hour is a variant orchestrated by Dvořák of a popular Czech hymn of praise to
Mary "A thousand times we hail Thee!" At a time when the plague was raging
through Prague, the bells are supposed to have sounded of their own accord at
the funeral of a poor washerwoman whose children had all died of the disease.
The carillon is connected to a keyboard, which enables other tunes to be played.

INTERIOR ⊘

The *santa casa* is surrounded by the **cloisters** originally erected around 1660 and
extended upwards by a storey by K.I. Dientzenhofer between 1747 and 1751. The
ground floor of the cloisters has confessional boxes, kneeling desks and pictures
of saints, while its ceiling is painted with scenes from the so-called *Loretto Litany*.
Richly decorated chapels are placed at the corners of the cloister and half way
along the north and south wings. The **St Francis Seraphim Chapel** in the northern wing
has a fine **painting** by **Peter Brandl** within an oval frame carved by Jäckel. In the
centre of this part of the courtyard stands a large-scale sculptural group by
JM Brüderle of the *Resurrection*.

★Santa Casa – The *santa casa* was originally quite a plain little building, but the
elaborate **stucco reliefs** covering its outer walls were added in 1664; they show
scenes from the life of the Virgin Mary as well as the miraculous flight of her home
from the Holy Land to Italy.
As in the Italian original, the simple, windowless interior is intended to replicate
the humble circumstances in Nazareth of the Holy Family. At one point the brickwork is purposely imperfect, imitating the effects of a thunderbolt which struck
the original building in order to punish a blasphemer. There are fragments of wall-
paintings, and, in the altarpiece, a darkened limewood figure of the *Virgin and
Child*. Several members of the Lobkowicz family, those great benefactors of the
Loretto, lie buried here.

★★★ Church of the Nativity

The Loretto church has one of the least altered Baroq interiors in Prague, as well as one of the most gorgeously decorated, with a particularly rich cast of statuary and oratories for the nobility not unlike theatre boxes. It was begun by Christoph Dientzenhofer in 1718, continued by his son Kili Ignác, and completed by the latter's kinsman Johann George Aichbauer in 173 The ceiling paintings include fine work by V.V. Reiner depicting the *Crucifixion (ne est to the altar)* and the altar incorporates a replica by Heinsch of Raphael's *Nativity*. In the side altars, the relics of St Felicissimus and St Marcia are clad, in somewhat macabre fashion, in the Spanish styles of the time, while their skulls are concealed beneath charming masks of wax. The church's acoustics are excellent, and concerts have long been held here, to which the delightful little musicians around the organ lend a pleasing visual, if not aural note.

In the centre of the southern wing of the courtyard is the **Chapel of St Anthony of Padua**, like its counterpart in the north wing with a picture frame carved by Jäckel. The sculptural group (copy) in the centre of this part of the courtyard represents the *Assumption of the Virgin Mary*. The chapel attracting most attention is the one in the southeastern corner, dedicated to Our Lady of Sorrows, whose early 15C statue adorns an altar; another altar presents the surprising spectacle of a bearded lady hanging from a cross *(see panel)*.

★★ Treasury

The Treasury was established in the earliest days of the Loretto's existence, and benefited enormously from the eagerness of the post-White Mountain nobility to display their Roman Catholic credentials by acts of pious generosity. Even though the collection was regularly depleted by confiscations ordered by impoverished Emperors, it still presents a stunning array of objects, including chalices, crucifixes, caskets, candelabras and crowns for statues of the Virgin Mary. In addition there are mitres, gloves, reliefs, filigree work, enamels, plate and figurines, but the most spectacular items are the glittering **monstrances**, among them the famous **Prague Sun★★** of 1699, designed by Fischer von Erlach; into its sunburst structure are worked no fewer than 6 500 diamonds which once decorated the wedding dress of Countess Kolovrat.

Sorrowful St Starosta

Starosta – or Wilgefortis to give her her non-Czech name – appears in legend as the Christian daughter of a heathen Visigothic ruler. Ordered by her father to make a marriage of convenience to a pagan prince, Starosta refused, and was thrown into prison. Her prayer to God that she might be made so ugly that her unwanted suitor would refuse her was answered; overnight she grew a magnificent beard. Father's fury knew no bounds, and he had her crucified. Since then Starosta has been the patron saint of unhappily married women, though her cult failed to catch on amongst traditionally rather sceptical Czechs.

Kapucínský klášter (Capuchin Monastery) – The north side of Loretto Square is taken up by the modest buildings of the **Capuchin monastery** of 1602, the first to be founded in the Czech lands; its monks were entrusted with the care of the Loretto Shrine, to which the monastery is linked by an overhead passage. The simple church houses a popular *Nativity* scene dating from 1700. The occupation of Prague by a Protestant Saxon army in 1632 was ended when the monks pulled down part of the adjoining city wall, thereby allowing Generalissimo Albrecht Wallenstein's Catholic besiegers to pour in. In the 1940s, the monastery was used as a prison, both by the Nazis, then by the short-lived, semi-democratic government of the immediate postwar period. The monks returned in 1990.

M. Guillou

MALÁ STRANA★★★

Lesser Quarter
Metro Malostranská

Bounded by the broad Vltava and the green slopes of the Petřín, and protected by the castle on the hill above, Prague's most perfectly preserved historic quarter seems hardly to have changed since the mid 18C. Its churches, burgher's houses and Baroque palaces rise from streets and squares first traced in the Middle Ages and scarcely altered since. Doorways lead to secret courtyards and terraced gardens and steps, ramps and stairways overcome the many changes in level. A wooden water-wheel turns lazily in the millstream, and the riverbank with its overhanging trees wears a rustic air. Among the scant reminders of the 20C are the tramlines which circle respectfully round the base of St Nicholas, the city's greatest monument of the age of the Baroque, before making their exit from Malostranské náměstí (Malá Strana Square), apparently through a palace doorway. The square marks an important station along the Royal Way, receiving the throngs of visitors coming off Charles Bridge and offering them a choice of routes up to the castle.

HISTORY

This part of Prague has always been dominated by the castle. The ancient routeway from the Hradčany heights to the riverside and to the ford leading to the Old Town attracted straggling settlements of merchants and other folk as early as the 9C. More substantial building began after the construction of the Judith Bridge around 1160; the Bishop moved his quarters down from the castle to a new palace adjoining the bridge tower and the Knights of Malta built their monastery opposite. In the mid 13C King Otakar II decided to consolidate these hitherto uncoordinated building projects and create a well-planned and easily supervised settlement to act as a counterweight to the rapidly developing commercial town (today's Old Town) on the far bank. A red tangle of walls was laid out connecting the bridgehead to the castle, the existing inhabitants – including the Jews – were persuaded to leave, to be replaced by artisans and merchants brought in from northern Germany. A central marketplace was laid out with a church – the Gothic forerunner of today's St Nicholas – as its centrepiece. A century later, Emperor Charles IV enclosed a vastly greater area of the Menší město pražské (the Lesser Town of Prague as it had become known) with the so-called "Hunger Wall", though most of this area has remained unbuilt.

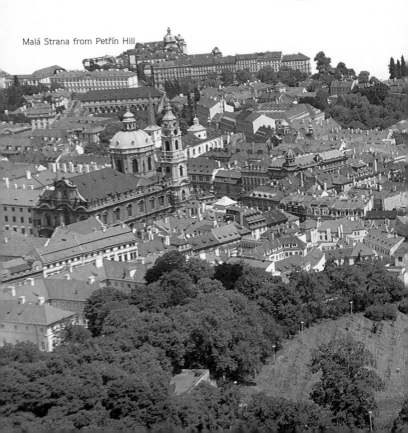

Malá Strana from Petřín Hill

Having survived destruction by war and fire, in the second half of the 16C the Lesser Town began to attract noblemen eager for a town residence within easy reach of the Castle. This process intensified in the following century, when new urban palaces were built and older ones renovated in Baroque and later Rococo style. Now known as Malá Strana, the town lost its commercial character and became an enclave of aristocrats and their servants, as well as builders, craftsmen and artists, many of them from northern Italy. The late 18C and 19C saw a decline, as the nobility concentrated their attention on their estates and the court in Vienna. **Malá Strana** became lost in a dream of its own past. Palaces and other fine buildings were subdivided to form lodging-houses. Some acquired a new lease of life in 1918 when Prague became the capital of the newly-founded country of Czechoslovakia and suitable premises for embassies were required. Under Communism, further subdivision occurred when the city council, hard-pressed to find housing, crammed its tenants into expropriated properties. This gave the area a unique social mix, under threat now as restitution returns buildings to their former owners.

★ **Malostranské náměstí** (Malá Strana Square) – The sloping square is divided into a lower and an upper half by **Sv.Mikuláš** (St Nicholas' Church★★★) *(see p. 198)*. This magnificent Baroque structure dominates the square but does not overwhelm it, thanks partly to the other buildings which share its central position and help domesticate its vast bulk. Among them is *no 28/5*, the Rococo Dům U kamenného stolu (House at the Stone Table), whose ground floor is occupied by one of the city's most venerable cafes, the Malostranská kavárna. Less inviting than this pretty Rococo building is its neighbour, the extremely plain Jesuit college of 1691, now part of the University.

With its traffic, its important tram stop and streams of pedestrians on their way to and from the castle, the square always seems busy. Aristocratic palaces set much of the tone of the square, but something of its original more homely atmosphere persists on the south side, which still consists mostly of burgher's houses with deep arcades, and, at *no 1/272*, a fine example of a pavlač or galleried courtyard. An unostentatiously Cubist house stands close to the beginning of Karmelitská Street, widened a century ago amid much controversy to accommodate the tramlines. Further up the slope, *no 10/262* the **Dům U zlatého Iva (The Golden Lion)** is an outstanding example of an unaltered Renaissance town house.

Similar buildings once characterised the western side of the square, but these had to make way for the **Lichtenštejnský palác** (Lichtenstein Palace), a grand edifice built for Karl von Lichtenstein, the Catholic convert who presided over the 1621 execution of Protestant rebels in Old Town Square. Remodelled in neo-Classical style in 1791, the palace now houses an Academy of Music; previous tenants have included Mozart's friends the Dušeks and the philologist Josef Dobrovský. The building also served as headquarters for the Swedes (in 1648), the Bavarians (in 1741) and General Windischgrätz (in 1848).

Among the properties confiscated after 1621 was the Renaissance-cum-Baroqu
Palác Smiřických (Smiřický Palace) on the north side of the square. It was here tha
the Protestant noblemen conspired in 1618 to carry out the Second Prague Defe
nestration. Prominent among them was their host, Jan Albrecht Smiřický, who wa
thought of as a possible candidate for the throne of Bohemia once the hated Hap
burgs had been vanquished. The adjacent **Šternberský palác** (Sternberg Palace) begu
in 1684 was the home of Count **Kaspar Maria von Sternberg** (1761-1838); a friend o
Goethe, this personifiation of aristocratic Bohemian patriotism kept open hous
for the intellectual elite of his day and was the leading light in the founding of th
National Museum in 1818. His home was the repository for the works of art assen
bled by the Society for Patriotic Friends of the Arts, the basis of today's Nation
Gallery collections.

On the eastern side of the square, the Renaissance **Malostranská radnice** (Malá Strar
Town Hall) lost its function when Prague became a united city in 1784; a fe
years later it lost the trio of Baroque towers which had been its chief ornamer
Today it houses the Malostranská beseda, the cultural centre of this part of tow
Also dating from Renaissance times is *no 23/37*, the **Kaiserštejnský palác** (Kaiserste
Palace), famous as the residence between 1908-14 of the opera singer Ema De
tinnová (Emmy Destinn).

① MALÁ STRANA NORTHEAST

★Sv. Tomáše (St Thomas' Church) ⊙ – *Josefská 8/28*. The **church** and monastery o
St Thomas was founded in the 13C by the Augustinians. Burned down by the Hu
sites in 1420, it was rebuilt and became fashionable in court circles; aristocra
and artists are buried here. Much remodelled by Kilián Ignác Dientzenhofer
1723-31, it nevertheless retains the proportions of a great Gothic church beneat
its lavish Baroque surfaces. With huge scrolls and broken pediments, the facac
has all the drama Dientzenhofer was capable of, while the splendid interior wa
decorated by some of the greatest artists of the Prague Baroque like VV Rein
(ceiling paintings), Karel Škréta (painting of the Holy Trinity), Brokoff and Qu
tainer. Dientzenhofer himself designed the High Altar with its paintings o
St Thomas and St Augustine by **Rubens** (originals now in the National Gallery
Among those laid to rest here is the sculptor Adrian de Vries and the defenestrate
Catholic councillor Jaroslav Bořita of Martinic.

The Augustinians first brewed beer here in 1358 and a tasty black beer is st
served in the monastery vaults today (U sv. Tomáše).

Sv. Josefa (St Joseph's Church) ⊙ – *Josefská*. Uniquely in Prague, St Joseph's has
Baroque facade of Flemish type, with banded rusticated columns framing a dr
matically vertical sequence of doorway and window openings and statuary. Set
back from the road, apparently in order to preserve the ancient lights of the adjc
ning Lobkowicz Palace, it was built for the Carmelites between 1683-91, probab
by a member of the Order from Leuven (Louvain) in what is now Belgium. Benea
its oval cupola, the centrally planned interior is unusually plain, though there a
paintings by Peter Brandl and carvings by MV Jäckel.

Mostecká (Bridge Street) – It is easy to imagine the coronation procession making i
way along well-proportioned Mostecká, as fine an introduction as can be imagine
to Malá Strana. From the towers which guard this end of Charles Bridge, this pa
of the Royal Way slopes gently down, then rises past a succession of Baroque ar
Rococo town houses towards the magnificence of St Nicholas' Church. Standing o
from more modest edifices is *no 15/277*, the **Kaunický palác** (0), now the Yugosl
Embassy, a splendid seven-bay structure with attic statuary by Platzer.

Dům U tří pštrosů (Three Ostriches House) – *Dražického náměstí No 12/76*. The lit
square is named after Jan of Dražic, a 14C ecclesiastic who resided in splendo
in the Bishops' Palace which stood here until it was sacked by the Hussites i
1420. The famous **Three Ostriches House** stands here, its upper windows level wi
the carriageway of Charles Bridge. Now a hotel, in 1597 it was bought by J
Fuchs, by royal appointment supplier to the court of ostrich feathers. It was
who commissioned paintings of the birds and their feathers to adorn the facac
but the twin gables, a Baroque touch, were added later, around 1657. Anoth
luxury enterprise, Malá Strana's first coffee house (the city's second), was inst
lled here in 1714 by an Armenian businessman, Deodat Damajan.

U lužického semináře (Lusatian Seminary Street) – Completed by Kilián Ignác Dier
zenhofer in 1728, the **Lusatian Seminary** at the junction with Míšeňská Street w
built for theological students from Lužice (Lusatia); Czechs have always felt an af
nity with this region in eastern Germany with its Slav minority, the Lusatian Sorl
Jäckel's statue of St Peter, the patron saint of Lusatia, beckons from the corn
of the building. The street widens out into an attractive small square; the buildir
on its southeastern side back directly on to the Kampa Island mill-race (t
Čertovka or Devil's Brook) close to its junction with the Vltava.

Vojanovy sady (Voyan Gardens) ⏱ – Exotic trees and shrubs flourish in the favourable microclimate created by the high walls of these delightful gardens. Part of the grounds of the medieval Bishop's Palace, they subsequently passed into the hands of the Carmelites from St Joseph's, whose monastery they adjoin. Now a public park, they have a grotto-like Chapel of St Elias, a further chapel dedicated to St Theresa, and a Nepomuk statue let into the wall.

Klárov – What is now a busy traffic intersection with its trams and Metro station was the very first part of Malá Strana to be built up, a district of ferrymen and fisherfolk. Well-used tracks led to fords across the Vltava, and it was here that the first wooden bridge was built. Something of the former atmosphere can be sensed in the little riverside park just to the south of Mánes Bridge.

Opened in 1978, Malostranská Metro not only pays tribute in many ways (statuary, ironwork) to its Baroque setting, but also, and no doubt uniquely among the world's underground railway stations, has a walled garden. The garden is overlooked by the **Valdštejnská jízdarna (Wallenstein Riding School)**, a spacious structure used by the National Gallery for important temporary exhibitions.

Zahrady pod Pražským hradem (Gardens below the Castle) ⏱ – *Access through the Ledebour Palace, Valdštejnské náměstí 3/162, and from the Southern Gardens of the castle* – Winding westward from Klárov, Valdštejnská Street is bounded on one side by the blank walls of the Wallenstein Garden and on the other by a series of fine Baroque palaces. Now housing foreign embassies and departments of state, the palaces are perhaps less remarkable than their glorious terraced gardens, recently restored and reopened to the public.

Malá Strana from the Ledebour Garden

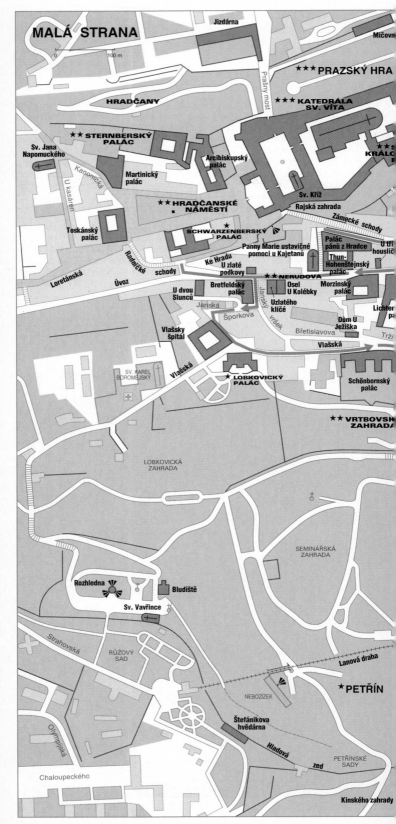

MALÁ STRANA

Jízdárna

Míčovn

★★★ PRAŽSKÝ HRA

Prašný most

HRADČANY

★★★ KATEDRÁLA SV. VÍTA

★★ STERNBERSKÝ PALÁC

Sv. Jana Napomuckého

Arcibiskupský palác

★★ KRÁLC

Martinický palác

U kasáren

Kanonická

Sv. Kříž

Rajská zahrada

★★ HRADČANSKÉ NÁMĚSTÍ

Zámecké schody

Toskánský palác

★ SCHWARZENBERSKÝ PALÁC

Palác pánů z Hradce

U tří housliс̌

Loretánská

Radniční schody

Ke Hradu U zlaté podkovy

Panny Marie ustavičné pomoci u Kajetánů

Thun-Hohenštejnský palác

Úvoz

★★ NERUDOVA

Morzinský palác

U dvou Slunců

Bretfeldský palác

Osel U Kolébky

Lichter pa

Jánská

Šporkova

Jánský vršek

U zlatého klíče

Dům U Ježíška

Vlašský špitál

Břetislavova

Trži

Vlašská

SV. KAREL BOROMEJSKÝ

Vlašská

★ LOBKOVICKÝ PALÁC

Schönbornský palác

★★ VRTBOVSK ZAHRADA

LOBKOVICKÁ ZAHRADA

SEMINÁŘSKÁ ZAHRADA

Rozhledna

Bludiště

Sv. Vavřince

Strahovská

RŮŽOVÝ SAD

Lanová draha

Olympijská

NEBOZÍZEK

★ PETŘÍN

Štefánikova hvězdárna

Hladová

Chaloupeckého

zed

PETŘÍNSKÉ SADY

Kinského zahrady

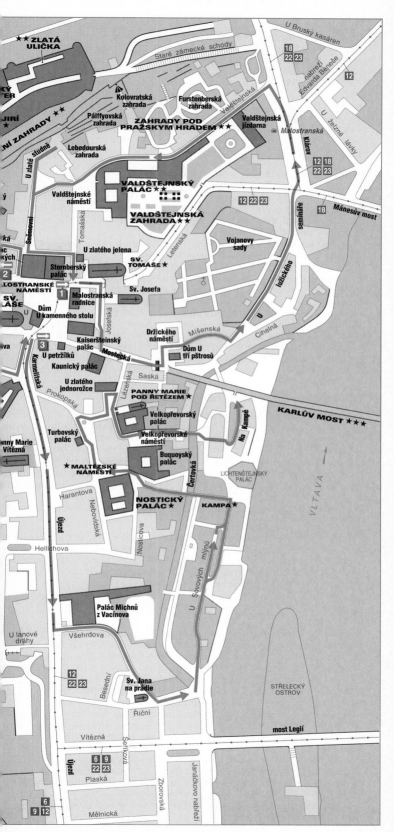

★★ ZLATÁ ULIČKA

Staré zámecké schody

U Bruský kasáren

18 22 23

12

nábřeží Edvarda Beneše

JIŘÍ ★

NÍ ZAHRADY ★★

Kolovratská zahrada

Furstenberská zahrada

Pálffyovská zahrada

ZAHRADY POD PRAŽSKYM HRADEM ★★

Valdštejnská jízdarna

Malostranská

U železné lávky

Lebedourská zahrada

U zlaté studně

VALDŠTEJNSKÝ PALÁC ★★

Valdštejnské náměstí

Tomášská

VALDŠTEJNSKÁ ZAHRADA ★★

12 22 23

12 18 22 23

18 Mánesův most

seminář

lužického

Šternoví

U zlatého jelena

Letenská

Vojanovy sady

SV. TOMÁŠE ★

Sternberský palác

LOSTRANSKÉ NÁMĚSTÍ

1

Malostranská radnice

Sv. Josefa

Dům U kamenného stolu

Josefská

Držického náměstí

Mišenská

Cihelná

U

3

Kaiserštejnský palác

Mostecká

Dům U tří pštrosů

U petržílků

Kaunický palác

Saská

Karmelitská

U zlatého jednorožce

Lázeňská

PANNY MARIE POD ŘETĚZEM ★

KARLŮV MOST ★★★

Prokopská

Velkopřevorský palác

Na Kampě

Turbovský palác

Velkopřevorské náměstí

nny Marie Vítězná

Buquoyský palác

★ MALTÉZSKÉ NÁMĚSTÍ

Čertovka

LICHTENŠTEJNSKÝ PALÁC

VLTAVA

Harantova

Nebovidská

NOSTICKÝ PALÁC ★

KAMPA ★

Újezd

Hellichova

Nosticova

U Sovových mlýnů

Palác Michnů z Vacínova

U lanové dráhy

Všehrdova

12 22 23

Besední

Sv. Jana na prádle

Říční

STŘELECKÝ OSTROV

Vítězná

Seříkova

most Legií

Újezd

6 9 22 23

Plaská

Janáčkovo nábřeží

Zborovská

6 9 12

Mělnická

For centuries, the cliff-like slope to the south of the castle was kept free
building in order to preserve a clear field of fire. Vineyards and orchards we
planted, and later dwellings and workshops sprang up along what is no
Valdštejnská, then the main road to the east. These were burnt down in t
great fire of 1541, making way for aristocratic residences, the predecessors
today's palaces. The first efforts to beautify the steep slope were made towar
the end of the 16C, with relatively modest gardens in Renaissance style. The
beginning at the very end of the 17C and continuing into the 18C the who
hillside was progressively remodelled into a series of architectural gardens
great virtuosity, using the whole panoply of Baroque techniques, terraces an
retaining walls, steps and stairways, statuary and fountains, loggias an
gazebos, as well as plants.

The decline of the gardens set in as early as the 19C. A first attempt at resto
tion, in the 1950s, was dogged by faulty workmanship and subsidence. T
gardens, opened to the public and providing an alternative approach to the cast
had to be closed again. The more recent restoration has been carried out w
great attention to detail, but has inevitably removed much of the patina of a
which was part of the gardens' charm.

A splendid **Sala terrena** is the main architectural feature of the **Ledebour Garden**; pr
bably designed by FM Kaňka at the end of the 17C, it has murals by VV Rein
and is used for occasional concerts. Another mural by Reiner once covered t
imposing retaining wall; showing a battle with the Turks, it was replaced in t
1950s by a Socialist Realist mural depicting the 1945 Liberation, which in tu
has given way to less controversial climbing plants. A symmetrical stairway lea
upwards through the terraces to a little pavilion just below the castle wall. Fro
this level there is a magnificent view of the red-tiled rooftops of Malá Strana a
of the city's hundred spires. Eastward are further Baroque delights: first com
the **Little Pálffy Garden**, then the **Pálffy Garden** with its central stairway and tunnel, a
finally the **Kolowrat Garden**, with its delightful gazebo. Beyond, the naturalistic **Fü**
tenberg Garden *(not open to the public)* with its mature trees and shrubs offers
contrast in landscape style.

★★**Valdštejnský palác** (Wallenstein Palace) – *See p. 212.*

Sněmovní (Parliament Lane) – Once the main approach to the castle from the sou
this is now a quiet little quarter, centred on the tiny square which, as a rare bil
gual Czech and German sign recalls, was once named Fünfkirchenplatz (Pětikoste
náměstí). Markets were held here before the focus of the expanding town shift
to Malostranské Square in the 13C. Charming **U zlaté studně** (Golden Well Lane) us
to climb up to a famous panoramic restaurant of the same name but is now a c
de-sac. Parliament Lane gets its name from *no 4/176*, one of several palaces bu
by the Thun family; home of the Bohemian Assembly in Austro-Hungarian days
then housed the Senate of interwar Czechoslovakia and the Communist Council
the Czech Republic.

U zlatého jelena (The Golden Stag) – *Tomášská no 26/4.* Two great artists collab
rated on the design of this exceptionally fine **Baroque burgher's house**, completed
1726; its architect was none other than Kilián Ignác Dientzenhofer, while Fer
nand Maxmilian Brokoff was responsible for the superbly evocative **sculpt**
depicting the encounter of St Hubert with the stag.

2 MALÁ STRANA NORTHWEST

Thunovská Street and Nové zámecké schody (New Castle Steps) – The narr
street and the steps and ramps beyond run parallel to Nerudova (Neruda Stree
forming a short but steep alternative route to the castle. The upper part of t
route was laid out in 1674, though the plan to make it part of the Royal W
between Old Town and castle by adorning it with sculptures like those on Char
Bridge came to nothing. The Renaissance **Thunovský palác (Thun Palace)** rising cli
like from the cobbles has housed the British Embassy since 1920. Built into t
hillside, it has a terrace garden reached from an upper floor and overlooked fro
the Castle; in the 1920s, the elderly but agile President Masaryk is supposed
have conferred with the ambassador by scaling a ladder attached to the cas
wall. The British connection goes back to 1630, when the palace's owner w
Walter Leslie, the mercenary general who was one of Wallenstein's assassi
Among the other fine Renaissance and Baroque buildings lining street and ste
the **Palác pánů z Hradce** (Palace of the Lords of Hradec) is outstanding. Now joir
to the Italian Embassy whose main entrance is on Nerudova, it has a highly p
turesque, many-gabled skyline; the massive central gable carries the coats
arms of the Kolowrat family.

Nerudova (Neruda Street) – Castle Steps may be the shortest way up to the castle, but it is no surprise that ceremonial processions preferred to climb this splendid street, the final stretch of the Royal Way linking the Old Town to the Hradčany heights. Nerudova has all the elements of picturesque townscape; fine examples of Baroque palaces and burghers' houses, a continuous change of level, a street whose width is never constant, and a mounting sense of anticipation as glimpses are gained of the monumental edifices of Hradčany. The details too are perfect, not only the many delightful house signs, but also medallions, sculptures, splendid doorways, and a floorscape of sturdy cobblestones.

Though the street has been colonised by souvenir shops, it still has something of the atmosphere evoked by its most distinguished resident, the writer **Jan Neruda** (1834-91). Sometimes compared to Dickens, Neruda was famous for his Povídky malostranské *(Tales of the Malá Strana)*, populated by an array of sharply observed urban types. The street took his name in 1895; earlier it had been called Spur Street, from the skid-like brakes lowered by coachmen to stop their vehicles running out of control on the steep descent.

At the corner with Zámecká stands *no 2/205*, its ground floor occupied by one of the city's most venerable pubs, U kocoura (The Tom Cat). Among several pretty Renaissance or Baroque houses on this north side of the street, *No 12/210* U tří housliček (The Three Little Fiddles) has a particularly famous sign, recalling the dynasty of violin-makers who worked here in the 17C and 18C. Almost facing each other are two extremely grand palaces, both the work of Santini. Now the Romanian Embassy, the **Morzinský palác** (Morzin Palace) of 1713-4 *(south side)* has twin portals representing *Night* and *Day*, allegorical statues of the Continents atop the balustrade, and superb figures of Moors (a play on the family name) supporting the balcony, the work of Ferdinand Maximilian Brokoff. Opposite, the Italian Embassy is housed in the **Thun-Hohenštejnský palác** (Thun-Hohenstein Palace), completed around 1725 for Count Kolovrat who demanded of Santini a residence which would "enhance the beauty of the city as well as my own comfort". The portal has huge eagles designed by Matthias Bernard Braun, as assertive in their own way as Brokoff's moors. *No 11/253* U červeného beránka (The Red Lamb) has a particularly fine house sign.

The early 18C **Panny Marie Matky ustavičné pomoci u Kajetánů (Church of Our Lady of Perpetual Succor)** ⊘ is also known as the Church of the Theatines. Its design was in the hands of various architects, but the dominant imprint is that of Santini, especially in the boldness of the façade.

The street continues with fine buildings of more domestic scale, with house names including *no 27/243* U zlatého klíče (The Golden Key), and *no 34* U zlaté podkovy (The Golden Horseshoe). In *no 32/219* is Malá Strana's first **pharmacy**, now in the care of the National Museum. At the corner with **Jánský vršek** (St John's Hill), *no 33* the **Bretfeldský palác** (Bretfeld Palace) strikes a grander note, as befits a building which in the late 18C was a sparkling centre of social life, attracting guests like Casanova and Mozart.

At *no 47/233*, U dvou Sluncǔ (The Two Suns), an elaborate Secession plaque records that this was the home where Jan Neruda spent his early days, above the tobacconist's shop belonging to his father.

At this point the street widens out, inviting a decision about which way to continue. Bearing slightly left is **Úvoz**, the ancient highway leading to Strahov and the countryside. Almost directly ahead, Radnické schody

Nerudova: The Thun-Hohenstein Palace

Y. Latronche/WOSTOK PRESS

(Town Hall Steps) climb up through the buildings to the upper end of Hradčans
náměstí (Hradčany Square). Most visitors follow the route once taken by the c
ronation procession, wheeling round the hairpin bend and toiling up **Ke Hradu**, t
ramp cut into the rock face in 1663 to ease the approach to the castle.

Italian quarter – Occupying the lower ground to the south of Nerudova is a cha
ming little backwater whose irregular streets, alleyways and culs-de-sac speak
its ancient origin. Only incorporated into Malá Strana in the mid 17C, it was know
as the Obora, and had its own town hall and parish churches. From the late 1(
it became the centre of Prague's Italian community, made up of artists, archited
and craftspeople of all kinds who dominated the city's building trades for ma
years.

The focal point of the Obora was around the junction of Jánský vršek and Šporkc
Street. The churches have disappeared, but house *no 1/323* U tří zlatých kor
(The Three Crowns), once the town hall, still stands, though rebuilt at the end
the 18C. Among the many fine buildings, *no 10/320* at the very end of Šporkov
is a splendid Baroque house with exceptionally rich stuccowork. The heart of wh
was the Italian community is marked by the early Baroque **Vlašský špitál** (Italian Hc
pital), now the Italian Cultural Centre, which stands at the corner of Šporkc
and Vlašská (Italian Street), an old routeway connecting Malá Strana with t
Petřín.

★**Lobkovický palác (Lobkowicz Palace)** – *Vlašská no 19/347*. Now the Germ
Embassy, the **Lobkowicz Palace** was designed by Giovanni Battista Alliprandi at t
very beginning of the 18C and had an extra storey added by Ignazio Pallia
in 1769. The street façade on the north side of the palace is relatively pla
but Alliprandi based his striking **design for the garden front** *(not open to the pub
but visible from the lane at the rear of the palace)* on Bernini's never implement
plan for the Louvre in Paris. An oval projection, three storeys high, with
splendid sala terrena on the ground floor, extends into the garden, flanked
boldly conceived concave wings. Complementing the palace was one of Pragu
finest formal gardens, laid out on the site of the vineyard belonging to
George's Convent; at the end of the 18C it was converted into a naturalis
English-style park.

The Lobkowicz Palace saw remarkable scenes in the summer of 1989, when hu
dreds of East Germans abandoned their Trabants and Wartburgs in t
surrounding streets, and sought asylum in the embassy and its grounds. Th
plight aroused intense interest among the Czech public, and their subseque
removal to West Germany by closed train through the German Democratic Rep
blic heralded the fall of Communism.

Schönbornský palác (Schönborn Palace) – *Tržiště no 15/365*. Begun in 1643, this w
one of Prague's first Baroque **palaces**. It was lived in by Count Rudolph Collorec
who had benefited from his betrayal of his chief, Generalissimo Wallenstein. Rem
delled by Santini between 1715-8, the palace later suffered the fate of many
Malá Strana's palaces and was divided up into apartments, one of which in 19
provided short-term lodgings for Franz Kafka. The palace is now the Embassy
the USA. Terraced gardens extend up the slope to the south, dominated by
delightful little pavilion converted from a wine cellar.

Opposite the Embassy is the narrow entrance to Břetislavova Street, once a re
light district, guarded by the Baroque Dům U Ježíška (Infant Jesus) House, possil
the work of Santini.

★★**Vrtbovská zahrada (Vrtba Garden)** ⊘ – *Karmelitská no 25/373*. A modest doorw
on the western side of Karmelitská Street gives access to a courtyard, beyo
which is one of Prague's finest Baroque gardens.

In 1631, the nobleman Sezima of Vrtba joined two town houses together to ma
himself a palace; one of the houses had been confiscated from Kryštof Harant
Polžice and Bezdružice, executed with the other Protestant rebels on Old Tov
Square in 1621. A century later, the architect František Maxmilián Kaňka rem
delled the building, and above all created a masterpiece of a terrace garden on t
steep slope to the south. Closed off and neglected for many years, then comp
hensively restored, the garden lacks the charming patina of continuous use a
care, but remains a supreme expression of Central European Baroque landsca
art.

The approach is via an archway topped by a Hercules sculpted by Matthias Berna
Braun, whose workshop was responsible for the rest of the garden's rich endc
ment with **statuary**. The lowest level consists of a parterre flanked by an **aviary** a
a **sala terrena**, with murals by V.V. Reiner. Concealed steps lead to the next level,
elaborate **parterre**, from which a further, much grander stairway rises on either s
of the central axis. The principal array of statuary, arranged along a balustra

makes a fascinating foreground to one of the finest **views**★★ of Malá Strana and the city beyond. Higher still, a geometrically subdivided glacis slopes up to a grotto-like belvedere, from whose upper level there is an even more stunning urban panorama, as well as a close-up view of the garden pavilion of the Schönborn Palace.

③ SOUTHERN MALÁ STRANA

Busy **Karmelitská** (Street of the Carmelites) and its continuation, Újezd, follow the-alignment of the old highway connecting Malá Strana with other places along the left bank of the Vltava and with southern Bohemia. Neither street was included within the Romanesque walls of Malá Strana, while Újezd, which was also the name of the district, was cut in two in the 14C when Emperor Charles IV built the "Hunger Wall" and a new town gate. In the 17C and 18C the area was much sought after as a convenient location for noble families to build their town palaces, of which several still stand, like *no 18/379* (Thun-Hohenstein), *no 16/380* (Muscon), and *no 14/382* (Špork).

Panny Marie Vítězné (Church of Our Lady Victorious) ⊘ – *Karmelitská no 9/385* – In a city where Baroque art and architecture are so inextricably associated with the Counter-Reformation, it comes as a surprise to find that the very first church to be built in the new style was for a congregation of German Lutherans. Begun in 1611, and originally dedicated to the Holy Trinity, the church was renamed following the Battle of the White Mountain in 1620, when it was handed over to the Spanish Carmelites, one of whose number had sermonised the Catholic troops before their decisive defeat of Bohemian Protestantism. Between 1636-44 the church was extensively remodelled; its layout was completely reversed, with the altar relocated to the west end in order to allow the church's principal façade to face the street.

A conventional example of early Baroque architecture, the church enjoys international fame, particularly in Iberia and Latin America, as the home of the Bambino di Praga, the **Infant Jesus of Prague**★. This tiny waxwork figure with its crown and its regular change of costume was presented to the Carmelites in 1628 by an aristocratic lady of Spanish descent, Polyxena of Lobkowicz. Miraculous powers were soon attributed to the Infant; it was supposed to have protected the city from the plague and from destruction during the Seven Years War, it answered prayers and healed the sick. Poetry and celebratory accounts spread the figure's fame; one poem in praise of Prague's Little Jesus was written by Paul Claudel during his service here as French consul. Elaborate costumes were presented by admirers, one set by Empress Maria Theresa, who is supposed to have sewn hers herself, another, more improbably, by the Communist North Vietnamese government.

The Bambino di Praga presides over an altar in the north aisle of the otherwise sombre interior, in a sumptuous silver case among figures carved by Peter Prachner. Its state of frozen infancy has a grotesque parallel in the church's crypt, where a combination of favourable temperature and air-flow has mummified the corpses of a number of Carmelites and benefactors of their Order.

Palác Michnù z Vacínova (Michna Palace) – *Karmelitská no 40/450.* Several noble families including the the Kinskys and the Thuns have been associated with this palace since it was begun as a Renaissance villa in 1580, but it was Pavel Michna of Vacínov who rebuilt it in Baroque style on a grand scale in the mid 17C. The palace subsequently served as an arsenal and military hospital until it was acquired by the Sokol organisation in 1918 and renamed Tyršův dům (The Tyrš Building) after the movement's founder. One of the building blocks of modern Czech identity, the Sokol was the intensely nationalistic, Slav-oriented gymnastic movement of the late 19C and early 20C, banned by both the Austrians and the Nazis. The building houses the **Tyršovo muzeum tělesné výchovy a sportu** (Tyrš Museum of Physical Culture and Sport) ⊘. Nearly opposite, as its name suggests, U lanové dráhy (Funicular Way) leads up to the lower station of the lanovka, the Petřín funicular railway.

Sv. Jana na prádle (Church of St John at the Wash-house) – Together with the adjoining hospice, this tiny church makes a prettily rustic scene. Once the parish church of the Újezd district and one of Malá Strana's oldest places of worship, it dates from the early 12C, though in the 13C it was rebuilt in Gothic style and its choir was added in the 17C. In 1787, when the hospice was closed, the church became a public wash-house.

Kampa (Kampa Island) – The island is separated from the "mainland" of Malá Strana by the Čertovk **(Devil's Brook)**, an artificial channel constructed in the Middle Ages to drive the wheels of water-mills. Three mills still stand: the Sova Mill on the Vltava, much enlarged over the years and now derelict, the Hut Mill on the Čertovk, and the Grand Prior's Mill, also on the Čertovk, its picturesque waterwheel visible from Charles Bridge and from the footbridge leading to Velkopřevorské náměstí (Grand Prior's Square).

The Devil's Brook from Charles Bridge

The abode of ferrymen and of masons working on Charles Bridge, the Kam
remained largely free of building because of the constant risk of flooding. Most
it was given over to gardens and orchards belonging to the palaces on the far si
of the brook; in 1940 these were amalgamated to form a public park which h
been a favourite place for city centre dwellers to relax ever since, not least becau
of the wonderful views across the Vltava to Charles Bridge and the Old Town.

★ **Maltézské náměstí (Maltese Square)** – The name of the square recalls the long pr
sence in this part of Malá Strana of the Knights of Malta.
The fortified and fully sovereign enclave of this Crusader Order was establish
close to the bridgehead as early as 1169, and remained under the jurisdiction
the Order's Grand Prior well into the 19C. The Order was also known as the Knigh
of St John, after their patron saint; his statue, originally part of a fountain, stan
at the northern end of the square. Aside from the flow of traffic, and with
wealth of well-preserved Baroque and Rococo buildings, the area made an id
setting for Miloš Forman's film *Amadeus.* Building *no 8/480* was for many yea
the city's post office, the terminus for the stage coach from Vienna, and the reas
why this part of Malá Strana was once Prague's hotel district. Among the famo
who stayed locally was Beethoven, whose 1789 sojourn at the Golden Unico
Hotel is commemorated by a plaque at *no 11/285* Lázeňská Street.
Now the Japanese Embassy, *no 6/477,* the Rococo **Turbovský palác (Turba Palace)** is
particularly fine example of the work of the architect Josef Jáger, but the southe
part of the square is dominated by the huge early Baroque **Nostický palác (Nostiz Palace**
built around a courtyard in 1660-70, probably by the architect of the Černín Palac
Francesco Caratti. The balustrade statuary consist of copies of works by Brokoff, wh
the splendid portal is a later, Rococo addition. Regular chamber concerts are held
the palace, carrying on the cultural traditions of the Nostiz family; their library a
art collection were internationally famous, **Františck Antonín Nostic** (1725-94) was t
builder of the Estates Theatre, and among the many intellectuals supported by t
family was Josef Dobrovský. The Nostiz Palace is now the Netherlands Embassy.

★ **Panny Marie pod řetězem (Church of Our Lady beneath the Chain)** ⊘ – The great Rom
nesque basilica built by the Knights of Malta was mostly demolished in the l
14C to make way for an equally imposing Gothic church. But the Hussite troub
intervened, and the church was never completed, though the stumps of its tw
towers stand, their austere masonry massively buttressed, a reminder of a mc
austere age among the 18C charm of Malá Strana. Beyond, an open area w
remnants of the Romanesque arcades leads to the what was the choir of the Got
church, thoroughly Baroquised in the mid 18C. Škréta's high altar painting ce
brates the role of the Knights in the defeat of the Turks at the naval Battle
Lepanto in 1571.

Velkopřevorské náměstí (Grand Prior Square) – Two of Malá Strana's finest Baroc
palaces dominate this tranquil square. Completed in 1728 by Giuseppe Scotti,
Velkopřevorský palác (Grand Prior's Palace) is the residence of the Grand Prior of t
Knights of Malta. Used in Communist times as the national Museum of Musical I
truments, it has now been restituted to the Order and is once more severe
territory. Its larger neighbour on the far side of the square is the **Buquoyský p**

(Buquoy Palace), designed by Jean-Baptiste Mathey around 1632, and rebuilt by František Maximilián Kaňka in 1719. Prague was sufficiently important in Austrian times to have a French consul, housed here; since 1919 the building has been the French Embassy. The representative, not of a country, but of international youth culture, is depicted on the graffiti-covered wall opposite; the image of **John Lennon**, originally a defiantly spontaneous gesture during the last years of Communism, is now a tourist attraction, subject to restoration.

Na kampě (Kampa Island Square) – Of indefinable, partly ovoid shape, this delightful square with its lime trees is bordered by Baroque and Rococo houses of great charm, among them *no 1/498* U modré lišky (The Blue Fox), now the Estonian Embassy.

MUCHOVO Muzeum★
New Town
Panská 7, Metro Můstek or Náměstí Republiky

Often thought of as the quintessential representative of Parisian Art Nouveau, **Alfons Mucha** (1860-1939) was a Moravian who felt that his true mission in life was to point the way to a future in which the ideals of Czech nationalism would fuse with those of Slavonic and world brotherhood. While his turn of the century Parisian posters have been reproduced by the million, the *Slovanská epopej (Slavonic Epic)* cycle of paintings to which he devoted the last 30 years of his life remains little known, despite – or perhaps because of – its huge size and scope. But Mucha was active in in many spheres of the fine and decorative arts; the **exhibition** opened in 1998 in the 18C Kaunic Palace gives some idea of his many-sided talents, with sections devoted to his work in Paris, his less famous posters of Czech subjects, his oils, drawings and pastels. Fully aware of Mucha's international fame, the museum has labelling in English as well as Czech, video presentations, and a well-stocked shop.

Mucha poster

Alphonse/Alfons Mucha

Mucha was born in 1860 in the small town of Ivančice in southern Moravia. Failing to secure a place in the Prague Academy, he followed his own artistic path, eventually studying in Munich and Paris. A sudden rise to fame came with his rapidly sketched 1895 poster for **Sarah Bernhardt**'s *Gismonda*. Mucha became the toast of Paris, sharing a studio with Rodin and Gauguin, and promoting Art Nouveau design as a bridge between the fine arts and everyday needs. But, uneasy with what he came to regard as the decorative superficiality of Art Nouveau, he longed to rediscover his Slav roots, which he did, literally, by returning to Prague in 1910. Supported by the American millionaire Charles R Crane, he set to work on the grandiose concept of his *Slavonic Epic*, a cycle of 20 huge canvases depicting highly mythologised episodes from Czech and Slav history. At the same time he threw himself enthusiastically into the affairs of the nation, decorating the Mayor's Parlour in the Municipal House, preparing stained glass for the cathedral, even designing banknotes and calendars for the new republic of Czechoslovakia. His death in 1939, after questioning by the Gestapo, was an occasion for national mourning.

NA PŘÍKOPĚ ★

MOAT Street – Old Town (north side)/New Town (south side)
Metro Můstek/Náměstí Republiky

One of Prague's busiest downtown streets, Na příkopě follows the line of the Old Town walls between the Golden Cross at the foot of Wenceslas Square and the Municipal House on Náměstí Republiky. When the walls were demolished the moat was drained but not filled in. It became a useful dumping ground for all kinds of ordure, a lurking place for vagabonds, and a trap for unwary coachmen trying to negotiate the narrow road which ran alongside. Eventually, in 1760, it was levelled and a well-treed boulevard laid out in its place. In the late 19C, lined with prestigious banks and offices, it became the main focus of German life in Prague, the place where the Sunday promenade took place and where students from the German university would sport their colours in the hope of provoking passing Czechs. Right up until the Second World War, literary lions thronged the greatest of all Prague cafes, the Continental, with its choice of 250 newspapers and magazines. Cleared of traffic and trams, the Moat still has some notable historic buildings and is reinventing itself as a prestige shopping street.

FROM EAST TO WEST ALONG THE MOAT

The street starts off soberly with a pair of interwar bank buildings. To the south is the massive, symmetrical, curving facade of the **Česká národní banka** (Czech National Bank). To the north, the semi-circular portal of the **Komerční banka** (Commercial Bank) with its semi-circular portal makes a modest companion to the flamboyance of the neighbouring **Prašná brána** (Powder Tower) *(see p. 111)*.

Vernierovský palác (Vernier Palace) – *No 22/859 (south side)*. Named after its late 17C owner, Baron Vernier de Rougemont, this big Baroque palace was given a Classical façade at the end of the 18C. As the "Deutsches Casino" in the late 19C and early 20C it was the stronghold of Prague Germans and seat of the Concordia cultural association (called the Discordia by Max Brod, though in his memoirs he recalls the unforgettable experience of hearing Rilke reading his poems here). After 1945 it became the **Slovanský dům** (Slavonic House) and is currently under reconstruction.

★**Živnostenská banka (Investment Bank)** – *No 20/858 (south side)*. Designed by Osvald Polívka and completed in 1896, this splendid neo-Renaissance structure was built as the prestigious headquarters of the Zemská banka/Provincial Bank. Ranking with the other great national monuments in the city centre like the National Museum and the National Theatre it was lavishly decorated inside and out by artists of the calibre of Mikoláš Aleš, Stanislav Sucharda, Max Švabinský and Bohuslav Schnirch. The main feature is the central banking hall at first floor level, reached by a stairway

Stern Secession statuary high above Na příkopě

guarded by two Slav warriors in bronze. Rising through two stories from its mosaic floor to its stained glass ceiling, the hall has an extraordinarily rich decorative scheme which must have convinced any investor of the enormous potential of the Kingdom of Bohemia; there are statues representing the country's regions, allegories of rivers, the coats of arms of towns, and lunettes evoking qualities like thrift, industry, welfare and the unity of capital and labour.

The bank is linked by two bridges across Nekázanka Street to a later building *no 18/857*, also by Polívka, in a style marking the transition from historicism to Secession, completed in 1910 and with mosaics by **Jan Preisler**.

Sv.Kříže (Church of the Holy Rood) ⊙ – *(south side)*. Its massive portico gives the facade of this little neo-Classical church at the corner of Panská Street an impact all out of proportion to its size. It was completed in 1824 by Georg Fischer, architect of the Customs House in Náměstí Republiky. The interior with original furnishings has all the restrained elegance of the period. The church was linked to the Piarist monastery and its school which numbered Max Brod and Rilke among its pupils.

Myslbek – *(north side)*. Completed in 1997, this multiplex with its striking steel and glass facade represents the contemporary face of Na Příkopě.

Československá obchodní banka (Czechoslovak Trading Bank) – *No 14/854 (south side)*. There could hardly be a greater contrast than between the exuberant decoration of the Živnostenská banka and the sobriety of this bank, completed in 1933 by B Bendelmayer. A bronze bust of Božena Němcová (1820-62) is a reminder that the much-loved author of Babička *(Granny)* lived and died in the building which once stood on this site, the "Three Linden Trees" lodging-house.

Dům U černé růže (Black Rose House) – *No 12/853 (south side)*. The building that stood on this site in the early 15C was given by the Hussites to their German-speaking allies, one of whom, Nicholas of Dresden, met martyrdom at the stake for propagating the teachings of John Huss in nearby Saxony. The building's neo-Renaissance façade of 1847 coexists with an interwar glass and concrete gallery running through to Panská Street by the Functionalist architect Oldřich Tyl.

Palác Sylva-Taroucca (Sylva Taroucca Palace) – *No 10/852 (south side)*. Not all of Na příkopě was redeveloped in the course of the 19C and 20C. Dating from 1751, this magnificent Rococo palace, now a casino, was a joint project by **K.I. Dientzenhofer** and **Anselmo Lurago**, its liveliness enhanced by cornice sculptures by Ignaz Platzer the Elder. The splendid stairway has further work by Platzer as well as plasterwork by Giovanni Bossi and frescoes by Václav Ambrozzi.

Komerční banka (Commercial Bank) – *No 3/390 (north side)*. Completed in 1908 by Josef Zasche for the Bank of Vienna, the severe granite facade and austere sculptural decoration of this building had a great influence on other architects and designers, turning them away from the florid excesses of Secession style. Opposite, No 4/847 with its richly modelled facade was the city's first purpose-built department store, completed around 1870. In Communist times it was the city's prime fashion store, the Dům elegance (House of Elegance).

NÁRODNÍ DIVADLO★★
NATIONAL THEATRE
Národní třída 2 New Town Metro Národní třída Trams 6, 9, 17, 18, 21,22

rhaps the greatest landmark of the Czech National Revival, this great neo-Renaisnce structure was the "gift of the nation to itself", as the inscription over the scenium arch – *Národ sobě* – recalls; the money for the building was raised by a scription to which virtually every Czech, however humble, made their contribution. e foundation stone – taken from Mount Říp where Čech, the legendary father of nation, had first gazed out over the promised land of Bohemia – was laid in 1868, d the theatre was opened on 11 June 1881 with a performance of Smetana's opera *uše*. Nine days later the building was a shell, gutted by a fire accidentally started workmen. Undaunted, the nation rallied round, and within nine months the funds reconstruction had been collected. Special "theatre trains" brought people from parts of the country to admire the great edifice they had paid for.

The National Theatre Generation – The theatre's designer was the architect **Josef Zítek**, followed by **Josef Schultz** who supervised reconstruction after the fire. There are three main elements, the theatre itself with its massive roof, the **Prozatímní divadlo** (Provisional Theatre) of 1862 which now houses the actors wardrobe, and the annexe called the Schulzův dům (Schulz Building).

The National Theatre

The theatre was lavishly decorated by the best Czech artists and sculptors of t
day, known ever after as "The National Theatre Generation". The pavilions to eith
side of the entrance arcade are adorned with Roman chariots designed by **Bohus**
Schnirch, while the statues on the wall facing the embankment are by **Myslbek**. T
ornate interior is decorated with paintings by **Aleš** and **Ženišek** celebrating the A
and the Czech Nation. Seating 1 700, the main auditorium has an allegorical ceili
painting by Ženišek while the curtain recalls the role of the Czech people in helpi
to create this great national institution.

Between 1977-83 the National Theatre was extended eastwards along Náro
třída by means of the **Nová scéna**, a building whose façade of glass blocks has r
met with universal approval and which has even been likened to bubble-wrap.

NÁRODNÍ MUZEUM★

NATIONAL MUSEUM Prague 1 New Town
Václavské náměstí 68 Metro Muzeum

Forming a magnificent terminal feature to the vista up Wenceslas Square, the mor
mental building of the **National Museum** has become an unmistakable symbol of Prag
and of the Czech nation.

The origins of the institution of which this is the headquarters were aristocratic a
patriotic. It was founded in 1818 by Count Kaspar Sternberg with the support of t
Castle Burgrave, Count Kolowrat, and its first collections were those donated by s
dious noblemen keen on contributing to a complete "scientific picture of our Bohem
fatherland". At first the collections were housed in a variety of more or less unsuita
premises around the town, but in 1885 the construction of a bespoke neo-Renaissar
building was begun to the design of Josef Schulz, on the site of the Old Town g
which stood at the top of Wenceslas Square. The huge edifice was opened five ye
later; its lavish architectural treatment and its array of statuary celebrating the nat
and its famous offspring immediately earned it equal ranking to the capital's other gr
national monument, the Národní divadlo (National Theatre), completed in 1883. It v
a particularly humiliating blow to Czech pride when Soviet soldiers raked the museur
facade with cannon fire in the course of the 1968 invasion.

The museum's resources are immense. However, some of its riches are on disp
elsewhere *(see index)* and much is in store, though there is a full programme
temporary exhibitions, oft
of great interest. On disp
here – in part in their centu
old showcases – are exhibi
from the departments of P
history and Natural Histo
and the building is also
home of a scientific libr
of more than three mill
volumes.

Breaking the Monday rule

All over the Czech Republic, museums and
galleries close on Mondays. The National
Museum is the great exception, opening its
doors on Mondays, but remaining closed on
Tuesdays.

EXTERIOR

The museum's majestic presence is enhanced by the massive walls, steps and ramps which link it to Wenceslas Square, though their effect is diminished by the intense flow of traffic along the southbound carriageway of the *Magistrála* expressway. The principal facade, with basement rustication, Corinthian columns and corner cupolas, is 104 m long. Above it, the square central tower carries a 70 high dome and lantern. The fountain has reclining figures (left to right) of the country's two great rivers, the Elbe *(Labe)* (male) and the Vltava (female), presided over by Czechia herself, and other allegorical personages appear by the entrance, along the balustrade and to either side of the main tower.

INTERIOR

The vestibule is imposing enough, but the galleried main **stairway,** lit from above and with four flights of stairs reaching to the first floor, is truly monumental. Facing outward from the piers of the upper gallery are bronze busts of founders and benefactors, while in the spandrels below them are medallions depicting various rulers of the Czech kingdom. Between this vast interior space and the front of the building and directly beneath the dome is the equally awe-inspiring **Pantheon★,** intended to honour the nation's great and good. In the segments beneath the dome, allegorical oil-paintings by Vojtěch Hynais represent Science, Art, Inspiration and Power and Progress, while much bigger wall paintings by František Ženíšek and Václav Brožík show scenes from the nation's history featuring ploughman Přemysl, apostle Methodius, Emperor Charles IV, and humanist Komenský. Around the splendid circle of mosaic flooring are posed 47 sculptures and busts of such figures as martyr Hus, historian Palacký, composer Dvořák, and statesman Masaryk. There are no generals, but two women, the writer Božena Němcová and the poetess Eliška Krásnohorská.

Exhibits ⊘

First floor

Prehistory of the Czech lands and Slovakia – a major presentation of regional archeology in its European context, from Paleolithic times to the beginnings of the medieval kingdom of Bohemia.

Numismatics – the development of money from the earliest times to the present, plus medals, orders and awards.

Mineralogy and Petrology – one of the world's most important collections, with more than 10 000 specimens of rocks and minerals including precious stones.

Second floor: Zoology – A collection of more than 5 000 items, ranging from the 22.5 m skeleton of a fin-whale to the native fauna of the Czech lands including its 200-plus bird species. Among special features are the marsupials of Australia, including the extinct thylacine. Here too is the *Barrandeum,* housing the extraordinarily extensive fossil collections made by the indefatigable Joachim Barrande, who came to Prague as tutor to the Comte de Chambord, pretender to the French crown, but went on to become the great pioneer of Bohemian geology.

NÁRODNÍ TECHNICKÉ MUZEUM★★

NATIONAL TECHNICAL MUSEUM Kostelní 42, Prague 7 Holešovice

-am 1 from Metro Vltavská or Tram 26 from Náměstí Republiky to Letenské náměstí

used in a plain, purpose-built building of 1942 on the edge of Letná Plain, the ional Technical Museum displays a vast array of fascinating items, reminders of leading role that the Czech lands have often played in the advancement of nce, technology and industry. The heart of the museum is the great Transport l, its floor the domain of road vehicles and locomotives, while aircraft in frozen ht hang beneath its high glazed roof, but the other specialised galleries all have r own fascination. The origins of the collections go back to the enthusiasm of h progressively minded 19C people as Vojtěch Náprstek, whose own museum initially devoted to industrial progress, but the present institution, then known he Technical Museum of the Kingdom of Bohemia, was founded in 1908. Only action of its riches are on display, but its vast reserve stock is regularly drawn n for temporary exhibitions of high quality. A particularly valuable resource is museum's fine collection of drawings and other material illustrating the History Architecture.

VISIT ⊘

Basement – *(Guided tour available in English and German)*. The Metallurgy exhibition tells the story of ironworking from Antiquity to modern times, but the main feature of the basement is the kilometre and more of underground galleries, a **recreated coal and ore mine**. Originally laid out in the early 1950s in order to promote mining and encourage recruitment into the industry, the comprehensive displays of machinery and equipment have now acquired an historic character of their own. But, given the long history of mining and mineral extraction in this part of Central Europe, there are exhibits of far greater antiquity than these, among them a 15C-16C "hund", a primitive underground railway vehicle. A diorama of intense late medieval mining activity in Jáchymov in the Ore Mountains contrasts with a huge model of a north Bohemian landscape devastated by the impact of open-cast lignite extraction.

Ground floor – The **chronometry** exhibition has a fabulous array of timepieces from sundials to digital clocks, while **Interkamera** has 2.500 items which together tell the **story of photography and film**, including an example of an Edison revolving studio and the Lumiére projector used for Prague's first movie shows. The cinema and accommodation for temporary exhibitions are on this floor.

Transport Hall – Galleries running round the walls of the hall are filled with transport memorabilia giving a comprehensive view of transport by road, river, sea, rail and air, but the main attraction is the superb array of road and rail vehicles and of aircraft *(the country's main collection of aircraft is on show in the Letecké muzeum)*. Among the fragile-looking early flying machines suspended from the ceiling is Igo Etrich's **Zanonia glider** of c 1905 and the **Bler monoplane** in which Jan Kašpar flew from Pardubice to Prague in 1911. The "**Tractor**" biplane was one of several such machines which served with the Czechoslovak Legions as they fought their way out of Russia in 1918-9, while the tiny French **Pou du ciel** ("flying flea") was the interwar equivalent of a motor scooter. A number of streamlined sports planes are evidence of Czechoslovak achievements in this field.

The earliest steam engine on display is the massive **Kladno**, built by the Vienna-Györ works in 1855 for use on the railway linking Prague with Buštěhrad. It a crude and heavy machine compared with the thoroughbred **express locomotive no 375007** of 1911, a product of the Prague-Libeň workshops. Outstanding among the railway rolling stock is the **Imperial saloon car**, made in Prague and presented to Emperor Franz Josef by the House of Representatives of Bohemia for his 18

Jubilee. Its interior, of neo-Baroque opulence, is most matched by the vehicle built for the ill-fated Archduke Franz Ferdinand, a palace on wheels which eventually became part of the official government train and was still in service in 1959.

The most venerable automobile on display is the **Benz Viktoria** of 1893, while the **NW Präsident** of 1895 which made a successful journey to Vienna in the same year, is the grandfather of all the vehicles made later at the famous Tatra works at Kopřivnice in Moravia. From the interwar years, when the Czechoslovak motor industry was the fifth largest in the world, are examples of marques such as Praga, Lauren and Klement, Walter and Praga as well as Tatra. The big black Tatra 80 built for President Masaryk in 1935 is severely conventio

Veteran Skoda

Ph. Gajic/MICHELIN

compared with the streamlined, air-cooled **Tatra 77a** of only two years later, a pioneering machine capable of 150kph which was much sought after by German officers during the Occupation. The prestige of much-maligned Škoda was enhanced by the 130RS of 1978, an unbeatable rally performer in the late 1970s and early 1980s.

First floor – With a number of interactive exhibits, the **Noise Ecology** exhibition gives a fascinating introduction to the study of acoustics. An exhibition on Telecommunications is currently in preparation.

Second floor – The **Astronomy** exhibition has objects from as far back as the 15C, but its high point is the wonderful collection of objects evoking the Prague of Emperor Rudolf II and his retinue of Renaissance stargazers. Here are sextants used by Keppler and Tycho Brahe, a sundial by Erasmus Haberemel, and a superb celestial globe made by Blaeu, a pupil of Brahe.

NÁRODNÍ Třída★

NATIONAL Avenue New Town/Old Town
Metro Můstek or Národní třída

ke Na Příkopě, this broad street was laid out along the line of the walls of the Old wn when the defensive moat was filled in. Its first name was New Avenue, then rdinand Avenue in honour of the former Emperor. Its present name dates from the unding of the new state of Czechoslovakia on 28 October 1918. This momentous ite is also celebrated, as 28 října, in the name of the short street linking Národní to e foot of Wenceslas Square. In the early 20C, the city's Germans having appropri- ed Na příkopě for their Sunday promenade, the Czechs held their *korzo* on Národní, nich meets the river at two of the city's great institutions, the National Theatre and e Slavia café.

nlike pedestrianised Na Příkopě, Národní has kept its trams and other traffic, giving a quite distinct flavour; lined with stores and institutional buildings of a predomin- ntly early 20C character, the street has been the scene of some of the century's most teful events and demonstrations.

FROM WENCESLAS SQUARE
TO THE NATIONAL THEATRE ALONG NÁRODNÍ

An island of buildings separates 28 října from Jungmannovo náměstí, and another building, a pretty Rococo structure, stands in isolation in the pedestrianised area to the rear of the Wenceslas Square Baťa store. Tucked away in a corner is a real curiosity, the world's only **Cubist street lamp**, a *jeu d'esprit* in chiselled concrete, prob- ably designed by Emil Králíček around 1912.

★**Panny Marie Sněžné (Our Lady of the Snows)** ⊘ – Begun in 1347, this great church was intended by Emperor Charles IV to dominate the lower part of the New Town, but building was brought to a halt by the Hussite Wars and only the choir was ever completed. With a height of 30 m it is imposing enough, the city's greatest Gothic structure other than the cathedral, well able to accommodate the Baroque furnishings subsequently added to the interior. The radical priest Jan Želivský preached here, and it is here that he was entombed after his execution in 1422.

Jungmannovo náměstí (Jungmann Square) – The square and its pensive statue com- memorate **Josef Jungmann** (1773-1847), one of the key figures of the Czech National Revival. A tireless writer and translator, Jungmann more than anyone else estab- lished the Czech language as a modern, expressive medium of communication, not least through his monumental 120000 entry Czech-German dictionary of 1834-9. On *Jungmannova*, the street also named after him, *no 30/748*, the former **Mozarteum**, was one of the first truly modernist buildings in Prague. Completed by **Jan Kotěra** in 1913 and now housing an art gallery, it was a multi-functional building with a concert hall which later became the home of DF Burian's "total theatre", *Divadlo B*.

★**Palác Adrie (Adria Palace)** – *(south side)*. Built by for the Italian insurance company *Riunione Adriatica di Sicurtá* between 1922-4, this fantastical fortress-like struc- ture with its boldly modelled façades is the most ambitious project carried out in the Rondo-Cubist style unique to Czechoslovakia. The architects were **Pavel Janák** and Josef Zasche, while the extensive sculptural decoration was by **Jan Štursa**, **Bohumil Kafka** and others. The building was famous as the home of the basement theatre of the *Laterna Magica* (now Theatre *Za branou II*), reached via a

Adria Palace

splendidly ornate *pasáž*; it was here in November 1989 that a chain-smoking Vác▮ Havel and his Civic Forum comrades closeted themselves while planning the mov▮ which led to the Velvet Revolution.

Palác Porgesů z Portheimu (Porges z Portheimu Palace) – *No 38/37 (south side* This 15-bay late Baroque palace, once the home and workshop of the **Brok▮** dynasty of sculptors, has a plaque commemorating the stay here in the winter 1799-1800 of the great Russian commander Suvorov.

No 26/63 – *(south side)*. Built in 1970-4 as a department store with the rousi▮ name of *Máj* (May), this multi-storey structure (now *Tesco*) presents a rather bla▮ façade to Národní. By contrast, its rear, almost entirely glazed facade gives c▮ tomers using the escalators a fine view of the bustling activity filling the squa▮ around the Národní Metro station.

No 16/118 – *(south side)*. In the arcade of this little Baroque palace which w▮ probably the work of FM Kaňka is a small sculpture of imploring hands, the mc▮ ument to the "Massacre" of 17 November 1989, when a student demonstratic▮ one of the key events leading up to the Velvet Revolution, was brutally put do▮ by riot police.

★**Sv. Voršily (St Ursula's Church)** – *(south side)*. Built 1698-1704 for the Ursuli▮ Convent by Marco Antonio Canevale, this was one of the earliest High Baroq▮ churches in Prague. Its layout, with a central doorway and internal spaces ru▮ ning parallel to the street, was the first of its kind. The splendidly restored ▮ terior is particularly ornate, with statues by F Preiss, an altar painting of St U▮ sula by K. Liška, and an *Assumption* by **P. Brandl**. Part of the convent has lo▮

The "Massacre"

One week after the breaching of the Berlin Wall in November 1989, a demonstration took place which was to lead to the resignation of Czechoslovakia's Communist government and the subsequent Velvet Revolution. Prague's students wished to commemorate the 50th anniversary of events which took place on 17 November 1939, when German police invaded dormitories and arrested more than 1 000 students; several were shot, the remainder sent to a concentration camp, and all Czech institutions of higher education were closed down.

With official approval, thousands of young people set off on 17 November 1989 on a peaceful march from the National Cemetery at Vyšehrad. A breakaway group decided to continue the march along Národní towards Wenceslas Square. They were first halted, then subjected to a vicious, unprovoked attack by riot police. Television pictures of police wielding batons on bloodied heads, and rumours of a dead student being spirited away in a van caused popular outrage and led directly to the far bigger demonstrations heralding the end of the regime.

been a well-known restaurant, but encroachment by the expanding National Theatre on property restituted after 1990 to the Ursulines has led to complex legal wrangling.

★ **Nos 7/1011 and 9/1010** – *(north side)*. This pair of office buildings are among the city's most elegant edifices of the Secession period. Both were designed by Osvald Polívka, *no 7* for the Prague Insurance Co. in 1903-6, *no 9* in 1906-8 for the well-known publisher F. Topič. The harmonious façades combine clear structure with profuse – but not too profuse – ornamentation using lettering, stucco, mosaic, statuary and relief panels.

Café Slavia – *No 1/1012 (north side)*. This famous café at the corner of Národní and the Vltava embankment enjoys superlative views over the river towards Malá Strana and Hradčany. As a haunt of intellectuals it had an exceptionally long period of glory, beginning when Smetana sat at a table composing *The Bartered Bride* and ending only in the early 1990s when it closed its doors on its clientele of former dissidents and secret policemen. Now reopened, it has yet to re-establish its reputation.

★ **Národní divadlo (National Theatre)** – *See p. 159*.

The underground labyrinth at *no. 20* Národní is the home of Reduta, Prague's most famous stronghold of jazz. As well as the clubroom where President Clinton played saxophone to an audience including Czech President Havel and Prime Minister Klaus, there is a music store, cinema, gallery, and black theatre.

Ph. Gajic/MICHELIN

Decorative lettering, Národní Třída 7

165

NOVÉ MĚSTO ★
NEW TOWN

Bounded by the Vltava at both extremities, the **Nové Město** (New Town) wraps its
around the Old Town, covering an area several times the size of the city's ancie
core. As is frequently the case in Prague, the "newness" is relative; the New Tov
was laid out in the mid 14C on the orders of a ruler determined to transform the c
and to make it a fitting "capital" for the Holy Roman Empire. The Gothic cathedr
and the great bridge across the river formed part of **Emperor Charles IV's** vision f
Prague, but the conception and construction of the New Town was his greate
achievement, perhaps the most extraordinary feat of urban planning in the whole
medieval Europe. Its success can be gauged by its endurance; many of the landmar
planned six and a half centuries ago still act as focal points and the city's life still flo
along the streets and squares laid out by Charles' surveyors, above all in **Václav**
náměstí (Wenceslas Square).

Practical considerations as well as prestige played a role in Charles' plan. The C
Town was becoming overcrowded, with little separation of living space from noisc
activities such as tanning, brewing, metalworking and slaughtering, hardly a suitab
setting for the new university the Emperor had in mind. In 1347 he signed the dc
ument laying the legal foundation for the New Town; it promised the citizens "honc
freedom, well-being, joy and protection against all violent conflict". The small pr
offered generous tax exemptions for those taking up residence, provided that th
respected an array of ordinances; construction work had to start as soon as a p
was assigned and had to be completed within 18 months and even the buildi
materials to be used were specified. Buildings soon began to line the broad ne
streets, the first structures going up at the corner of present-day Jindřišská Stre
and **Wenceslas Square**. The original name of Wenceslas Square was the **Horse Market**, whi
together with two other great market spaces helped articulate the whole scheme a
give it coherence. In the north was the **Hay Market** (still with the same name – Se
ovážné náměstí – today), balanced in the south by the **Cattle Market** (now called Karlc
náměstí in honour of the New Town's founder).

Within the astonishingly short space of two years, the whole area of the New Tov
had been enclosed by a 3.5 km stretch of impressive fortifications, linked to improv
defences at Vyšehrad, Malá Strana and Hradčany and pierced only by three gates a
a tower. The huge labour force used to build these defences was saved by Char
from unemployment and destitution by being drafted to work on the so-cal
"Hunger Wall" on Petřín Hill.

People quickly saw the advantages of moving to the New Town, though the Je*
whom Charles wished to attract there preferred the reassuringly familiar confines
the ghetto. Most of the new inhabitants were Czechs, drawn from the countryside
from the Old Town, whose affairs were still largely under the thumb of German pa
cian families. Within a decade, the New Town's success could be gauged by t
presence of a hundred or more butchers shops, a figure not exceeded before the 19
And it was not until the 19C and the demolition of the fortifications that Prague fina
burst the bounds set for it six and a half centuries before, in the visionary project co
ceived by one of its most revered rulers.

The Magistrála – The line of Charles IV's fortifications is followed by this gre
north-south urban expressway, which has caused much environmental controvers
and seems to draw in much of the city region's through traffic. Crossing the de
Nusle ravine on a spectacular bridge, it runs through the southern New Town
Legerova and Sokolská Streets, then hems in the **Národní muzeum** (National Museu
– *see p. 160*) and **Statní opera** (State Opera – *see p. 192*) before passing the Hla
nádraží (Main Railway Station – *see below*) and continuing on an elevated secti
towards the **Hlávkův most** (Hlávka Bridge) *(see p. 220)*.

★**Hlavní nádraží (Main Station)** – With the exception of the **Obecnú dům** (Municij
House), this is Prague's greatest public building in Secession style, intended
introduce the city to its visitors with as much panache as possible. It consists o
twin-towered central hall flanked by symmetrical wings with their own towers, a
is formidable enough in scale to have survived the assault of the expressway a
the addition of a vast new concourse in the 1970s. Beyond the huge glazed ar
of the central hall is a splendid semi-circular **dome** with characteristically proft
Art Nouveau decoration and a glimpse down into a central well of commuters sc
rying to and from the platforms. The station has had more than one name;
Austro-Hungarian days it honoured Emperor Franz Josef, then in the fi
Czechoslovak Republic, US President Wilson. Under Nazism and Communism
became plain Main Station (Hlavní nádraží), a name it is still generally known I
though a plaque records the reinstatement of its prewar title (Wilsonovo nádra
when Wilson's successor, George Bush, came here in 1991.

*Make the most of your **Michelin Green Guide**
by consulting the key on page 9.*

NOVÝ SVĚT★

NEW WORLD Hradčany

Tram 22 to Brusnice or Pohořelec

ut off by the Baroque fortifications from the world outside, this isolated part of the
astle District is old world rather than new. It has a village-like charm, with crooked
reets and alleyways, flights of steps, old houses, fine trees, and secluded gardens
dden behind high walls. The area takes its name from Nový svět, the straggling
reet which once meandered between the castle and the countryside beyond, but
hich is now a virtual cul-de-sac.

the very edge of town, and first built-up in the 16C, Nový svět was where the castle
rvants were squeezed into squalid lodgings. Later it attracted a more refined kind of
tainer; both Tycho Brahe and his colleague and competitor Johannes Kepler are sup-
osed to have lived here while waiting for superior accommodation to be assigned to
em by Emperor Rudolph II. In more recent times the area has been colonised by
tists and writers, and so far has resisted the pressures of commercialisation.

Evening light in Nový Svět

Černínská – Running roughly parallel to the Baroque fortifications, this narrow
cobbled street drops gently downhill from Loretánské náměstí (Loretto Square)
along the wall of the Capuchin Monastery of 1602 *(See p135)*. A delightful miniature statue of St John Nepomuk atop a garden wall to the left seems to welcome
visitors to the area.

Nový svět – Mostly on the south side of the twisting cobbled street, Nový svět's
buildings range from the humblest of single-storey dwellings to substantial town
houses. *No 25/90*, **U zlatého pluhu** (The Golden Plough), was the birthplace in 1857
of František Ondříček, a celebrated violinist, while *no 1/76*, **U zlatého noha** (The
Golden Griffin), was the joint residence of **Tycho Brahe** and **Johannes Kepler**. Tycho is
supposed to have complained to the Emperor that his work was impossible because
of the continual ringing of the Capucins' bells; the indecisive Rudolph first ordered
the monks to be expelled, than relented when they presented him with a fine
painting. The adjacent early 18C building with its attractive stucco façade is
U zlaté hrušky (The Golden Pear), a famous restaurant, which, together with its
garden opposite, has something of the atmosphere of a country inn.

Sv. Jana Nepomuckého (Church of St John Nepomuk) ☉ – Completed in 1729, this
was the first church to be built by **Kilián Ignác Dientzenhofer**. Serving the adjacent
Ursuline convent, it has splendid ceiling paintings by VV Rainer depicting the dramatic life of the saint.

*Use the index at the end of the guide to locate the text
describing a particular sight.*

OBECNÍ DŮM★★★

MUNICIPAL HOUSE Náměstí Republiky 5/1090, Old Town
Metro Náměstí Republiky

No expense was spared at the beginning of the 20C to make the Obecní dům (Muni‹
ipal House) a focal point of the expanding city, with salons, concert halls, restauran‹
and reception rooms fit for a burgeoning metropolitan life suffused with the spirit ‹
Czech nationalism. In a key position next to the Powder Tower on the edge of th‹
Old Town, the Municipal House was closed for a thoroughgoing restoration for thre‹
years from 1994; though accusations have been made of over-restoration, this gre‹
symbol of turn-of-the-century Prague once more glitters in all its Secession glory.

HISTORY

Towards the end of the 14C, following a great fire at the castle, Václav IV built
royal palace at the point where the ancient trade route from the east entered the O‹
Town. The Bohemian kings resided here for a century or so before returning ‹
Hradčany, whereupon the palace became a seminary, then a barracks, before fallin‹
into disrepair and eventually being demolished in 1902.
The idea for a multi-purpose building which would accommodate a variety of activitie‹
add to the prestige of the growing city and act as a counterweight to the German don‹
inance of Na Příkopě had already been canvassed, and in 1903 the architects **Anto‹
Balšánek** and **Osvald Polívka** were commissioned to carry out the work. As had been th‹
case at the National Theatre, a whole generation of artists collaborated on the projec‹
their efforts resulting in extraordinarily rich effects inside and out, though by the tim‹
of the building's completion its design and extravagant ornamentation was considere‹
outdated, if not decadent. At the same time the most advanced technical services we‹
fitted, including pneumatic message delivery and cleaning by suction.
On 28 October 1918, the independence of Czechoslovakia from Austria-Hungary w‹
proclaimed at the Municipal House, a fact commemorated by a stylish memorial plaq‹
by **Ladislav Šaloun** on the corner of the building. The Municipal House is the home ‹
the Prague Symphony Orchestra and it is here that the Prague Spring Festival is he‹
alded every year with a rousing performance of Smetana's *Má vlast*.

EXTERIOR

Balšánek and Polívka had to contend with an awkwardly shaped site and the pro‹
imity of the venerable Powder Tower. Their building is an irregular diamond shap‹
in plan, with a principal façade of two wings of unequal length which meet at ‹
portal of the utmost ostentation. Topped by a glazed copper dome, the edifi‹
draws its inspiration from the great neo-Baroque monuments of late-19C Paris li‹
Garnier's Opera, but its decoration is almost entirely in the spirit of the Prag‹
Secession.
The most eye-catching feature of the **portal** is the colourful **mosaic** in the semi-circ‹
of the gable. Based on a painting by Karel Špillar, it depicts the *Apotheosis ‹
Prague*, and is bordered by a lengthy exhortation in gilt letters from the pen ‹
the poet Svatopluk Čech "Hail to thee, Prague! Stand steadfast against Time a‹
Malice as you have withstood the storms of ages". To either side of the gable a‹
groups of statues by Šaloun representing the *Humiliation of the Nation* and (wi‹
a copper eagle) its Revival. The balcony below with its jewel-like metalwork is su‹
ported by columns topped by figures bearing lanterns. Elsewhere on the faça‹
are more allegorical figures as well as the floral ornamentation so characteristic ‹
the Secession; among the heads between the first floor windows are two repr‹
senting *Motoring* and *Aeronautics*.

INTERIOR

The **ground floor** and **basement** of the building, easily accessible to the public at larg‹
are largely given over to places of refreshment. To the right of the foyer with ‹
reliefs of Flora and Fauna by **Bohumil Kafka** is the high-ceilinged and elegant **Fr‹
couská restaurace** (French Restaurant), its decor a harmonious fusion of gleami‹
fittings and pale wood. Among the paintings is a charming *Prague Welcoming H‹
Guests* as well as allegories of *Hop-growing* and *Viticulture*. To the left of the foy‹
is the equally spacious **Café**, especially well-frequented in summer when it opens ‹
doors on to the pavement. Though the clientele may have changed, it still h‹
something of the atmosphere of a typical establishment from the early years of t‹
20C. At the far end, completing the opulent effect, is an illuminated fountain w‹
a resident nymph.
Close to the foot of the grand double stairway is the original porter's lodge, wh‹
beyond is a shop, a small café and the ticket office.
Other stairs, with ceramic panels depicting scenes of old Prague, lead to the ba‹
ment, where a wall fountain plays in the vestibule. The **American Bar** with its supe‹
central chandelier, designed like many of the building's light fittings by **F Křižík**

decorated with reproductions of rustic scenes originally drawn by Mikoláš Aleš. Beneath the vault of the **Plzeňská restaurace** (Pilsen Restaurant) is appropriately dark beer hall furniture as well as cheerful paintings like *Bohemian Harvest* in ceramic frames.

The planning and decoration of the more functional spaces of the Obecní dům was given as much attention as the rest of the building, as is evident from the treatment of the lifts, cloakroom, pool hall, stairways and the main foyer on the first floor. From here splendid doorways lead into the building's prestigious core, the **Smetanova síň** (Smetana Hall), a multi-purpose 1300-seat space used for balls, receptions and fashion shows as well as concerts. The hall is a splendid confection of stucco, statuary and painting, top lit through a central circular window and other areas of stained glass. On both sides of the proscenium arch, dynamic sculptural groups by Šaloun represent *Vyšehrad* and *Slavonic Dances*, while allegories of *Music, Dance, Poetry and Drama* appear in the ceiling and wall paintings. A medallion of Smetana graces the great organ.

★**Ceremonial Rooms** – *Guided tour in various languages*. The building's ornamental sumptuousness reaches fresh heights in this suite of rooms on the first floor.

The **Patisserie** is an appetising confection of mirrors, pastel colours, pale wood, and stuccowork like icing, while the decor of the **Moravian-Slovak Saloon** is inspired by folk motifs from the eastern part of the Czech lands, though its aquarium, fed by snails, is a unique feature. The **Božena Němcová Room** honours this much loved author with a seated figure of the central character from her most famous novel, *Babička (Granny)*. The exotic decoration of the **Oriental Room** includes coloured glass embedded in the stuccowork; it was called the Serbian Room until Austria-Hungary declared war on that country in 1914.

The **Grégr Hall** is one of several larger spaces named after prominent personages of the National Revival. Originally called the Debating Hall, it has a minstrels' gallery, an allegorical ceiling painting and walls of artificial marble with paintings by F. Ženíšek. The **Palacký Hall** features a bust of the great man by **Myslbek** and paintings by **Jan Preisler** evoking the *Golden Age of Mankind*.

The ceremonial core of the building is the Primátorský sál, the hall named for the city's Lord Mayor or *Primátor*. Its decor, the crystallisation of an intense Czech patriotism, was the responsibility of that most acclaimed of Secession artists, **Alfons Mucha** (though the prominence given here to his talents was resented by some of his contemporaries). The ceiling fresco of a mythic eagle and joyful Slavs is carried on pendentives depicting virtues, all of them represented by figures from Czech history. Thus *Independence* is personified by King George of Poděbrady, *Justice* by John Huss, *Militancy* by one-eyed Hussite general Jan Žižka. The solemn message of the three wall-paintings is reinforced by lettering of the utmost elegance proclaiming such slogans as "With strength towards freedom, with love towards concorde". Mucha also designed the stained glass and the curtains with their elaborate hand-pulls were sewn by students under his supervision.

The **Rieger Hall**, with its pantheon of worthies, and the large **Sladkovský Hall** with its silk-like wallpaper, complete this wonderful series of Secession spaces.

On the attic floor, the circular **Hollar Room** leads to top-lit halls used for exhibition purposes.

The Lord Mayor's Parlour in the Obecní dům

R. Mazin/DIAF

Náměstí Republiky (Republic Square) – Despite its architectural incoherence, Náměs
Republiky is one of Prague's focal points, situated at the interface between C
and New Towns, with a Metro station and an important tram stop. Facing t
Obecní dům is the stern grey facade of **U Hybernů**, built in 1811 by Georg Fisc
and a rare example in Prague of an Empire-style building; on the site of
monastery once inhabited by Hibernian ie Irish monks, it served for many years
the Custom House. To the north is the characteristically modest mid-17C **Capuc
Church of St Joseph**, opposite which is one of the city's main department stores, **Kot**
built along Swedish lines in the 1970s.

Hybernská – This street leads directly from Náměstí Republiky to **Masarykovo nádr**
(Masaryk Station). Prague's first railway terminus, it still has the original stat
building which was the centre of much jubilation on 20 August 1845 as the fi
train steamed in.

Hybernská has a number of fascinating buildings. *No.10/1001*, the **Hotel Central**
1899-1901, with leafy stucco about to envelop its elegant oriel, was one of t
city's first buildings designed in Secession style. On the opposite side of t
street is the 18C **Šporkův palác** (Sweets-Sporck Palace), carefully modernised
the versatile modernist architect Josef Gočár in the 1920s. The former **Pa
kinských** at *no 7/1033* was originally built by Carlo Lurago in the mid 18C;
1907 it became the headquarters of the Czech Social Democratic Party, anc
was here in 1912 that Vladimir Ilyich Lenin presided over an illegal conferer
of the All-Russian Social Democratic Party. In 1920 the building and its su
roundings were the scene of violent disturbances as the Czechoslovak sociali
split into Communist and centrist factions. After the 1948 coup, the Soc
Democratic Party was absorbed by the Communists, who took over the buildir
replaced the Baroque statuary with suitably proletarian figures and in 19
installed the Lenin Museum, now defunct.

Other memories are associated with building *no 16/1004* on the corner
Hybernská and Dlážděná, the **Café Arco**. In the early part of the 20C this was t
stronghold of the literary lions of German-speaking Prague, among them Fra
Werfel, Max Brod, Franz Kafka and Egon Erwin Kisch. The lion-tamer, hea
waiter Počta, shared their fame. The acerbic Karl Kraus christened the mos
Jewish clientele the "Arconauts", putting them down in a famous but untrai
latable line *"Es werfelt und brodet und kafkat und kischt"*.

Na Poříčí – Unlike ruler-straight Hybernská, this busy street of shops, hotels a
offices follows an erratic course eastwards from Náměstí Republiky, betraying
ancient origins. Meaning "By the River", Na poříčí linked the Old Town to the riv
side settlement known as St Peter's. Now forming the northern part of the N
Town, this was a quarter dominated from the mid 11C by German traders, who
church, Sv.Petra na Poříčí, rebuilt in Gothic and then neo-Gothic style and witl
free-standing bell-tower, still stands.

The outstanding building on Na Poříčí is *no 24/1046*, the former **Legio Bai
(Bank of the Legions★)**. Perhaps the city's finest example of the "Rondo-Cubi
style of the early 1920s, it has a monumental facade heavy with the circu
forms typical of this short-lived architectural movement. At first floor level a
remarkable sculptural reliefs by **Jan Štursa** and **Otto Gutfreund**, inspired by t
exploits of the Czechs and Slovaks who fought on many fronts in World W
One in the hope of liberating their country from Hapsburg rule. The lavish a
colourful decoration of the interior culminates in the **banking hall** with its supe
curved glazed roof.

OLŠANSKÉ Hřbitovy★

OLŠANY cemeteries Prague 3 Žižkov
Metro Flora and Želivského

Beyond the suburb of Vinohrady, covering a vast area where the village of Olšany or
stood, are Prague's largest cemeteries, the resting place of many of the city's me
famous figures. Beneath the canopy of venerable trees, the tombstones and mem
rials illustrate changing tastes in the aesthetic commemoration of the dead.

Olšanské hřbitovy (Olšany cemeteries) ⏱ – First laid out after the great plague
1680 and covering an area of several hectares, Olšany comprises ten individu
cemeteries, the older ones of which are now treated as historic conservation are
Among the various buildings the oldest is **Sv. Rocha** (St Roch's Church), built in 168
perhaps to a design by Jean-Baptiste Mathey. Despite the existence of the Sla
Cemetery on Vyšehrad, the list of eminent people buried resembles the natio
roll-call of honour. The tombs of such figures as **Josef Jungmann**, several memb

of the Mánes family, and the writer Eliška Krásnohorská attract pilgrims, but the most visited grave is that of **Jan Palach**, the tragic student who burnt himself to death in January 1969 in protest at the 1968 invasion.

On the far side of broad Želivského street are a number of military cemeteries as well as a Russian Orthodox cemetery. The **Orthodox church** was built in 1925 mainly to serve Prague's large interwar community of White Russian emigrés. Nearby are graves of soldiers of the anti-Soviet Vlasov Army, deemed "unpersons" during the Communist era, and kept from public view, while the memorials to Red Army soldiers were maintained immaculately. There are Tsarist bones here too, those of soldiers who fell in the Napoleonic Wars. Other sections are devoted to the graves of Czechoslovak legionaries and airmen, citizens who perished in the Prague Uprising of May 1945, and there is even a small British war cemetery.

Nový židovský hřbitov (New Jewish Cemetery) ⊘ – This extensive cemetery is Prague's third great Jewish burial ground, laid out in 1881 when the graveyard in Žižkov had no more space. With its ivy covered trees and space for expansion which was never necessary, it's a poignant place. The most visited grave, in plot 21, is that of **Franz Kafka**, which can be seen through the grille in the wall about 200 m east of the entrance when the cemetery is closed. His unusual memorial stele commemorates not just him but the parents who outlived him together with his three sisters who perished during the Occupation. Opposite his grave on the cemetery wall are plaques in memory of other Prague Jews, including Max Brod.

PETŘÍN ★

PETŘÍN HILL Malá Strana

Lanovka/funicular railway from Újezd to Petřín or Tram 22 to Pohořelec

omplementing the densely built-up historic quarters of Malá Strana and Hradčany, e gardens, orchards and woods of Petřín Hill help maintain the illusion of a city emingly untouched by modernity and still contained within its ancient boundaries. ouping together the Strahov, Seminary and Kinských Gardens, the Petřín is one of ague's most important parks, a glorious embayment which rises steeply to the ateau sweeping down from the White Mountain.

the past the hill played many roles. Its quarries provided the limestone from which any of Prague's medieval buildings were constructed. In the 1360s it was enclosed Emperor Charles IV's **"Hunger Wall"**, built to relieve unemployment. Vineyards nded here right up to the 18C. In the troubled times after the Thirty Years War the ll was a lurking place for robbers and deserters. But the Petřín always offered some the finest views over Prague, and in the early 19C, thanks to the efforts of ener-tic Count Chotek, it became a public park. A network of paths was laid out, some gzagging up and down the slopes, others providing easily graded contour walks. e little lanovka, the water-powered funicular railway, crawled up the hill for the

P. Wysocki/EXPLORER

The Petřín orchards in winter

first time in the Jubilee year of 1891, hauling visitors up to the *Rozhledna*, built imitation of the Eiffel Tower. In the 20C the woodland began to grow out of contr and the orchards to decay, though these are now being rescued by a long-term co servation and replanting programme and can still be relied upon to stage their splend springtime show of blossom.

ON FOOT FROM STRAHOVSKÝ KLÁŠTER (Strahov MONASTERY) TO KINSKÉHO ZAHRADY (KINSKY GARDENS)
About 2.5 km

Vineyard – At the viewpoint just below Strahov Monastery, a symbolic vineyar has been planted in memory of the extensive vineyards which once clad the slope here.

Rozhledna (Viewing tower) ⊘ – The tower was promoted by the Czech Tourist Clu whose delegates to the Paris International Exposition of 1889 had been impresse by the Eiffel Tower. 299 steps lead to the top. The view takes in the whole Prague and in clear weather – so it is claimed – the far-off Alps can be seen well as the Giant Mountains in northern Bohemia.

Bludiště (Mirror Maze) ⊘ – The distorting **mirrors** of the **maze** produce their infallib hilarious results. Supposedly resembling the medieval Vyšehrad Gate, the fancif mock-Gothic structure in which it is housed was the Tourist Club's pavilion at th 1891 Expo. Somewhat incongruously, it also contains a large-scale **diorama** evokir the battle of 1648 in which the Prague students stopped the Swedish soldiery fro crossing Charles Bridge.

Sv. Vavřince (Church of St Lawrence) ⊘ – There was a church on this spot as early the 12C and though the present building is a Baroque structure dating from arour 1740, it incorporates some Romanesque masonry. Next to the church is a Calva Chapel with a Holy Sepulchre and sgraffito to a design by Mikoláš Aleš. Anoth chapel, oval in form, terminates an early 19C via sacra with Stations of the Cros

Štefánikova hvězdárna (Štefánik Observatory) ⊘ – Reached through a gap in the Hung Wall, and attractively set among rose gardens, the observatory was opened 1928. It has telescopes which can be used by the public as well as an exhibitic on astronomy and is named after Milan Rastislav Štefánik (1880-1919), the Slova aviator and astronomer who was one of the founders of independent Czechosl vakia.

Lanová dráha (funicular railway) – Popularly known as the *lanovka*, the **funicular** w originally water-powered, then electrified in 1932. Neglected in the postwar perio it was damaged by a landslide and closed for many years, but is now fully restore It links the lower station at Újezd in Malá Strana with an upper station among th rose gardens. A halfway station gives access to *Nebozízek* ("Little Auger"), panoramic restaurant housed in a building which was once one of a number substantial vintners' residences scattered among the Petřín vineyards.

Sv. Michal (St Michael's Church) – Beyond the Hunger Wall stretch the Kins Gardens, landscaped in Romantic style with statuary, pools, and rocky outcrop and incorporated into the Petřín parklands in 1905. Lost in a clearing high u among the trees is this little Orthodox timber church with its trio of belfries. poignant reminder of the forgotten province of Carpatho-Ukraine, attached Czechoslovakia in 1919 and snatched from it by the Soviet Union in 1945, th church once stood among the Carpathian mountains in the village of Medvědovi – the place of bears. It was brought here in one piece in 1928 on behalf of th Ethnographic Museum.

Vila Kinských (Villa Kinsky) – Despite its present dilapidated state this large Empir style villa exudes an air of neo-Classical sophistication in utter contrast to th rusticity of the timber church on the slopes above. Built between 1827 and 183 for Count Rudolf Kinský by the Vienna architect Heinrich Koch, it was converte early in the 20C into the Ethnographical Museum, but is now closed. By the vil is a memorial to the actress Hana Kvapilová, while close to the entrance is charming statue of a young girl by Karel Dvořák entitled *"Fourteen"*. **Náměs Kinských** (Kinsky Square) used to bear the name Square of the Red Army Tankme and a Soviet T34 tank, supposedly the first to enter to the city in May 194 occupied a place of honour. After the Velvet Revolution no-one really knew wh to do with it, but after it had been painted pink, not once, but twice, the emba rassing tank was removed.

Visiting monuments and other buildings will be far more interesting once you have read the chapter in the Introduction on Art and Architecture.

Muzeum POLICIE ČR★

The national Police Museum is housed, somewhat incongruously, in the former Augustinian convent attached to one of the most fascinating of the churches founded in the New Town by Charles IV.

★Panny Marie a Karla Velikého na Karlově (Church of Our Lady and Charlemagne) – Seen from the Vyšehrad side of the Nusle valley, a landmark cluster of red cupolas rises over the fortifications originally raised by Emperor Charles IV to protect the New Town. The church to which they belong was begun by Charles in 1358 in honour of his great predecessor Charlemagne, its octagonal layout recalling that of the Imperial Chapel at Aachen. The spectacular vault of the nave, 24 m across, was completed by **Bonifaz Wohlmut** in 1575. The Baroque period left lively wall paintings, a grotto-like Bethlehem Chapel, and a staircase designed by Santini.

★Muzeum Policie (Police Museum) ⊘ – The museum *(some labelling in English and German)* draws something of a veil over the activities of the police – conventional and secret – during the Communist period, and to the regret of some visitors, the famous stuffed Alsatian Blek is no longer on display; working with the prestigious force guarding the border, Blek was responsible for the arrest of many a fugitive attempting to slip beneath the Iron Curtain. After reminding visitors that the first organised force was formed under Louis XIV of France, the museum concentrates on relatively non-controversial themes including History, Traffic Police, Criminology, and Interpol. Among the nuggets of historical information is the revelation that, like the other citizens of former Austria-Hungary, Czechs drove on the left, at least until the Germans arrived in 1939. There are plenty of evocations of horrible or spectacular crimes, and even a reconstruction of the chaos of a burgled apartment.

Some of the rooms of the former convent retain their splendid stuccoed ceilings. In the garden is a helicopter, a launch, and a children's traffic playground.

POŠTOVNÍ Muzeum

Dating originally from the early 16C, this building houses a fine collection of stamps and other memorabilia. Its philatelic interest is complemented by the charming 19C decor of some of its rooms.

Few traces remain outside the building of the source of miller Michalovic's wealth; the mills which stood here for centuries had all been demolished by the early 20C and the Vltava embankment around the approaches to the Štefánik Bridge has been comprehensively tidied up. Something of the picturesque atmosphere of past times, when the riverside was the domain of millers, fishmongers and loggers, is evoked by the early-17C **water tower** and the older buildings crouching nearby.

To the south of the Postal Museum, **St Clement's Church** is one of the city's oldest, dating from the 11C, though it has been much rebuilt.

The Museum ⊘ – The collection has a natural emphasis on the philately of Czechoslovakia and its successor countries, the Czech Republic and Slovakia. Even those with little interest in stamps may be fascinated by the way in which the collection illustrates the often tormented course of Czechoslovak history. There are Austrian stamps overprinted in Czech as the First Republic was born, stamps from Hitler's Protectorate of Bohemia-Moravia and from the puppet Slovak Republic, and stamps illustrating the building of Socialism. There is much other material too, including Austrian stamps, British *Penny Blacks* and other rarities. The stamps are stored and exhibited on the ground floor, together with various items of postal memorabilia including uniforms, souvenirs, and artwork.

The rooms on the upper floor are used for temporary exhibitions but much of their appeal comes from the delightful **wall and ceiling paintings** carried out in 1847 by the painter Josef Navrátil for Václav Michalovic, the prosperous miller whose residence this was. Apart from its splendid tiled stove, the Green Room is relatively plain. The mural paintings in the larger **Alpine Room** offer wonderfully Romantic panoramas of mountain scenery, and a wishful northerner's view of the charming denizens of the Mediterranean world beyond the Alps. The third room has a fine ceiling, while the **Theatre Room** is Rococo in character with pretty vignettes from plays and operas and a self-portrait of the artist.

PRAŽSKÝ Hrad★★★
PRAGUE Castle – Hradčany
Tram 22

The sight of Prague Castle crowning the long ridge rising over the Vltava and the re
roofs of Malá Strana is unforgettable. Even to those with no knowledge of Bohemia
history the silhouette of the great citadel speaks eloquently of temporal and eccles
astical power exercised for more than 1 000 years. Every age has marked th
Hradčany, from Czech princelings barely emergent from the age of legends, to th
rulers of the Holy Roman Empire and the totalitarian tyrants of the 20C. The lat
medieval vaults of the Vladislav Hall are supported on far older, Romanesque foun
dations, while the austere façades of the 18C contain interiors elegantly adapted
the early years of the 20C for the first President of democratic Czechoslovakia.

The undisputed spiritual and political focus of the nation, the Hrad is a town with
a town. The great Gothic cathedral looks down on lesser churches and on a pres
dential palace linked by streets and squares, courtyards, stairs and alleyways to humb
dwellings as well as other palaces, while the margins of what has been called th
"Bohemian acropolis" are softened by a wreath of gardens. Within the walls are son
of the country's greatest treasures: the cathedral guards not only the rarely show
Crown Jewels but is a gallery of artworks in its own right, St George's Convent is
splendid home for the national collection of medieval, Renaissance and Baroque a
and enough is on show in the Castle Gallery to recall the glories of Emperor Rudolp
II's unparalleled collections. Post-1989 policy has been to open up the castle to th
public as much as possible; gardens which were once off-limits now welcome summ
visitors, there are exhibitions and concerts and crowds always gather to watch th
serio-comic midday ceremony of the Changing of the Guard.

HISTORY

Early Slav stronghold

The first Czech ruler to fortify the rocky spur above the Vltava was Prince Bořivoj
(c 852-884), who, in the last years of the 9C
moved his residence here from his earlier stronghold at Levý Hradec a few miles downstream.
By the time of his death he had built the
Church of the Virgin Mary, only the second Christian place of worship to
be established in the Czech
lands; its remains have been excavated and can be seen from
the passageway to the Bastion
Garden. Protected by an
earthen bank and a timber palisade, Bořivoj's stronghold extended over virtually the whole
area of today's castle; its only
stone building was the church,
the prince and his retinue re-
siding in a timber structure
which was the forerunner of
the Royal Palace, his followers in dwellings
half sunk into
the ground.
More stone
churches were
soon added, the
predecessor of
St George's
Basilica around
920, the Ro-
tunda of St Vitus
a decade later. In
973, the castle
became the seat
of the newly es-
tablished Prague
bishopric, the
rotunda was ele-
vated to cath-
edral status, and
a convent added

St George's. In the mid 11C the original primitive defences were replaced by walls
to 5 m in height, together with a number of gate-towers. A century later the walls
ere raised to a height of up to 14 m and a fine new palace, all of 50 m long, was
uilt of pale limestone.

mperial residence

hough the energetic King **Otakar II** (1228-78) had continued improving the castle's
efences and had extended the Royal Palace, by the time the future **Charles IV** (1316-78)
ished to reside in Prague the castle was in a semi-derelict state, and temporary accomodation had to be provided for him in the Old Town. Even before succeeding to the
rone in 1346, Charles set about making the castle a fit place for an Emperor to reside;
s numerous improvements included a sumptuous French-style Gothic **palace** to replace
takar's edifice, which had burnt down in 1303. A chapel was added to a design by
etr Parléř, and the castle's glory was proclaimed far and wide by the gilding applied to
e roofs of its towers. Its role as the spiritual as well as political centre of the country
as affirmed by the start of work in 1344 on the great new Gothic cathedral.

ecline and revival

hough work continued on the castle under Charles IV's son **Wenceslas IV** (1361-1419),
is monarch preferred to live in the **Royal Court** on the site in the Old Town now occu-
ed by the **Obecní dům** (Municipal House). The castle suffered badly during the chaos
f the Hussite Wars, and subsequent rulers continued to live in the Royal Court, until
1483, frightened by the riotous behaviour of the citizenry, **Vladislav II** (1456-1516)
oved back to the security of the Hradčany heights. Appointing the gifted **Benedict
ed** as castle architect, Vladislav had the long-neglected fortifications replaced by
odern defences which included the **Daliborka**, the **White Tower**, and the massive **Powder
wer** or Mihulka. The Royal Palace was given its definitive form, with Ried's magnif-
ent **Great Throne Hall** (later known as the Vladislav Hall) as its centrepiece.

Rudolphine citadel of culture

The most colourful period in the castle's history began with the reign of
Hapsburg Emperor **Rudolph II**
(1552-1612). His predecessors
had begun the process of trans-
formation which turned a Gothic
castle into a Renaissance palace.
Ferdinand I (1503-64) laid out
extensive gardens on the far side
of the deep ditch known as the
Stag Moat, crowning them with
the elegant Italianate Royal **Summer Palace** or Belveder. Archduke **Ferdinand of Tyrol**
(1529-95) and his archi-
tect **Bonifaz Wohlmut** added
the splendid **Ball-game Hall** to
the gardens and took ad-
vantage of the great fire
of 1541 to carry out
much rebuilding.

Under Rudolph ex-
tensive building
took place at the
western end of the
castle, mainly to
house the Em-
peror's ever-
growing collec-
tions of art
objects and cu-
riosities of all
kinds, but his
reign was less
notable for its
architectural
achievements
than for the cas-
tle's role as a

M. Guillou

175

crucible of culture. Around the reclusive Emperor gathered a cosmopolitan swarm painters, sculptors, scholars, scientists, craftsmen, cavaliers and alchemists, all ea to satisfy his unquenchable curiosity about the nature of the world as well as to p der to his sometimes questionable tastes.

Decline and revival

After Rudolph's forced retirement in 1611, the castle lost its role as Imperial resider though the dramatic defenestration precipitating the Thirty Years War took place h and there was a brief moment of courtly gaiety during the short rule (1619-20) of Fr erick, "the Winter King", and his Stuart wife Elizabeth, who scandalised and fascina Central Europeans with her low-cut dresses and uninhibited behaviour. The Saxon ar was billeted here in 1631, in 1648 many of the castle's treasures were carried off the Swedes, and it was battered by Prussian guns in the siege of 1757. It had beco a white elephant, posing problems of use and maintenance; when royalty came here it did only occasionally, furniture and fittings had to be borrowed from elsewhere make them feel at home. After the Prussian siege, Empress **Maria Theresa** (1717- employed the architect **Nicola Pacassi** to bring some semblance of eighteenth century or into the place. By eliminating the castle's post-medieval silhouette of towers and turr dormers, gables and cupolas and replacing the picturesque chaos with a series of rat bland, late Baroque façades, he succeeded in tying the great complex together and largely responsible for the face the castle wears today. But Maria Theresa was succeed by her son **Joseph II** (1741-90), to whom all symbolism was superfluous and who co find no better use for the castle than as an artillery barracks.

The last coronation ceremony took place on Hradčany in 1836, when Emperor Fe nand V was crowned King of Bohemia in the cathedral. But from the middle of the 1 the Czech National Revival began to breathe new life into the neglected complex. W began on the completion of the cathedral, and in 1918 the founders of Czechoslova saw the castle as a national symbol, the only possible choice for the residence of the P ident of the new Republic. The first holder of that office, **Tomáš Garrigue Masa**

How to scale the Hradčany heights

The easiest way to approach the castle is to take the no 22 tram. You can get off either at the Pražský hrad stop, or better still at Královský letohrádek, the stop for the Royal Summer Palace and then walk through the Royal Gardens. Either way you enter the castle across the Stag Moat and into the Second Courtyard. Alternatively you could stay on the tram as far as Pohořelec and make your way down through Hradčany Town to the ceremonial entrance at the western end of the castle.

The steep climb can be made in various ways on foot. Staré zámecké schody/Old castle Steps begin not far from Malostranská Metro station and enter via the eastern gateway by the Black Tower. The slightly older Nové zámecké schody (New Castle Steps) begin above Malostranské náměstí (Malá Strana Square) and emerge close to the castle's western entrance. A longer alternative is to climb Nerudová (Neruda Street) and turn right up the steep cobbled ramp known as *K Hradu*.

1850-1937) was a more than worthy successor to previous rulers, employing the architectural genius **Josip Plečnik** to adapt the castle to its new vocation as the focal point of a
modern, democratic state *(see panel)*. During the period of the German Protectorate of
Bohemia-Moravia of 1939-45, the castle remained the residence of the powerless President Hácha, but its symbolic and ceremonial importance was exploited by the Nazis on
every possible occasion; in 1941, poor Hácha had to hand over the seven keys giving
access to St Wenceslas' crown and the Cathedral Treasury to Reichsprotektor Heydrich.
During the period 1948-89, the blank walls of the castle seemed an apt metaphor
for the remoteness and inhumanity of the Communist system, though many of its interiors remained open to the public and much devoted archeological and restoration
work took place. Since 1989, the aim of the authorities has been to restore the castle's
symbolic continuity with the past and make it more accessible to the public.

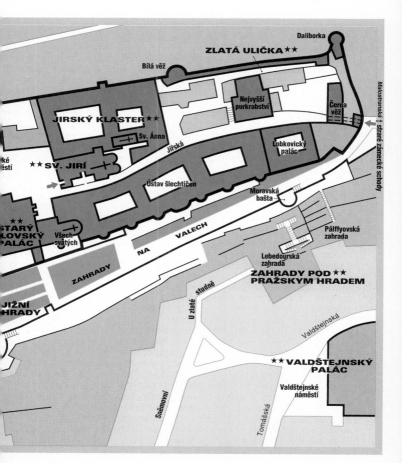

177

CASTLE COURTYARDS AND INTERIORS ⊙

Entrance tickets for the castle interiors accessible to the public are on sale inside th Chapel of the Holy Cross in the Second Courtyard. Note that the ticket is not valid fc the National Gallery's Collection of Early Bohemian Art in St George's Convent.

First Courtyard – This *cour d'honneur* watched over by the famous pair of bat tling giants dwarfing the blue-uniformed guardsmen is the usual place from whic to begin a visit to the castle. The sweep of cobbles down from Hradčany Squar and the smooth paving of the courtyard belie the fact that this whole area wa once defended by a natural ravine, moats and bridges, long since swept away i favour of what is now an inviting ceremonial entrance. The gateway is surmounte by a Rococo grille with the initials of Maria Theresa and Joseph II; the giants ar copies of the originals sculpted in 1771 by Ignaz Platzer. Platzer was also respon sible for the martial trophies decorating the attic gables of Pacassi's late-Baroqu façades which define the three sides of the courtyard. Incorporated into the centra block is the early Baroque **Matyášova brána** (Matthias Gate), a theatrical-looking sand stone structure modelled on the triumphal arches of Antiquity and completed i 1614. The 25m-tall flagpoles of Moravian pine were installed by Plečnik, wh boldly created two new openings *(only occasionally open to the public)* off the pas sageway leading to the Second Courtyard. To the right, a ceremonial stairway lead up to the castle's sumptuously furnished **State Rooms**, to the left is the monument: Sloupová síň (Hall of Columns) or **Plečnik Hall**, a lofty space of great calm and repos with three superimposed rows of pale granite columns.

Second Courtyard – The harmonious, perhaps monotonous appearance of the spa cious courtyard is entirely due to Pacassi's extensive 18C remodelling. Pacassi wa also responsible for the Kaple svatého kříže (Chapel of the Holy Cross), which wa adapted in 1852 as a private chapel for the former Emperor Ferdinand V, the charmin but simple-minded Hapsburg who was made to abdicate in 1848 in favour of h nephew Franz Josef and who chose Prague Castle as his retirement home. The cour yard has focal points in the shape of a substantial Baroque **fountain** with figures c Hercules and other deities, a Baroque well-head and a modern lion fountain.

A covered passageway leads to the formal Zahrada na baště (Bastion Garden) t the west, redesigned by Plečnik in the 1920s; part of the north wall of the pas sageway is glazed, allowing a view down into the foundations of the 9C Churc of the Virgin Mary.

The central wing separating the Second and Third Courtyards houses administrativ offices and stands on the site of the earthen rampart which divided the main part c the early Slavonic stronghold from the outer bailey; a new Postmodern canopy wit a delightful sculpture of a winged leopard marks the ceremonial entrance to this win The north wing is pierced by a passageway leading to the causeway over the dee ravine known as the Stag Moat which protected this flank of the castle. Pacassi facades conceal a complex building history which began with the construction c royal stables and continued in Emperor Rudolph's time with the addition of super galleries to house his vast collections. The Rudolph Gallery and the 48 m lor **Spanish Hall** are now used for ceremonial purposes, while the **Obrazárna Pražkéł hradu★ (Prague Castle Gallerya)** ⊙ *(See panel)* has been accommodated in attractive adapted premises on the lower floor.

Rudolphine remains: the Castle Gallery

In pursuit of his passion for paintings, Emperor Rudolph II employed a galaxy of court artists and sent his agents all over Europe in search of fine works to add to his ever-growing collection. By the end of his life he had amassed a total of some 3 000 pictures and other works of art as well as an array of curiosities, but this extraordinary heritage was soon dispersed by his successors. Much was removed to Vienna, much was appropriated by corrupt courtiers, and much was plundered, notably by the Swedish soldiery in 1648, who left only empty picture frames and the skeleton of a rhinoceros. The collection was built up again in the late 17C and early 18C, but the impoverished Imperial treasury was again and again tempted to sell off works and at a famous auction in 1782 the last items were dispersed. But, not least due to a fund established by President Masaryk in the 1920s, the castle collection has been re-established, and even includes a number of pictures once admired by Rudolph II. Among the minor works are a number of masterpieces; they include a sensitive *Head of a Girl* by Rudolph's court painter Hans van Aachen, a wonderfully quizzical *Portrait of Frau Schreyvogel* by Jan Kupecký, several canvases by Cranach the Elder, Bartholomeus Spranger, Tintoretto, and Veronese, a *Portrait of Lady Vaux* by Holbein the Younger, *The Centaur Nessus Abducting Deianira* by Guido Reni, and a *Young Woman at her Toilet* by Titian.

Third Courtyard – The Third Courtyard is completely dominated by the soaring stonework of the **Sv. Víta (Cathedral of St Vitus★★★)** – *(see p. 200),* whose west front rears up suddenly just a few metres from the mouth of the tunnel leading through from the Second Courtyard.

Like the other courtyards, the Third Courtyard is defined by Pacassi's austere ar-

> ### Victuals at the Vicarage
> The row of houses along the north side of Vikářská Street includes a couple of former vicarages, now converted into a café and a restaurant, a welcome addition to the rather sparse facilities of this kind within easy reach of the Castle.
> Other places of refreshment within the Castle precinct include a restaurant in the Bastion Garden, and a café and a self-service snack bar close to the entrance of Golden Lane.

chitecture, though to the north the narrow street along the northern flank of the cathedral is bordered by humbler buildings. Some of these accommodated the cathedral's vicars, hence the street's name of Vikářská. An opening leads through to the massive **Prašná věž (Powder Tower)**, also known as the Mihulka, built as a gun emplacement towards the end of the 15C by Benedict Ried. As its name suggests, it was used as a gunpowder store; it survived the serious damage caused when its contents blew up in 1648 as a result of the Swedish soldiers' carelessness. It now houses a variety of displays, among them a replica of an alchemist's laboratory.

On the far side of the cathedral, Pacassi's **South Wing** features a splendid portico surmounted by a balcony used by the President to greet crowds on ceremonial occasions. Otherwise it was Plečnik who was largely responsible for the present appearance of the Third Courtyard. Eliminating the previous changes of level, he laid out the present paving, built the canopy covering the excavated foundations of the Romanesque basilica which was the forerunner of the cathedral, and installed, (not without mishap, since its top broke off) the great granite obelisk intended as a memorial to the dead of the First World War. The **Býčí schodiště (Bull Staircase★)** in the southeast corner is Plečnik's work too; it consists of several flights of stairs tunnelling down through the South Wing to the gardens far below, and is entered through a superb **canopy** inspired by the architecture and mythology of pre-Classical Crete. The Gothic sculpture of an elegant **St George** spiking the dragon is a copy of the original in the National Gallery.

The Baroque building at the southwestern corner of the cathedral is the **Staré Proboštsví** (Old Deanery), incorporating fragments of the Romanesque Bishops' Palace and with a figure of *St Wenceslas* by Bendl adorning one corner.

★**Starý královský palác (Old Royal Palace)** – Once the heart of court life, the Old Royal Palace is now a museum piece, all the Presidential and other functions having been removed long ago to the western ranges of the castle. Some idea of the great antiquity of the castle is gained as the successive layers of the Palace are explored. Entrance is from the Third Courtyard, where Pacassi covered the older facade with one of his own incorporating a balcony and an Eagle Fountain to which Plečnik added details of his own. Beyond, the **vestibule** has Romanesque stonework turned red by the great fire of 1541. To the left is the **Zelená světnice** (Green Chamber), with coats of arms and a Baroque fresco depicting the *Judgement of Solomon,* as well as the so-called **Vladislav Bedchamber** with colourful Gothic vaulting and further coats of arms. These are insignificant preludes to the grandeur of the **Vladislavský sál (Vladislav Hall★★★)**, in its time the largest secular vaulted space in Central Europe. Built between 1492-1502, it is the masterpiece of **Benedict Ried**, castle architect to Ladislav II, a sublime fusion of Late Gothic fantasy and the dawning Renaissance. Particularly when seen from outside, the walls and great rectangular windows are entirely Renaissance in spirit, though on the north side they coexist with Gothic arches and tall buttresses with tapering pinnacles. Inside, the ribs of **Ried's vault** writhe weightlessly into space, forming gloriously star or rose-like patterns as they meet at a height of 13 m above the floor. The architect's intention seem entirely playful rather than functional, but in fact this constellation of slender stonework does hold up some of the weight of the roof. Some 62 m long by 16 across, the great hall replaced Charles IV's Gothic Throne Room. It was used for a whole variety of purposes; assemblies, balls, coronation feasts, royal audiences, even for tournaments, since the participants were able to spur their steeds up the Riders' Staircase. A famous print by Rudolph II's court engraver Aegidius Sadeler shows all the paraphernalia of an antiques fair, with dealers at their stalls, groups of courtiers and connoisseurs standing around, and the Emperor himself contemplating a purchase in the background. In the 20C the hall acquired a new tradition, that of lending the appropriate solemnity to the election of the country's president.

There are fine views over Prague from the **outside terrace** along the southern front of the Vladislav Hall.

The Vladislav Hall

From the southwestern corner of the hall a doorway leads to the **Ludvíkův palác** (Louis Wing), added by Ried in the first decade of the 16C and housing the officers of the Bohemian Chancellery. Lower-ranking personnel occupied the first room, the Council of Governors the second room, from whose windows two of their number were forcibly ejected in 1618 in Prague's Second Defenestration *(see panel)*. A spiral staircase with Gothic vaulting leads up to the Imperial Council Chamber. It was here that the sequel to the Defenestration was played out, when in 1621 the 27 noblemen who had participated in the rebellion of the Bohemian Estates against Imperial authority were sentenced to death.

From the eastern end of the Hall steps lead up through a Renaissance portal to the gallery of **Všech svatých** (All Saints Church), built originally by Peter Parler for Charles IV, but rebuilt after the fire of 1541 with a feeble Renaissance vault replacing the one designed by Parler. The church has a very dark altarpiece by VV Reiner, and its northern chapel houses the tomb of St Procopius, one of the country's patron saints.

The Second Defenestration of Prague

Tension between the Protestants and Catholics of early-17C Bohemia came to a head in 1618. Convinced that Emperor Matthias in Vienna was aiding and abetting Catholic attempts to strip Protestants of their privileges and reduce the traditional authority of the Bohemian Estates, the fiery-tempered Count Thurn led a delegation up to the castle and broke into the offices in the Louis Wing from where the Catholic Governors ruled in the absence of the Emperor. Heated discussion soon turned to action. Governors **Vilém Slavata of Chlum** and **Jaroslav Bořita** of Martinic, both known for their intransigent Catholicism, were dragged to the window. Facing death, they pleaded for a confessor, but their pleas fell on unsympathetic ears. Martinic was ejected first, while Slavata managed to delay his fall for a few moments by hanging on to the sill until someone broke his knuckles with the hilt of a dagger. For good measure, their secretary, **Filip Fabricius** was thrown out too. Surprisingly, all three survived the considerable fall, evaded the random shots fired at them from above, and made themselves scarce. The Catholic version of the event has them miraculously borne up by a solicitous Virgin Mary, while the Protestant, possibly more credible version has their fall broken by the thick layer of ordure accumulated in the moat. For his pains, Fabricius was later raised to the nobility, with the title of Von Hohenfall (Sir Philip of High Fall).

Sensing the significance of the moment, the Old Town mob rioted, burning Catholic churches and pillaging the Jewish Quarter, events foreshadowing the greater horrors of the Thirty Years War, the outbreak of which was marked by this defenestration.

Successive doorways in the north wall of the hall lead to the Diet Hall, the Riders' Staircase, and the rooms of the New Land Rolls. The **Stará směmovna** (Diet Hall) was rebuilt after the 1541 fire by Bonifác Wohlmut, who renewed the Gothic vaulting in deference to his predecessor Ried. The room is laid out as if for a meeting of the Diet, with a throne for the monarch, seats for the nobility and clergy, and a sort of pen for the representatives of the towns, who between them were only allowed a single vote. The scribe sat in a splendid Renaissance gallery. The **Nové zemské desky** (New Land Rolls) recorded the proceedings of the Diet, which had the force of law; reached by a staircase, the walls and vaults of the rooms housing them are splendidly decorated with the painted coats of arms of the Clerks of the Rolls. The first part of the **Jezdecké schody** (Riders Staircase) has a Renaissance vault, the second, steeper part has **Gothic vaulting**★ by Ried of even greater virtuosity than the hall itself. The Riders' Stairway leads to an exit from the Palace, or to steps descending into its Gothic and Romanesque depths. The outstanding interiors here include the **Charles Hall**, with models of the castle at various stages of its development and copies of the Parler sculptures from the Cathedral, and the **Hall of Columns** of Wenceslas IV with elegant vaulting of around 1400.

Jiřské náměstí (St George's Square) – The rough paving of the square is in contrast to the sophisticated surfaces laid down in the other squares of the castle by Plečnik. The square offers an amazing view of the east end of the cathedral with its semi-circle of ambulatory chapels and the complex system of buttresses supporting the roof of Parléř's choir.

★ **Jiřský klášter (St George's Convent)** – See p. 117.

EASTERN PRECINCT

The sense of the Hradčany as a town within a town is most strongly pronounced at the eastern end of the castle, with its lanes, steps and alleyways leading past rickety cottages as well as noble palaces.

Ústav šlechtičen (Home for Distressed Gentlewomen) – With a fine pillared portico facing St Georges' Square and forming much of the southern side of **Jiřská** (St George's Lane), this was originally the palace of the powerful **Rožmberk** (Rosenberg family). Its four tall towers feature strongly in early views of the castle, but in 1755 it was rebuilt in sober style by Pacassi as a refuge for impoverished female members of the aristocracy and now houses administrative offices.

★ **Zlatá ulička (Golden Lane)** – Legends crowd as thickly around **Golden Lane** as do today's tourists. The quaint little dwellings sheltering beneath the castle's outer wall are supposed to have housed alchemists engaged in making gold, but in fact the cobbled alleyway's name has a more prosaic origin, and refers not to savants but to craftsmen; the castle lay outside the jurisdiction of the Prague guilds, and the poorly paid castle guardsmen supplemented their meagre earnings by turning to trade, including goldsmithing. Kafka found its atmosphere congenial and stayed here for a while, but nowadays the lane is home to a flourishing trade in superior souvenirs.

Golden Lane

Castle defences – Above Golden Lane runs a sentry-walk, while to the west is t[...] **Bílá věž** (White Tower), part of Benedict Ried's late 15C strengthening of the castle[...] northern defences; the English alchemist Edward Kelley once languished here. [...] the east is another tower built by Ried, the **Daliborka**, where another prisoner, t[...] knight Dalibor, is supposed to have whiled away his sentence by playing so swee[...] on the violin (an instrument only invented long after his death) that crowds gat[...] ered to listen. The finale of the fortifications is formed by the **Černá věž** (Bla[...] Tower), a Romanesque structure which once guarded the castle entrance, but [...] now bypassed. Beyond today's entrance with its pair of blue-uniformed sentries[...] splendid viewpoint is laid out on the site of the medieval Barbican.

Lobkovický palác (Lobkowicz Palace) – Just within the castle precinct at the foot [...] St George's Lane, this Baroque palace houses the conscientious but uninspiring **Natio[...] History Exhibition of the National Museum** ⊘. With some original items, reproductions a[...] lengthy explanations (*in Czech, but translations available in various languages*), t[...] displays trace the country's history from the earliest times to the mid 19C. There a[...] some interesting original interiors. Perhaps the most intriguing items are the carefu[...] crafted reproductions of the Crown Jewels of the Kingdom of Bohemia.

Muzeum hraček (Toy Museum) ⊘ – The private enterprise successor to the Cor[...] munist-era House of Czechoslovak Children, the museum occupies the **Nejvy[...] purkrabství** (Palace of the High Burgrave), the castle's most senior official. Its prese[...] appearance, with Renaissance sgraffito imitating stonework, dates from a mid-16[...] rebuilding.

GARDENS AND NORTHERN PRECINCT

★★ **Jižní zahrady (South Gardens)** – Running the whole length of the castle's southern fro[...] and offering magnificent views, this series of very different gardens was unified [...] the careful touch of Castle architect Josip Plečnik in the 1920s. His additions, form[...] and Classical in style, are set off by the fine trees which he was careful to spare.

The most dramatic approach to the gardens is from the castle's Third Courtya[...] down the steps of the **Bull Staircase**, but the gardens can also be entered from t[...] east as well as from the west, where Plečnik created an opening in the battlement[...] brick wall at the top of New Castle Steps. From here a monumental stairway lea[...] down to the **Rajská zahrada** (Paradise Garden) first laid out by Archduke Ferdina[...] for his private use in 1562. At its centre is a massive granite **bowl**, placed by Plečn[...] to represent the female principle, a counterpart to the masculine principle symbo[...] ised by the monolith in the Third Courtyard. The charming little **Matthias Pavilion** w[...] its pointed roof dates from 1617. Beyond stretch the **Zahrady na valech** (Bastion Ga[...] dens). On the far side of[...]

little colonnaded **belvedere** [...] slim pyramid stands abo[...] a stairway leading down [...] the **Hartigovská zahrada** (Ha[...] tig Garden) with i[...] Baroque music pavilio[...] The gravel area beneath t[...] Bull Staircase is the settin[...] for occasional concert[...] Sandstone columns belo[...] the Louis Wing of the [...] Royal Palace mark the sp[...] where the heaps of ordu[...] broke the fall of Governo[...] Slavata and Martinic follo[...] ing the Second Defenestr[...] tion. Close to the easte[...] entrance to the garden[...] the **Moravská bašta** (Moravi[...] Bastion) is dominated by[...] slender column topped by[...] gilded sphere with lightni[...] flashes. Steps descend to [...] oval stone table, a qu[...] nook much favoured [...] President Masaryk, a[...] from here there is access [...] the series of terrace[...] Baroque gardens belongi[...] to the palaces below t[...] castle (see p. 149).

The Paradise Garden

M. Ivory/MICHELIN

Presidential palace

Throughout the 1920s and into the early 1930s, the Slovene architect Josip Plečnik (1872-1957) worked with Tomáš Masaryk to transform Prague Castle into a fitting residence for the president of a democratic and progressive republic. Plečnik was an unusual choice, a deeply religious man working in a largely secular state, a lover of the Classical past but neither a traditionalist nor a sympathiser with the avant-garde ambitions of most of his Czech colleagues. The individual path he trod has led him to be hailed as a precursor of Post-Modernism, but Plečnik resists rigid labelling. His work at the castle includes the remodelling of the Presidential apartments and the creation of the monumental Sloupová síň (Pillar Hall), but it is perhaps the courtyards and gardens which most perfectly reveal his modest genius. He was responsible for the clever manipulation of the levels of Third Courtyard, which ironed out its awkward slope at the same time revealing the foundations of the Romanesque basilica, for the Bull Stairway which connects the courtyard with the South Gardens, and for the Gardens themselves, including the Bastion Garden. Neither Nazis nor Communists liked Plečnik's style, but his sensitive additions to the castle are now seen as a model of how to adapt an historic complex to contemporary needs.

Northern Precinct – The plateau to the north of the **Jelení příkop** (Stag Moat) became an integral part of castle life as Hrad(any evolved from a medieval fortress into a Renaissance residence and its denizens sought light, air, and greenery. The deep cleft of the Stag Moat is a natural ravine, offering wonderful protection to the Castle's northern flank. It was first bridged in 1540, with a two-storey structure, the upper deck reserved for the perambulations of the monarch. In 1770 it was replaced by the present causeway. The stags which once inhabited the moat were not replaced after they had all been killed and eaten by the occupying French army in 1743.

★**Královská zahrada (Royal Gardens)** – See p. 137.

★**Belveder (Královský letohrádek) (Royal Summer Palace)** – See p. 106.

Královská Jízdarna (Royal Riding School) – The charming street running north from the causeway is dominated by this fine example of the utilitarian architecture of the Baroque period, built by Jean-Baptiste Mathey in 1695. Horses are no longer led through their paces here, but the building makes an excellent setting for temporary exhibitions.

Beyond the Riding Hall were once further gardens of a functional rather than decorative nature, including vineyards, orchards, fishponds and a pheasantry.

RUDOLFINUM★

Alšovo nábřeží.í 12 Old Town Metro Staroměstská

ompleted in 1884, this monumental neo-Renaissance structure gave late-19C Prague ot only the first-rate concert hall it had hitherto lacked but also splendid exhibition ɔaces. It was designed by **Josef Zítek** and **Josef Schultz**, winners of an architectural competition sponsored by the Savings Bank of Bohemia; the competition had envisaged ʋo buildings, but Zítek and Schultz cleverly combined the concert and exhibition ɪnction in a single edifice. The building's name commemorates Austrian **Crown Prince dolf**, but Praguers prefer to link it with a Rudolf more intimately associated with ague, the art-loving **Emperor Rudolf II**.

A palace for the arts – The main façade recalls that of another great late-19C riverside edifice, the National Theatre, though the Rudolfinum's five arcades are glazed. The building has a fine array of statuary; the seated figures are by Antonín Wagner, the lions and sphinxes gracing the side entrances are by Bohuslav Schnirch, while the rooftop composers are the work of various sculptors.

Inside, the **Dvořák Hall** with its Corinthian columns supporting a conical ceiling has exceptionally fine acoustics and seating for 1 200.

The wrong nose

The fact that the statues on the roof of the Rudolfinum included one of the Jewish composer Mendelssohn was unacceptable to the Nazis. Orders were given for the offending item to be removed, but it proved difficult to identify. Racial science came to the rescue, and the one with the most prominent nose was taken down. Faces reddened when it turned out to represent Richard Wagner. (From Jiří Weill's 1960 story *Mendelssohn Is on the Roof.*)

In 1896 the Rudolfinum saw the premiere of Dvořák's symphony *From the N[e] World*, conducted by the composer himself. Later it became the home of the **Prag[ue] Philharmonic**, but after the First World War was converted to house the **Parliam[ent]** of the new Czechoslovak Republic. During the Occupation the Rudolfinum was t[he] seat of the German administration, then after the war, renamed the House [of] Artists, housed the Prague Conservatory and Academy of Music as well as the Ph[il]harmonic. In the 1990s it was comprehensively restored.

Náměstí Jana Palacha (Jan Palach Square) – The majestic Rudolfinum dominates t[he] northern side of this square, laid out in the late 19C as part of the city's effo[rt] to give the riverside a more dignified appearance. To the south, also in neo-Rena[is]sance style but far less imposing is the **Vysoká škola uměleckoprůmyslová (Decorative A[rts] College)** of 1884, to the east the **Philosophy Faculty** of the university, built 1929 in[a] strangely traditional style quite at odds with the prevailing modernism of the tim[e,] while to the west is the Vltava, crossed by the coolly elegant **Mánesův most** (Mán[es] Bridge) of 1914.

MUZEUM BEDŘICHA SMETANY★

Smetana Museum
Novotného lávka 1 Old Town Metro Staroměstská

At the very end of the Novotného lávka, the jetty protruding into the Vltava ju[st] upstream of Charles Bridge, this handsome neo-Renaissance building is now a muse[um] devoted to the composer **Bedřich Smetana** (1824-84). Designed by Antonín Wiehl a[nd] completed in 1887, the building originally contained machinery which drew wa[ter] from the river for distribution round the city. It was then converted into offices [for] the water board, and finally, in 1936, made into the present museum, which und[er]went a complete reorganisation in the late 1990s. The prolific sgraffito work on t[he] facade depicts in some detail the robust defence of the Old Town against the Swe[des] in 1648.

The first part of the museum surveys the composer's life. Born in 1824 in t[he] eastern Bohemian town of Litomyšl, Smetana was the son of a brewer employ[ed] by the famous Thurn und Taxis concern. He lived in a number of places in Bohe[mia] and spent time in Sweden as director of the Göteborg Philharmonia, but his mo[st] significant years were spent in Prague, where he died in 1884, a victim of depre[s]sion and mental instability.

A second section recalls Smetana's part in establishing a distinctively Czech musi[cal] tradition and his particular fascination with the country's **folklore**. His role in vario[us] musical associations like the **Hlahol choir** and the **Umělecká beseda** is recalled, as w[ell] as his participation in the great concert marking the laying of the foundation sto[ne] of the National Theatre. The constant murmur of the **Vltava** outside the buildin[g is] a reminder both of its original purpose and of the composer's great tone po[em] *Má vlast*.

A final section has musical instruments and illustrations of operas, a reminder th[at] Smetana virtually founded Czech opera single-handed, with works like *The Bra[n]denburgers in Bohemia*, *The Bartered Bride*, *Libuše*, and *Dalibor*.

To help in planning your stay in Prague, study the plan of Principal Sights (p. 1[?] and the plan of Walks in Prague (p. 98).

STARÉ MĚSTO★★★

OLD TOWN

Metro Staroměstská, Můstek, Náměstí Republiky

ounded by the bend of the Vltava and the boulevards laid out where defensive alls once stood, Prague's Staré město (Old Town) has a long history evident erywhere in its labyrinth of streets and squares. Baroque-fronted buildings rise ver cellars which were once the ground floor of Romanesque and Gothic houses, d a galaxy of churches has an equally ancient origin. This was the burghers' wn, quite distinct from the rulers' citadel on the far side of the river and the istocratic quarter squatting beneath it. Among its medieval population of adesmen, merchants and craftsmen, a sense of civic pride grew and flourished, hile its churches produced radicals of the stamp of John Huss and its university s quota of restless students, often ready to challenge the authority of cathedral d castle.

The great symbol of civic consciousness is the **Staroměstská radnice** (Town Hall) dominating **Staroměstské náměstí** (Old Town Square), the wide expanse of which stands in such contrast to the surrounding warren of streets and passageways. The roads radiating from here run northwest (Kaprova) to ancient fording places, west (Karlova) to the medieval bridges, northeast (Dlouhá) to the foreign merchants' quarter, and east (Celetná) towards the gateway guarding the approach from Kutná hora. The tightly constricted passageway of Melantrichova winds southwards to where a bridge once crossed the moat into the open country which has long since been covered by the buildings of the New Town. Two arches of the little bridge (Můstek) were uncovered when Prague's underground railway was being built, commemorated in the name of today's busy interchange station between Underground lines A and B. Line B runs eastward beneath Na příkopě (Moat Street), laid out in the 18C along the line of the Old Town's 13C semi-circle of defensive walls, towers and ditches.

The haphazard growth of the Old Town gave rise to a street pattern calculated to puzzle visitors and lead them astray, but there are exceptions to this irregularity. One is the area just inside the walls; called **Havelské město** (St Havel's Town), this was a planned piece of urban infill, laid out by 13C surveyors on rectangular lines to provide the city with spacious market squares and desirable residences. Centuries later the **Havelská market** still flourishes. A much later attempt at planning transformed the area to the north of Old Town Square once occupied by the ghetto. By the end of the 19C the **Josefov** or Jewish Town, once among the largest and most famous in Europe, had become a warren of streets and unsanitary courtyards. A bold turn-of-the-century redevelopment scheme called the *asanace* swept most of it away, leaving a handful of **synagogues** and the **Old Jewish Cemetery** stranded among smart new apartment blocks.

For many years the Old Town ignored its riverside setting, and the banks of the Vltava were given over to watermills, timber yards and rubbish tips. This began to change when in 1847 what is now **Smetanovo nábřeží** (Smetana Embankment) was the first of a number of riverside improvements. At the end of the 19C the area north of the bridge was reclaimed for a series of prestigious public buildings, among them the **UPM** (Decorative Arts Museum) and the **Rudolfinum** concert hall, which were arranged around what is now **Náměstí Jana Palacha** (Jan Palach Square).

Little that has happened in the 20C has changed the character of the Old Town. A number of fine modern buildings have been sensitively inserted into the ancient townscape, foremost among them the **Cubist Black Madonna House** close to the medieval **Powder Tower**. The shape of Old Town Square was altered, seemingly for ever, when the north wing of the Town Hall was burnt down during the 1945 Liberation, exposing the splendid façade of Baroque **St Nicholas Church** to the Gothic towers of the **Týn Church** on the far side of the square. More than ever the square itself remains one of the city's focal points, with crowds gathering to watch the **Town Hall's** famous **orloj** (astronomical clock), enjoy the efforts of buskers or indulge in people-watching from the base of the **Huss statue** or from one of the many open-air cafes and restaurants. One of the achievements of the Communist regime was to remove through traffic from most of the Old Town, making it a delight for leisurely exploration on foot, though vehicles and traffic still clog the north-south route along the riverside. Though much remains to be done in the way of restoration, many fine buildings have emerged from neglect and there are any number of fascinating interiors to be explored, like the Gothic complex of **St Agnes Convent**, now the home of the national collection of 19C Czech art, the **medieval palace of the Lords of Kunštát** and **Poděbrady** with its Romanesque cellars, or the labyrinth of low-ceilinged rooms of the ancient **Golden Ring House**, an intriguing home for the city's 20C art gallery.

STAROMĚSTSKÉ Naměstí★★★
OLD TOWN SQUARE Old Town
Metro Staroměstská

Fringed by historic houses and presided over by two great churches and the tall tow
of the Town Hall, this spacious cobbled square is the very heart of the Old Tov
From all directions, streets first traced in medieval times funnel people into what
Prague's most popular gathering-place; youngsters congregate around the impos
memorial to John Huss, a dense crowd assembles every hour to gaze up at the famc
astronomical clock, footsore tourists refresh themselves in the many restaurants a
outdoor cafes, while souvenir sellers and street performers provide an extra dash
noise and colour. The square has a theatrical quality, enhanced at night by floc
lighting, and it comes as no surprise to learn that in the past it has been the sta
of some of the most dramatic moments in Bohemian history.

HISTORY

By the 13C, the square was lined by substantial Romanesque town houses and w
firmly established as a conveniently central market place for the traders who had pr
viously conducted their business by the riverside. Tournaments were held here, at c
of which, in 1321, King John of Luxembourg was severely injured. From the mid-14
with the building of the Town Hall, the square's civic and ceremonial function grew

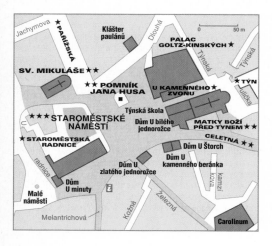

importance. In 1437 se
eral dozen Hussites we
hanged here, but t
most fateful executio
were those which fc
lowed the defeat of t
Protestant Estates at t
Battle of the White Mou
tain. On 21 June 1621,
deafening drum-rolls,
aristocratic "rebels" we
expertly beheaded on
scaffold draped in bla
while three commone
were hanged. The unfo
tunate Dr Jessenius, Re
tor of the Carolinum, s
fered the addition
indignity of having h
tongue cut out before h
head was removed. H
and several others we
drawn and quartere
their body parts being e

hibited on Žižkov Hill, while a dozen heads were stuck on spikes on the Old Tov
Bridge Tower. In 1650, the raising of the Swedish siege of two years previously w
commemorated by the erection of a column in honour of the Virgin Mary Victoriou
The Marian column presided over the centre of the square until 1915, when it w
joined by the memorial to John Huss; in the frenzy accompanying the declaration
Czechoslovak independence in 1918 it was torn down by a nationalist mob who r
garded it as a symbol of Hapsburg rule.

The Nazis recognised the symbolic importance of the square by draping Huss in blac
but the huge V (for Victory) they set among the cobbles failed to save them fro
defeat in May 1945, when one of their last acts was the destruction of the astr
nomical clock and the east wing of the Town Hall.

Hardly had the wartime damage been cleared up, when, on a cold and gloomy d
in February 1948, 80000 demonstrators filled the square to hear Communist Prir
Minister Gottwald proclaim the demise of democratic Czechoslovakia.

THE SQUARE

An irregular rectangle in shape, the square seems not to have been planned b
to have evolved more or less organic way like the Town Hall itself *(see belov*
Nevertheless it once possessed a certain visual coherence; despite their differe
ages, its houses were of broadly similar character, and the narrow streets enter
at an angle, preventing space from leaking away. The façade of St Nicholas' Churc
never intended to be seen from a distance, was discreetly hidden down a si
street. But during the *asanace* of the ghetto in the first decade of the 20C, t
north side of the square was redeveloped and an incongruous vista opened

E. Baret

The Huss Memorial by Ladislav Šaloun

along Pařížská třída (Boulevard de Paris) towards the river and Letná Plain. The burning-down of the east wing of the Town Hall in the fighting of May 1945 rudely revealed the façade of St Nicholas, and has left a gap which has never been filled, despite a number of imaginative proposals for a replacement.

The square is almost entirely given over to pedestrians, though in the not too recent past it was a busy traffic hub and an important tram route once passed this way.

★**Pomník Jana Husa (Huss Memorial)** – On its massive plinth, the memorial is dominated by the tall and erect figure of John Huss, the reformist preacher burnt as a heretic in 1415 *(see p. 108).*

Seeming to gaze into a future in which the injustices of his day have been overcome, Huss appears the very essence of fearlessness and integrity. His calm contrasts with the more dynamically sculpted figures at his feet, who represent his followers, Czechs forced into exile, and a mother and child symbolising the National Revival.

The monument is perhaps the most ambitious sculptural group of the Czech Secession. The work of **Ladislav Šaloun**, it was begun in 1903 and owes something to the monumental works of Auguste Rodin, who had been introduced to the Prague public at a well-attended exhibition in 1902. After a long gestation period, the memorial was unveiled on 6 July 1915, the 500th anniversary of Huss' martyrdom, but due to Austrian officialdom's anxiety about the rising tide of Czech nationalism, all ceremony was banned.

John Huss had been a devotee of the Virgin Mary, and for three years his monument and the Marian column of 1650 stood beside one another, between them representing the country's two great Christian traditions. But for extreme nationalists, the column had come to represent the forces repressing Czech nationhood. On 3 November 1918, a crowd set out to destroy the symbols of Austrian rule. Swift action by the authorities saved the Nepomuk statue on Charles Bridge, but the Marian column was torn down. Stored in the National Museum's Lapidarium, its stonework awaits the outcome of a campaign by the Association for the Restoration of the Marian Column.

★**Staroměstská radnice (Town Hall of the Old Town)** ⊙ – Although the Old Town had been granted its charter around 1230, it was only in 1338 that the burghers received permission from King John of Luxembourg to build a **town hall**. Funds were insufficient for a completely new building, so a existing structure was acquired, a corner house dating from the previous century. As the town prospered, the town hall was extended, westwards by the acquisition of adjoining properties, upwards, by the raising of a great tower over the modest corner house, and northwards by the so-called east wing, which, after being rebuilt more than once, was totally destroyed in May 1945, along with the irreplaceable city archives.

Exterior – A single bay is all that remains of the east wing. Built of stone, the corner house incorporates a mid-14C chapel on its first floor, to a design by Peter Parler. It has a splendid **oriel window★** and a statue of the Virgin Mary.

The Astronomical Clock

Below, 27 **crosses** set in the paving commemorate those executed on this spot 1621. Nearly 70 m tall, the **tower** was begun not long after the purchase of th house; the present roof and gallery were added in the early 19C. A projection bu on to the south side houses the world-famous *orloj* or astronomical clock *(se below)*. Immediately to the west of the clock is a richly carved Late Gothic **port** dating from around 1470-80 and possibly the work of Matěj Rejsek. The adjoinir window has the coats of arms of the city and of the Czech lands. The next buildir was purchased from the merchant Kříž as early as 1360 to accommodate th expanding activity of the city council; its superb first floor Renaissance **window**, wi the Latin inscription *Praga caput regni* (Prague, capital of the kingdom), w added around 1520. Further west still, a building belonging to Mikeš the Furri was added in 1458; it now has a 19C neo-Renaissance façade. Its arcaded Empir style neighbour U kohouta (The Cockerel) became city property in 1830. Finall projecting southwards, the **Dům U minuty** (Minute House) was added in 1896, aft Franz Kafka's family had lived there for seven years; originally a late-Goth structure, it was rebuilt in the mid 16C and given exceptionally fine sgraffi decoration.

★★★**Orloj** (Astronomical Clock) – A potent symbol of magic Prague, the clock attrac a constant stream of admirers and, as the hour comes round, a substant crowd gathers. The clock strikes, and the show begins, reminding all prese of the steady passing of life and time. The Apostles, together with Chr himself, turn and turn around, Death waggles his hourglass, Turk, Jew ar Vanity perform their parts, and a cockerel pops out cuckoo-like to bring t parade to an end.

These fascinating figures are quite recent, carved in 1948 to replace those lc when the clock was destroyed in 1945. The sculptor was stopped from carvir Judas in the likeness of a prominent Nazi collaborator. But the clock had be completed long before the original figures were added, in the 17C. It was fii installed by the royal clockmaker, Nicholas of Kadaň, around 1410, repaired a improved by Master Hanuš around 1490, and perfected by Jan Taborský in t mid-16C. Legend has it that the proud burghers were so protective of the secre of its mechanism that Hanuš was blinded lest he reveal them. His revenge co sisted of having himself led up the tower by an apprentice boy, then plunging t hand into the works, immobilising them for a long time to come.

The central dial of the clock has three hands to indicate not only the passage the hours but also the position of sun, moon and planets according to medie cosmology. The lower dial is a delightful calendar of the months, its vignett reproductions of the originals painted by by Josef Mánes in 1865 and now in t Muzeum hl.m. Prahy (City Museum) (see p. 113).

Interior – Replaced at the beginning of the 20C by a new building in Mariáns náměstí (Marian Square), and restored after the devastation of 1945, the To Hall is nowadays only used for exhibitions and ceremonial purposes. On the grou floor is a gallery for temporary exhibitions, together with a branch of the F (Prague Information Service), while the adjacent vestibule has mosaics to desig by Mikoláš Aleš showing the legendary foundation of the city. On the upper floor, the antiquity of the Town Hall can be sensed in the George of Poděbrady Room where there are massive beams and traces of late medieval wall-paintings. The modern Brožík Hall has a huge picture by this 19C history painter depicting John Huss at his trial in Constance and another showing the election of King George. The Courtroom retains medieval panelling, while the Mayor's Parlour was completely refurbished after the 1945 conflagration. An opening in the vestibule to the Chapel allows a close-up look at some of the carved figures of the Astronomical Clock. The stiff climb to the top of the Town Hall tower is highly recommended for its wonderful **view★★** of the city as a whole, the bustling activity in the square and the convoluted rooftops of the Old Town.

Southern side of the square – Some of the grandest burghers' houses in the whole of the city grace the curving southern side of the square, their varied dates and the differing treatment of their facades in no way impairing their magnificence as an urban ensemble. They include *(west to east):*

– No 20/548 **U zlatého jednorožce** (The Golden Unicorn); in 1848 a music school was founded by Smetana in this building with a Romanesque basement, part of a Gothic portal, and a vestibule with Late Gothic vaulting by Matěj Rejsek;

– No 17/551 **U kamenného beránka** (The Stone Lamb), with a Renaissance portal and gable, a fine carved house sign, and a plaque recording Einstein's stay here;

– No 16/552 the **Štorch Building**, built in the late 19C in neo-Renaissance style for a famous publisher, with frescoes by Mikoláš Aleš including St Wenceslas on horseback.

East and north sides of the square – The pale colouring and the domestic scale of the arcaded buildings in front of the Tyn Church make a striking foreground to its great dark mass of stonework.

– No 15/603 **U bílého jednorožce** (The White Unicorn), the corner house with Celetná Street, was the birthplace of Mozart's Prague friend and opera singer Josefina Dušková;

– No 14/604 **Týnská škola** (Týn School) has pretty Venetian gables. It functioned as a school for five hundred years and among its teachers was the architect Matěj Rejsek. A passageway leading off its arcades gives access to the western portal of the Týn Church;

– No 13/605 **U kamenného zvonu★ (House at the Stone Bell)**. The most remarkable domestic building in the square, the House at the Stone Bell hid its real nature beneath a Baroque façade for many years. In reality it was a medieval, palace-like tower house, quite possibly the residence for a while of King John of Luxembourg's consort, Queen Eliška. Begun in the late 13C, it was greatly extended and beautified in the 14C, with much carving, mural painting, and statuary. All this was hidden or destroyed towards the end of the 17C, and only discovered in the 1960s, when reconstruction was stopped while experts agonised over what state to return such an important building to. Eventually most of the Baroque additions were removed, and the building restored to its Gothic state, including a tall chisel roof. It now stands in all its rebuilt medieval glory, a prestigious home for temporary exhibitions.

Palác Goltz-Kinských★ (Goltz-Kinsky Palace) – This is one of the city's finest Rococo palaces, a prestigious home for Count Goltz who had no qualms about projecting it out into the square beyond the approved building line. It was completed in 1765 by Anselmo Lurago, who used plans drawn up earlier by Kilián Ignác Dientzenhofer. Statues by Platzer crown the attic, while below the twin pediments, twin portals are linked by a splendid balcony; it was from here that Communist Prime Minister Gottwald delivered his fateful speech in February 1948 marking the death of the short-lived postwar democratic republic. Now housing the graphic collections of the National Gallery *(temporarily closed)*, the building has manifold associations with Kafka. At one point his father's shop was on the ground floor, the family flat above, and another part of the building housed the German grammar school attended by the young Franz.

– No 7/930, the **former Convent of the Pauline Order** on the north side of the square at its junction with Dlouhá Street, is a splendid Baroque structure by Giovanni Domenico Canevale, completed in 1684. Its Baroque neighbours to the west were all pulled down in the course of the *asanace*, and replaced with the present buildings. In very much the same florid style as the prestige structures lining Pařížská (Boulevard de Paris) is the middle building, *no 6/932*, designed by Osvald Polívka in 1900.

Sv.Mikuláš (Church of St Nicholas) ⊘ – Completed in 1737, its monumentality accentuated by its gleaming whiteness, this resplendent Baroque church only became one of the dominant structures in Old Town Square when the buildings which once largely screened it from view were demolished.

Faced with the problem of constructing a church in what was then a narrow stree its architect, Kilián Ignác Dientzenhofer built high, flanking a great cupola wit twin towers. The centrally planned interior, of equally pristine whiteness, is complex display of architectural virtuosity with spectacular stuccowork by Bernar Spinetti. The inside of the cupola is painted with frescoes by P. Asam depictir the life of St Nicholas.

Together with its predecessors on the site, the church has had a varied histor The first church was erected by German merchants who moved here from the original settlement in Na Poříčí in the early 13C; before the construction of tl Town Hall their building served as council chamber as well as the Old Town's pari church. For more than 200 years the church was a stronghold of Hussitism, befo being handed over to the Benedictines, whose monastery it adjoined. Betwee 1871-1914 it served the city's Russian Orthodox community, then had a brief sp as a garrison church. In 1920 it became the seat of the newly-formed Czechoslova Church, a neo-Hussite foundation which it was hoped would become the natior church of Czechoslovakia.

Adjoining the church at the corner with Maiselová is the site of the Baroque hou in which Franz Kafka was born. Rebuilt at the time of the asanace, the buildir now houses the small-scale **Expozice Franze Kafky** ⊘, with displays on Kafka's life a works. A somewhat tortured-looking bust of the author by Karel Hladík is attache to the façade.

★★**Matky Boží před Týnem (Church of Our Lady of Týn or Týn Church)** ⊘ – Despite lower parts being hidden by the houses crouching in front of it, the **Týn Church** the most assertive building in the square, with its twin towers rising 80 m ov the paving and capped by an array of steeples and sharply pointed belfries of dec edly sinister appearance.

The church is the city's most important Gothic place of worship other than t cathedral. Built from about 1360 onwards, it replaced an early Gothic church, its a replacement for a 12C Romanesque structure serving the foreign merchants from the nearby Týn Court or Ungelt★ *(see p. 207)*. For many years it was a focal po of reform; Konrad Waldhauser and Milíč of Kroměříž preached here in the la 14C, and in the next century it was the seat of the only Hussite archbishop, J of Rokycany. The Hussite King, George of Poděbrady endowed it with the symb of the Utraquist movement, a golden chalice. This, together with a statue of t king himself, adorned the gable between the towers until 1623, when, in a gestu of Catholic triumphalism, it was melted down and made into the halo for the stat of the Virgin Mary which replaced it.

Some of the construction work on the church was carried out by the workshop of Petr Parléř. Dating from around 1380, the most splendid achievement of its craftsmen is the carving of the Crucifixion in the tympanum of the north portal facing Týnská Lane (original now in the National Gallery). The interior of the church is currently undergoing restoration, which should enhance its previously somewhat dark and gloomy appearance and allow its rich fusion of Gothic, Baroque and Renaissance structure and decoration to be more fully appreciated. The aisles, of equal height to the nave, retain their Gothic vaulting, while that of the nave was reconstructed in Baroque style following the great fire of Prague in 1679. Among the Gothic furnishings are a stone canopy of 1493 carved for the tomb of the Hussite Bishop Mirandola by Matěj Rejsek, presbytery sedilia with portraits of King Václav IV and his Queen, a Calvary and a Madonna and Child of about 1400, a pulpit of around 1450 and a pewter font of 1414. Renaissance features include a superbly carved *Baptism of Christ* of 1520 *(to the right of south portal)* and the polished red granite tombstone of Tycho de Brahe, in which the unfortunate astronomer's attenuated nose (sliced off in a duel) is clearly visible. The Baroque imprint is decisive, notably in the form of the altarpieces painted by Karel Škreta of which the most striking is the Ascension forming part of the High Altar. High up in the wall of the south aisle is the little window belonging to the house on Celetná Street in which the young Kafka lived for a while.

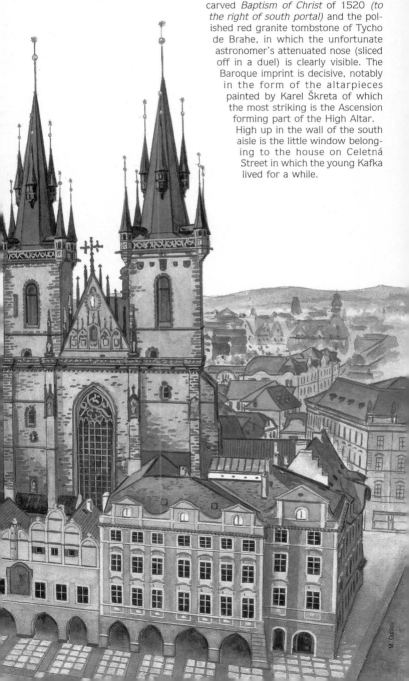

Státní OPERA★

STATE Opera
Wilsonova 4 New Town Underground Muzeum

In response to the construction by the Czechs of the monumental building
the National Theatre, Prague's prosperous and cultured German communi
financed this equally splendid but rather smaller structure, originally called th
Neues Deutsches Theater. The choice of architects was an inevitable one: th
indefatigable Viennese duo of **Helmer and Fellner**, responsible for theatres an
opera houses all over the Austro-Hungarian Empire. Behind the neo-Classic
façade with its Pegasus statue is a delicious neo-Rococo interior, entire
restored in 1973.

The theatre was the scene of much musical innovation. Prague was introduce
here to the music of Richard Strauss and Gustav Mahler. Between 1911 an
1927 the theatre's Austrian director, Alexander Zemlinský promoted conten
porary German music, with compositions by Ernst Křenek and Arno
Schoenberg. In 1924 Hindemith conducted the premiere of his *The Wait*, an
in 1936 Shostakovitch's *A Lady Macbeth of Mtsensk* was given its first perfo
mance outside the Soviet Union.

After the Second World War the theatre became the home of the company calle
the Opera of the 5 May and its avant-garde orchestra. It was subsequently rename
the Smetanovo divadlo (Smetana Theatre) before becoming the State Opera.

STAVOVSKÉ Divadlo★

ESTATES Theatre
Ovocný trh 1 Old Town Metro Mùstek

Founded by Count Nostiz in 1781 as Prague's first permanent theatre, the green an
cream neo-Classical building of the Stavovské divadlo (Theatre of the Estates) dom
nates **Ovocný trh** (Fruit Market).

The Fruit Market, along with the **Uhelný trh** (Coal Market) to the southwest, forms pa
of **Havelské město** (St Havel's Town), a planned extension to the Old Town carried ou
in the mid 13C, the rectilinear pattern of its streets and building plots still markin
the townscape of today. On the south side of Rytířská (Knight Street) remains of th
original medieval tower dwellings have been incorporated into later buildings. As we
as the Estates Theatre, St Havel's Town encompasses the ancient buildings of **Charl
University**, a fine parish church, and not least, the most accessible of the city's ope
air markets.

★**Stavovské divadlo (Estates Theatre)** ⊘ – Named after its founder, the theatre opene
on 21 April 1783 with a performance of Lessing's play *Emilia Galotti*, but it is fo
the triumphal premiere of Mozart's opera *Don Giovanni* on 29 October 1787 tha
it will always be remembered *(see panel)*. Subsidized by the Diet, the assembly o
the Bohemian Estates (nobility, clergy, burghers), the theatre changed its name t
the Estates Theatre in 1799, eventually putting on performance in Czech as we
as in German, though it became exclusively German again in 1861 with the ne
title of the Theatre Royal. In 1920, in the course of violent anti-German and ant
Jewish disturbances, it was taken over by force by actors from the National Theatr
and became an wholly Czech establishment. The Communists renamed it the T
Theatre, after Josef Kajetán Tyl, the composer of *Kde domov můj? (Where is m
home?)*, the tune which became the Czech national anthem, but this venerab
institution has now reverted to its late-18C name.

The premiere of Don Giovanni

A couple of operas based on the tale of Don Juan had already been performed
in Prague when, in early 1787, Mozart was asked by the Nostiz Theatre to
compose an opera on the same subject for the following autumn. He set to
work, but two days before the premiere, the overture was still not written. The
story has it that the composer's wife Constanze had to keep him awake with
strong coffee throughout the night of the 27 October while he scribbled away
against the clock. From the Bertramka where the couple were staying, the completed overture was rushed to the copyists and distributed to the orchestra just
in time for the premiere on the 29th. The performance of *Il dissoluto punito os-
sia il Don Giovanni* was a triumph, the general agreement being that nothing
quite like it had ever been seen in Prague before. Mozart revelled in the city's
adulation, declaring *"Meine Prager verstehen mich!" (My Praguers understand
me!)*. The city still reveres him, though the constant performance of his most
popular works for the tourist audience is no guarantee of quality.

Carolinum – *Ovocný trh 3.* The university founded by Charles IV in 1348 and named after him was the first in Central Europe. At first it had no premises of its own, but in 1383 it moved into the Gothic mansion which still serves as its ceremonial centre today and in which occasional exhibitions open to the public are staged. Fragments of the original building to survive Baroque reconstruction and war damage include a medieval portal known as the Hus Gate, two bays of its Gothic arcade, and a wonderful **oriel window**★ looking out onto the side of the Estates Theatre.

The university has shared to the full in the country's turbulent history. Originally it was divided into four so-called "nations" with equal privileges, but in 1409, in the year of John Huss' rectorship, a royal decree gave the "Bohemian nation" priority. Even though many of these Bohemians were German-speakers, their fellow-Germans from beyond the frontiers felt unwelcome and decamped en masse, many of them setting up a rival university in Leipzig. The university's reputation as a hot-bed of heresy came to an end after the Battle of the White Mountain in 1620; the Rector, Jan Jessenius, was one of those put to death in Old Town Square in 1621, his tongue having first been cut out, and a year later the university was handed over to the Jesuits. In 1882 growing national tensions led to a split into a German and a Czech university, each faction claiming to be the true heirs of Emperor Charles IV. After all Czech institutions of higher learning had been suppressed by the Nazis in 1939 the final closure of the Deutsche Universität in Prag in 1945 came as no surprise.

★**Sv.Havel (Church of St Havel or St Gallus)** ⊘ – This handsome Baroque church with its undulating west front designed by Santini in 1727 incorporates some of the stonework of its predecessor, the Gothic parish church built for the mostly Bavarian immigrants who were the first inhabitants of the newly-founded St Havel's Town. It contains the tomb of one of the greatest artists of the Prague Baroque, Karel Škréta, but its greatest treasure is a complex Crucifixion scene of 1726 sculpted in wood by F.M. Brokoff.

Melantrichova (Melantrich Street) – Named after a famous 16C Czech printer and publisher, this street teases the crowds of pedestrians which throng it by narrowing to the width of an alleyway before allowing them to escape into the broad spaces of Old Town Square. On the corner with Kožná Street stands the birthplace of the "rushing reporter" (Rasender Reporter) Egon Erwin Kisch, its most distinctive feature being a splendid **Renaissance portal**★ with the two bears which give the house its name.

ŠTERNBERSKÝ Palác
NÁRODNÍ Galerie★★

STERNBERG Palace - Old Masters Collection of National Gallery

Hradčanské náměstí Hradčany Tram 22 to Pražský hrad

‍anding in the shade of its far more flamboyant neighbour, the Archbishop's Palace, ⁊e town mansion built by Wenzel Adalbert Sternberg (Václav Vojtěch Šternberg) at the ⁊rn of the 18C is the home of the fine national collection of Old Master paintings. ‍ernberg was among the wealthiest men in Prague, rich enough to build not only ⁊is spacious town residence but also the great palace at Troja on what was then the ‍untrified edge of the city. His architect was Giovanni Battista Alliprandi, who based ‍s work on plans by Domenico Martinelli, and completed his commission in 1707. ‍pproached down a cobbled passageway along the western flank of the Archbishop's ‍alace, the building is arranged around a courtyard. Its most distinctive features are ⁊e spacious vestibule and a grandiose pavilion facing the garden front and crowned ⁊ an oval dome. Some of the interiors retain their original decoration, and the palace ‍st manages to evoke some sense of its past as an aristocratic residence.

‍wards the end of the 18C, another Sternberg, Count Franz Josef, was a leading ‍gure in the revival of Bohemian cultural life, a member of the Patriotic Association ⁼ Friends of Art, an aristocratic confraternity which established the country's very ‍st art collection with the aim of *"raising the fallen artistic taste of the public"*.

★NÁRODNÍ GALERIE ⊘

To begin with the collection was housed in the Černín Palace, then from 1814 to 1871 in the Šternberg Palace, to which, after spells elsewhere, the European (ie non-Czech) works finally returned in 1947. In 1995 the Šternberg Palace lost its superlative collection of modern European art, which was integrated with the national collection of Czech art in the Trade Fair Palace *(see p.214)*. As one of the National Gallery's principal roles in Communist times was to act as a repository for confiscated property, the post-1989 process of restitution has resulted in a number of key works being returned to private owners, but the Šternberg Palace can still offer a fine survey of Old Master paintings from most European schools, with particular strengths in the art of the German Renaissance and 17C painting from the Low Countries.

Adam and Eve by Cranach

DAGLI ORTI

First floor – The fir rooms have numerous n nor Italian works from t 14C to the 16C. A five-pa altarpiece by Antonio V varini and Giovanni d'Al magna from the mid 1! includes its original fram and there is also an impo ing St Peter by Vivarini. splendid hook-nosed bu of *Lorenzo de Medici* is Antonio del Pollaiuo (1431-98). The smaller Ita ian primitives make an i teresting prelude to the co lection of Greek, Venetia Dalmatian and Russia icons of various dates ar to a number of early Egyp ian portraits.

Canvases from the Lo Countries include a *Lame tation* by Dieric Bou (1410/20-1475), a triptyc of the Adoration of th Magi by Geertgen tot Si Jans (1460/65-1490/93 much cut up but still wi fine portraits of donors s among meticulously de tailed townscapes and lan

scapes. Another triptych is by Joos van Cleve (c 1464-1540), but the most fasci ating pictures in this section are perhaps **St Luke Drawing the Virgin Mary★** by Ja Gossaert (c 1478-1533/6), where the figures are located in an elaborate archite tural setting, and a lovely *Virgin and Child* of c 1520 by unknown Netherlandis master. A grotesque *Weeping Bride* of c 1540 is by Johannes Sanders va Hemessen.

A number of paintings by contemporaries and by other members of the **Breugh** family try vainly to make up for the return to its original Lobkowicz owners what was one of the gallery's greatest prizes, Pieter Breughel the Elder's Ha making, now to be seen in the palace at Nelahozeves outside Prague.

Second floor – Among the German Renaissance paintings are works of really hig quality, including several pictures by **Cranach the Elder** (1452-1553) among them superb **Adam and Eve★** and a exceptionally foolish *Old Man* whose young female con panion has her eye set firmly on his purse. There are panels from the Hohenbu Altarpiece by Holbein the Elder (c 1465-1524), a *Portrait of a Man* by Cranac the Younger (1515-86) and a **Martyrdom of St Florian★** by Albrecht Altdorfer (c 148 1538), in which the unfortunate saint is being beaten to death by stave-wieldir thugs.

In Hans Baldung Grien's (c 1485-1545) **Beheading of St Dorothy★**, the subject awa her fate with calm.

The undoubted star of this section, however, is Dürer's ambitious **Feast of the Ro Garlands★★**. A wonderful fusion of North European and Mediterranean art, this just celebrated picture was painted in 1506 for the German merchants' church Venice; among the distinguished crowd assembled to watch the Virgin crownir Emperor Maxmilian and the Infant Jesus performing the same ceremony for th Pope stands the none-too-modest artist himself, posing with a parchment bearir his initials. A century later, Emperor Rudolph II took a great fancy to this pictur after organising its purchase he had it wrapped in carpets and brought across th Alps on the shoulders of four stalwart porters. It is one of the few great painting from Rudolph's extensive collection to have remained continuously in Prague.

The prestige of the Šternberg family is celebrated in the so-called **Antique Cabinet,** room decorated some time after 1707 by Johann Rudolf Bys with an illusionist ceiling painting incorporating a stereometric star (Stern means star in German rising heavenwards.

The **Italian Renaissance** paintings include a Tintoretto (1518-94) of *St Jerome*, po traits by Bronzino (1503-72), and an appealing *Virgin and Child, Zacharia Elisabeth and the Infant St John the Baptist* by Vincenzo di Biagio Catena (c 147C 1531). The finest Italian Baroque work is of *Salome with the Head of St John th Baptist* by Guido Reni (1575-1642).

St Jerome appears again in a sensitive study by Ribera (1591-1652) and there is a *Praying Christ* by El Greco (1541-1614).

Another preserved early-18C Šternberg interior is the sumptuous **Chinese Cabinet**, with lacquer walls by the decorator Jan Vojtěch Ignác Kratochvíl who had an Imperial monopoly of this technique.

Italian Rococo works include pictures by Guardi and Tiepolo, while among the Flemish paintings are two by Rudolph II's court artist Roland Savery (1576-1639), the *Earthly Paradise*, filled with abundant animal life, and a *Landscape with Birds*. Rubens is represented by a *Study of a Man's Head*. Among the Dutch artists, Ruysdael is well represented, and there are two fine portraits of a *Botanist* and an *Old Woman* by Jan van Ravesteyn (1570-1657).

The great oval-shaped chamber in the centre of the northern wing of the palace houses a number of masterpieces. There are more works by Rubens, The *Martyrdom of St Thomas* and a *St Augustine*, a **St Bruno★** and an *Abraham and Isaac* by Van Dyck (1599-1641), a portrait of **Japsec Schade van Westrum★** by Frans Hals (1581/5-1666), and a superb Rembrandt of a **Scholar in his Study★**. The double portrait by Joseph Wright of Derby (1734-94) of **Perez Burdett and his Wife Hannah★** is full of human sympathy.

The permanent exhibition concludes with an array of minor works, the most charming of which are a pair of portraits by Bartolomeus van der Helst (1613-70) showing himself and his wife as participants in a pastoral play.

On the cover of the **Michelin Green Guides**, *the coloured band on top indicates the language:*
pink for English
blue for French
yellow for German
orange for Spanish
green for Italian etc.

STRAHOVSKÝ Klášter★★
STRAHOV Abbey Hradčany
Strahovské nádvoří, Tram 22 to Pohořelec

From all over Prague the twin towers of Strahov beckon, rising over the woods and orchards of Petřín Hill and seeming to announce the beginning of the Bohemian countyside. The abbey's splendid hilltop site was indeed on the very edge of town when was founded in the mid 12C, at a point where the road from western Bohemia egan to descend towards the castle. From the very start Strahov was an internationally renowned centre of culture; its long history has left an architectural complex tretching from the Romanesque to the 18C Enlightenment, while its libraries and icture collection are among the great sights of Prague.

HISTORY

seems to have been the founder's way with words that garnered royal support for he abbey in its early days. In 1140, Bishop Zdík of Olomouc described the site to rince Vladislav II in the most fulsome terms, comparing the city of Prague to erusalem and Strahov to Mount Zion. The ruler's approval was given, the first Premonstratensian monks arrived from the Rhineland in 1142, and by the 1180s a great omanesque abbey dominated the heights. Its first name was indeed Zion, only later hanged to Strahov (from the Czech "stráž" meaning "guard") in recognition of its trategic location at the western approach to the city. The location was a mixed lessing; the monastery was regularly subjected to sacking and burning. But it was lways rebuilt and the loss of its treasures made good. In the middle of the Thirty ears War the remains of St Norbert, the founder of the Premonstratensian Order and ne of the patron saints of Bohemia, were rescued from Protestant Magdeburg and rought here with much ceremony.

owards the end of the 18C, at a time when Joseph II was shutting down monaseries all over the Empire, Abbot Meyer was able to save Strahov by emphasising its alue as an institution of learning. Far from being dissolved, Strahov grew, not least t the expense of the great abbey of Louka in Moravia, whose confiscated library was nstalled here. But the monks were unable to resist the pressures of later, more ruthss modernisers; in 1950 the Communist regime expelled them and converted the bbey into the **Museum of Czechoslovak Literature**. With the restitution of the abbey to the remonstratensian Order after the Velvet Revolution, the future of this unique instiution with its literary archive of more than seven million items is in doubt.

ABBEY PRECINCT

The precinct can be approached from Petřín Hill, via a passageway between th
buildings on the south side of Pohořelec Square, or through its main entrance
the west, a splendid Baroque gateway of 1742 with a statue of St Norbert. Imm
diately to the left is the **kostelík sv.Rocha** (Chapel of St Roch), built 1603/11
Rudolph II in gratitude for Prague's escape from the plague which raged in th
country but spared the capital. Despite its Renaissance detailing, the chapel exer
plifies the continuing survival of Gothic structural ideas in 17C Bohemia. It is no
used as an exhibition hall.

Beyond, the precinct has something of the rustic air of a country estate, wi
cobbles, grass, trees and a range of working buildings, including a wine cell
which is now a restaurant. A late 17C column with a statue of St Norbert stan
among the trees at the eastern end of the courtyard.

Nanebevzetí Panny Marie (Church of the Assumption of Our Lady) – Like much
the rest of the abbey, the church retains Romanesque stonework beneath th
rebuilding and redecoration carried out in later times. Here, the decisive impri
is that of the mid-18C, when reconstruction was supervised by Anselmo Lurag
but the church retains the basic structure of a Romanesque basilica with aisl
of equal height to the nave. The relatively sober Baroque facade has a fir
statue of the Immaculata by Quittainer. The interior was sumptuously redec
rated at the time of the reconstruction; above the pews and side altars in da
wood and gilt the creamy stuccowork by Palliardi frames paintings of scen
from the life of St Norbert (*side walls*) and of Our Lady *(ceiling)*. There a
altar paintings by Willmann and Liška and statuary by Platzer and Quittaine
The relics of St Norbert are preserved in an Empire style sarcophagus. Th
church's landmark towers date from Renaissance times, but were remodelle
by Lurago in 1743-51.

STRAHOVSKÁ KNIHOVNA/STRAHOV LIBRARIES ⊘

The Strahov Libraries comprise two of the finest interiors ever dedicated to th
storage and display of books, the **Teologický sál (Theological Hall)** of 1671-79, and th
Filozofický sál (Philosophical Hall) of 1782-84. The Theological Hall adjoins the we
wing of the abbey cloisters, while the Philosophical Hall was built, appropriate
enough, on the site of an old storage building. Its architect, Ignaz Palliardi, ga
it a neo-Classical facade with a pediment incorporating a medallion of Empero
Joseph II, to whose gracious dispensation the abbey and its libraries owed the
continued existence.

The vestibule to the libraries has showcases in which intriguing items from th
abbey's cabinet of curiosities can be seen. The libraries themselves can only b
viewed from their entrances.

★★★**Philosophical Hall** – This dimensions of this splendid space were tailored by Pa
liardi specifically to accommodate the bookcases brought here from the dissolve
abbey at Louka. Fifteen metres high, they are a masterpiece of ornamental ca
pentry, carved in walnut by Jan Lachofer and with a single gallery. The magnifice
ceiling painting is the last great work of the Viennese **Franz Anton Maulpertsch** (172
96), who had been responsible for a similar project at Louka, subsequent
destroyed. Painted when he was already 72 years old, it has as its subject th
History of Philosophy, encompassing not only Biblical figures but personages fro
Bohemia's Christian heritage like St Ludmila and St Wenceslas as well as hereti
thinkers of the French Enlightenment like Voltaire and Diderot, shown as bein
cast into Hell.

★★★**Theological Hall** – While the rectilinear design of the Philosophical Hall is at on
with the rational outlook of the late 18C, the Theological Hall designed by Gic
vanni Domenico Orsini more than a century earlier evokes an earlier, mor
mysterious world of learning and speculation. Its broad barrel vault, richly orn
mented with stuccowork, presses down on the bookcases, while a procession
ancient globes stalks through the centre space. Dating from 1720s, the ceilin
paintings in their stucco frames are devoted to the theme of True Wisdom, the
message spelt out in Latin captions. Behind bars in some of the bookcases ar
volumes whose heretical or otherwise undesirable contents caused them to be p
on the Church's Index of prohibited works.

★**Strahovská obrazárna (Strahov Picture Gallery)** ⊘ – Built up mostly in the course of th
19C, the abbey's fine collection of artworks was confiscated under the Commu
nist regime. Many works have now been restituted, some of them from the Nation
Gallery, and are now shown on the upper floor of the cloisters. The works c

Strahov: the Theological Hall

display range from wonderful examples of Bohemian Gothic painting by the Masters of Vyšší Brod and Litoměřice to Renaissance and Baroque masterpieces by van Aachen, Spranger, Škréta, Brandl, and Reiner. Maulpertsch's sketch for the ceiling of the Philosophical Hall is also on display, but the greatest treasure is perhaps the icon-like **Strahov Madonna★★**, painted by an unknown Bohemian master around the middle of the 14C.

SV. MIKULÁŠE★★★
ST NICHOLAS' Church – Malá Strana
Metro Malostranská Tram 22

One of the great achievements of High Baroque church architecture, St Nicholas ris
proudly from the centre of Malá Strana Square, a colossal presence held in place
the lesser buildings which crowd around it. While the detail of its architectural desig
is outstanding, and its interior is one of the most sumptuously decorated the city h
to show, the church's role in the wider townscape of Prague is no less striking,
great dome and slender bell-tower forming "the pivot on which the city silently turn
(Brian Knox).

A motley collection of buildings had always occupied the middle of Malá Stra
Square, dwellings, market stalls, a council house and a school, as well as a coup
of churches, St Wenceslas' (Romanesque) and St Nicholas' (Gothic). After the Ba
tle of the White Mountain in 1620 the Jesuits gained control of the centre of t
square, demolishing most of the existing structures, extending their college (no
part of the University), but continuing to worship in the old Gothic Church of
Nicholas until its grandiose replacement was ready for use, a process which last
many years and involved several generations of architects. Planning was under w
by 1672 and the foundation stone was laid the following year, but
1679 the architect, Giovanni Domenico Orsi died. He was succeede
by Carlo Lurago, then in 1703 the work passed into the hands
the **Dientzenhofer** dynasty. In 1703 Kryštof Dientzenhofer beg
work on the nave, which was completed by his son, Kilián Igná
who between 1737 and his death in 175
also built the chancel and the
metre high dome. Finally, in 175
the bell-tower was added k
Anselmo Lurago, Kilian's son-i
law. But even now the great pr
ject was not finished; the deco
ation of the interior went on un
1775, a mere two years befo
Emperor Joseph II ordered the d
solution of the Jesuit Order.

Mozart played on the church's ma
nificent organ, and it was here
14 December 1791, a few days aft
his death, that a requiem Mass w
held for him, the crowd spilli
out into the square.

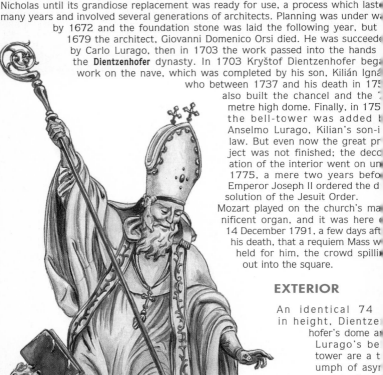

EXTERIOR

An identical 74
in height, Dientze
hofer's dome a
Lurago's be
tower are a t
umph of asyr
m e t r i c a
compositio
their visual relationsh
constantly changing
the viewer moves arou
the city. The contrast b
tween their basic shapes
heightened by the convex
of the dome and its drum a
the concave surfaces of t
bell-tower.

Facing the upper pa
of the square, t
slope of which
cleverly tak
up by thr
flights
steps, t
main faça
is chara
terised by

M. Guillou

further interplay of convex and concave, producing an undulating effect which is enhanced by sharply defined sills and balustrades, broken pediments, and obliquely set columns and pilasters. Statuary by Johann Friedrich Kohl is fitted into this complex but harmonious scheme; it includes Fathers of the Church, the Jesuit saints St Ignatius and St Francis Xavier, saints Peter and Paul, and, in the gable above the Hapsburg eagle, St Nicholas himself with the device JHS – *Jesus Habemus Socium* (Jesus is our Ally).

The bell-tower ⊙ can be climbed for a close-up look at roof-top statuary and a fabulous **view★★★** over Malá Strana and the city as a whole.

INTERIOR ⊙

The Jesuits set out to stimulate faith by sensational spectacle, and the interior of St Nicholas' is nothing if not theatrical, using all the resources of light, colour and movement to create an effect which is almost overwhelming. The rhythmic columns of Kryštof Dientzenhofer's **nave**, lined with gesticulating saints, lead the eye inexorably towards the vast central space beneath the dome designed by his son. High above, the structure of the vault dissolves into the painting by Johann Lukas Kracker of the *Apotheosis of St Nicholas*, at nearly 1 500 m² one of the largest ceiling paintings of its kind anywhere. Kracker not only painted, but also moulded the plasterwork, creating even greater *trompe l'oeil* effects. To the left is the Chapel of St Barbara, with a fine **Crucifixion** by Karel Škréta and wall frescoes, one of which shows a young Jesuit monk apparently looking through a window into the church. To the right is the Chapel of St Anne, beneath its floor the family vaults of the Kolovrats,

the noble family who paid much of the cost of the construction of the church.

Above is the magnificent organ, with heavenly musicians playing beneath more *trompe l'oeil* painting, here showing St Cecilia.

The crossing is dominated by Platzer's four giant figures of the Fathers of the Church, one of them making short work of his devilish opponent with his crozier. Above the Fathers are smaller figures of the Virtues. Platzer was also responsible for the gilded figure of St Nicholas above the high altar. The most extraordinary single feature however is Richard Georg Prachner's **pulpit** of 1765; a coral-like craft in gilt and rocaille, it seems ready to be borne away on celestial currents by its attendant *putti*. High above, light floods in through the tall windows below the cupola, whose fresco, a *Celebration of the Holy Trinity*, was completed in 1752 by Palko.

Paul Claudel responded to the splendours of St Nicholas in the introduction to his drama *Shoe of Satin (Soulier de satin)*: "the whole structure is an act of grace which immediately draws us in, where everything is peace, joy, and not simply a smile, but an outburst of laughter".

M. Guillou

Built over the remains of its Romanesque predecessors, its towers and pinnacles risir effortlessly over the castle's enclosing walls, Prague's glorious Gothic Cathedral is th country's greatest shrine, the coronation church and mausoleum of kings and quee and the repository of Bohemia's symbol-laden crown jewels. The cathedral's foundatio stone was laid in 1344, but five centuries had to pass before the vast edifice was of cially completed in 1929. Its sometimes austere, sometimes richly inventive architectu is complemented by an array of decorative features, from sumptuous Renaissance ar Baroque tombs to extraordinarily colourful stained glass from the early 20C; embellis ment of the building continued even in the Communist era, despite the regime's sco for the Church. In the early 1950s the cathedral's future Archbishop, **František Tomáš** (1899-1992), was incarcerated for several years in a labour camp; during the period "normalisation" he kept in touch with opposition groups and was instrumental, ju before the Velvet Revolution in 1989, in securing the canonisation of the Blessed Agn of Bohemia *(see p. 104)*. He celebrated the triumph of the revolution with a speci Mass in the cathedral, and in 1990 was able to welcome Pope John Paul to Prague.

HISTORY

The guiding spirit behind the cathedral's creation, his presence sensed in the ve fabric of the building as well as proclaimed by specific features, is **Charles IV** (131 78). While still a prince, he was present at the ceremony in 1344 at which th foundation stone was laid by Ernest of Pardubice, whose appointment by the Po as first Archbishop of Prague affirmed the city's importance as a growing, westwar

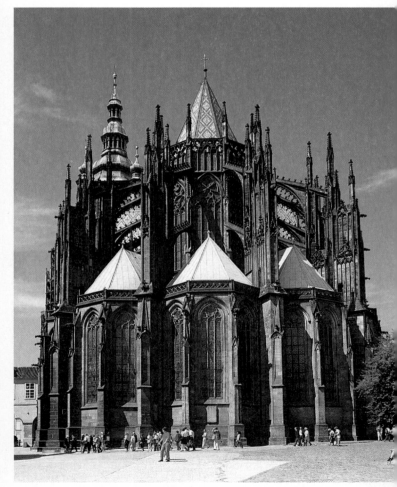

St Vitus' Cathedral: east end

iented city. As King, then from 1355 as Holy Roman Emperor, Charles presided
er the expansion and beautification of his capital, with the new cathedral as its spir-
ual centre. Given his French upbringing, it was natural for him to choose as his
chitect **Matthew of Arras**. By the time of Matthew's death in 1352, he had completed
uch of the east end of the cathedral, in a style and layout which harked back to the
ench Gothic of half a century earlier. In his place Charles appointed the 23-year-old
ter Parler (Petr Parléř in Czech), member of a dynasty of master-masons responsible
r work on the new cathedral at Cologne. Original, energetic and resourceful, Parler
mpleted Matthew's choir, throwing over it a vault of inspired design, whose airy
etwork of ribs integrate space rather than sub-dividing it. He also closed off the west
d of the choir with what was intended to be a temporary wall, a "provisional" solu-
n which had to last for nearly half a millennium.
ork on the cathedral continued after Parléř's death in 1399, but only in a sporadic way.
1421 the Hussites stormed in to plunder the rich furnishings and decoration, though
ey found that their opponent Emperor Sigismund had beaten them to some of the
oils, having melted down the cathedral treasure to pay his troops. Two centuries later,
1619, similar destruction was wrought by fanatical Calvinists, and in 1757 the cathe-
al was badly damaged in the course of the Prussian siege. Perhaps fortunately, thoughts
completing the cathedral in Baroque style came to nothing. It was only in the mid 19C,
ith the revival of enthusiasm for all things Gothic, that a concerted effort was finally
ade; a "Union for the Completion of the Cathedral" was founded in 1859 and a start
ade by removing Baroque accretions to the choir. The country's most eminent expo-
ent of neo-Gothic, **Josef Mocker** (1835-99) oversaw much of the work. The vaulting of
e new nave was completed in 1903, after which the emphasis shifted to fittings and
rnishings, with contributions from many of the major artists of the early 20C. In 1929,
e millennial anniversary of the slaying of the country's patron St Wenceslas, amid great
remony, the Cathedral of St Vitus was reconsecrated.

EXTERIOR

The sudden soaring sight of the cathedral's sheer **west front** with its tall twin towers
seems too much for some visitors to take in as they emerge, blinking, from the tunnel
linking the castle's Second and Third Courtyards. This is of course the 20C face of the
great building, though at first glance the Gothic illusion is complete, such was the commitment of Mocker and his fellow-architects to the style of their medieval predecessors. Close inspection reveals fascinating details, such as the **bronze reliefs** of 1929 by
Otakar Španiel on all three doorways depicting scenes from the building of the cathedral *(central door)* and the lives of St Vojtěch *(left door)* and St Wenceslas *(right door)*.
It's now best to walk around the northern flank of the cathedral, which presses up

close to the humbler buildings in its shade, to **Jiřské
náměstí (St George's Square)**.
From here it is possible to
appreciate the lengths Petr
Parléř went to ensure that
the purity and simplicity of
his **choir** was as little dis-
turbed as possible by structural elements; an array of
pillars, pinnacles and flying
buttresses, a veritable *"forest of stone"* (V. Dudák),
rises over the wreath of ambulatory chapels to support
the vaulting of the choir and
enable as much light as possible to penetrate its glazed
walls.

The Third Courtyard is re-
entered beneath the over-
head passageway which en-
abled the monarch to pass
directly from the Old Royal
Palace to the Royal Oratory
overlooking the cathedral
choir. The courtyard is
dominated by the Cathe-
dral's splendid **southern
tower**; 96.5 m high, it was
begun by Parléř's succes-
sors, and given a Renais-
sance gallery and triple
cupola in the mid 16C.

J.-P. Garcin/DIAF

Cathedral door: Murder of St Wenceslas

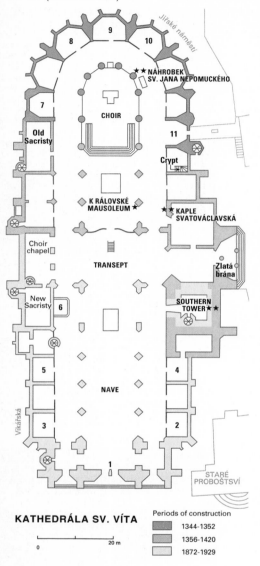

KATHEDRÁLA SV. VÍTA

Periods of construction
- 1344-1352
- 1356-1420
- 1872-1929

0 ⊢———⊣ 20 m

The cupola was remo[d]elled to its present di[s]tinctive shape in 177[ ] and is topped by [a] gilded Bohemian lion. To the east of the bas[e] of the tower are th[e] three arches of the f[a]mous **Zlatá brána (Golde[n] Portal)**, completed b[y] Parler in 1367 as th[e] ceremonial entrance [to] the cathedral. Above [it] is a superb **Venetian m[o]saic★★** depicting th[e] *Last Judgement*; Chri[st] sits in judgement in [a] mandorla, to the le[ft] the saved, to the rig[ht] the damned, dragge[d] by demons into the fir[es] of Hell. In the spandre[ls] of the central arch a[re] the figures of Charles [IV] and his consort. Th[e] vestibule inside is pr[o]tected by a grille wit[h] **bronze reliefs★** of 195[ ] depicting in earth[y] fashion the labours [of] the seasons as well a[s] the signs of the zodia[c] the work of th[e] renowned decorativ[e] artist Jaroslav Horejc.

INTERIOR ⊘

Access to the choir ar[d] crypt of the cathedral [ ] by the ticket giving a[d]mission to the variou[s] parts of the castle.

Nave – The neo-Goth[ic] nave was criticised aft[er] its completion for it[s] academic coldness, b[ut] is now seen, like the re[st] of the 19C and 20[C] work, as an organic pa[rt] of the great buildin[g] suffused with since[re] respect for the achievement of the medieval builders who began its construction. [It] follows closely the patterns established by Petr Parléř in the choir, like the **net vaul[t]ing** or the placing of **sculptural portraits** high up in the gallery; among the busts ho[n]ouring those who contributed towards the cathedral's completion is one by Ja[n] Štursa of Josef Mocker. But perhaps the most striking feature of this part of th[e] cathedral is the modern **stained glass★★**. František Kysela was a pioneer in this fiel[d] his western rose window (**1**) of 1928 with its 25 000 pieces of glass shows the *Cr[e]ation of the World*. Kysela also designed the window of the **Thun Chapel** (**4**) *(3rd o[n] right)* to illustrate Psalm 126 *"He that soweth in tears shall reap in joy"*, as well a[s] the window of the **Chapel of St Agnes** (**3**) *(1st on left)* depicting the Eight Beatitude[s] Other side chapels with fascinating modern glass include the Chapel of St Ludmila (**2**) *(1st chapel on right)* with Max Švabinský's *Descent of the Holy Ghost*, but the wi[n]dow that attracts most attention is the one in the **New Archbishops' Chapel★** (**5**) *(3r[d] on left)* showing scenes from the lives of SS Cyril and Methodius; completed by A[l]fons Mucha as late as 1931, it is still in the Secession style long since abandoned b[y] other artists but none the less appealing for that. Archbishop Tomášek is buried her[e] In a very different spirit from Mucha's work is the **altarpiece** (**6**) carved in a varie[ty] of woods by the sculptor František Bílek, an impassioned statement of sufferin[g] and redemption. The figure of Christ Crucified was completed in 1899, th[e] remaining features in 1927.

Crossing and transepts – Almost completely filling the north transept is the Renaissance organ loft, the work in 1561 of the cathedral architect Bonifác Wohlmut, which originally closed off the western end of the choir and was moved here in 1924. The Rococo organ dates from 1763. Splendid Baroque statues of Bohemia's patron saints are attached to the columns of the crossing, and appear again, more spectacularly, in the south transept in the cathedral's largest window; rising over the ceremonial entrance to the cathedral *(normally closed)* and the Golden Gateway and depicting the *Last Judgement*, its glass is to designs by Max Švabinský.

Choir – *Tickets must be shown at the entrance to the north choir aisle.* This is the heart of the medieval building created by Matthew of Arras and Petr Parléř, the place where the latter carried out the bold experiments which treat the space of the vault in a unified way rather than dividing it up into separate bays as the structure would normally dictate; his network of diagonal ribs allows the eye to roam unhindered. Parléř's originality was also expressed in the **Old**

Stained glass by Mucha

Ph. Gajic/MICHELIN

Sacristy *(second choir chapel in the north aisle)*, where part of the vault springs from a carved boss suspended in space. High up in the gallery (and difficult to see) are portrait **busts**★★ from the Parléř workshop; unusually realistic for medieval sculpture, they include Charles IV, and, remarkably, Parler himself as well as Matthew of Arras.

Enclosed by an elaborate grille, the pale marble **Royal Mausoleum**★ dominates the centre of this end of the choir. The work of the Netherlander Alexander Colin, it was commissioned by Maxmilian II in 1566 to honour his parents, Ferdinand I and Anne Jagiello, as well as to link the relatively recently installed Hapsburg dynasty with the earlier kings of Bohemia. Thus Ferdinand, Anne, and Maxmilian himself have recumbent effigies atop the tomb, while the side panels depict previous rulers whose remains were moved to the crypt beneath the mausoleum, among them Charles IV and his four wives.

With the Chapel of St Anne (**7**) *(3rd chapel in the choir north aisle)* begins the semi-circle of chapels around the east end of the cathedral, part of the work completed by Matthew of Arras. Attached to the choir arcade are **relief panels**★ in wood, showing the flight of the Winter King, Frederick of Palatinate, and his Stuart Queen Elizabeth following the defeat of his forces at the Battle of the White Mountain in 1620; one of the most fascinating early depictions of Prague, they show the monarchs' enormously long wagon train wending its way through the streets of Malá Strana, across the Vltava, and out through the eastern gateway of the Old Town. Close by, the majestic 1895 statue of the kneeling Archbishop Cardinal Bedřich Schwarzenberg is by Josef Myslbek.

Several of the chapels have **Gothic tombstones** of early rulers of Bohemia carved by the Parler workshop: Princes Bořivoj II and Břetislav II are buried in the Chapel of St John the Baptist (**8**) *(last chapel before the axial chapel at the east end)*. Princes Spytihněv II and Břetislav I in the Chapel of the Virgin Mary (**9**) *(axial chapel)*, but the most striking are the figures of those most powerful Přemyslid kings, Otakar I and Otakar II (**10**) *(first chapel after the axial chapel)*. But the Přemyslids are easily upstaged by the extraordinarily ostentatious **Baroque solid silver tomb**★★ of St John Nepomuk, occupying much of the space of the ambulatory. Completed in 1736 to a design by Fischer von Erlach,

Tomb of St John Nepomuk

Ph. Gajic/MICHELIN

it shows the saint atop his coffin, supported by angels, and is supposed to have consumed something like two tons of the precious metal. The baldachin above was donated by Empress Maria Theresa.

Just beyond this extravaganza are counterparts of the wooden panels on the far side of the choir, here depicting the destruction of the cathedral's decoration in 1619 by Calvinist image breakers.

The **Royal Oratory**★ (11) was completed some time after 1490 by cathedral architect Benedict Ried; it has rustic ornamentation in the form of branches as well as jolly figures of miners, a reminder of the source of the kingdom's great wealth. Entered via steps down from the adjoining chapel, the **Crypt** is a mysterious space; on display are not only sinister-looking polished granite cylinders containing the remains of rulers, among them Charles IV, but also fragments of the ancient churches which preceded the cathedral on this spot, the pre-Romanesque rotunda and the basilica.

★★**Chapel of St Wenceslas** – *No access; can be viewed only from doorways.* The chapel was built in 1365 by Petr Parléř on the site of the tomb of Wenceslas, the Přemyslid prince and saint whom Charles IV wished to honour as his predecessor and thereby strengthen the hold of his own dynasty on Bohemia.

The northern doorway to the chapel has a bronze lion knocker, supposedly the one grasped by the dying Wenceslas as he was struck down by his treacherous brother, but in fact of later, 14C date. Beyond the doorway, the rectangular space is much larger than the other chapels and has a striking star vault. But it is the opulent decoration of the chapel which most conveys the intense veneration Charles had for the country's patron saint and which elevates it to the level of the most sacred space in the whole cathedral.

Two cycles of **paintings** cover the walls. Those below the ledge date from the period of the chapel's construction and show *Christ's Passion*. They are set in a lavish matrix of semi-precious stones and gilded stucco. The Crucifixion is flanked by the kneeling figures of Charles IV and his fourth wife, Elizabeth of Pomerania. The upper cycle, attributed to the workshop of the Master of Litoměřice and dating from around 1509, depicts scenes from the life of St Wenceslas. An elegant limestone **statue** of the saint, by a member of the Parléř family, flanked by two painted angels, stands above the altar. The shrine of Wenceslas is mostly a modern reconstruction.

A small doorway gives access to the staircase to the **Crown Chamber** where the **Crown Jewels** of the Bohemian monarchs are held, among them the magnificent St Wenceslas Crown made for the coronation of Charles IV. Objects of extreme veneration on the infrequent occasions when they are exhibited, the crown jewels are protected by seven locks, their keys dispersed among different authorities of Church, State, and city.

Tower ⊘ – 287 steps lead to the viewing gallery of the cathedral's southern tower, from where there is a stunning close-up view of the building's external structure as well as a wonderful **panorama**★★ of the castle and the city in its setting.

*Admission times and charges
are given at the end of the guide.*

TRÓJA★★

Bus 112 from Metro Nádraží Holešovice to Zoo. Waterbus (summer only).
On foot across Stromovka Park (Výstaviště/Exhibition Park entrance),
crossing the River Vltava via Cisařský ostrov.

A scattering of hamlets in a rustic setting of vine-clad slopes (a few token vines remain) was given the collective name Trója (Troy) when Count Václav Vojtěch Šternberk (Wenzel Adalbert Sternberg) built his great summer palace here in the 18C.

★★TROJSKÝ ZÁMEK (TROJA PALACE OR CHÂTEAU) ⊙

Access via the main gateway. If arriving by bus, ignore the side entrance, go to the right and down towards the river, if on foot from the far side of the river, go to the left from the footbridge.

Several birds with one stone – Count Sternberg reckoned that it would do his standing at court no harm if he could entertain his sovereign in pleasant surroundings after hunting parties in the Stromovka, the royal park on the far side of the river; at the time the Stromovka had no amenities of this kind, not even a simple pavilion. A farm belonging to the Sternbergs provided an eminently suitable site, and construction began in 1679, even though the family had not yet built a palace in town.

Being able to entertain on a royal scale would not only enhance the name of Sternberg, it would also prove his loyalty and help the cause of the Bohemian nobility, whose image had been tarnished following the failure of the Estates Rebellion and the Battle of the White Mountain.

An ambitious architectural project – On the advice of the Archbishop of Prague the Count employed a then little known architect, the Frenchman **Jean-Baptiste Mathey** (c 1630-1696, *see Introduction to Art*). Considerable manipulation of ground levels was necessary in order to align the main axis of the palace and its garden on the castle, in deference to the sovereign. This also meant that guests arriving by boat would have plenty of time to admire the building and its setting. After landing, they would walk through parterres in the French style before arriving at the terrace, climbing the monumental external stairway and then going straight into the heart of the palace, the Great Hall on the first floor.

A Franco-Italian fantasy – Despite the disappearance of some of the features created by Mathey, his overall concept is still intact.

Gardens – The formal gardens, now recreated at the cost of some loss of atmosphere, consist of parterres centred on a great fountain and an upper terrace bounded by a wall with huge vases designed by Bombelli. To one side is a large orchard, also laid out on formal lines, with radiating avenues, a circular maze and an open-air theatre.

Palace – The rigorously symmetrical design of the palace was based on concepts recently developed by Fontana and Bernini. Lit by two storeys of windows, the whole of the monumental central block is occupied by the **Great Hall**. To either side is a lower wing flanked in turn by corner pavilions extending into the garden. Above rise low towers containing the internal staircases. The main axis of the complex is

Trója: Garden front with monumental stairway

continued on the north side, where stables flank a central semi-circular stairway and a small gateway which once led into the vineyards. To enhance the scale of his building, Mathey used a Colossal order picked out in red, a colour also applied to window frames and cornices. Only the great external stairway and the doorways were in exposed stone, thereby accentuating their impact.

Stairway – The focal point of the main axis, the stairway provides the only direct access from ground level to the Great Hall. Its horseshoe shape was inspired by the great stairway at the Chateau of Fontainebleau outside Paris. The superb array of **sculpture★** shows the gods of Olympus casting the Titans into Hell. Flanked by Zeus and Hera, the uppermost balustrade offers a vista over the gardens towards Hradčany. This splendid gigantomachia symbolising the terrestial and divine order was the work of the Dresden sculptors **Johann Georg Heerman** and his nephew Paul, followers of Bernini

Interior
Descriptions of the decor are available in each room in a number of languages.

The Marchetti, father and son – From Trento in northern Italy, **Francesco Marchetti** and his son Giovanni Francesco, were responsible for ceiling paintings as well as for oil paintings, of which only those in the chapel (1690) have been preserved. Without exception, their work celebrates the genius and the glory of the Sternberg family, showing them in the company of the Olympians, in allegorical compositions (Truth, Victory), proclaiming the Virtues (Obedience, Wisdom, Loyalty) or triumphing over Vice (Evil, Envy, Folly...). The eight-sided Sternberg star appears frequently. The pretentious and complex iconography fails to conceal deficiencies in general composition and the portrayal of gesture; the Count was disappointed and turned to others to decorate the Great Hall.

★★★**Great Hall** (1691-7) – Originally from Flanders, the brothers **Abraham** and **Isaac Godyn**, entered the Count's employment in 1690. After they had successfully decorated the corridors with trompe l'oeil architectural wall paintings, Sternberg was sufficiently impressed to order them to proceed with the painting of the Great Hall, the project dearest to his heart. Their frescoes, glorifying the Hapsburg dynasty and the Christian faith, are on an epic scale. Some of the most telling are those which show the Turkish invaders of Central Europe being soundly defeated. The Godyns were masters of *trompe l'oeil* technique, treating space in a superbly dynamic way by the use of multiple point of view.

The three rooms linked to the Great Hall have lovely wall paintings of landscapes in Chinese style by an unknown artist.

Painting collection – The palace houses a selection of the Prague City Council's very extensive collection of **19C Czech paintings**, among them many works by the history painter Václav Brožík.

Zoo ⊙ – The entrance to the City Zoo is opposite the side access to the palace. The zoo's glory days were in the interwar period when a number of enclosures were designed by the Functionalist architect Josef Fuchs, but it is still popular especially with children.

UMĚLECKOPRŮMYSLOVÉ Muzeum★
DECORATIVE ARTS Museum 17 listopadu, Old Town
Metro Staroměstská

The last of the array of prestigious "neo-historical" public buildings intended to grace the streets of late-19C Prague, the palace housing part of the nation's decorative art heritage was designed by Josef Schulz, architect of the National Museum, and opened in 1900.

VISIT

The Collections – The origin of the collections goes back to the late 19C, at a time when great efforts were being made to promote craftsmanship in the applied arts; and the museum's early exhibitions – first housed in the nearby Rudolfinum – were mainly intended to encourage high standards in contemporary production rather than serving as a historical record. But over time gifts and acquisitions swelled the museum's holdings to such an extent that it is now one of the best endowed institutions of its kind in Central Europe. Display space remains a problem, and it is particularly unfortunate that the permanent exhibition here goes no further than the end of the 19C; the achievements of 20C Czech artists and artisans working in the decorative arts were quite exceptional, but the visitor hoping to admire their distinctive contribution to Art Nouveau, Cubism or Art Deco must rely on temporary exhibitions since most of the museum's stock remains in store (*but see p. 11*, **House at the Black Madonna**). Nevertheless, the works on display here give a more than adequate overview of the arts and crafts from late medieval times to the late 19C. The emphasis is on products from the Czech lands and neighbouring countries, though items from France,

The UPM has two further attractions: a basement café and, from some of its windows, an unusual, detached view down into the Old Jewish Cemetery.

Italy and other countries are featured as well. As is to be expected, Bohemian glassware is strongly represented, but there are marvellous objects of all types, including textiles, ceramics, articles in silver and gold, lace and clocks.

The halls – The technique of *pietra dura* (inlay of semi-precious stones) was particularly admired during the reign of Emperor Rudolf II, and in **Hall I (Renaissance)** there are exquisite panels in this material depicting Prague Castle and the medieval town of Český Krumlov. **Hall II** is dedicated to the **Early Baroque period;** presided over by a bust of Emperor Franz Josef and with lunette paintings celebrating the achievements of the city's Chamber of Commerce, it is as remarkable for its luxuriant decoration as for the items displayed. As well as fine porcelain and faience, **Hall III (Baroque and Rococo)** is dominated by splendid furniture, including massive desks and building-sized bookcases. Fine furniture is a feature too of **Hall IV (Classical, Empire, Biedermeier and Second Rococo),** with outstanding examples of the characteristic Biedermeier use of pale wood and bold and simple forms like the Vienna desk of c 1830.

UNGELT (Týnský dvůr)★

Týn Court Old Town

Metro Náměstí Republiky

Only accessible through gateways at either end, this secluded medieval courtyard still has the atmosphere of a world apart. From the very beginnings of commercial life in the Old Town in the 11C, the Týn was an enclave for foreign, mostly German merchants, the place where they lodged and carried out their business, enjoying the protection of the monarch and subject to their own laws. In return, they were not allowed to trade anywhere else in town; their goods were unloaded here, weighed and subjected to customs duty, the *"ungelt"* in archaic German. Close at hand was the Týn Church where they worshipped and the hospital where they were cared for. These medieval arrangements continued right up to the 18C. After being closed for many years for restoration, the Týn Court is reverting to something like its ancient raison d'etre, with a hotel and restaurants mostly patronised by visitors from abroad.

Granovský palác (Granovský Palace) – This magnificent Renaissance residence with its first floor loggia was built around 1560 by Jakub Granovský of Granov, the chief customs officer. The interior of the loggia has paintings of mythological and biblical scenes.
None of the other buildings in the cobbled courtyard match this splendour, but there are plenty of minor delights, such as the statues of saints Wenceslas, Nepomuk and Florian on House *no 7/642* U černého medvěda (The Black Bear).

Courtyard in Karlín by Jan Smetana (1942)

UNGELT (Týnský dvůr)

★**Dům U zlatého prstenu (Golden Ring House)** ⊘ – *Týnská 6*. As well as housing part of the extensive collection of 20C Czech art owned by the City of Prague, the Golden Ring House has one of the most fascinating Prague **interiors** accessible to the general public. The building's origins go back to the 13C, and in its warren of rooms there are features dating from most periods of its complex history, including fragments of medieval wall-paintings. Immensely long in plan, the building hugs the fortress-like wall of the Týn Court, while from its windows there is the occasional intriguing glimpse of the towers of the Týn Church. Giving an overall view of the evolution of Czech art through the modern period second only in interest to that on display in the **Veletržní palác (Trade Fair Palace)** *(See p. 214)*, the collections are arranged thematically on three floors. Labelling and interpretation is in both Czech and English and is constantly stimulating as well as occasionally baffling. Most of the well-known figures are represented, from **Max Švabinský**, **Antonín Hudeček** and **Jan Zrzavý** in the early years of the century, via the **Surrealists** of the 1930s and the members of **Group 42** from the 1940s to more recent painters, sculptors and creators of installations. There are colourful stage designs by Bedřich Feuerstein for Karel Čapek's play *RUR* and meticulous reconstructions of Zdeněk Pešánek's light-kinetic sculptures of the late 1920s. The bullet-riddled little sculpture *Hands* by Eva Kmentová recalls the trauma of the Soviet-led invasion of 1968. The basement is devoted to a range of disturbing and unsettling works by young contemporaries, among them the lead-coated quarters of Krištof Kintera's Plumbař a Golem-like creature whose lumbering progress through the city streets is shown on videotape.

★**Sv. Jakuba (St James' Church)** ⊘ – *Malá Štupartská*. One of the city's great religious edifices, St James' adjoins the monastery founded by the Minorite Order in 1232, though the church itself was not completed until the late 14C. The bones of this Gothic building remain, beneath lavish layers of Baroque decoration; the church was partly destroyed in the great fire which swept the Old Town in 1689, then rebuilt between 1690-1702, the work on the interior being carried out between 1736-39.

The façade has a trio exuberant **stucco reliefs**, the work of Ottavio Mosto in 1695. Depicting events *(left to right)* from the lives of St Francis, St James and St Anthony, the apparently chaotic scenes reveal themselves as harmonious compositions centred on the calm figure of each of the saints.

Inside, the church has a total length only exceeded in Prague by the cathedral, legacy of its Gothic origin. Its height too is exceptional, despite the insertion of a Baroque barrel vault several metres lower than the original structure. The decoration is superb, culminating in ceiling paintings by FQ Voget and a monumental altar painting of the *Martyrdom of St James* by VV Reiner, its frame, of almost unbelievable richness and complexity, by M Schönherr.

Wordly success and misery both have memorials here. In the north aisle, the monument to **Jan Václav Vratislav of Mitrovice★** was designed by Fischer von Erlach with figures by Ferdinand Maxmilian Brokoff. Dating from 1714, it shows the Grand Prior of the Maltese Order and High Chancellor of Bohemia about to leave this life supported by a female figure. Death shakes his hourglass and another lady is lost in mourning, but the great man's fame, inscribed by an angel in the stonework above, seems safe for all eternity. In contrast to this pomp, a decomposed arm hanging from the west wall commemorates a thief; legend has it that a statue of the Virgin Mary gripped the wretch firmly as he reached to steal her jewels, and that he could only be released by having his arm sliced off.

The operation may have been performed by a member of the butchers' guild whose church this was, and which they defended vigorously against attack on more than one occasion.

To help in planning your stay in Prague, study the plan of Principal Sights (p. 12) and the plan of Walks in Prague (p. 98).

VÁCLAVSKÉ Náměstí★★★
WENCESLAS Square New Town
Metro Můstek or Muzeum

ising gently for about half a mile towards the famous statue of the country's patron
int and the broad facade of the National Museum, this great urban space with its ability
absorb half the population of Prague has the dimensions of a boulevard rather than a
uare. Originally laid out in the 14C as the **Horse Market**, it developed in the late 19C as
e city's main commercial and entertainment centre and became the focus of many of
e events marking the modern history of the Czech people. Through traffic has been
moved and the once ubiquitous trams now only make a quick dash across the middle
the square, but the ever-present crowds of shoppers, sightseers, strollers and night-
vls are proof that Wenceslas Square remains the city's strongly beating heart.

HISTORY

eading from the walls of the Old Town to a new city gate, the Horse Market was the
entral space in Charles IV's concept for the New Town. But it took a long time for build-
g to catch up with the expansiveness of the Emperor's vision and any real architectural
ity had to await the modern
ge. Closer to the city's com-
ercial core, the lower part of
e square developed first,
hile for many years its upper
eaches were lined with the
umblest of dwellings as well as
eing the site of a gallows. A
rst **Wenceslas statue**, by the
ulptor JJ Bendl, rose in the
iddle of the Square in 1689.

1848, by which time fine
alaces, hotels and commercial
uildings dominated the town-
ape, the statue was the focal
oint of the open-air Mass
hich helped precipitate the
evolutionary events of that
teful year. The upsurge of pa-
iotic feeling at this time also
d to the Horse Market receiv-
g its present, more dignified
ame.

y 1890, the old Horse Gate
hich once led directly into the
ountryside had been demol-
hed, its site occupied by the
onumental National Museum,
nd by the early 20C there was
doubt that the city's centre
gravity had shifted decisively
Wenceslas Square. It was here
at avant-guard architects built
e great palaces of the modern
ge, multi-purpose complexes

Wenceslas statue by Myslbek

ke the Koruna Palace at the corner with Na Příkopě or the Lucerna Palace, the creation
Václav Havel, grandfather of the playwright who was elected president in 1989. The
ague *pasáž* came into its own, tunnelling deep into the interior of such buildings, link-
g with other parts of the city centre, and creating a semi-secret, partly underground
orld of bars, boutiques, dance halls and cinemas. The square was given its decisive ar-
itectural imprint in this period, becoming an apt symbol of the progressive, independent
ew nation of Czechoslovakia by day, and by night, with its array of neon signs, a colour-
l backdrop to a nightlife which was among the most sophisticated in Central Europe.

ll the parades, processions and demonstrations of the 20C have passed through
enceslas Square: Czechoslovak legionnaires accompanying President Masaryk on his
iumphant return from exile in 1918, German occupation troops in 1939, banner-
earing Communist masses on May Day, Soviet tanks in 1968, and, more recently,
pturous crowds applauding Václav Havel and Alexander Dubček as they proclaimed
e triumph of the Velvet Revolution.

THE SQUARE

The best overall view of Wenceslas Square is from the terrace in front of the
National Museum, though this can only be reached safely via the underpasses
beneath the southbound carriageway of the Magistrála urban expressway. Beyond
the statue of Wenceslas the 60 m wide boulevard, lined with lime trees, slopes

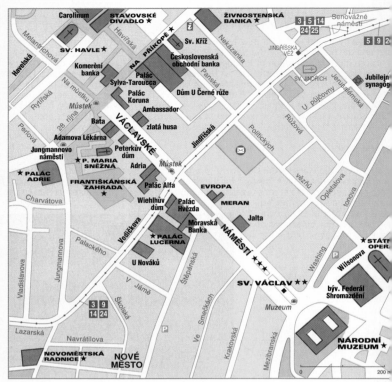

gently downwards towards the boundary of the Old and New Towns. Here it form a T-junction, the **Golden Cross**, with the broad streets laid out along the line of t Old Town fortifications, to the right Na Příkopě, to the left 28 října and Národn

Beneath the paving is the important Metro station Můstek (little bridge) name after the medieval bridge which crossed the moat at this point, and whose remain can be seen underground; the bridge is recalled too in the name, **Na můstku** (Bridg Approach) leading northwards into the Old Town, flanked by two very differe structures, the late 18C **U zlatého úlu (Golden Beehive)** building to the west and t Postmodern ČKD office building to the east.

All the streets centred on the Golden Cross are pedestrianised, funnelling stream of people to this focal point of the city. Many pause here, attracted by the outdo performers, the sausage stalls or simply by the constantly changing scene.

Palác Koruna (Koruna Palace) – *No 1/846 (east side)*. Turning the corner with N příkopě in great style, this monumental structure was completed for the Koru (Crown) insurance company in 1914. Marking the transition from Secession to A Deco, it does indeed have a jewel-like crown atop its tower, flanked by stern all gorical figures, while its airy *pasáž* is lit from above by a beautiful glass a concrete cupola. But the interwar Automat, a famous New York style self-servi buffet, has long since gone.

Bată – *No 6/774 (west side)*. Tomáš Bată made his fortune supplying the Austr Hungarian army with boots in the First World War. A paternal industrialist, continued to prosper in newly-founded Czechoslovakia, planning a utopian tow Zlín, for his workers, and building this masterpiece of Functionalist architectur the prototype of Bata shoe-stores around the world, in 1927.

Adamova lékárna (Adam Pharmacy) – *No 8/775 (west side)*. A Secession building 1913 with Cubist details and a splendid pair of sculpted figures supporting t balcony.

Peterkův dům (Peterka Building) – *No 12/777 (west side)*. This Early Secession building by Jan Kotěra dates from 1899 and was a landmark in the development Czech modern architecture, abandoning all historical references in favour of inspired synthesis of clear function and lyrical but restrained ornamentation. The co struction of this and other relatively tall modern buildings ended the previous visu dominance of this part of the square by the Church of Our Lady of the Snows.

Ph. Roy/HOA QUI

Hotels Ambassador and Zlatá husa (The Golden Goose) – *Nos 5/840* and *7/839 (east side)*. A famous pair of Art Deco hotels, dating from just before the First World War.

Palác Alfa (Alfa Palace) – *No 28/785 (west side)*. A multi-purpose Functionalist building of 1929 with a *pasáž* linking through to the Franciscans' Garden *(see below)* and Vodičkova Street. Deep underground, the Alfa cinema was Prague's largest, with seating for 1 200. *No 26/784*, the Adria, is the last of Wenceslas Square's Baroque hotels.

★ **Františkánská zahrada (Franciscans' Garden)** ⓒ – *Access from the Alfa pasáž or from Jungmannovo náměstí*. This delightfully secluded little park originally formed part of the adjoining Franciscan monastery attached to the Church of Our Lady of the Snows. First laid out in the 14C, it remained in the possession of the monks until 1950, when it became a public open space. Re-landscaped in 1992, it is extremely popular with all those escaping the noise, pollution, and hard pavements of the city centre, but still retains something of the atmosphere of a medieval garden. At its northern end is a little Baroque pavilion, embedded in a recreated herb garden.

Vodičkova (Vodička Street) and Jindřišská (St Henry's Street) – Crossing the square at right angles, these two streets are one of the New Town's important arteries, with a busy tram route. Between here and the Golden Cross, an vast underground esplanade was built as part of the grandiose public works associated with the Metro. Jindřišská runs eastwards past the main post office towards the free-

---

Revolution Balcony

Dating from 1912, *no 36/793* Wenceslas Square is best known as the Melantrich Building, after the famous Prague Renaissance printer. During the Velvet Revolution of November 1989 it housed the offices of Svobodné Slovo *(The Free Word)*, the first newspaper to throw off the shackles of Communist control. The building's balcony was offered to the leaders of Civic Forum, the umbrella organisation co-ordinating the astonishingly rapid progress of the revolution. On the afternoon of the 24th, a purposeful delegation emerged from the bowels of the Laterna Magica, the underground theatre in Národní (National Avenue) where the Forum was holding its smoke-filled sessions. Striding through the labyrinth of passageways and arcades behind Wenceslas Square, the little group was headed by Václav Havel, the dissident playwright soon to be elected President, and none other than Alexander Dubček, the much-loved former Prime Minister and hero of the Prague Spring of 1968. Dubček's appearance on the Melantrich balcony was the signal for a "roar such as I have never heard" (Timothy Garton-Ash) from the crowd of several hundred thousand gathered in the square. But despite their affection and enthusiasm, it was clear that the kindly Dubček was a man from the past; his desire to complete the work of 1968 by building "socialism with a human face" jarred with rapidly developing reality, and it was Havel who was to preside over the creation of a new political order in which liberal values were to dominate.

standing belfry of Sv. Jindřicha (St Henry's Church), while a short way alon
Vodičkova at *no 30/699* is U Nováků, the former Novák department store, con
pleted 1904 and now a casino; its wonderful **Secession facade★** has a large ar
colourful mosaic by Jan Preisler with allegories of Trade and Industry as well a
delicious little stucco cameos of wriggling frogs.

Wiehlův dům (Wiehl Building) – *No 34/792 (west side)*. An exuberant example o
the Czech neo-Renaissance style, built 1895-96, with colourful murals, gable
turrets, an oriel window and a belfry.

Moravská banka (Bank of Moravia) – *Nos 38-40/794-795 (west side)*. Called a
"architectural monster" at the time of its completion in 1918, this assertive buildin
lords it over the corner with Štěpánská Street. Crowned by a fantastical cupola ar
with an array of decorative features including stylised heads of warriors, it has
pasáž connecting with what is probably the most extraordinary building comple
associated with Wenceslas Square, the **Palác Lucerna (Lucerna Palace★)**. Linkin
Štěpánská and Vodičkova and developed between 1907-20 by Václav Havel, th
engineer grandfather of the Velvet Revolution's president, it is the epitome of th
Prague *pasáž*, an almost self-contained world of apartments, shops, snack bars an
places of entertainment, rising nine storeys above ground and with no fewer tha
four basement levels, on one of which is Prague's most prestigious dance ha
(check). A bust of engineer Havel presides over one of the elegant staircases.

★Grand Hotel Evropa and Hotel Meran – *Nos 25-27/865-825 (east side)*. Bu
1903-5 to replace the original hotel on this site, the Archduke Stephen, the Evrop
and Meran together make up one of the great landmarks of the Prague Secessio
The detailing of the building, inside and out, is of the greatest elegance and de
cacy. Above the glazed arches of the ground floor, the facade has intrica
metalwork, leaf ornament and lettering, and a gable filled with glittering mosa
and topped by a fairy lantern, the work of L. Šaloun. Inside, the famous café whe
Kafka gave the one and only public reading of his work, is a delight of sumptuo
wood inlay, cut glass mirrors and exquisite lighting, and other interiors are equa
lavish.

Hotel Jalta – *No 45/818 (east side)*. Completed in 1956, the Jalta is as repr
sentative of its time as the Evropa. Proof that not all Soviet influence was negativ
it is Prague's finest example of a building in so-called Socialist Realist style, wit
a distinctive air of discreet luxury about its finishes and fittings.

★★Wenceslas Statue – Familiar throughout the world, the equestrian statue of th
country's patron saint is the masterpiece of Josef Václav Myslbek (1848-1922
Conceived in 1887, the statue was decades in the making, the final flanking figur
only being added in the early 1920s; representing Bohemia's patron saint
Ludmila, Agnes, Procopius and Vojtěch, they stand at the corners of the massi
plinth of polished granite which has little decoration other than the words of th
medieval chorale *"May we and our descendants not perish"*.
Wenceslas himself, an alert figure astride his sprightly steed, a pennant flutterin
from his upright lance, was in place by 1913, and thus able to witness the birt
of independent Czechoslovakia in 1918. Since then the statue has become Pr
guers' favourite rendezvous, as well as the focus of the nation's attention in tim
of peril. Nearby, a small memorial to the Victims of Communism recalls that it wa
nearby that tragic student Jan Palach set himself on fire in January 1969 in prote
at the continuing Soviet occupation of his country.

★Národní muzeum (National Museum) – See p. 160.

Wilsonova (Wilson Street) – *No 2/52*. Built 1966-72 between the two carriagewa
of the Magistrála expressway to house the Federal Parliament of Czechoslovaki
this overbearing structure incorporates a fragment of the old Stock Exchange, a
that is left of an entire street frontage. The National Museum is reflected eerily
its expanses of bronzed glass.

VALDŠTEJNSKÝ Palác★★

WALLENSTEIN Palace Valdštejnské náměstí 4/17 Malá Strana
Metro Malostranská

This huge palace crouching at the foot of the castle was the earliest and the large
of all the Baroque palaces to be built by those who profited from the expulsion
Bohemia's Protestant nobility following the Battle of the White Mountain in 162
Concealed for the most part behind high walls, its vast scale, the ostentation of i
formal gardens and the lavishness of its interiors evoke the complex character of i
owner, the secretive, ambitious, and immensely rich generalissimo Wallenstein, wh
as commander of the Emperor's armies, plotted against his master and even ha
boured thoughts of succeeding to the Bohemian throne.

Albrecht von Waldstein (Wallenstein) (1583-1634)

Offspring of a noble family from northern Bohemia and known in Czech as Albrecht Václav Eusebius z Valdštejna, Wallenstein (Waldstein) had a military and politcal career which dazzled the world but which ended in his ignominious assassination at the hands of an Englishman, a Scotsman and an Irishman. His rise to power was at first financed by marriage to an elderly but immensely rich widow, then by the astute purchase of confiscated Protestant estates at knock-down prices. The Emperor elevated his brilliant and apparently loyal commander to the highest aristocratic rank in 1624, and the newly-created Duke of Friedland (Frýdlant) ruled like a king from his miniature capital city of Jičín in the centre of his vast land-holdings in northeastern Bohemia. From his mother's Prague home, the Smiřický Palace in Malá Strana Square, he planned the construction of his new city centre residence, demolishing two dozen houses, a brickworks and one of the city gates in the process. The palace, of unprecedented size, was built quickly between 1624-30. It soon became the scene of lavish receptions and entertainments, while in the background astronomers and astrologers laboured to cast their master's horoscope in ever-greater detail, for Wallenstein, despite his mastery of the material world, was a fervid believer in the occult.

Though aware of Wallenstein's intrigues with the Empire's enemies, Ferdinand II long thought him indispensable, but eventually ordered his execution. Wallenstein was cornered in Cheb (Eger in western Bohemia): roused from his slumber, he was run through by the halberd of Captain Walter Devereux and his body carried away wrapped in a carpet.

★PALACE ⊘

The extensive complex of buildings grouped around a series of courtyards and the formal garden was designed by Andrea Spezza, Niccolo Sebregondi and Giovanni Pieroni. The main facade of the palace is 60 m long; with its late Renaissance dormer windows and a trio of Mannerist portals which hardly interrupt the remorseless run of the many windows, it dominates **Valdštejnské náměstí** (Wallenstein Square). Beyond are interiors which housed the Wallenstein family until their flight in 1945 (though an ancient aunt stayed on, tolerated by the Communist regime and even made an honorary citizen of Prague before finally dying at the age of 104). Today the palace is the home of the **Czech Senate**, and few members of the public ever see the imposing **Great Hall** with its superb stucco work and its ceiling painting by Baccio di Bianco showing Wallenstein as Mars the God of War. The **Valdštejnská jízdárna** (Wallenstein Riding School) at the far end of the garden has been converted into a gallery in which the National Gallery holds important temporary exhibitions.

Wallenstein Palace: gardens and *sala terrena*

R. Holzbachova, P. Bénet

213

★★GARDEN (Valdštejnská zahrada) ⊘

With its formal parterres and hedged avenues, the axial layout of the garde
cleverly increases the garden's apparent size within its confining walls. The wo
derful upward view encompassing castle and cathedral also amplifies the sen
of space and is perhaps suggestive of Wallenstein's overweeing ambition. Th
garden extends eastwards towards the Riding School, in front of which the
is a large, calm pool with a Hercules fountain, but the greatest concentratic
of interest is at the western end, where Pieroni's superb **Sala Terrena★★** brin
garden and palace together. Below a hipped roof with dormers, three gre
arches open into a spacious interior with a vault whose rich stuccowork fram
paintings in which arms and armour feature prominently. The equal in grande
and elegance of any of its Italian counterparts, the loggia looks out onto a gia
dinetto dominated by a fountain with a charming Venus statue. Beyond, a
avenue is formed by two lines of superbly dynamic **bronze statues★★**, the ma
terpieces of Rudolph II's court sculptor **Adrian de Vries**, though the ones on displ
are modern reproductions of the originals looted by the Swedish soldiery
1648. To one side is an aviary and a grotto, in whose walls of drippir
stonework grotesque faces peer and grimace.

Wallenstein's garden weaves a special magic as the setting for **open-air summ
concerts**.

VELETRŽNÍ Palác

MUZEUM MODERNÍHO A SOUČASNÉHO UMĚNÍ★★

Trade Fair Palace: Museum of Modern and Contemporary Art Dukelských hrdinů 47
Holešovice, Prague VII
Trams 5, 12, 17 to Veletržní

The progressive spirit of interwar Prague is nowhere expressed more strongly than
this huge palace of glass and concrete, now the home of the National Gallery's s
perlative collections of modern art.

Cleopatra by Jan Zrzavý

O. Palan/Narodni Galerie V Praze

It's well worth the short tra
ride to the inner-city distri
of **Holešovice** in order to see t
works by many of the gre
figures of modern Europea
art, but while names like Ga
guin, Picasso, Cézanne, Klim
Schiele, Miró and Kokosch
may be the biggest draw,
visitor should neglect t
work of 20C Czech artist
whose contribution to t
development of 20C art is
less significant for havi
remained little known for f
too long.

THE PALACE

Although Bohemia was t
most industrialised part
the Austro-Hungarian En
pire, Prague lacked a worl
class industrial exhibiti
centre until after the fou
dation of the new state
Czechoslovakia in 1918.

1924 the architects Oldřich Tyl and Josef Fuchs were commissioned to build t
Trade Fair Palace, whose vast scale and avant-garde design astounded Le Corbusi
when he was shown round shortly after its completion in 1928. Regarding hims
as the fount of all wisdom as far as Functionalist architecture was concerned, t
Swiss-born architect had to admit that the building's designers had put into pra
tice what he himself had only dreamt of achieving. Occupying a whole city bloc
the building's main features were the **Great Hall,** intended to house displays of hea
machinery, and the **Small Exhibition Hall★** rising through eight storeys of open galleri
Below ground was a cinema, while the roof had a terrace restaurant and café. Af
the Second World War, Czechoslovakia's trade fairs were transferred to Brno, and t
great building was used for a variety of unsuitable purposes, among the

storage space for the western consumer goods, which under Communism could only be bought with hard currency at special shops. When a great fire devastated the ill-maintained building in 1974, the surrounding streets are supposed to have been awash with whisky and fine French wines. The building might have been demolished, but in 1978 the decision was taken to adapt it to house the modern collections of the National Gallery which had never had a fitting home. Appointed to oversee the complex work of reconstruction, the architectural group SIAL had to overcome many problems before the galleries could finally be opened to the public in 1995.

The Great Hall is only used for occasional exhibitions while other parts of the building are not accessible to the public. The permanent collections and other temporary exhibitions occupy gleaming white galleries running off the Small Exhibition Hall; beneath its glass ceiling, this immaculately restored space can now be appreciated as one of the foremost interiors of the heroic period of modern architecture, its spacious balconies making a stimulating setting for displays of contemporary sculpture and installations.

★MUZEUM MODERNÍHO A SOUČASNÉHO UMĚNI ⊘
(MUSEUM OF MODERN AND CONTEMPORARY ART)

Retain your ticket; it must be presented at the entrance to each floor of the gallery. Temporary exhibitions may be mounted on the first and fourth floors, while the permanent exhibition is on show on the second and third floors. Works are rotated and not all those mentioned below may be shown at any one time.

★**Third floor: Czech Painting and Sculpture 1900-1960** – Czech painters and sculptors responded to most of the major movements of European art in the first half of the 20C as well as making strikingly original contributions of their own. Much of the work on display here is all the more fascinating because of its unfamiliarity.

Symbolism – The *Black Lake* cycle of paintings of 1903-5 with their almost monochrome depiction of slim youth and pale horse seen against the background of a dark and mysterious lake are among the best-known works of **Jan Preisler** (1872-1918). Though his own house is now his museum with a fine selection of his work *(see p...)*, **František Bílek** (1872-1941) is well represented here by some of his impassioned, forceful carvings, among them the *Parable of the Great Decline of the Czechs* of 1898. **Antonín Hudeček** (1872-1941) used landscape to convey subtleties of mood, as in *Full Moon* of 1899 or *Evening Silence* of 1900, in contrast to the turbulent panoramas of Prague painted by **Antonín Slavíček** (1870-1910), like the *View towards Trója* of 1908. Sculpture from this period includes fine work by Stanislav Sucharda (1866-1916), **Bohumil Kafka** (1878-1942) and by **Ladislav Šaloun** (1870-1946), the creator of the Huss memorial in Old Town Square. Among several works by **Jan Štursa** (1880-1925) is the touching *Melancholic Girl* of 1906 as well as the pathetic *Drowned Cat* of 1904.

Expressionism – The outstanding figure here is **Jan Zrzavý** (1890-1977), whose wistful visions like *Valley of Sorrow* of 1908 and *Meditation* of 1915 are sometimes spiced with humorous eroticism, as in the case of the invitingly reclining *Cleopatra II*★ of 1919-57.

Emil Filla (1882-1953) is represented with several paintings, including his *Reader of Dostoyevsky*★ of 1907, and there are a number of early paintings including the droll *Triple Portrait* of 1907 by the happily named Cubist **Bohumil Kubišta** (1884-1918).

František Kupka (1871-1957) is now internationally renowned as a superb colourist and pioneer of abstraction. His artistic evolution can be traced here, from early representational works like *Family Portrait*★ of 1910 to the abstraction of *Cosmic Spring*★ of 1913-4.

Cubism – Evidence of Prague's place as Europe's major centre of Cubism after Paris includes paintings by Filla, **Václav Špála** (1885-1946), Otakar Kubín (1883-1969), and especially by **Kubišta** (*Branik Quarry* 1910-1, *Still Life with a Skull* 1912, *St Sebastian*★ 1912, and *The Smoker*★, a wry self-portrait of 1910). **Otto Gutfreund** (1889-1927) explored the possibilities of Cubist sculpture in an array of striking works, including the huddled *Anxiety*★ of 1911 and the splendidly tormented bust of *Don Quixote*★ of 1912.

Civilism – In his later work Gutfreund turned to a kind of Realism well adapted to public sculpture and building decoration. His monumental *Family*★ of 1925 is a key work in this category, while smaller, polychrome sculptures include cheerful tributes to work like *Business* or *The Spinner*. There are sculptures in a similar spirit by Karel Dvořák (1893-1950) (*Girlfriends* 1924) and Bedřich Stefan (*Girl drinking Absinthe* 1924).

Cosmic Spring by František Kupka

Abstraction and Surrealism – Kupka continued to dominate abstract painting, his magnificent canvases overshadowing delicate paintings like *Composition with Circles* of 1936 by Vojtěch Preissig (1873-1944). A persistent theme in Czech art until the 1950s, Surrealism enthused painters such as **Josef Šíma** (1891-1971) (*Nameless Painting*), **Toyen** (Marie Čermínová 1902-80) (*Fright* 1937), and **Jindřich Štyrský** (1899-1942) (*Acacias* 1931), while Zdeněk Pešánek (1896-1965) produced highly original **kinetic illuminated sculptures** like *Reclining Torso*★ of 1937. Works by later Surrealists include the *Perpetuum Mobile for Winding Up Colors* of 1940 by František Hudeček (1909-90) and the truly terrifying *Man with Instrument* of 1945 by Ladislav Zívr (1909-80). Hudeček and Zivr were members of **Group 42** which continued to work and exhibit during the Occupation, taking the desolation of the modern city as a principal theme as in *Last Stop* of 1944 by Jan Smetana (1918-) or *Station with Windmill*★ of 1941 by Hudeček.

Postwar – The array of sculpture includes fascinating work by artists such as Olbram Zoubek (1926-) *(Shot Dead)* and Ing Arch Ivo Loos and Ing Jindřich Malátek) and a tender *Couple* by Zdeněk Paler (1927-96).

Second Floor

★★ **19C and 20C French Art** – Visitors are greeted by Rodin's monumental *Age of Bronze* of 1875-7, sometimes described as "the first modern sculpture". Other sculptures include a Cubist *Woman's Head* of 1909 by Picasso, and, in sensuous contrast, Junoesque *Pomona* of 1910 by Maillol, but it is the paintings which command the greatest attention, a near-comprehensive selection of modern French art. There are works, some of them of the highest quality, by Courbet, Corot, Delacroix, Daumier, Pissarro, Renoir, Lautrec, Van Gogh, Seurat, Signac, Cézanne, Dégas, Derain, Gauguin, Matisse, Bonnard, Utrillo, Léger, Vlaminck, Dufy, and Valadon. In the early years of the 20C the art historian and collector Dr Vincenc Kramář championed the cause of Cubism, and thanks to his pioneering purchases the gallery has an exceptionally fine array of **Cubist paintings**★★ by **Braque** and **Picasso**.

★★ **20C European Art** – Artists from many European countries are represented including Edvard Munch (1863-1944) (*Dance on the Shore* 1900), Marc Chagall (1887-1985) (*The Circus* 1927), Joan Miró (1893-1983) (*Composition* 1933), Giorgio de Chirico (1888-1978) *(Still Life)*, and Henry Moore (1898-1986) (*Sculpture in Two Parts No 10, Interlinked* 1968). The core of the collection however consists of works by Central European artists like **Egon Schiele** (1890-1918), **Gustav Klimt** (1862-1918), and **Oskar Kokoschka** (1886-1980), Paul Klee (1879-1940), Max Pechstein (1881-1955), Karl Hofer (1878-1955), and Karl Schmidt-Rottluff (1884-1976). The I tle town of Český Krumlov in southern Bohemia inspired a number of sombre pictures by Schiele, among them *Dead City* of 1911, while Kokoschka painted several vivid panoramas of Prague such as the *View of Prague from Dr Kramář's Villa* of 1934-5.

★ **Czech Art 1960-95** – The horror of works like Kurt Gebauer's horned *Dwarf Dog* of 1985 and the graffiti-like *July Escape to the Mountains* of 1967 by Jiří Načeradský contrast with the wit and irony expressed in *Great Dialogue* of 1966 by Karel Nepraš or the field of twitching chronometers in Ivan Kafka's *On Potent Impotence* of 1989-95.

VINOHRADY
Vinohrady, Prague II and X
Metro Náměstí mírů or Jiřího z Poděbrad

etween the National Museum and the Olšany cemeteries stretches this densely built-
) inner-city district of apartment blocks, interspersed with the occasional park and
number of sights of more than local interest.

'hen the name Královské Vinohrady (Royal Vineyards) was given to the area in
id 19C it still consisted largely of open land, strung with tree-shaded avenues and
terspersed with farmsteads and rustic inns frequented by townsfolk on summer
undays. The new name recalled the vineyards planted by order of Emperor Charles
' in the 14C, most of which had long since disappeared. By the time the district was
corporated into Greater Prague in 1920, the fields too had vanished, buried beneath
)untless blocks of flats in Secession style, the product of an extraordinary building
)om at the turn of the century. Vinohrady was a good address, while its inhabitants
ere solid middle-class citizens able tolerant of the occasional intellectual also
tracted to the area. **Jan Kotěra** (1871-1923), Prague's greatest turn-of-the-century
rchitect, built his villa here in 1909, and between 1924 and 1938 the house shared
/ the brothers **Josef** (1887-1945) **and Karel Čapek** (1890-1938) saw informal gather-
gs of Czechoslovakia's elite of writers, artists, business leaders and politicians, among
em Presidents Masaryk and Beneš.

ne area had already suffered the loss of its royal epithet, when under Communism
endured decades of near-neglect. But the crumbling stucco is now being restored
id Vinohrady is regaining its reputation as a desirable residential area, close to the
ty centre and with a heritage of domestic Secession architecture unrivalled elsewhere
Prague.

Náměstí míru (Peace Square) – Despite the speed at which it was developed, the Vinohrady district was laid out in a planned fashion, with a coherent hierarchy of streets and thoroughfares, parks and gardens, and a focal point in the form of this spacious square, a natural location for a number of important community buildings.
The Náměstí míru Metro station is the deepest – (53 m) – on the city's underground railway system.

Divadlo na Vinohradech (Vinohrady Theatre) – Completed in 1907 by Alois Černý, this was only the second theatre in Prague to be devoted to productions in Czech and it retains its important role in the life of the city. It's an imposing building in a vaguely Renaissance style with Secession ornamentation and a richly decorated interior. The winged sculptures atop the façade represent *Opera* and *Drama.*

Sv. Ludmila (Church of St Ludmila) ⊘ – This great brick neo-Gothic church dominates the square and its twin towers, 60 m high, are visible from many parts of the city. It was built between 1888-93 to designs by the architect Josef Mocker, better known for his restoration of historic buildings. The austerity of the brickwork is complemented by the opulence of the decoration by Mocker's contemporaries; the entrance has a tympanum by Myslbek, while inside are polychrome walls and vaults, together with statues of the country's patron saints, fine stained glass, ceramic panels and superb altarpieces.

Riegrovy sady (Rieger Park) – Vinohrady is built on ground rising eastwards from the city centre. Laid out on some of the steeper slopes, **Rieger Park** offers fine views over the city between its trees.

Náměstí Jiřího z Poděbrad (King George of Poděbrady Square) – A sculpture of George of Poděbrady, the "Hussite King", adorns the façade of a building at the corner of Mánesova(Mánes Street), but this busy square is dominated by an extraordinary church, the masterpiece of the castle architect of the interwar period, **Josip Plečnik** (1872-1957).

★**Chrám Nejsvětějšího Srdce Páne (Church of the Most Sacred Heart of Our Lord)** ⊘
Like all Plečnik's work, the temple-like church draws on tradition but reinterpre
it in a highly original way. Above the simple, spacious nave rises a broad but th
42 m- high tower flanked by slender pyramids and punctuated by an great tran
parent clock. The building is clad in dark brickwork studded with granite block
evoking a kingly cloak of ermine in apparent reference to the square's royal ass
ciations. The restrained decor of the interior includes altarpieces and statua
designed by Plečnik and executed with exquisite workmanship by his collaborator
Below ground is a barrel-vaulted, mysterious undercroft.
The building met with a mixture of guarded approval and incomprehension in
interwar Prague dominated by avant-garde and Functionalist ideas. Nowadays,
well as playing a central role in the life of the Vinohrady district, the church is
place of pilgrimage for students of architecture who see in Plečnik a precursor
Postmodernism.

The VLTAVA

Prague is unthinkable without its lovely river, which, far from separating the differe
parts of the city, unites them with a glorious array of bridges, islands, embankmer
and promenades which offer endless ways of experiencing the waterside. Further fa
cinating perspectives can be enjoyed aboard a pleasure steamer or other craft.

HISTORY

The Vltava rises high among the dark conifers of the Bohemian Forest, then flov
north before merging with the Elbe (Labe) near Mělník some 40km downstream fro
Prague. Flowing entirely within the country, it's the dearest of rivers to Czech hear
while its beauty, meaning and moods are familiar to millions around the world throu
its lyrical celebration in the second movement of Smetana's *Má vlast*. In the past i
been a contrary companion for city dwellers, subject to sudden and violent flood
destroying bridges and embankments and shifting islands from one part of its bed
another. At the end of the 13C, in near desperation, the level of the Old Town w
laboriously raised a whole two metres in an attempt to counter the constant floodi
(the main reason why the Romanesque and Gothic ground floors of many buildin
are now at basement level). Navigation could be perilous, and was hindered in tl
river's upstream gorges by the presence of rapids. The principal traffic was timbe
brought downstream in the form of rafts, some of them lashed together in convo
up to 200 m long. Early prints show bold raftsmen piloting their crude craft throu
the gaps in the weirs which are still a feature of the river today. Much of the emban
ment was given over to timber yards; in Langweil's famous town model in the Ci
Museum *(See p. 113)* the huge piles of timber look like nothing so much as gre
apartment blocks lining the riverside.

The Vltava

e first watermills appeared as early as the 10C; eventually there were dozens of
em, grouped around the various weirs or fed by artificial channels like Kampa
and's Čertovka (Devil's Brook). Some mills were used to draw water up into a series
towers, from where it was fed into conduits supplying important buildings and
blic fountains.

til the 19C the riverside remained a strictly functional area, the domain of dyers,
nners, slaughtermen, fishmongers and others whose trades required a reliable water
pply and separation from respectable residential areas. Great mounds of rubbish
cumulated, providing a home of sorts for scavengers and other people living on the
argins of society. But from the 1840s onwards, when Smetanovo nábřeží (Smetana
nbankment) was completed, the riverside was gradually tidied up, though even
day stretches remain in Malá Strana where its ancient, semi-natural appearance is
eserved, a rare sight in a metropolitan European city.

e Vltava remains a working river. Steamers and barges still pass through the locks
tween Children's Island and Malá Strana, though most of the traffic is further down-
ream; Prague is an important inland port, linked via the Labe/Elbe to the waterways
northern Germany and far-off Hamburg. Upstream, the building of dams and hydro-
ectric power stations has tamed the river's destructive powers and converted the
ce turbulent stream into a series of placid lakes, thronged with bathers and boaters
summer.

FROM VYŠEHRAD TO ŠTVANICE ISLAND

★Vyšehrad – *See p. 220.*

Výtoň – *New Town bank*. This 16C customs house is all that remains of the ancient
village of Podskalí, the home of fisherfolk and raftsmen. It was the headquarters
of the New Town's excise men and its was from here that they collected the
charges levied on timber floated down the river.

Palackého most (Palacký Bridge) – From his elaborate Secession **monument** on the
New Town bank, the seated figure of the great Czech historian František Palacký
(1798-1876) looks out across the bridge named after him. Completed in 1876,
the bridge was originally graced by sculptures of figures from Czech mythology by
Myslbek, but after being damaged in the Second World War the statues were
removed to Vyšehrad where they can be seen today.
Below the embankment linking Palacký Bridge and Jirásek Bridge is the main
landing-stage for pleasure steamers.

Jiráskův most (Jirásek Bridge) – Named after the author of historical plays and novels,
Alois Jirásek (1851-1930), this reinforced concrete bridge was completed in 1932. Overlooking it from the New Town bank is the Postmodern **"Dancing Building"** *(See p. 131)*.

Dětský ostrov (Children's Island) – This long and narrow island with its playgrounds
and sports facilities is separated from the mainland by the navigation channel and
lock. Dating from 1483, the **water tower** once supplied the fountains of Malá Strana.

Slovanský ostrov (Slavonic Island) – Attractively landscaped and with its restored
bandstand, the island is a popular place to relax. In the 19C it was the scene of
important cultural and other events, mostly patriotic in nature; the Pan-Slav Congress which prefigured the 1848 Revolution was held here as was many a musical
premiere, including that of Smetana's *Má vlast*. Concerts are still held in the Žofín,
the multi-purpose hall rebuilt in neo-Renaissance style in 1884; its name recalls the
mother of Emperor Franz Josef, Archduchess Sophia, after whom the island was
once named. In strange but stimulating juxtaposition stand the ancient, blackened,
onion-domed **water tower** and the **Mánes Building**, a pristine white Functionalist structure which links island and mainland and was built in 1930 to house the famous
Mánes artistic group.
The river is at its widest – (330 m) – at the weir just upstream.

Masarykovo nábřeží (Masaryk Embankment) – *New Town bank*. An almost continuous wall of mostly Secession style apartment blocks defines the meeting point of
city and river. Their characteristically opulent ornamentation reaches a peak at
no 16/248, the **Hlahol Choir** building, and at *no 32/224*, the **Goethe-Institut**, until 1990
the Embassy of the German Democratic Republic.

Most Legií (Bridge of the Legions) – Built 1899-1901 in a mixture of neo-Baroque
and Secession styles to replace an earlier chain bridge, the **Bridge of the Legions** provides access to Střelecký ostrov (Shooters' Island), until 1948 the domain of the
city's marksmen. In 1890 the island was the scene of the first mass celebration of
May Day by a crowd of some 35 000 working people, reason enough for the bridge
to be renamed "May 1st Bridge" during the Communist period. There are wonderful views of river, Charles Bridge and city from the parkland at the northern
end of the island.
On All Saints Day, a wreath in memory of those lost to the river is laid at the statue
celebrating the Vltava and her tributaries at the Malá Strana end of the bridge.

Smetanovo nábřeží (Smetana Embankment) – *New Town bank*. This was the fir
stretch of riverside to be "improved" in the 1840s under the direction of the ene
getic town planner Count Chotek. It offers a wonderful panorama over the Vltav
towards Charles Bridge, Malá Strana and the castle. The elaborate neo-Goth
memorial in the gardens on the landward side of the embankment was erected 1
commemorate Emperor Francis I, whose statue has long since been removed.

Novotného lávka (Novotný Jetty) – Ending in the neo-Renaissance building housir
the **Smetana Museum** *(See p. 184)*, this line of buildings was once a complex of wate
mills, fed from the weir stretching diagonally across the river. The tall tower wit
its spire and cluster of turrets is the first of all the city's water towers, dating fro
1489 but much rebuilt over the years.

★★★ **Karlův most (Charles Bridge)** – *See p. 132*.

Mánesův most (Mánes Bridge) – Completed in 1914 on the site of an old fer
crossing, the Mánes Bridge commemorates the artist Josef Mánes, though it ha
also carried the names of Crown Prince Rudolph and assassinated Archduke Fran
Ferdinand. Motifs by the artists František Bílek and Jan Štursa relieve its rathe
sober appearance. It joins the Old Town at **Náměstí Jana Palacha** (Jan Palach Square
where the riverside is laid out along formal lines with monumental building
including the **Rudolfinum** *(See p. 183)*, in contrast to the near-natural appearanc
of the Malá Strana bank opposite.

★ **Čechův most (Svatopluk Čech Bridge)** – Bearing the name of the lyric poet Svatoplu
Čech (1846-1908), this splendid Secession structure is the city's most elaborate
decorated river crossing after the Charles Bridge. Built in 1908 to a design by Ja
Koula, it has beautiful ironwork and a whole array of ornamental features, includir
statues elegantly poised on its piers. An equally elaborate tunnel beneath the **Let.
Plain** *(See p. 140)* at the northern end of the bridge was planned but never buil
while for a few short years in the 1950s the massive Stalin statue stared acros
the bridge and down Pařížská (Boulevard de Paris) towards Old Town Square.

Švermův most (Jan Šverma Bridge) – A modern structure, erected in 1951 to replac
an earlier bridge, and named after a Czech Communist MP who died in the cours
of the Slovak National Uprising of 1944.

Ostrov Štvanice (Štvanice Island) – Weirs and sluices guard the approach to th
large island whose many recreational facilities include a winter stadium and tenn
complex. The graceful northern section of the **Hlávkův most** (Hlávka Bridge) whic
crosses the island was built between 1909-12 by the architect Pavel Janák an
has medallions by Otto Gutfreund, Cubist-style kiosks and monumental statues b
Jan Štursa representing *Humanity* and *Work*.

VYŠEHRAD★

Prague IV

Metro Vyšehrad or Tram 3, 17, 21 to Výtoň

Guarding the southern approach to Prague, the fortress rock of Vyšehrad confines th
waters of the Vltava to a relatively deep and narrow channel before the river broader
out again to the north. The dark cliffs are crowned by a twin-towered church, a cou
terpoint to the cathedral on the Hradčany heights visible on the far bank to the nort
Steeped in myth and history, Vyšehrad became a focal point of patriotic feeling whe
in the late 19C, it was chosen as the site of the Slavín, the Czech national cemetery. E
the early 20C the tide of suburban development was lapping at the base of the hea
land, among the new buildings a number of fascinating examples of **Cubist architecture**.

HISTORY

Vyšehrad is intimately associated with the legendary beginnings of Czech history an
the rise of the Přemyslid dynasty; it is supposed to have been here that **Princess Libu**
(Libussa) fell into a swoon and foresaw the founding of Prague, "a city whose sple
dour shall reach unto the stars", and it was from here that warriors went forth to c
battle with their Amazonian opponents in the "War of the Maidens".
More verifiable than these inventions of poets and chroniclers is the choice of Vyšehra
as a place of residence by a number of the early rulers of Bohemia, who evident
preferred it to Hradčany. In the 10C Boleslav II had a mint here, and there are trac
of a church of the same date beneath the ruins of the **Romanesque Basilika sv. Vavřin**
(Basilica of St Lawrence). Though Hradčany had returned to favour by the middle
the 12C, its royal associations were revived by Emperor Charles IV, who rebuilt th
decayed palace and incorporated a pilgrimage to Vyšehrad into the coronation cer
monies. In later years the headland grew in importance as a military **strongho**
Destroyed by the Hussites in 1420, it was given elaborate Baroque fortificatio
in the mid 17C to which the French added extensive casements a century late

it by the time of the Austro-Prussian War of 1866 fortresses like Vyšehrad were dundant; abandoned by the military, Vyšehrad was taken up by patriotic Czechs, eir national feelings strengthened by an extraordinary outpouring of art, music and iting inspired by Libuše and other legends of the glorious Czech past. The national metery of the Slavín was developed from the 1870s onwards. The Church of Peter and St Paul was lavishly rebuilt, and the whole hilltop landscaped.

šehrad continued to exercise its spell throughout the 20C. In 1939 half the population of Prague attended the reburial in the national cemetery of the lyric poet **Karel nek Mácha** (1810-36), his remains disinterred from his home town of Litoměřice iich the Munich settlement had made part of Germany. And on a November day If a century later it was from here that the students set off on the demonstration at was to precipitate the Velvet Revolution of 1989.

TOUR

Vyšehrad can be approached from the Metro station of the same name via the Tábor Gate or from Výtoň tram stop on Rašínovo nábřeží/Rašín Embankment via Vratislavova Street and the Cihelná Gate or by the more direct steep paths from the riverside.

Vyšehrad Metro station – To cross the 40 m deep Nusle ravine, Prague's underground railway is brought overground, slung beneath the deck of the modern road bridge.

Kongresové centrum Praha (Prague Congress Centre) – Also known as the **Palác kultury (Palace of Culture)**, this huge edifice looking northwards across the Nusle ravine towards city and castle was one of the largest and most prestigious building projects undertaken by the Communist regime. Completed in 1980, it has an array of facilities including a main hall with 3000 seats and almost rivals Hradčany in its dominance of the townscape.

Táborská brána (Tábor Gate) – Protected by steep slopes on three sides, Vyšehrad is guarded on the fourth by an outwork to which this mid-17C gate gives entry. On the right between here and the Leopold Gate are the remains of part of the Gothic fortifications, the Špička Gate.

Leopoldova brána (Leopold Gate) – The architect Carlo Lurago was involved in the design of this splendid Baroque gate, completed around 1670.

Rotunda sv.Martina (St Martin's Rotunda) – Built around 1070, this Romanesque rotunda stood at the heart of the urban settlement which developed on Vyšehrad until all civilians were expelled when the Baroque fortifications were built. Converted into a storehouse and powder magazine, the rotunda was almost swept away in its turn when road improvements were proposed in the 19C, but was saved by the efforts of Count Chotek and thoroughly, perhaps over-thoroughly restored.

Nové děkanství (New Deanery) ⊘ – The building contains a small exhibition on the history of Vyšehrad. (Another small exhibition of drawings is housed in the bastion overlooking the Vltava). In the park opposite are the **Devil's Pillars**, which may be the remains of a prehistoric astronomical clock.

Myslbek statues – Brought here from Palacký Bridge where they suffered war damage and were threatened by road improvements, the four groups of sculptures by the creator of the Wenceslas statue, Josef Václav Myslbek (1848-1922) include, appropriately enough, the figures of Libuše and Přemysl, her ploughman husband.

Dvořák's tomb in Vyšehrad Cemetery

Sv. Petra a Pavla (Church of St Peter and St Paul) ◎ – Dating from the end of the 1
and progressively altered and restored over the years, the church had its final a
very thorough rebuilding in neo-Gothic style at the hands of Josef Mocker in t
1880s. The interior too was remodelled in the same style, with bold polychron
decor.

★**Vyšehradský hřbitov (Vyšehrad Cemetery)** ◎ – Developed from the 1870s onwa
the cemetery, once a humble parish graveyard, shelters the remains of some 6
of the great and good of the Czech nation. Few military men or politicians featu
among the figures from the arts, academe and literature, though there are
number of women, among them the writer Božena Němcová and the opera sin
Ema Destinnová (Emmy Destinn). Some of the funerary monuments are outstandi
creations in their own right by sculptors such as František Bílek and Bohumil Kaf
those by Ladislav Šaloun include that of Dvořák.
A neo-Renaissance arcade defines part of the boundary of the cemetery, but
centrepiece is the Slavín, the mausoleum containing the remains of the especia
worthy, including the painter **Alfons Mucha**. It is presided over by a winged gen
and statues representing the *Grieving Nation* and the *Joyful Nation*.

Ramparts – It is possible to walk almost right round the Vyšehrad ramparts. T
views are magnificent, both upriver towards the cliffs at Bráník and Barrand
and northwards across the New Town, Smíchov and Malá Strana to the castle.

Cihelná brána (Brick Gate) – Completed in 1842, the gate is also known as
Prague Gate or the Chotek Gate, after its builder. Here is the entrance to the Ca
mates, a fascinating series of claustrophobic spaces which were once use
prosaically, as a vegetable store and now house an informative exhibition
Prague's fortifications.

★**Cubist Buildings** – In the first decade of the 20C there was pressure to deve
the Vyšehrad district as a prestige residential area. The project faltered, but
number of houses were commissioned at the foot of the fortress from **Josef Choc**
(1880-1956), an architect working in the uniquely Czech Cubist style.
At *no 3/49* Libušina Street is the **Vila Kovařovič**. Occupying a triangular site betwe
the embankment, Vnislavova and Libušina Streets the villa was completed
Chochol in 1913, who, even more uniquely, laid out a Cubist garden to comp
ment his inventive creation. Further south along the embankment at Rašínc
nábřeží *no 6-10/42, 47,71* is a short terrace of three family houses, intended
be a modern, modest version of a Baroque palace. Away from the riverside,
Neklanova Street no 2/56, Chochol built an apartment block, but further along t
street, dramatically exploiting the corner site and the upward slope is anoth
apartment block, **no 30/98**. Its soaring corner column leads to a crystalline corr
which seems about to develop into one of those star vaults so typical of Bohem
Gothic architecture.

VÝSTAVIŠTĚ

EXHIBITION Park Holešovice, Prague 7
Tram 5, 12, 17

Originally laid out for the great Jubilee Exhibition of 1891 at the eastern end of St
movka Park, Prague's exhibition grounds were renovated and extended for th
centenary in 1991. The 1891 Expo was one of the most ambitious and successful
its time. With 146 pavilions displaying the technical marvels and curiosities of the tir
it was attended by two million visitors, many of them arriving on a combined trip
new-fangled funicular and electric tram.
Now extending over an area of 36 h at the eastern end of Stromovka Park, the ex
bition park not only hosts trade fairs and exhibitions of all kinds, but has a popu
funfair and all kinds of outdoor and indoor facilities. The place buzzes on summ
weekends, especially on Saturday mornings when an amazing variety of goods
offered for sale at the outdoor market.
Nearby is the Planetarium, while one of the original pavilions of 1891 houses the Natio
Museum's **Lapidárium**, the country's finest collection of statuary and stonework.

★★**Lapidárium** ◎ – Housed and attractively displayed in one of the original neo-Baroc
pavilions from 1891, some 400 pieces from the collections of the National Muse
give a fascinating picture of the development of sculpture and the mason's skill fr
medieval times to the end of the 19C. Much that is on display is of the very high
quality. Because of the risk of environmental and other damage, many of works t
play such an important role in the Prague townscape are in fact reproductions;
Lapidarium offers the chance to enjoy the originals of many famous pieces at cl
quarters. Other masterpieces have been rescued from demolished buildings or fr
monuments that have fallen out of favour. Completing the picture are numero
plaster casts of important works, as well as house signs and many other items.

Room 1 – The oldest items in the collection are **11C columns** decorated with bold plaited motifs from the Hradčany basilica, the predecessor of today's cathedral, while the fiercely-roaring early **13C Lions of Kouřím** are the country's most venerable free-standing sculpture.

Room 2 – Plaster casts of the famous **14C portrait busts** from the triforium of the cathedral, including those of Petr Parléř and Matthew of Arras as well as Emperor Charles IV, his four wives, and other royalty, are more than matched by the superb **Old Town Bridge Tower sculptures★★**, rearranged in appropriately hierarchical fashion. Charles IV appears again in the guise of Roman Emperor, accompanied by the country's patron saints. The battered original of the knight Bruncvík from Charles Bridge is here too.

Room 3 – The room is dominated by the remains of the magnificent **Krocín Fountain★**, the equal of any of the great urban fountains of the Italian Renaissance, which graced the Old Town Square from 1591 to 1862.

Room 4 – The **Slavata Gate** with its two bears once formed the portal to one of Prague's finest Baroque gardens, while the **Atlas** figure by Braun is the original of the one at the entrance to the Vrtba Gardens. Here too are the originals of some of the finest Charles Bridge **statues★**, including **St Ignatius of Loyola** and **St Francis Xavier** by Brokof and **St Ivo** by Braun.

Room 5 – Fragments give some idea of the appearance of the Baroque **Marian Column** which stood in Old Town Square until its destruction in 1918.

Room 6 – Further Baroque works include the original equestrian statue by Bendl of the country's patron saint which stood in Wenceslas Square until its removal in 1879.

Room 7 – Among the 18C and 19C works are the charming *Lovers beneath a palm tree*, once part of a fountain by František Lederer.

Room 8 – Among the monuments to great figures whose fame has dimmed are those of Emperors Franz I and Franz Josef and Marshal Radecký (Radetzky), the popular Czech-born general who routed the Hapsburg's enemies on many an occasion. The work of the Max brothers, his splendid **statue★** was cast from captured Italian guns and formed a central feature of Malá Strana Square until its removal in 1919.

Průmyslový palác (Palace of Industry) – This vast and splendid structure in steel and glass was built to house the principal exhibits of the 1891 Expo and is still the dominant feature of the Exhibition Park today. A cousin to the reduced-scale Eiffel Tower erected on Petřín Hill in the same year, the technically advanced steel structure is partly clad in neo-Baroque clothes, with domed towers flanking the main facade, a central tower 51 m high and allegorical statuary above the entrance. In February 1948, as part of the preparations for the forthcoming *coup d'état*, 8 000 trade union delegates were crammed into the palace and persuaded to endorse Communist Prime Minister Gottwald's revolutionary demands; thereafter the building – renamed Congress Palace – became the venue for all Communist Party congresses.

More recent major buildings include: the striking silver **Pyramida** (Pyramid), used for musical shows as well as for exhibitions, and the cylindrical **Spirála** (Spiral Theatre).

Křižíkova fontána (Křižík Fountain) – Surrounded by modern exhibition pavilions is this extraordinary fountain, the recently rebuilt and modernised creation of František Křižík, a prolific inventor and the guiding spirit behind the 1891 Expo. Computer control of 50 pumps, 3 000 nozzles and 1 248 floodlights ensures a spectacular light and water show for more than 6 000 spectators.

Ph. Roy/HOA QUI

Palace of Industry

Maroldovo panorama (Marold Panorama) ⊘ — An ambitious late-19C attempt
"virtual reality" can still be admired in this pavilion. It was built in 1898 to accom
modate the huge circular painting by Luděk Marold depicting one of the decisi
conflicts of the Hussite Wars. At the Battle of Lipany in 1434 the followers of tl
radical Prokop Holý were soundly defeated by the forces of the more modera
Hussites who were ready to compromise with the established order. The chaos al
confusion of battle in all its detail is wonderfully evoked by the huge painting, 30
in diameter and 11 m high.

Stromovka (Royal Game Park) — The royal game preserve was originally establishe
in the early 14C and later linked by an avenue of chestnut trees to the cast
Sliced up by railway lines, eaten into by Exhibition Park and with its weste
extremity transformed into a villa district (now the embassy quarter), it still exten
over more than 1 km² and with its fine stands of trees and its extensive pa
network is much appreciated by Praguers, especially at weekends.

Under the rule of Rudolph II a 1100 m-long tunnel, the **Rudolfova stoka**, was cc
structed to channel water from the Vltava underneath Letná Plain into the parl
central lake, an extraordinary engineering achievement for its time and still inta
Other reminders of the park's kingly past include the derelict Královská dvořa
(Royal Lodge), rebuilt in neo-Gothic style in 1855, and, in a similar style al
perched above a precipitous slope, the **Letohrádek** (Summer Palace), which no
houses the periodicals section of the National Museum. Close to Exhibition Park
the **Planetárium**, a purpose-built postwar building with displays on the mysteries
the universe, a cinema, and the technically advanced "Cosmorama".

ŽIŽKOV

Prague III

Bus 207 from Metro Staroměstská or Metro Florenc to U Památníku

This resolutely working-class inner city district lies at the foot of Žižkov Hill, a roc
spur just east of the city centre which was the scene of a famous Hussite victory
1420. The area was rapidly built up in the last decades of the 19C, following the cc
struction of the main railway lines which flank the hill to both north and south. T
closely-packed tenements soon filled up with people from the Bohemian countrysid
attracted by the relatively high wages offered in the factories, gasworks and railw
yards. Before being incorporated into Greater Prague in 1920, Žižkov with its pop
lation of over 70000 was the third largest city in the Czech lands. Radical tra
unionism took hold in these conditions, earning the area the name of "Red Žižkc
and ensuring a consistently high Communist vote at election times. Despite its comm
heritage of Secession style apartment blocks, the area is still quite distinct in soc
terms from neighbouring, middle-class Vinohrady. Žižkov is also a stronghold
Prague's Romany population, while its raucous pubs draw serious drinkers from
over town. Over the dingy streets loom two of the city's most visible features, t
TV Tower and the **National Monument**.

ŽIŽKA'S HILL

The western end of the long and narrow ridge gives a commanding view over t
whole of Prague, a fact taken advantage of over the centuries by a number of m
itary men. The Swedes bombarded the city from here in 1638, the Prussia
likewise in 1756, but the battle which has the greatest resonance among Czec
is the one that took place on 14 July 1420. In response to the Pope's call fo
crusade against the heretical Hussites, Emperor Sigismund had led a motley fo
drawn from all over Europe to Prague, stationing them on Letná Plain a
Vyšehrad. One-eyed Hussite general **Jan Žižka** (1360-1424), heavily outnumbere
drew up his peasant army on what was then known at Vítkov Hill, fortifying t
ridge with ditches and with a stockade partly built with pews ransacked from
nearby church. Ordered by the Emperor to attack, the heavily armed Imper
cavalry overcame the first obstacles, but was then checked at the last barrier
Žižka's men (and some women) fighting with fanatic ferocity. Žižka ordered
counterattack from the flank. With little space to manoeuvre, the cavalrymen we
soon overcome, many of them plunging to their deaths down the rocky flanks
the hill, while others drowned trying to escape across the Vltava. Forced to wat
this disaster from the far side of the river, the Emperor retired speechless to
tent, while the victorious Hussites celebrated their victory by stuffing a number
their prisoners into barrels and setting them on fire.

The hill was given the victor's name, as, centuries later, was the burgeon
borough, many of whose street-names (Husitská, Taborská) recall the glories
the Hussite era.

Národní památník (National Memorial) – This huge granite slab of a structure with its **equestrian statue of Jan Žižka** dominates the hilltop and can be seen from all over Prague.

The idea of building a memorial to Žižka went back to the years before the First World War. By the time architectural competitions had been held and the funds gathered, the project had expanded, and was now intended to celebrate the independence Czechoslovakia had gained in 1918 and the role of her Legionaries in securing it. Designed by Jan Zázvorka, the great structure was built between 1926 and 1932, complemented by an austere building housing a military museum and archive near the foot of the hill.

The sculptor **Bohumil Kafka** began his colossal **Žižka statue★** in 1931 and worked on it for many years, somehow concealing it from German eyes during the Occupation. What is generally reckoned to be the largest statue of its kind in the world was finally put in place in 1950, the mace-wielding general and his mighty steed rising 9 m from their plinth and weighing all of 16.5 t.

In the early years of Communism, the Memorial became a Party shrine. The interior decoration by some of the most prominent artists of the prewar period was supplemented by works in Socialist Realist style, like the bronze doors depicting the revolutionary struggles of the Czechoslovak people. The remains of the Unknown Soldier were accompanied by the body of the country's first Communist president **Klement Gottwald** (1896-1953), mummified by means of the same techniques used to preserve the corpse of Lenin in Moscow's Red Square. But despite the experts' best attentions, Gottwald's remains gradually disintegrated and in 1962 had to be cremated. After 1989 all traces of Gottwald and his fellow dignitaries were removed and the memorial awaits a new use.

★**Armádní muzeum (Army Museum)** ⊘ – *U památníku 2.* With a wealth of weapons, uniforms, posters, documents, models and dioramas, works of art and all kinds of military memorabilia, the up-to-date displays of the museum give a fascinating account of much of the troubled 20C history of this part of Central Europe, though nearly all labelling is in Czech only. Episodes such as the role of the Czechoslovak Legions on the Russian, French and Italian fronts in the First World War, the break-up of the country after the Munich settlement in 1938, the struggle at home and abroad in the Second World War, are all tellingly evoked.

Televizní vysílač (Television Tower) ⊘ – *Mahlerovy sady 1.* The casing containing antennae for TV, radio and telecommunications rises more than 216 m above the old Jewish cemetery which was partly cleared to make way for this extraordinary three-legged science-fiction structure so much at odds with its suburban surroundings. Restaurants and a viewing platform (93.5 m above ground) give a superb **panorama★** over Vinohrady, Žižkov and the whole of Prague, best enjoyed in the morning while the sun is still in the east.

*The plans in the **Michelin Red Guide Europe** are brought up to date annually and show:*
– main approach roads, ring roads and bypasses
– new roads
– car parks
– one-way streets
– location of hotels and public buildings
It is an invaluable aid for drivers in large and medium sized towns and cites.

Karlštejn Castle

Day
Excursions

Day excursions from Prague

With a total area of 78864 km², the Czech Republic is quite a small country, its greatest east-west length no more than 500km, its maximum north-south width around 250km. Within this compass is an extraordinary wealth of visitor attractions, historic towns, castles and mansions, forests, rivers, lakes and uplands. Prague lies roughly at the centre of Bohemia, making it at least theoretically possible to undertake a day trip to any destination in that province. But the provincial capital of Moravia, Brno, is only 2 hr by motorway from Prague, bringing this city and its surroundings within range as well.

The destinations described in alphabetical order in this chapter have been selected from the very wide range of possible excursions which could be undertaken in a single day from Prague, and include outstanding attractions drawn from the whole of Bohemia and from southern Moravia. Tour operators run coach trips to many of them, while others are best reached by car. If using public transport or intending to make a thorough exploration of all the sights described in a particular place, you might consider spending a night away from Prague, and a limited choice of hotels and restaurants has been listed with this in mind.

CASTLES AND COUNTRY HOUSES

A feudal land in many respects well into the 20C, Bohemia has countless examples of aristocratic residences scattered across the whole of the country. The range is complete, from medieval castles perched on crags to ostentatious Renaissance palaces or country houses set in parkland. Many were taken from their owners even before the Communist *coup d'etat* in 1948; these remain in state ownership, often as more or less well maintained museums of themselves. A conducted tour is normally the only way to visit such places and its timing may not be particularly convenient. Brochures and souvenirs are variable in quality and quantity. Those residences nationalised after 1948 are the subject of restitution, though many owners, after taking one look at a

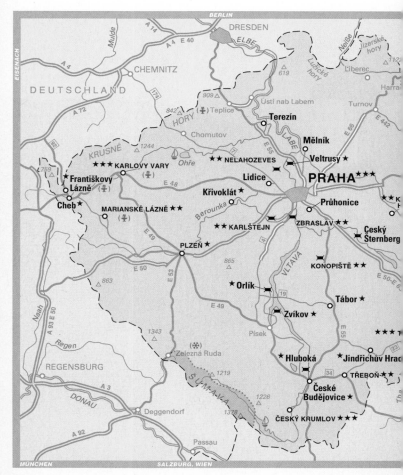

crumbling complex of buildings, have politely refused the offer and returned to comfortable exile. Others, like the different branches of the Lobkowicz family at Nelahozeves and Mělník, have re-possessed with alacrity, filling rooms with restituted heirlooms and developing visitor facilities with enthusiasm.

Castles to the south...

A clutch of castles to the south of Prague are so near to the capital that they could (almost) all be visited in the course of a single day. Its romantic silhouette familiar from many a tourist brochure, the famous royal castle of **Karlštejn** is the most popular trip, even though its greatest treasures are no longer on show. More rewarding perhaps is **Konopiště**, the Bohemian home of Hapsburg Archduke Franz Ferdinand, furnished much as he left it to make his fateful journey to assassination at Sarajevo in 1914. Nearest of all to Prague is **Zbraslav**, not really a castle but a magnificent 18C monastery, now the home of the superlative national collection of Asiatic art. Just down the motorway towards Brno is **Průhonice**; the castle itself is not open to the public, but its magnificent park is, its arboretum one of the finest in Central Europe. Furthest away, but easily reached from the motorway is **Český Šternberk**, high on its crag overlooking the River Sázava.

And castles to the north...

The Renaissance castle of the Lobkowicz family at **Nelahozeves** houses what is perhaps the finest private art collection in the Czech Republic. At its foot stands the humble village birthplace of **Antonín Dvořák**. Nearby is a very different residence, **Veltrusy**, the summer villa of the Choteks, a delightful Baroque building in an English style park filled with follies and garden pavilions. The town of **Mělník** on its hilltop above the confluence of the Vltava with the Elbe is worth a trip in its own right, but most visitors come here for the castle owned by the other branch of the Lobkowicz family and to taste the wines grown all around.

To the west of the capital, isolated amid the vast forests which were once the hunting preserve of medieval kings is **Křivoklát**, as romantically located as Karlštejn and with a far more authentic medieval air.

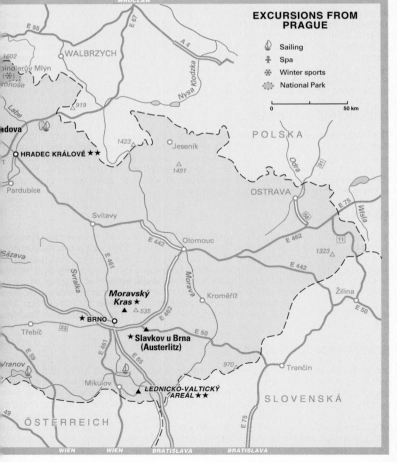

THE BOHEMIAN TRIANGLE

The tradition of visiting a spa in order to cure your ills or simply to relax in pleasant surroundings is a long one in the Czech lands. There are spa towns throughout the country, but the greatest and most prestigious concentration is in the far northwest, where **Carlsbad** (Karlovy Vary), **Marienbad** (Mariánské Lázně), and **Franzens bad** (Františkovy Lázně) make up the renowned "Bohemian Triangle". Each still operates as a serious spa, with patients undertaking a variety of cures, most but not all not all based on the therapeutic properties of the waters. Each has its own legacy of wonderful buildings: greater and lesser hotels, trim pensions and villas, churches for the different denominations, and superb colonnades sheltering the springs. Marienbad is laid out around a park, while Carlsbad is set in a deep and winding valley. The smallest of the trio, Františkový Lázně is surrounded by heath and forest and is close to historic **Cheb**, the "Bohemian Nuremberg" which was once the miniature capital of the Egerland region.

Places of Memory

Some of the darkest memories of the Nazi occupation of the Czech lands are recalled in two places north of Prague. In revenge for the assassination of Reichsprotektor Heydrich, the mining village of **Lidice** was destroyed, its population murdered or deported. Lidice became a world-wide symbol of Nazi brutality and Czech suffering, and though a new settlement was built nearby, the site of the old village remains much as it was in 1942. In the same year the fortress town of **Terezín** was cleared of its inhabitants and turned into a ghetto for the country's Jews, from which most were transported to the death camps further east.

SOUTHERN BOHEMIA

Much cherished by local connoisseurs of Czech landscape, this is a rural area of lakes and woodland bounded by forested uplands along the border with Austria. The Hussite town of **Tábor** forms the gateway to the region, whose capital is **České Budějovice**, its great square laid out in the 13C. A galaxy of smaller medieval towns includes **Třeboň**, **Jindřichův Hradec**, and UNESCO listed **Český Krumlov**. Exquisite **Telč**, just over the border in southern Moravia, is also on the UNESCO list. Castles abound, not only in the towns (Krumlov's is the largest outside Prague) but deep in the countryside too, like **Orlík** and **Zvíkov**. On its hilltop outside Budějovice, **Hluboká** is modelled on England's Windsor Castle.

THE HOME OF BEER

The motorway west from Prague leads straight to Bohemia's second city, industrial **Plzeň** (Pilsen). Founded in the 13C and with an historic core centred on the country's largest square, the town is worth exploring in its own right, but it is Pilsen's associations with beer and brewing that bring most people here, to tour the great Prazdroj (Urquell brewery), visit the brewery museum, or simply to drink what many regard as the world's best beer in its place of origin.

EASTERN CITIES

Most Czech towns were founded in the Middle Ages. Free from commercial pressures during the Communist period, their medieval centres are often well preserved, though sometimes in a rather dilapidated state. To the east of Prague two such places are outstanding: the silver-mining town of **Kutná Hora** spent much of its medieval wealth on fine buildings like St Barbara's Cathedral, while **Hradec Králové** not only has an intact historic core but also an early-20C town centre which is a masterpiece of modern urban planning. Nearby, monuments dot the battlefield of **Sadowa** (or Königgrätz), the scene in 1866 of the decisive and bloody encounter of the Austrian and Prussian armies.

SOUTHERN MORAVIA

Something of the distinctive personality of the Czech Republic's other province can be sensed in its capital, **Brno**, which despite its industrial and commercial dynamism has retained much of its historic identity. To the north of the city is the limestone country of the **Moravský kras** (Moravian Karst), with its spectacular caves and chasms, while to the south the vast tracts of UNESCO designated parkland around **Lednice** and **Valtice** are unique in extent, architectural heritage and ecological richness. Almost within sight of Brno is the fateful battlefield of **Slavkov** (Austerlitz) where Napoleon won his famous victory in 1805 over his Austrian and Russian opponents.

BRNO ★

202km southeast Population 386 000

Though its origins go far back to the early Slav fortress established on Petrov Hill, the bustling capital of Moravia is one of those cities that has consistently looked to the future. As the first industrial city in the Hapsburg Empire, in the 19C it acquired a skyline of textile factory chimneys causing it to be known as the "Austrian Manchester". Modern concepts of heredity and genetics owe everything to Gregor Mendel (1822-84), the Brno monk who conducted his researches in the city's Augustinian monastery. In the interwar period the city was second only to Prague in its enthusiasm for all that was modern and progressive in the arts, particularly in architecture, and the period gave the city an unparalleled legacy of functionalist building, much of it the responsibility of the local architect **Bohuslav Fuchs** (1895-1972). The splendid **BVV/Exhibition Park** laid out at that time was used during the Communist regime to showcase the country's technological and industrial achievements, a tradition which continues. Since 1989, the pace of life has quickened, less from any great influx of tourists than from an exploitation of the city's strategic position at the centre of the eastern part of the country, close to the Austrian border and nearer to Vienna than Prague. Good communication links in all directions are one asset, while others include a diversified economy, the presence of many educational institutions, and a vibrant cultural life. Forvisitors, the city is not only a good base for exploring this part of the Czech Republic but has preserved enough of its past to make it a destination in its own right.

Brno is easy to visit. The city's extensive Baroque fortifications were demolished in the 19C and replaced by a more or less complete circle of landscaped boulevards and public buildings like those of Vienna's Ring. Within the circle, the compact old town is almost entirely given over to pedestrians. Among the stimulating mixture of structures old and new a number of churches are outstanding, notably Gothic Sv. Jakub (St James') and Baroque Sv.Tomáš (St Thomas). Two squares, **Zelný trh** (Vegetable Market) and **Náměstí svobody** (Liberty Square) are useful reference points in the maze of streets, and the unmistakable outline of the **Cathedral** rising over **Petrov Hill** is another. Rising higher still is the height crowned by the **Špilberk**, the city's famous fortress.

Staying in Brno

Befitting its business-like image, Brno has its share of international style executive hotels, among them the International *(Husova 16, ☎ 05 42 12 21 11)* which has the advantage of a fine location at the foot of Špilberk Hill on the edge of the old city centre. But the connoisseur's choice must be the Royal Ricc *(Starobrněnská 10, ☎ 05 42 21 92 62-4)*; in an immaculately restored town house in the very heart of the old city this exquisite hotel has a limited number of luxurious rooms, each furnished individually with antiques and modern works of art. The Ricc also has an excellent restaurant and a wine bar.

Travellers' addresses

ŠPILBERK HILL

★**Špilberk** – Once kept bare to provide a clear field of fire, the steep slopes of the Špilberk hill are now quite thickly wooded. The lowering fortress astride the summit dates from the late 13C, though most of the present structure derives from 18C and 19C rebuildings. Over the centuries the Špilberk resisted attacks by Hussites, Swedes, Prussians and Saxons, but it fell without a fight to Napoleon on two occasions, first before the Battle of Austerlitz in 1805 and then again in 1809, after which the French Emperor ordered its outer defences destroyed. But the Špilberk is remembered more for its role as a prison than as a fortress; for many years it was the most notorious gaol in the Austrian Empire, earning itself the title of "prison of nations". Under long-term restoration, it now houses sections of the city museum, which give an excellent introduction to Brno's history and its artistic heritage as well as to the Špilberk itself. A tour of the clammy casemates is a spine-chilling evocation of the conditions in which prisoners once lived.

★**Muzeum města Brna** (City Museum)

Prison of Nations - Displays give a full account of the Špilberk's role as an imperial prison. Its principal function was to contain the "enemy within", the patriotic representatives of the Italians, Poles, Hungarians and others who strove for the rights of their nations within the Empire. But there are also reminders of the limitations of Austrian ruthlessness; Metternich once remarked that the revelations of the Italian patriot Silvio Pellico in his book *"My Prisons"* had caused Austria greater shame than any lost battle, and in 1853 Emperor Franz Josef ordered the prison closed. In 1939 the Gestapo were quick to open it up again, and there are a number of mementoes of their particular brand of unlimited ruthlessness.

Brno in the Špilberk – This section covers important chapters in the city's history from early medieval times to the 20C with a fine array of well-displayed models, documents, paintings and prints, arms and uniforms, furniture and many other items. The Swedish siege of 1645 is brought to vivid life in contemporary oil paintings, while the city's industrial rise can be traced back to the earlier activities of its flourishing guilds. Until the early 20C, Brno was Brünn, a majority German city, and the activities of such rival organisations as the Czech Sokol and the German Turnverein are recalled.

★ **City Gallery** – **From Renaissance to Modernism** – The highlight of the pre-20C collection is a series of charming portraits from the Biedermeier era, proclaiming the confidence of the prosperous city worthies of the time, but it is the 20C painting which commands the greatest attention, with fine canvases by local artists such as Josef Kubíček (1890-1972), Jaroslav Král (1883-1942), and Antonín Procházka (1882-1945), representatives of the lively left-wing artistic community which flourished in Brno in the interwar years. The gallery's paintings and sculpture are complemented by well-chosen pieces of furniture and other objects. A final section, **New Brno 1919-39**, celebrates the city's interwar fame as a centre of modern architecture and design.

BRNO

Beethovenova	X 2	Kapucínské náměstí	Y 10	Panenská	Y 21
Běhounská	X 3	Komenského náměstí	X 12	Petrská	Y 22
Besední	X 4	Malinovského náměstí	XY 14	Poštovská	Y 23
Divadelní	Y 6	Masarykova	Y 15	Radnická	Y 24
Dominikánská	Y 7	Mečová	Y 16	Silingrovo náměstí	Y 25
Františkánská	Y 8	Měnínská	Y 17	Starobrněnská	Y 26
Jakubské náměstí	X 9	Minoritská	Y 19	Středová	Y 27
		Mozartova	X 20	Zámečnická	Y 29

Moravská galerie	Y	Kapucínský kostel	Y	Sv. Tomáše	X
Moravský kras	X	Špilberk	Y	Vila Tugendhat	X
Náměstí svobody	Y	Stará radnice	Y	Zelný trh	Y
Parnas	Y	Sv. Jakuba	X		
Petrov	Y	Sv. Petra a Pavla	Y		

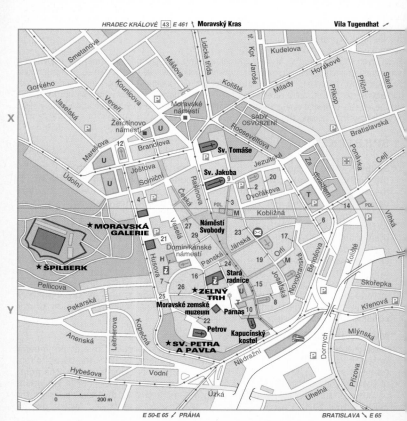

CITY CENTRE

★**Zelný trh (Vegetable Market)** – Brno's sloping **Vegetable or Cabbage Market** has been a centre of urban life since the Middle Ages. Lined by buildings in contrasting styles, it has a Trinity Column and a **Parnassus Fountain** of 1695, an extraordinary grotto-like creation by the Viennese architect Fischer von Erlach. The **Moravské zemské muzeum** (Provincial Museum) is housed in the splendid Baroque Diettrichstein Palace; its collections cover the prehistory and natural history of Moravia in great detail, and among its great treasures is the squat and fecund figure of the Venus of Věstonice, 27 000 years old. Just to the south of the square, the **Kapucínský kostel** (Capucin Church) has a **crypt** housing Brno's strangest curiosities, the air-dried and mummified corpses of monks and benefactors.

Stará radnice (Old Town Hall) ⊘ – As in Prague, Brno's Town Hall had as its core a medieval private house, around which it expanded until eventually, in the early 20C, more spacious premises had to be found elsewhere. Beneath its fine Renaissance tower with a viewing gallery, the Town Hall has many fascinating features, including a superbly carved **portal** of 1510 by the Brno-born sculptor Anton Pilgram and a Renaissance arcade. Suspended from the ceiling in the passageway by the Tourist Information Centre is the famous **Brněnský drak** (Brno Dragon), jaws agape. The Dragon is in fact an Amazonian crocodile, given to the city by Archduke Matthias in 1608. Nearby is another oddity of about the same date, the **Brněnské kolo**, a wooden wheel carpentered together and rolled from Lednice (40 km away) to Brno in the space of a single day, all in pursuit of a bet.

★**Katedrála sv. Petra a Pavla** (Cathedral of St Peter and St Paul) - Atop the Petrov hill, the cathedral with its bulky nave and slim towers and spires is visible from far beyond the city boundary. Originally Gothic, the cathedral was burnt down in the course of the Swedish siege of 1645; it was rebuilt in Baroque style, then re-Gothicised in the 19C.

★**Moravská galerie (Provincial Gallery)** ⊘ – Decorative Arts *Husova 14*. The gallery's collections are distributed around a number of sites. This neo-Renaissance palace houses one of the country's finest collections of decorative arts, furniture, porcelain, glass and much else from the Middle Ages to modern times.

★**Moravská galerie (Provincial Gallery)** ⊘ – 20C Czech Art *Pražák Palace, Husova 8*. The palace has space for important temporary exhibitions as well as providing a fine setting for a representative collection of the country's modern art. Local personalities such as Antonín Procházka naturally feature strongly (his curious Cubist Cat graces the catalogue's cover), but nearly all the country's foremost painters and sculptors of the 20C are present, from František Bílek to Jan Zrzavý.

Náměstí svobody (Liberty Square) – Funnel-shaped, the city's largest square was once the market place for the German, Flemish and Walloon colonists who settled on the edge of the established town in the early 13C. The plague column at the northern end of the square dates from 1680. At the southern end, the Renaissance Schwanz House *(no17)* had its sgraffiti renewed in the 1930s; nearly opposite, *no10* has a heavily-accented façade held up but monster atlantes, known as the The Four Numbskulls (U čtyř mamlasů).

IN ČERNÉ POLE *1 km north*

★★**Vila Tugendhat (Tugendhat House)** ⊘ – *Černopolní 45*. One of the great masterpieces of 20C architecture, the white villa on its elevated site overlooking its garden and the city beyond was completed by the German architect **Ludwig Mies van der Rohe** in 1930 for the newly married **Fritz** and **Greta Tugendhat**. As well as demonstrating Mies' obsession with fine materials and insistence on the highest standards of workmanship, the building exemplifies most of the principles of architectural Modernism: interpenetration of space, integration of inside and outside, and expression of function. The heart of the villa is the living area, a vast and subtle

---

Brno-Enfield

Brno's gunsmithing traditions go back a long way, but few are aware that one of the British Army's most familiar 20C weapons originated here. Designed in Brno in 1937, the highly-effective air-cooled light machine gun known as the Bren was produced in large numbers in Britain's Royal Enfield factory and equipped several generations of British infantrymen during the Second World War and after.

The Tugendhat House

space with a spectacular free-standing wall of onyx. The progressive-minded and Jewish Tugendhats had to flee Brno in 1938; their home was misused by the Nazis, and its restoration only really began in the 1980s.

In 1992, Czechoslovak government leaders meeting here took the fateful decision to split the country into separate Czech and Slovak republics.

EXCURSION

★**Moravský kras (Moravian Karst)** – *c 25km north of Brno.* This tract of limestone country has all the characteristic forms of karst scenery, sink-holes, underground rivers, chasms and caves with wonderfully developed stalactites and stalagmites. The most popular visitor destination is the **Punkevní jeskyně (Punkva Caves ⊘)**, where the tour includes the 138 m-deep Macocha Chasm and a trip along the underground Punkva River.

ČESKÉ BUDĚJOVICE★

139km south – Population 99 500

The commercial, industrial and cultural centre of southern Bohemia, České Budějovice has preserved its medieval street pattern intact, and the town's life is still focused on the magnificent central square laid out in 1265 on the orders of King Otakar II.

HISTORY

Wishing to consolidate the growing power of his kingdom in the face of potential opposition from the powerful local **Lords of Vítkov** as well as to secure his southern border, **King Otakar II** had his surveyor choose a site for a royal town at the confluence of the Vltava with the River Malše. Protected by the rivers as well as by moats and stone walls, and quickly populated by local Czechs and by colonists from Austria and Bavaria, the town was a success, becoming a centre for crafts and for trade between Austria and Bohemia, particularly for salt from the Salzkammergut. Largely German in character, Budějovice tended to side with royalty rather than rebels, resisting the Hussites and taking the Imperial side in the Thirty Years War. The town's key location was confirmed when the Vltava was made navigable downstream to Prague and when, in 1832, the European continent's first major horse-drawn railway linked it to Linz, 129km away. Industries came to the town, among them the world-famous Hardmuth pencil factory, drawing its supplies of graphite from local deposits. **Brewing** flourished as it had done ever since the town was founded, to the extent that the town's German name, Budweis, was appropriated by a Milwaukee brewery for its very different product. Today the delicious, slightly sweet-tasting beer from the **Budějovický Budvar brewery** is exported all over the world. The growth of industry in the 19C brought an influx of Czech population from the surrounding countryside, and by the start of the 20C the long-standing German dominance of urban life had come to an end.

SIGHTS

★★**Náměstí Přemysla Otakara II** (**King Otakar II Square**) – This splendid urban space really is a square, with four sides each measuring 133 m. Although the focal point of the chequerboard pattern of streets, it lies somewhat to the south of the true centre of the oval-shaped medieval town. It is lined with arcaded burghers' houses, most of them rebuilt several times over since the town's foundation, but there are many fascinating details such as Gothic portals and traces of original sgraffito work. The most imposing building is the three-towered **Town Hall**★, a Renaissance structure rebuilt in Baroque style in 1730. Its lively facade has balustrade statues of the civic virtues, exceptionally fierce-looking gargoyles, decorative relief panels and coats of arms.

The square's classically simple grid of paving was designed in the 1930s by Pavel Janák, the Prague Castle architect. At the centre stands the superb **Samson Fountain**★, built between 1721 and 1726 to supply the town with water drawn from the Vltava. The figure of Samson overcoming the lion is supported by atlantes while mascarons spout water into the broad basin.

The square's arcades spread into the surrounding streets, where there are numerous fine old houses, many of them of Renaissance or Late Gothic date.

Černá věž (**Black Tower**) ⊘ – Set back from the square next to the Baroque St Nicholas' Cathedral, the tower reaches a height of 72 m. Completed in 1578, it served as a watch-tower and belfry and now offers a fine **panorama**★ over the town and its setting.

Masné krámy – *Krajinská 13*. Now a restaurant, the structure which once ran with blood from the butchers' stalls it was built to house dates from the mid 16C.

Dominikánský klášter (**Domincan Monastery**) – The monastery was founded at the same time as the town, though its lovely Gothic cloister and Church of St Mary date from about a century later.

Solnice (**Salt store**) – A substantial and splendid reminder of one of the important sources of the town's early wealth, the high-gabled salt warehouse was originally built in 1541 as a corn store and has also served as an armoury. Three strange faces stare out from the wall.

Rabenštejnská věž (**Rabenstein Tower**) – This highly picturesque 14C tower with its steeply pitched hipped roof is one of the few remaining elements of the once-elaborate town defences.

The square, České Budějovice

ČESKÝ KRUMLOV★★★

161km south — Population 14 500

Almost completely encircled by a great loop in the upper course of the Vltava, this exquisite little medieval town has always been dominated by the great castle built on the rocky ridge rising abruptly from the river. Persisting well into the 20C, the near-feudal rule of the castle lords and Krumlov's remote location on the fringe of the Bohemian Forest preserved it from the tourist gaze, as did the near-total neglect of the town's unique building heritage during the Communist period. Since 1989 Krumlov's extraordinarily picturesque location, its huge castle and its wealth of building from all periods has attracted an ever-growing stream of visitors. The new perils this brings in terms of loss of character through over-restoration and proliferation of souvenir shops may be countered by the UNESCO World Heritage status awarded in 1992.

Český Krumlov

HISTORY

The first to establish themselves on the crag overlooking the river bend were the powerful south Bohemian **Vítek** family, who fortified this naturally well-defended position with a formidable circular stronghold, which later became the base of the Renaissance tower which is such a dominant feature today. In the early 13C the little **Latrán** quarter grew up on the gentler slope to the east of the castle. When this proved inadequate to accommodate the growing population, a more ambitious urban settlement was laid out within the bend of the river. Focused on a central square, the town shows signs of its founders' attempts to give it a regular street plan, though the shape of the site and its extreme constriction meant that hardly a single street or alleyway could be persuaded to follow a straight alignment.

The Víteks' emblem of a five-petalled rose was also that of the **Rožmberk** (Rosenberg) branch of the family who succeeded to ownership of the castle and town in 1302. Their 300-year rule reached a peak in the 16C when much of the wealth gained through their development of silver mines, hop-fields, breweries and fishponds was used to convert the medieval castle into a sumptuous Renaissance residence. In 1622 the Rožmberks were succeeded by the Austrian **Eggenberg** family, who later in the century established a glittering provincial court life centred on their splendid Baroque theatre, miraculously intact today. The town too remained intact, despite occupation by foreign troops on more than one occasion.

After the death of the last Eggenberg in 1719, the **Schwarzenberg** family became the new lords. Their rule started splendidly, but towards the end of the 18C they abandoned Krumlov as their main residence. Nevertheless, traditions were maintained; a trumpeter sounded the hour from the castle tower and the Schwarzenbergs' private army of a dozen or so men paraded daily in their archaic white uniforms. Small industries established themselves in and around the town, without however damaging its character, which began to exert its spell on writers such as Rilke and Karel Čapek as well as on the Viennese artist **Egon Schiele** (1890-1918), who spent a summer in his mother's home town in 1911.

Krumlov was detached from Czechoslovakia in 1938 to become part of the Nazis' Ostmark (Austria); its Czech minority fled, and the Schwarzenbergs were expropriated by the Gestapo. The town fell to the US Army in May 1945. The postwar expulsion of its German inhabitants was made good by the return of the Czech population and by immigration from other parts of Czechoslovakia.

★★★CASTLE ⓥ *Free access to courtyards and gardens.*

Almost matching Prague's castle in sheer size and commanding presence, and, like Hradčany a virtual a town within a town, Krumlov Castle spreads its 40-odd buildings along the narrow ridge above the Vltava, linking them via courtyards, ramps, passageways and bridges to the splendid Baroque gardens occupying the flatter, higher ground to the west. The most prominent structure is the Renaissance tower soaring over the Lower Castle at the eastern end of the complex, but the Upper Castle, its grim 40 m high walls rising from the bare rock, has a forbidding quality all its own. Even more extraordinary is the multi-tiered bridge thrown across the ravine-like moat separating the main complex from the Baroque Castle Theatre and the gardens beyond.

Outer Bailey – The castle precincts are entered from the Latrán part of town through the **Červená brána** (Red Gate) with the Schwarzenberg coat of arms. The **First Courtyard** rising steeply westward still has something of the atmosphere of the days when the castle was the economic and administrative centre of the Schwarzenberg estates, a domain the size of a small kingdom. To the right is a medieval salthouse, to the left the pharmacy, a 14C building with Renaissance sgraffiti, the 16C stables, and the Gothic burgrave's residence. Other buildings including farm structures, a smithy, a brewery, a dairy, a coach-house and a hospital, line the well-treed area opening out to the right.

Lower Castle – The Lower Castle, built around the **Second Courtyard** or Inner Bailey, consisted of a 13C Gothic palace – the **Hrádek** – defended by a great round tower. The moat with its bears is crossed by a stone bridge, a replacement for a former drawbridge. Towards the end of the 16C the palace was rebuilt as a Renaissance residence and the squat tower was extended boldly upwards and given its arcaded gallery, elaborate cupola, and the rather garish decoration which has recently been recreated after being plastered over in the 19C. The **tower gallery** from which the Schwarzenberg trumpeters used to sound the passing hours is reached by a staircase contained within the thickness of the walls. It offers a wonderful **panorama**★★ over Krumlov's rooftops and beyond to the wooded heights of the Šumava (Bohemian Forest). To the south of the mid-17C fountain in the courtyard is the **Mint**; for a while Krumlov produced its own coinage, based on locally extracted silver, though the present mostly 18C building has generally been used as offices and archives. The late-16C **New Burgave's Residence** to the north rises over vast vaulted cellars and contains the castle library *(not open to the public)*. Guarding the ramp leading to the plain portal of the Upper Castle is the pretty Renaissance **Buttery**, its core a Gothic watchtower.

Upper Castle – A steep passageway winds up into the **Third Courtyard**, hemmed in on all sides by high walls. Like the **Fourth Courtyard** beyond, its gloom is partly relieved by late 16C murals of allegorical and mythological scenes. The homogenous character of this part of the castle belies its building history, which lasted from the 14C to the 18C. A good number of the innumerable **interiors** are accessible by means of a series of guided tours, one of which includes the many-tiered **cellars** in which King Wenceslas IV was allegedly held prisoner in 1394. Upstairs rooms are furnished in a variety of styles which give a good idea of how life was lived in the castle from Renaissance times to the 19C. There is a fine collection of **Brussels tapestries**★ as well as an opulent gilded **coach**★ made for the Eggenbergs in 1638, but the outstanding interior is the **Maškarní sál (Masquerade Hall)**★★. This fascinating ballroom was decorated in 1748 by Joseph Lederer with jolly scenes of revelry drawn from the Italian *commedia dell'arte* tradition. The brightly painted *trompe l'oeil* figures laugh and gesticulate, and many of them seem about to descend from their boxes and balconies, intent on drawing the spectator into their fun.

★★**Zámecké divadlo (Castle Theatre)** – The many-tiered covered bridge over the ravine includes a separate passageway leading to this uniquely well-preserved Baroque theatre. Built originally for the highly cultivated Jan Kristián (Johann Christian), the last of the Eggenbergs, in 1680, then remodelled in 1766, it has kept intact not only its auditorium, but also its scenery, lighting, costume collection and archives, and is thus able to provide a totally authentic setting for occasional performances of Baroque opera.

★**Gardens** – Jan Kristián Eggenberg was also responsible for the splendid Baroque gardens which are linked to the theatre building by a further covered bridge. Now restored to something like their original appearance, the gardens have formal parterres, a Neptune fountain with statuary, clipped hedges in strict geometric patterns, and, to the west, a naturalistic area with fine trees and a lake. There is also a summer and a winter riding school and the **Bellarie**★, a lovely Rococo pavilion now linked to a modern revolving theatre.

THE TOWN

Krumlov's narrow streets are lined with any number of fascinating old buildings, many of them dating from the late Middle Ages though with Renaissance and later features. It's best to wander at will; though the street layout seems quite confusing, Krumlov's compact size makes it impossible to get lost for long.

Náměstí svornosti (Concord Square) – The arcaded Renaissance **Town Hall** on the north side of the town's little central square has emblems of the Eggenbergs and Schwarzenbergs as wall as Krumlov's own coats of arms. On the west side of the square, the **hotel** assembled from a number of originally separate buildings has an a fine arcaded hall and numerous Late Gothic and Early Renaissance features. The **plague column** of around 1715 is by the Prague sculptor Jäckel.

★**Sv. Vita (St Vitus' Church)** – This splendid Gothic church with its slender tower and immensely tall lancet windows is the town's visual counterweight to the great mass of the Castle on the far bank of the river. Inside, the lofty nave has reticulated vaulting based on Petr Parléř's innovations in Prague's St Vitus' Cathedral. Close by in Horní ulice (Upper Street) are a number of fine buildings including the early-16C **Kaplanka** at *no 159* and the **Růže Hotel**, originally built in 1588 as a Jesuit seminary, its name – Rose – a reminder of the town's early rulers.

Muzeum ⊙ – *Horní 152*. Just on the town side of the deep cleft cut across the narrowest part of the isthmus is the district museum, whose collections of local interest include a model of the town and the fittings from a traditional pharmacy. Items relating to **Adalbert Stifter** (1805-68), the Austrian writer most intimately associated with the history and landscape of the Bohemian Forest and Southern Bohemia, are now displayed at his birthplace in Horní Planá (Oberplan) *(30km west)*.

Egon Schiele Art Centrum ⊙ – The dominant building in lens-shaped Široká (Broad Street) is the handsome municipal brewery dating from 1578. The international cultural centre now housed here takes its name from the short-lived Vienna artist, and as well as displaying a number of his original works stages important temporary exhibitions of 20C art.

Latrán – Once a separate township from Krumlov itself but always under the dominance of the Castle, the Latrán district consists essentially of a single street winding up from the river crossing towards the Castle and the **Budějovická brána** (Budějovice Gate), the town's only remaining gateway. Among the many fine houses lining the street, **no 39** is decorated with a late-16C mural known as the Rožmberk Horseman while **no 53** has alchemical symbols and murals depicting the Ages of Man. The side street known as Na Novém Městě (New Town) leads east to the Renaissance **brewery** and another lane gives access to the **Minorite Monastery** founded in 1350.

ČESKÝ ŠTERNBERK★

53km southeast – Population 150

The tiny settlement of **Český Šternberk** crouches at the foot of its castle crag on the left bank of the winding Sázava River. The second longest tributary of the Vltava (after the Berounka), the 220km-long Sazava rises in the Bohemian-Moravian Highlands between Prague and Brno. Much of its meandering course is highly picturesque, particularly where it cuts through the well-wooded schist plateau to the southeast of Prague, and the valley, traditionally reached by the extremely slow "Sázava Express", is a popular destination for weekenders and day-trippers from the city. No site along the river is more picturesque than the 13C castle founded by the Šternberk family.

★**Hrad (Castle)** ⊙ – Much rebuilt over the centuries, the stronghold of Český Šternberk was begun sometime before 1241 by Zdeslav of Divišov, who according to the fashionable custom of the time took a German name, in his case **Sternberg**, and adopted the emblem of the eight-pointed star ("Stern" in German) which has graced the family coat of arms ever since. The Šternberks became one of the most powerful families in the kingdom, acquiring vast tracts of Bohemia including the nearby domain of Konopiště, as well as building more than one fine palace in Prague itself. In the early 19C the great botanist Kašpar Maria Count Šternberk was one of the co-founders of the National Museum.

Strung out along the narrow rocky ridge above the Sázava, the castle has a fascinating profile, from the round tower at its southern end to the high walls of the imposing central block and the defences of the outer bailey to the north. Inside, the cramped site resulted in strangely shaped rooms, some with rich furnishings and elaborate stuccowork.

FRANTIŠKOVY LÁZNĚ★

194km west Population 5300

Named after Emperor Francis I, the smallest of the "Bohemian Triangle" of spa towns consists of a few elegant streets set in parkland dotted with pretty pavilions dispensing the waters from some two dozen sources. The beneficial properties of one of the springs had been known from the Middle Ages onward; for centuries it was portered to Cheb to be dispensed there, and the townspeople vigorously, sometimes violently opposed any attempt to bring visitors to the spring rather than vice-versa. Eventually an Imperial commission overruled their objections; in 1793 the spa was formally founded and given the name Franzensdorf, later Franzensbad in honour of Emperor Francis I.

Water from the cool springs is used to alleviate heart, circulatory and gynaecological problems, and there are also gas and mud treatments. In its heyday the spa attracted as glittering a clientele as any of its competitors; Goethe described Franzensbad as "paradise on earth" and it was here in 1808 that he began his liaison with the 23-year old Silvia von Ziegesar.

Náměstí miru (Peace Square) — All the elements which make up the spa's distinctive character can be appreciated from this spot, once called the Kurplatz.

The focal point is the little circular neo-Classical pavilion covering the **Františkův pramen (Francis Spring)**; built in 1832 it replaced an earlier building which itself had been a replacement for the original structure torn down by rioting water-carriers from Cheb in 1791. Close by is the **Plynové lázně** (Gas Bath) and the Colonnade of 1914, guarded by sphinxes. To the north is

Kaisergelb

The buildings of Františkový Lázně were originally painted in a variety of colours, but the present harmonious appearance of the spa owes much to the predominance of *"kaisergelb"* (Imperial Yellow), the restful light ochre colour still much in evidence over all the former Austro-Hungarian Empire.

the main boulevard, Národní třída, while to the south in the parkland is the grandiose interwar pavilion housing the **Glauberův pramen** (Glauber Spring). In the gardens to the west is the town's favourite resident, the little bronze cherub called František; the fish he holds is a symbol of fecundity, and female fertility is supposedly enhanced by touching him in the right place.

Národní třída (National Avenue) — The broad avenue rises gently towards the municipal gardens with their music pavilion and bandstand. Strict building controls regulated development here; the original buildings were all bath-houses, among them the hotel U tří Lílií (Three Lilies) of 1794, the residence of Goethe during his stay here *(see panel)*.

Muzeum ⊘ — *Dr Pohoreckého*. The modest collections of the local museum give an account of the spa's history and include an array of medical instruments and what is possibly the world's first exercise bicycle.

Coffee in spa style

Stylishly renovated, Goethe's favourite Franzensbad hotel U tří Lílií has a Philosopher's Café, a good place to pause for coffee during your stroll around the elegant town Národní třída 3. ☎ *0166542415*.

HLUBOKÁ Nad Vltavou★

133km south   Population 4 370

The little town on the Vltava 10km north of České Budějovice is one of the most visited places in the Czech Republic, less for of its own modest charms than for the great castle built by the **Schwarzenbergs** on the bluff overlooking the river.

★ **Zámek (Castle)** ⊘ – It was probably King Wenceslas I who built the first **stronghold** on this easily defended site. For the first few centuries of its existence the castle passed alternately from royal to aristocratic ownership, but eventually, in 1661 it was acquired by Johann Adolf Schwarzenberg. His descendant, Prince Adolf, fled the Nazis in 1939 and since 1945 Hluboká has been a state property. In the course of its long existence it was rebuilt several times, finally in the mid-19C in a Tudor Gothic style inspired by Windsor Castle. Like Windsor, its romantic silhouette floats enchantingly above the wooded banks of the country's longest river, and like Windsor, it has extensive gardens and a vast landscaped park in the English style. A choice of guided tours takes groups through a selection of the castle's 140 rooms. The lavishly furnished interiors display family portraits, fine paintings and splendid weaponry. Some have superb examples of panelling and other carving, there is a collection of Brussels tapestries and the dining room has a Renaissance ceiling brought from Český Krumlov.

★ **Alšova jihočeská galerie (Mikoláš Aleš Gallery of Southern Bohemia)** ⊘ – The castle is linked by splendid iron and glass Winter Garden to the Riding School, which houses the region's principal art gallery. The collections fall into three main categories: a fairly comprehensive collection of **20C Czech art** (not necessarily on show at any given time), 16C–18C Dutch paintings, and a magnificent array of **Bohemian Gothic paintings and sculpture★★**.

Hluboká: neo-Tudor stronghold of the Schwarzenbergs

★ **Lovecký zámek Ohrada (Ohrada Hunting Lodge)** ⊘ – This chateau-sized hunting lodge on the southern shore of the big Munický fishpond was built by Adam Franz Schwarzenberg at the beginning of the 18C. In 1842 it became the Austrian Empire's first Agriculture Museum, and today its fine interiors house extensive and fascinating exhibits on **hunting, fishing and forestry**, among them the last Bohemian bear together with the gun with which it was slain. The usual array of hunting trophies is upstaged by furniture made from fur and horn and by a huge rug made from the fur of forty foxes.

Michelin Maps are revised regularly.
Never travel with an out-of-date map.

HRADEC KRÁLOVÉ★★

Built on both banks of the upper Elbe at its confluence with the River Orlice, the regional capital of northeastern Bohemia is a trim, well-balanced town with a university as well as a wide range of industries. Its historic town centre is one of the country's finest, while the modern city is a model of early 20C town planning. In 1866 the Battle of **Sadová** or **Königgrätz** (the town's German name) was one of the bloodiest and most decisive ever fought by the Austrian Empire.

OLD TOWN

The core of historic Hradec Králové on its low rise above the flood plain is the funnel-shaped **Velké náměstí (Great Square★)**. Here, in a matrix of fine old

---

Staying in Hradec Králové

At entirely different ends of the scale are the Černigov *(Riegrovo náměstí 1494, ☎ 049 581 41 11, 370 56)*, a well-modernised Communist-era high-rise block opposite the railway station in the New Town, and the little Penzion U Jana *(Velké náměstí 137, ☎ 049 23 15 4, 24 155)* in the heart of the Old Town. Both have restaurants of similarly contrasting character.

---

burgher houses dating from medieval times onwards, are the city's major historic monuments, reminders of its long past and in particular of the royal *(králové)* status it enjoyed as the dowry town of Bohemian queens.

★**Katedrála sv. Ducha (Cathedral of the Holy Spirit)** – Brick-built and with twin 40 m towers, this is one of the country's outstanding Gothic churches, founded in the early 14C by the dowager Queen Elizabeth, widow of King Wenceslas II. Its present appearance is largely the result of the efforts of 19C restorers to remove all traces of a late 18C Baroque rebuilding. The cool, lofty interior houses a number of treasures, among them a Gothic pewter font and an altar painting of *St Anthony* by Petr Brandl.

★**Bílá věž (White Tower)** – Called white because of the pale sandstone used in its construction, the 72 m watchtower and belfry was completed in 1580. Its biggest bell is the country's second largest. The gallery offers a superb **panorama** over both old and new towns. The tower is attached to the little Baroque sv. Klimenta (St Clement's Church).

Biskupská rezidence (Bishop's Residence) – The stately High Baroque Bishop's palace was returned to church use in 1990 after having served as the regional art gallery. Linked to it over an archway is the pretty pink U Špuláků building, with a balcony, a statue of the Virgin Mary and a copper cupola.

Plague column – Unusually well-endowed with surrounding statuary, the plague column in the centre of the square dates from 1717.

★**Galerie moderního umění (Gallery of Modern Art)** ⊘ – With sculptures carved by Ladislav Šaloun guarding its entrance, the Secession-style building designed by Osvald Polívka in 1911 was originally a bank, but makes an excellent home for what is probably the most representative collection of **Czech 20C art** outside Prague. Virtually every prominent painter as well as a good number of sculptors are featured, from the founders of modern Czech art like Bohumil Kubišta and Jan Zrzavý, via Surrealists such as Josef Šíma and Toyen and members of Group 42 like Kamil Lhoták and Ladislav Zívr to abstract artists like Mikuláš Medek and members of the contemporary generation.

NEW TOWN

The development of Hradec Králové from the late 19C until well into the 20C was overseen by the two of the country's most able architect-planners, **Jan Kotěra** (1871-1923) and his successor, **Josef Gočár** (1880-1945). Thanks to their efforts, the city enjoyed an international reputation in the interwar period for the quality of its architecture, urban design, and parks and gardens, and even under Communism maintained higher standards of development than elsewhere. Between the Elbe and the railway station a kilometre to the west, a rationally designed web of streets and squares is lined with buildings designed in sober and decent style with the occasional playful touch. Even the riverside came in for special treatment, from Kotěra's **Pražský most** (Prague Bridge) of 1910 with its twin pavilions at either end to the colourful **vodárna** (power station) of 1914 a short distance downstream.

Sadová 1866

The day-long battle which took place in the rolling countryside northwest of Hradec Králové on 3 July 1866 resulted in the utter defeat of the Austrian army by its better-led and better-equipped Prussian adversary. Pushed back eastwards from the Bohemian frontier, the Austrians made a stand on the low ridge centred on the village of Chlum. For a while the Prussian advance was held up by a fierce artillery bombardment, but when the Austrian right wing counter-attacked, the troopers' white uniforms made them easy targets for Crown Prince Friedrich Wilhelm's Second Army, freshly on the scene. Mown down by the Prussians' breech-loaders, the Austrians fell back and were only saved from a complete rout by the bravery of their cavalry. More than 32 000 dead and wounded lay on the battlefield.

Defeat meant Austrian exclusion from the affairs of Germany, whose fate was to be determined by a triumphant Prussia, and many historians consider the battle to mark the beginning of the end for the Hapsburg Empire.

Memorials and cemeteries are scattered all over the extensive battlefield, but the best place to get something of the feel of this decisive conflict is at **Chlum** *(signposted off Highway 35, 10km northwest of Hradec Králové)*, where there is a small **museum** ⊘ and a **lookout tower**.

★ **Krajské muzeum východních Čech (East Bohemian Regional Museum)** ⊘ – *Eliščino nábřeží 465*. Looking across the Elbe towards the New Town, the dignified **museum building**★ in brick and stone by Ko těra was completed in 1912. A splendid example of sober late Secession style, it is decorated inside and out by some of the leading artists of the time; the stern-looking female guardians on either side of the entrance are by Stanislav Sucharda, while the monumental interior has stained glass by František Kysela and mosaics by Jan Preisler. A fascinating town model shows the Old Town still cut off from its surroundings by the formidable array of Baroque fortifications which were demolished in the late 19C/early 20C, but the main attraction is the exceptionally well-presented array of objects evoking everyday urban life throughout the ages.

CHEB★

189km west – Population 32 000

Only 5km from the Bavarian border on the banks of the Ohře River, Cheb (Eger in German) was once known as the Bohemian Nuremberg, mainly because of its picturesque townscape of streets and squares lined with ancient, high-roofed buildings and also because of the distinctive character of its former population, considered by some to be more German than the Germans themselves.

The town's history is particularly rich. Disputed between the Holy Roman Empire and Bohemia, in 1322 it was mortgaged to the Bohemian crown on condition that its independence was maintained "in perpetuity". For much of its existence it prospered from its strategic position on the frontier between the Germanic and Slav worlds, and it will forever be associated with the assassination in 1634 of warlord **Albrecht of Wallenstein**.

After the postwar expulsion of its German inhabitants, Cheb's physical fabric deteriorated rapidly, and has only partly been made good by the restoration carried out from the late 1950s onwards. It took until 1995 for the town's population to reach its prewar level again. Of Cheb's several churches, Gothic **Sv. Mikuláše** (St Nicholas) was added to in the 18C by the great architect **Balthasar Neumann**, born here in 1687. Baroque **Sv. Klary** was built by **Kryštof Dientzenhofer**, while early-15C **Sv. Bartolomej** (St Bartholomew) makes a fine setting for an exhibition of Gothic art. But the town's greatest single monument is the ruined Imperial Castle.

SIGHTS

★ **Náměstí krále Jiřího z Poděbrad (King George of Poděbrady Square)** – A harmonious composition of city-scale buildings of various dates, nearly all with characteristic steep roofs broken by rows of dormers, the funnel-shaped former market square has at its lower end a quaint agglomeration of houses known as the **Špaliček**★. Divided by a narrow lane and timber-framed additional upper stories, the Špaliček probably grew from the medieval market stalls which once clustered here. Two **fountains** grace the square: the upper one with a **Roland statue**, the guarantor of civic rights and privileges, the lower with a **Hercules statue**, also known as the "Wild Man". On the east side of the square the Baroque **Radnice** (Town Hall) with its stately interior houses the Galerie výtvarného umění (art gallery) with a representative collection of 20C Czech art.

★Chebské muzeum (Cheb Museum) ⊘ – Splendidly accommodated in a magnificent Gothic town house rebuilt around 1600, the museum founded in 1873 was one of the first of its kind in Bohemia, opened because of the exceptional public interest in the assassination here of Generalissimo Wallenstein. There are excellent displays on local history, but most visitors still come to see the **Wallenstein memorabilia**, including the stuffed horse shot from beneath him at the battle of Lützen and the pike used by his assassin, the English mercenary Captain Walter Devereux.

★Hrad (Imperial Castle) (Kaiserpfalz in German) ⊘ – The site overlooking a ford across the river seems to have been occupied from early times by a succession of Germanic and Slavonic tribespeople, then in the 10C by the Přemyslid rulers of Bohemia who built a stronghold defended by earth banks and a palisade. The first stone castle was erected in the early 12C, at the time when the area was being colonised by settlers from Germany. In 1179 the present structure was begun by **Emperor Frederick Barbarossa**, as one of several sites throughout his realm where he would periodically hold court. His roofless **palace** is still imposing, as is the massive **keep**, built of basalt and known as the **Černá věž** (Black Tower). The **Chapel** combines a lower, Romanesque chamber, and an upper, Early Gothic chamber with elegant columns, finely carved capitals and ribbed vaults.

KARLOVY VARY★★★

The opulent turn-of-the-century hotels, villas and spa buildings of this queen of spas fill the narrow winding valley of the little Teplá as it rushes down to join the River Ohře at the northern, more modern end of the town. Clad in glorious beechwoods, the steep slopes all around are threaded with the footpaths considered as essential a component of the cure as the ingestion of the mineral-rich waters spouting from Carlsbad's twelve springs.

> ### The thirteenth spring
>
> Unusually shaped green bottles bearing the name Becherovka can be seen in gift shops all over the Czech Republic, but the herbal liqueur invented in the early 19C by Jan Becher and nicknamed the 13th spring is probably tastes best in its place of origin.

HISTORY

Carlsbad's founding legend has the spring discovered in the mid 14C by Emperor Charles IV, when, in the course of a deer hunt his hounds fell howling into the hot waters, though it is quite possible that their therapeutic effects were known well beforehand. But naming the spa after an emperor never did the place any harm. Bathing was the mainstay of early cures, and it was only in the 17C that the drinking cure became established, with guests straining to swallow up to 70 cupfuls a day. As important as the cure was, the need to see and be seen and the guest lists kept annually recorded Carlsbad's increasingly starry status. In the late 18C and early 19C, the royal and aristocratic clientele was joined by members of the European cultural elite, among them Goethe, who came here no fewer than 17 times. In the course of the 19C, guests were drawn more and more from the increasingly prosperous middle classes. Carlsbad's Golden Age came at the turn of the century; its present appearance owes everything to the building boom of that period. As well as palatial hotels and residences, fine places of worship were built, prominent among them a splendid Orthodox churh for the many spa guests from Tsarist Russia.

Harder times followed the disaster of the First World War. The economic difficulties of the 1930s helped push the predominantly German population into the arms of the ultra-nationalist Sudenten German Party; it was at a meeting here in April 1938 that party leader Konrad Henlein made the Carlsbad Demands, an event helping to precipitate the Munich crisis and the break-up of Czechoslovakia. Nationalisation of the spa facilities after the Second World War drew a socially much broader-based clientele to Carlsbad, while the range of treatments was extended and made available all year round, very much on the Soviet model.

Russian spa guests once more figure prominently among Carlsbad's visitors, drawn from the post-Soviet business elite, happy to stay in a place where Russian language and ways are widely understood.

Taking the waters at Carlsbad

KARLOVY VARY

Bulharská	A	2	Mariánskolázeňská	B	9	Poděbradská . . . . AB 17
Divadelní	B	3	Mattoniho nábřeži.	B	10	Škroupova . . . . B 19
Drahomířino nábřeži.	B	4	Mlýnské nábřeži.	B	12	Tylova . . . . B 21
I.P. Pavlova	AB	6	Moravská	B	13	Varšavská . . . . A 23
Lázeňská	B	7	náměstí Republiky	B	14	Vřídelní . . . . B 24
			Nová louka	B	15	Vyšehradská. . . . . B 25

Park Antonína Dvořáka	B	Mlýnská kolonáda	B	Tržní kolonáda	B
Grand Hotel Pupp	B	Stará louka.	B	Vřídelní kolonáda	B
Hotel Thermal	B	Sv. Maří Magdalény	B		
Karlovarské muzeum.	B	Sv. Petra a Pavla	A		

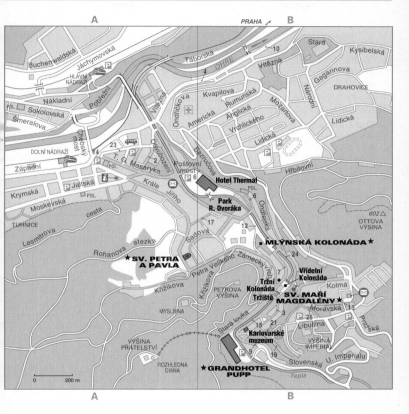

SIGHTS

Traffic is excluded from most of Carlsbad's streets, though overnight guests may ask for a pass permitting access to and from their hotel. Day visitors can park at the northern end of the town and make their tour on foot, or take the shuttle bus from the car park to the south. The sights are described below from north to south.

★**Mlýnská kolonáda (Mill Colonnade)** – Completed in 1881 by Josef Zítek, architect of Prague's National Theatre, the great colonnade running parallel to the Teplá stands at the heart of the spa, and shelters no fewer than five springs. Beyond the neo-Gothic Spa III to the north is the elegant cast-iron **colonnade** of **Dvořák Park**, and further still and far less elegant, the brutalist architecture of the **Thermal Sanatorium** of 1976, an indispensable venue nevertheless for many events including the annual International Film Festival.

Tržiště (Market Square) – The pretty **Market Colonnade** was built in 1883 as a temporary measure but lasted more than a century before being rebuilt in 1993. Close by is a Baroque **Trinity Column** of 1716, while between the colonnade and Emperor Charles IV's **Castle Tower** high above the Secession buildings of the **Castle Springs** are sadly derelict.

★**Sv. Petra a Pavla (Orthodox Church of St Peter and St Paul)** ⊘ – The glorious gilded onion domes of the Russian church rise among the ornate hotels and villas of the town's steeply sloping West End. At the edge of the woodland stands a statue of "Karel Marx"; a Mr Charles Marx from London came to Carlsbad more than once and, kept under discreet surveillance by the Austrian police, may have written some of the chapters of Capital in the soothing surroundings of the spa. But the museum once dedicated to him has been emptied of its exhibits.

Staying in Carlsbad

It's tempting to pass your time here among the Edwardian and other ghosts of that mother of all spa hotels, the Pupp, but for a more intimate and thoroughly pleasurable experience try the Embassy *(Nová louka 21, ☏ 0173223049)*, a medium-sized family-run hotel of great charm. Visiting film stars tend to eat in the hotel's cosy restaurant and it's advisable to reserve a table well in advance.

Vřídelní kolonáda (Hot Spring or Sprudel Colonnade) – Its architecture only somewhat less brutal than that of the Thermal, the colonnade houses Carlsbad's most spectacular spring, the **Vřídlo★**, spouting water at 72 °C up to 12 m in the air every few seconds from a depth of 2 000 m.

★Sv.Mář í Magdalény (St Mary Magdalen Church) – A masterpiece by Kilián Ignác Dientzenhofer, the twin-towered church completed in 1736 is a rare Baroque landmark among Carlsbad's predominantly 19C architecture.

Stará louka (Old Meadow Promenade) – Gradually being recolonised by international boutiques, this part of the **riverside** was once the preserve of the spa's most exclusive shops. On the opposite bank of the Teplá is the **Karlovarské Muzeum** (Carlsbad Museum) with good displays on regional and local history and plenty of reminders in the shape of glass, porcelain and guns, that Carlsbad was as famous for its crafts as much as for its waters.

★**Grand Hotel Pupp** – Founded by the confectioner Johann Georg Pupp who came to the town in 1775, this archetypal spa hotel in what might be called "wedding-cake" style became a Carlsbad institution. Favoured by the aristocracy, in 1912 the Pupp acquired a rival in the shape of the massive **Imperial Hotel** on the hill above, though the latter's clientele tended to be monied rather than blue-blooded.

EXCURSION

★**Loket** – *12km west. Population 3270.* "Delightfully situated" was Goethe's comment on this tiny medieval town, and Loket does indeed owe much to its location on a rock outcrop almost entirely enclosed by a tight loop (or elbow, "loket" in Czech) in the River Ohře. It owes even more to its curving main square and to the castle ⊘ whose walls shoot sheer from its craggy foundation. The **castle** a fine collection of the local porcelain.

Walking in the woods

The network of paths leading through the wooded surroundings of Carlsbad has a total length of more than 130km. There are any number of possible destinations and viewpoints, but the best excursion on foot for those with little time is to the splendid lookout point (Petrova vršina) named after Peter the Great, who rode bareback up the steep slope for a bet. The ascent can be shortened by taking the funicular *(lanovka)* from behind the Hotel Pupp.

Hrad KARLŠTEJN★★

KARLŠTEJN Castle

28km southwest

High above the winding valley of the River Berounka, Karlštejn Castle's romantic silhouette of towers and battlemented walls rising over the treetops is one of the great sights of Bohemia, attracting day visitors by the thousand from the nearby capital. Founded on 10 June 1348, the castle was one of Emperor **Charles IV's** visionary projects, intended like St Vitus' Cathedral and Prague's New Town to confirm his dynasty's spiritual and temporal status as rulers not just of Bohemia but of the Holy Roman Empire. Karlštejn was conceived less as a fortress than as a kind of sacred bunker, the repository for **crown jewels** and for the many **holy relics** assembled by the pious Emperor, among which was a fragment of the True Cross. Laid out in sequence on the steeply sloping site, the castle's buildings symbolise a pilgrimage which reaches its destination in the Great Tower; here, in the extraordinarily ornate Chapel of the Holy Rood, the Emperor would lose himself in mystic contemplation among the holy relics.

Seemingly built for all eternity, Karlštejn first lost its treasures, then its original appearance. Because of the Hussite troubles, the Imperial crown jewels were taken to Vienna, while the Bohemian crown jewels which had replaced them were removed to St Vitus' Cathedral at the start of the Thirty Years War. The castle lost its imperial role, was remodelled in Renaissance times, and eventually became little more than the head-quarters of the surrounding agricultural estate, many of its buildings used as barns and storehouses. In 1812 Emperor Francis I gave the first grant towards its restoration, and in the late 19C the great conservation architect **Josef Mocker** rebuilt it in what was fondly imagined to be its original, Gothic state.

TOUR ⊘

Guided tour only. No access to castle by motor vehicle. 1.5km on foot or by horse-drawn carriage from car parks in Karlštejn village. The need to protect the castle's most precious treasures from damage means that there is no access to the Chapel of the Holy Rood neither to St Mary's Chapel. Some of Master Theodoric's portraits can be seen at St George's Convent in Prague.

The long climb up from the village eventually reaches the western gateway to the castle. On the far side of the outer ward, another gateway leads into the **Purkrabský dvůr (Burgrave's Courtyard)** overlooked by the timber-framed early-16C residence of this high official. From here a battlemented spur with splendid views over the wooded valley runs westwards towards the **Well Tower** built over an 80 m-deep well. Another gatehouse leads to the Inner Ward, dominated by the **Císařský palác** (Imperial Palace); stables occupied its ground floor while the upper floors provided separate quarters for the Imperial retinue, for the Emperor and for his spouse (of whom Charles had four in the course of his life). In the sparsely furnished rooms there are displays on the Emperor and on the history of the castle as well as a number of artworks, among them a portable 14C Italian diptych. At a higher level stands the **Mariánská věž** (St Mary's Tower), containing St Mary's Church and the tiny **kaple sv. Kateřiny** (Chapel of St Catherine). The church has substantial remnants of its original Gothic wall paintings, probably by Nikolaus Wurmser of Strasbourg, showing scenes of the Apocalypse and of Charles receiving holy relics. Built into the thickness of the wall, the chapel is decorated in the same opulent style as the Chapel of St Wenceslas in St Vitus' Cathedral and the Chapel of the Holy Rood with wall-paintings set in a matrix of semi-precious stones. One of the paintings shows Charles with his wife Anna of Schwednitz. The Emperor would shut himself in the chapel for extended periods of contemplation before ascending to the holy of holies, the **Kaple svatého kříže** (Chapel of the Holy Rood). Reached across a covered bridge, this was the repository of the holy relics and marked the climax of the Karlštejn pilgrimage. It was decorated accordingly in an extraordinarily lavish manner. Beneath gilded vaulting glittering with stars of Venetian glass were more walls inlaid with semi-precious stones and set with 130 portraits from the studio of court painter **Master Theodoric**. Representing the heavenly host, these master-pieces depicted saints and martyrs, prophets and popes, as well as rulers including the great Charlemagne. Suffused with light filtering through more semi-precious stones filling the window spaces or from innumerable candles, the chapel evoked wonder in those privileged to worship in it, one medieval visitor concluding that it had "no equal in the whole world".

Zámek KONOPIŠTĚ★★

KONOPIŠTĚ Castle

40km southeast

This sombre stronghold set amid woods and parkland dates from the 13C but its present appearance and atmosphere owes everything to the dominant personality of Hapsburg **Archduke Franz Ferdinand**, who remodelled it in the years preceding his fateful assassination in Sarajevo in June 1914.

HISTORY

It was in the 1490s, that the local lord, Tobiáš of Benešov, began to build himself a fortress modelled on contemporary French practice, with sturdy round towers linked by massive walls. His stronghold passed through many ownerships and was subjected to several rebuildings; its owners included the Šternberks and, briefly, Albrecht of Wallenstein. But the decisive imprint was that of Archduke Francis Ferdinand, who acquired it in 1887 for the handsome sum of six million florins. With the help of expert restorer **Josef Mocker** the archduke set about returning it to an idealised version of its medieval appearance as well as creating a prestigious and comfortable residence and a showcase for his remarkable collections of artworks, arms and armour, and curiosities of many kinds. At the same time the castle was thoroughly modernised,

Heir to the Hapsburg throne

Nephew of Emperor Francis Joseph, Hapsburg **Archduke Francis Ferdinand d'Este** (1863-1914) inherited great wealth, considerable possessions and the title d'Este from his uncle the Duke of Modena. Following the suicide of Crown Prince Rudolph in 1889, it became Francis Ferdinand's destiny to succeed the ageing Emperor as ruler of the troubled, multinational Austro-Hungarian Empire. Energetic, determined, widely-travelled and fluent in Czech and Hungarian as well as German, the archduke threw himself into the task of adapting the ossified Hapsburg realm so that it could survive into the 20C, though his lack of real power was a source of continual frustration to him, as was the treatment of his adored wife, **Sophie Chotková**, whose rank as a mere countess led her to be ostracised in snobbish Viennese court circles; before receiving the Emperor's permission to contract his morganatic marriage, the archduke had to renounce his children's rights of succession.

Ill-starred Archduke Franz Ferdinand and his consort

Konopiště was Franz Ferdinand's favourite retreat. Ahead of his time in concern for historic conservation, he was deeply involved in the conscientious recreation of his medieval castle. Art objects were avidly added to his already substantial collections. Functional buildings and staff dwellings were ruthlessly swept aside in the re-landscaping of the castle's park and gardens. Game was slaughtered in epic numbers. Business was conducted at Konopiště too; the stay here in early June 1914 of Emperor **Wilhelm II** of Germany has sometimes been interpreted as the signal for the start of World War One. But Franz Ferdinand was essentially a man of peace; too conservative to really respond to the growing nationalism among the Empire's subjects, he was nevertheless one of the few members of its ruling elite to see the need for change and it was a bitter irony that it was his assassination in Sarajevo on 28 June 1914 that served as a pretext for Austria to declare war on Serbia.

with the last word in running hot and cold water, central heating, and even a lift. The grounds were redesigned, populated with statuary, planted with exotic trees and shrubs, and given a magnificent rose garden.

Konopiště's most prominent feature is the tall round tower at the southeastern corner, with its machicolations and conical roof Tyrolean rather than Bohemian in style. Close to its foot is one of the few post-medieval features not to have been swept away by the archduke and his architect, the Baroque gateway designed by F.M. Kaňka with statuary from the workshop of M.B. Braun.

Like all Hapsburg possessions, Konopiště passed into the hands of the Czechoslovak State at the end of the First World War. During the Second World War it served as an SS headquarters and was earmarked for eventual occupation by the sinister figure of Heinrich Himmler.

INTERIOR ⊘

A choice of tours is available, one concentrating on the collections, one on living quarters.

Most of the furnishings, fittings and art objects from Francis Ferdinand's day are in place, giving the castle an especially intimate and personal atmosphere, sometimes oppressively so.

A suite of sumptuously furnished **state apartments** occupies the first floor of the **south wing**, among them rooms named to evoke the visits made to Konopiště by Emperor William II and his retinue. The archduke's love of the hunt is evident throughout the castle, sensationally so in the adjacent corridor decorated with hunting **trophies**; Franz Ferdinand is reckoned to have shot one animal for every hour of his life. The **dining room** has preserved its 18C decor.

Konopiště game

Game is no longer slaughtered at Konopiště in such great numbers as in Franz Ferdinand's time, but the unpretentious Stará myslivna (Gamekeeper's Lodge) restaurant (☎ *030 1211 48*) in one of the old estate buildings can still provide a good helping of venison.

including a fine ceiling painting of the *Times of the Day* by FJ Lux, while the **pillar room** has a stucco ceiling supported by a single column. The rooms on the second floor are those once occupied by Franz Ferdinand and his family, among them the his **study**, the **master bedroom**, **Sophie's study**, and the children's rooms, including their **playroom**. The corridor has mementoes of the ten-month round-the-world voyage the archduke made incognito in 1892/3, which he described in his *Tagebuch meiner Reise um die Erde*.

In the western section of the castle's **north wing** is the **library**, the gentlemen's **smoking room**, its floor spread with the skins of bears shot by the SS, and the so-called **harem**, furnished in oriental style.

On the ground floor of the eastern part of the north wing is a suite of vaulted rooms with many reminders of the life lived by the archduke and his family, among them the **death masks** made of the tragic couple after their assassination. Above is the **chapel**, with a fine collection consisting mostly of late Gothic painting and sculpture. On the second floor is the **Armoury**★★, one of the finest of its kind, based on Francis Ferdinand's Modena inheritance. Among the extraordinary array of arms and armour, mostly from the 16C-17C, is a superb full set of **equestrian armour** made for the *Condottiere* of the Republic of Venice, Eneo Pio degli Obizzi around 1560. One of the archduke's more out-of-the-way obsessions, linked no doubt to his own struggles, was the legend of St George, and a somewhat depleted array of objects associated with the saint is on display.

KŘIVOKLÁT★

KŘIVOKLAT Castle

60km west

High above a tributary of the Berounka River among the endless forests which were once the favourite hunting ground of the Bohemian kings is this medieval castle, less frequented than Karlštejn but less restored too and with a more evocative atmosphere. Křivoklát's origins go back to a princely hunting lodge established here as early as the 11C. This was fortified in the 12C and rebuilt in stone in the 13C, when it became a centre of courtly life. The future Emperor **Charles IV** spent his early childhood here and returned to Křivoklát in 1334 with his young wife Blanche of Valois; as she lay in childbirth Charles is supposed to have released countless captured nightingales at the foot of the castle to cheer her with their song. Remodelled in Late Gothic style at the turn of the 15C-16C, the castle became the love-nest of Imperial Governor Ferdinand of Tyrol and his secret spouse, the low-born merchant's daughter Philippine Welser. It served intermittently as a prison, one of its most distinguished inmates being Rudolph II's disgraced alchemist **Edward Kelley**. In the late 17C Křivoklát lost its royal status; the last private owners were the princely Fürstenberg family, who restored it in the late 19C and early 20C, inevitably with the help of the eminent conservation architect **Josef Mocker**.

Tour – Perched on its crag and dominated by its great round tower, Křivoklát's outline epitomises all that is picturesque and romantic about Bohemian castles. Approached through a gatehouse and entrance tower, the inner bailey is flanked to the east by the **Royal Hall** with a balcony and splendid oriel window with busts of the Jagellion kings, late-15C work by Hans Spiess of Frankfurt. Spiess was also responsible for the rebuilding of the superb **Chapel** in the south wing of the inner bailey; it has a reticulated vault and wonderful stone carving, as well as stained glass and a superb Late Gothic altarpiece. The castle houses a collection of Late Gothic painting and sculpture as well as Fürstenberg portraits.

KUTNÁ HORA★★

70km east Population 21 700

Its wealth based on immensely productive silver deposits, Kutná Hora was one of the largest and busiest of medieval Bohemian towns, able to begin though not to complete St Barbara's, one of glories of the country's Gothic church architecture. The stagnation suffered later meant that much of Kutná Hora's fine heritage of historic buildings remained untouched by modern developments, a factor in the town's designation as a UNESCO World Heritage Site.

HISTORY

Kutná Hora's "silver rush" began in 1275, when prospectors flocked to the newly discovered seams in great numbers from all over Central Europe. The riches extracted from the soil underpinned the prosperity of the medieval Bohemian state and King Wenceslas II replaced the coinage then in use by the Prague *groschen* (cf English groat), minted here in the building known as the **Vlášský dvůr (Italian Court)**.

The Hussite troubles at the beginning of the 14C led to the flight of many of the German-speaking, Catholic miners, but the event which put an end to the glory days was the discovery in the early 15C of richer seams at Jáchymov in the Ore Mountains of northwestern Bohemia. In the 17C war and emigration left two-thirds of Kutná Hora's houses empty and though the town eventually recovered, it never regained its former pre-eminence.

SIGHTS

★★Velechrám sv. Barbory (St Barbara's Church) ⊙ – Intended to rival the nearby abbey at Sedlec, the great church on its prominent site high above the winding River Vrchlice was begun at the end of the 14C and dedicated to the patron saint of miners, sappers and artillerymen. Its first architect was **Jan Parléř**, son of the builder of Prague's St Vitus'. He was followed by Matyáš Rejsek and then in the mid 16C by **Benedikt Ried**, who was responsible for the superb roof in the form of a triple tent, floating above the building like "an encampment of angels" (Brian Knox).

Inside, Ried's design for the **nave vault★★** is likewise a triumph of Late Gothic inventiveness, with intersecting rib patterns of great beauty and complexity. The nave has a fine set of pews and a pulpit provided by the Jesuits as well as late medieval statues of the cardinal Virtues. The splendid organ case dates from the 18C and there are fine wall-paintings some of which show the work of miners and minters. Built by Rejsek, the choir has carved bosses depicting Christ crucified, the four Evangelists, and the emblems of the town's guilds. The altarpiece of 1552 has been replaced by a 20C replica. Rejsek's tomb can be seen in the southern part of the choir. The first of the ambulatory chapels has wall-paintings depicting the town's coat of arms and those of the miners responsible for operating the windlass which brought the ore up from the depths of the earth; it is to them that the chapel is dedicated. The next chapel is dedicated to the Smíšeks, a family who made an instant fortune from mining. The lower wall-painting shows them at worship, while the painting above depicts the Arrival of the Queen of Sheba; knowing that the timber from the bridge across the Cedron will one day be used to make Christ's cross, she fords the stream on foot.

Jezuitská kolej (Jesuit College) – The Baroque building of the college was designed by Domenico Orsi in the form of a letter F in honour of Emperor Ferdinand II. Its great size and its dominant position are typical of the Jesuit establishments built as bastions of the 17C Counter-Reformation.

Hrádek ⊙ – This 15C Gothic palace houses the **Mining Museum**, from which those with sufficient enthusiasm can don miner's gear and descend into the shafts and galleries below.

Sv. Jakuba (St James' Church) – Built between 1330 and 1380, this fine example of a hall church has an 82 m tower.

St Barbara's Church: the vault

Rejskovo náměstí (Rejsek Square) – Named after the architect and sculptor, the square has as its principal ornament a splendid twelve-sided **fountain** designed by him around 1495.

Sv. Jana Nepomuckého (Church of St John of Nepomuk) – Completed by FM Kaňka around 1754, the Baroque church has an exceptionally richly furnished interior.

★**Vlašský dvůr (Italian Court)** ⊘ – Much restored in the 19C, the Italian Court is where experts from Florence taught the locals the art of minting money. Wenceslas IV converted it into a royal palace, complete with chapel with a splendid oriel window of about 1400. The little **museum** has numerous examples of the coinage struck here.

Kammený dům (Stone House) – This high-gabled late Gothic building from the end of the 15C is one of the most distinctive of the town's patrician town houses.

Klášter Voršilek (Ursuline Convent) ⊘ – Kilián Ignác Dientzenhofer was the archictect of this convent, but of his grandiose design of 1734 only two wings were ever completed. Inside is a small exhibition of furniture and other 17C - 19C items.

★**Chrám Nanebevzetí Panny Marie (Abbey Church of the Assumption)** ⊘ – *In Sedlec 3km northeast*. Founded in 1142 by Cistercian monks from Waldsassen in Bavaria, **Sedlec Abbey** reached a peak of wealth and influence towards the end of the 13C, but its great Gothic church was sacked by the Hussites in 1421. A replacement was not begun until 1699; the first architect was Paul Ignaz Bayer, followed in 1703 by **Jan Blažej** (or Johann Blasius or even Giovanni Battista) **Santini-Aichl** (1667-1723), the highly original Prague architect of Italian descent. Santini added pinnacles to the exterior while inside he constructed a complex ribbed vault of medieval inspiration. This was the first example of the highly individual synthesis of Baroque and Gothic which he later applied throughout Bohemia, the origin of which was religious as much as aesthetic, the churchmen of the Counter-Reformation wishing to revive the glories of the great monastic establishments of the Middle Ages.

★**Kostnice (Ossuary)** ⊘ – *In Sedlec*. The cemetery chapel in the centre of the burial ground dates from the end of the 14C, though its was baroquised by Santini in 1708. As early as 1511 a blind monk had constructed pyramids from the bones of people buried here, but it was not until 1870 that František Rint created the present extraordinary array of patterns using the bones from some 40 000 burials. They include fantastical chandeliers and the coats of arms of the Schwarzenbergs, owners of Sedlec Abbey after its secularisation.

LEDNICKO-VALTICKÝ Areál★★

LEDNICE-VALTICE Complex
Lednice 250km (47km southeast of Brno)

For more than six hundred years the gently undulating countryside near Břeclav on the Austrian-Moravian border was the domain of the princely **Liechtenstein** family. Centred on their residences at Lednice and Valtice which were linked by a magnificent avenue, their vast estates were managed with great care; swamps were drained, flooding contained, ponds dug, avenues planted, gardens laid out and agricultural and forest productivity enhanced by every possible means. The result was a many-layered, park-like landscape of great aesthetic and ecological value, its international significance recognised in 1996 when the whole area was designated a UNESCO World Heritage Site. Among its treasures is an array of park buildings – temples, arches, towers, mock castles – unparalleled in Central Europe.

A princely dynasty

The first written record of the **Liechtenstein** family goes back to 1130, but their connection with this part of Moravia came a century later, when in 1249 Heinrich von Liechtenstein was granted the lordship of the town of Mikulov. In the 15C they acquired **Valtice** as well as **Lednice**, where they built a splendid summer residence. Attracted at first to Protestantism, the family reconverted to Catholicism under the ambitious **Karl I von Liechtenstein** (1569-1627), whose canny support of future Emperor Matthias in his struggle to overthrow his brother Rudolph II was rewarded by his elevation to princely status. Further honours followed his role in suppressing the revolt of the Protestant Estates of Bohemia in 1618 and supervising the trial of its leaders and their subsequent execution in Prague's Old Town Square in 1622; having thus distinguished himself as Governor of Bohemia, he was made a member of the Order of the Golden Fleece, the highest honour of its kind. He was now in a good position to purchase, at knock-down prices, the confiscated property of Protestant rebels; the wealth thus acquired paid for the lavish rebuilding of the palaces at Lednice and Valtice.

Further rebuildings and general improvement of the family's estates were carried out by Karl's descendants, but the greatest flowering of the Lednice-Valtice area came in the 19C. Architects and landscape designers were brought in from Vienna and abroad to supervise the rebuilding of the residence at Lednice in neo-Gothic style, the scattering of numerous park buildings throughout the estates, and the further beautification of parks and gardens.

By the end of the 19C the Lednice-Valtice landscape was complete, but the Liechtensteins only had a few more decades to enjoy it; wholly identified with Austria and then with Greater Germany, they fled at the end of the Second World War, emptying their great houses of many of their possessions.

TOUR

Allow a day. Bicycle hire and the use of waymarked cycle routes are one of the most pleasant ways of exploring the area.

★★**Zámek Lednice (Lednice Palace)** ⊘ – *Guided tour*. The origins of this great country house go back to a moated medieval castle guarding an important trade route between Austria and Moravia. This was replaced by a Renaissance residence in the 16C, which was rebuilt by Fischer von Erlach at the end of the 17C. Further rebuildings and extensions followed, but the present imposing structure is the result of the wholesale reconstruction ordered by Prince Alois Josef of Liechtenstein in 1846. After a study tour of England, home of the Gothic revival, his architect J. Wingelmüller set about giving the palace a fashionable medieval appearance, inside and out. One wing of the palace is formed by the great neo-Gothic **chapel**, intended also as the parish church of the village of Lednice.

The palace interior has wood carving of exceptional virtuosity, especially in the splendid **Library**★ with its spiral staircase made from a single oak felled on the estate, and other rooms demonstrate the romantic enthusiasm with which the Liechtensteins and their designers felt for all things medieval.

One wing of the palace houses the displays of the **Národní zemědělské Muzeum** (National Agricultural Museum), which as well as a few items on hunting, concentrates on countryside conservation.

The **grounds**★ have many fascinating features. Designed by Fischer von Erlach, the **Baroque stables**★ have a classical calm and repose altogether lacking in the grandiloquent architecture of the palace. They house an aquarium. The **gardens** in the immediate vicinity of the palace have a formal layout, with allegorical statues among the geometrical pathways and hedges. The 92 m long **glasshouse**, the first of its kind in the Austrian Empire, was built in 1845 by the Englishman Peter Desvignes. To the north of the palace a vast semi-natural **park** was laid out between 1805-11. Its 34 ha lake, studded with islands, is a haven for wildlife. The park forms the setting for one of the area's most fascinating structures, the splendid **Minaret**★, while to the east is the artificial ruin known as **Janohrad** (John's Castle). Both of these magnificent follies were built between 1797-1810 by Josef Hardmuth.

★**Zamek Valtice** ⊘ – *Guided tour*. The Liechtensteins made Valtice their principal seat in the middle of the 16C, but the Baroque appearance of the present splendid residence dates from a whole series of rebuildings carried out in the last decade of the 17C and much of the 18C. Fischer von Erlach was involved early on, Domenico Martinelli at a later stage. The **palace** stands on a low rise above the little town which it has dominated for so long. The **cour d'honneur** with Hercules statues and flanking stable wings is magnificent, as is the main facade of the palace itself with its central tower, military trophies above the cornice, and a portal decorated with statues of Wisdom and Justice and the Liechtenstein coat of arms. The restored interiors are sadly lacking in original furnishings, but there is fine **chapel** with *trompe l'oeil* frescoes.

Valtice town *(Population 3500)* – The sleepy little town has a broad main street with a fine late-19C town hall in traditional style as well as the monumental Early **Baroque Church** of the Assumption of the Virgin Mary. Valtice is the centre of one of the country's most renowned wine-growing areas, whose vines cover the gentle slopes rising towards the nearby Austrian border; Valtice was once called Feldsberg and belonged to Austria, but in 1920 a frontier adjustment assigned it to Moravia, part of the newly created state of Czechoslovakia.

★**Park buildings** – The number and quality of structures scattered over the Liechtenstein domain constituted one of the main reasons for the area's UNESCO designation. Many were designed by the Liechtensteins' architects Josef Hardmuth (1758-1816) and Josef Kornhäusel (1782-1860).

★**Kolonáda (Colonnade)** – *1km southwest of Valtice*. Inspired by the Gloriette in Vienna and completed in 1823 by Prince Johann I in memory of his father and brother Sited right on the Austrian border, it served under Communism as an observation post and was inaccessible to the public. Battered by time and vandals, it awaits restoration.

The Colonnade, Valtice

★**Dianin chrám (Temple of Diana or Rendez-vous)** — *1.5km east of Valtice*. The triumphal arch was built by Kornhäusel to plans by Hardmuth to serve as a hunting lodge among the woods planted by the Liechtensteins to stabilise the poor soils of the area. A little concert hall and ballroom are contained within the structure.

Tří Grácie (Three Graces) — *4.5km northeast of Valtice*. The horseshoe-shaped colonnade above the Prostřední rybník (Central Pond) has at its centre the figures of the Greek goddesses Athena, Artemis and Aphrodite, hewn from a single block of stone and incorrectly known as the *Three Graces*.

★**Hraniční zámeček (Border Castle)** — *At the western end of the village of Hlohovec, 5km north of Valtice*. Now containing a restaurant, this dignified neo-Classical structure was designed by Kornhäusel and completed in 1827 on what was then the border between Austria and Moravia as indicated by the inscription *Zwischen Österreich und Mähren* on its facade. It has a fine view eastwards over the bird-rich Hlohovecký rybník (Hlohovec Pond).

Apollonův chrám (Temple of Apollo) — *2km southeast of Lednice*. Crowning the sandy rise above the Mlýnský rybník (Mill Pond) and designed by Kornhäusel, the temple is decorated with sculpture devoted to the sun-god Apollo.

★**Minaret and Janohrad** — *See under Zámek Lednice above.*

Travellers' addresses

LIDICE

23km northwest Population 446

In reprisal for the assassination of Reichsprotektor Reinhard Heydrich on 27 May 1942 the nondescript mining village of Lidice was destroyed, its male inhabitants shot, its women and children sent to concentration camp. The Nazis boasted that corn would grow where Lidice once stood and that its name would be erased from the records forever. But the atrocity had the opposite effect. Lidice became a world-wide symbol of German cruelty and Czech suffering. The movement "Lidice Shall Live" began in England, while communities all over the world renamed themselves in honour of the destroyed village. After the war the site of Lidice became a much-visited memorial park alongside which a new village was built.

Frustrated in their search for the parachutists responsible for **Heydrich**'s killing *(see also p. 131)*, the German authorities used the flimsiest of pretexts to associate Lidice with the deed. Sealing off the village on the night of 9 June, armed police and

SS then herded all the men they had found into a farmyard where they were executed at dawn the following morning. Those absent on that fatal night were not spared: miners on the night shift were arrested as they left work and later murdered, as was a colleague confined to hospital with a broken leg. Supposedly the only man to escape death was an imprisoned murderer. Many of the women and children disappeared forever in the labyrinth of the camps, though a few youngsters thought suitable for "Germanisation" were given to SS foster-parents.

The emptied village was burned to the ground and its remains bulldozed by Wehrmacht engineers.

> **Memorial park** – Below a colonnade and a bastion, the ground where Lidice once stood slopes gently southwards then rises again. The mass grave of the village's menfolk can be seen, and foundations remain of the church and other buildings. There is an extensive rose garden. The exhibits in the small **museum** ⊘ are poignant in their evocation of the utterly ordinary life lived in Lidice before its brutal annihilation.

MARIÁNSKÉ LÁZNĚ★★

Marienbad

160km west Population 15 300

Its stucco hotels and spa installations set in lavish gardens and surrounded by glorious woodlands, world-famous **Marienbad** wears a sedate air, but is nevertheless the youngest of the three spa towns of the "Bohemian Triangle". Some 600 metres above sea level on the edge of the vast Slavkovsk les, the conifer-covered tract of granite upland once known as the Emperor's Forest *(Kaiserwald)*, Marienbad enjoys a fresh climate, and its waters are cool too; flowing from some 40 springs, they are unique in their variety and are used to treat a variety of ills, including kidney problems and obesity.

HISTORY

For centuries the healing powers of the area's springs remained a secret only known to local people familiar with the few paths that led through the dense forest and across treacherous boglands. The first written record of the springs' existence dates from 1528, when Emperor Ferdinand asked the local landowners, the monks of **Teplá Abbey** for samples of water to be sent to Prague, but it was only towards the end of the 18C that the Abbey's doctor, **Johann Josef Nehr** (1752-1820) made a thorough analysis of the waters and erected the first spa building at his own expense. The first season of the spa was formally opened in 1808, based on Mary's Spring, so-called after a portrait of the Virgin Mary given by a patient in gratitude for his cure. After initial hesitation, Teplá Abbey threw itself behind the development of the spa, with its energetic **Abbot Karl Kaspar Reitenberger** (1779-1860) playing a decisive role.

In the last decades of the 19C and the start of the 20C the linking of Marienbad to the European railway network brought about its heyday; the spa flourished as never before or since, its guest list matching that of Carlsbad in its parade of illustrious names. It was at this time that the town was largely rebuilt and given its attractive turn-of-the-century appearance.

At the war's end the town lost some of its aristocratic cachet, but guests continued to come, a all-time peak attendance being registered in 1929. With the Munich settlement of 1938 Marienbad was incorporated into Germany, and in the Second World War became one big military hospital. Like much of western Bohemia it was liberated by US troops in 1945. The Communist regime made spa facilities available to a wider public, and by the 1960s cures were being taken all year round, rather than just during the season.

SIGHTS

★**Křížový pramen (Cross Spring)** – This delightful neo-Classical temple to health dates from 1811. It is built over the oldest spring still in use, whose water has an unusually high mineral content and a strong purgative effect. The pavilion's distinctive cupola is topped by a double cross, a reminder of the role of Teplá Abbey in the foundation of the spa.

★★★**Colonnade** – The splendid curving colonnade of cast-iron construction is one of the finest examples of 19C spa architecture still in existence. It was completed in 1889 in neo-Baroque style and comprehensively and faithfully rebuilt between 1973-81. It is linked to the Cross Spring and the colonnade of the **Karolínin pramen** (Caroline Spring) by a tastefully landscaped **promenade.** At the centre of the promenade stands the computer-controlled **Singing Fountain★**, whose spectacular performance is enhanced by illumination in the evening.

Marienbad: the Colonnade

★ **Nanebevzetí Panny Marie (Church of the Assumption)** – Thirty-three steps symbolising Christ's 33 years on Earth lead up to the portal of this monumental church, built in neo-Byzantine style on a polygonal plan by the Munich architect J. J. Guthensohn in 1844.

★ **Goethův dům (Goethe House)** ⏱ – *Goethovo náměstí 11*. That indefatigable frequenter of spas, **Johann Wolfgang von Goethe** (1749-1832), visited Marienbad on four occasions, getting to know Abbot Reitenberger and entering into long and learned discussions about geology and botany with fellow-guest Count Kaspar Sternberg. It was in Marienbad that he fell passionately in love with the "pretty child" Ulrike von Levetzow.

On his third visit to the town, Goethe stayed in this house, then called The Golden Grape. Dating from 1818, it has kept its external appearance, while inside the great writer's rooms form part of an exhibit which traces his long-standing fascination with Bohemia, its natural history, its inhabitants, and its language, which he attempted to learn. The house is also the local **museum**, with many fascinating exhibits including a number of horrific kidney stones left here by sufferers.

Outside, a modern statue of Goethe surveys the verdant square named after him.

★ **Skalníkovy sady (Skalník Gardens)** – These luxuriant gardens laid out along the course of the little Třebísk stream form the green heart of the spa town, linking many of its important buildings and representing a tamed and beautified version of the woodland all around. They are named after their creator, **Václav Skalník** (1776-1861), a landscape architect who became Marienbad's third mayor. In a central position stands the memorial to the 1945 Liberation by the US Army. On the southern side of the park rise the towers of the **Nové lázně** (New Spa), a pompous neo-Renaissance building of 1896. To the west, pollution-free trolley-buses glide along Hlavní třída (Main Street), lined by fine turn-of-the-century structures including several of the town's most prestigious hotels. Further west still, on the slope above, is the Anglican church, now used for exhibitions, and its more flamboyant neighbour, the **Pravoslavný kostel sv. Vladimíra (St Vladimir's Orthodox Church)**, built in 1901 for the spa's many Russian visitors.

By Royal Appointment

One of Marienbad's favourite guests was Great Britain's **King Edward VII** (1841-1910) who between 1897 and 1906 came here every August. As well as working off some of the effects of his hearty lifestyle, he played golf, attended services in the Anglican church, conferred with his fellow-monarchs, and also found time to make discreet visits to Mizzi Pistl, a pretty young milliner.

EXCURSION

★ **Klášter premonstrátů (Teplá Abbey)** – *13km east*. Founded in 1193, and with close links to the Premonstratensians' foundation at Strahov in Prague, the abbey at **Teplá** ⊘ had a long history of fires, sackings, and dissolutions, and most recently under the Communist regime, underwent conversion to an army barracks. Currently being restored, it is once again the popular day trip it was in the time of Goethe, who bequeathed it his substantial collection of minerals. Fairly completely baroquised by the Dientzenhofers, the abbey church nevertheless kept its twin Romanesque towers. The monastery **library**★ is spectacular, with fabulous stucco work and several layers of bookcases reached by balconies.

MĚLNÍK

39km north Population 19700

Visible from far away across the plains, the ancient town of Mělník crowns the isolated hilltop above the meeting-point of Bohemia's two great rivers, the Vltava and the Elbe (*Labe* in Czech). Beneath its castle and church tower grow the vines which produce some of the country's most famous wines.

HISTORY

Mělník's origins go back to a stronghold built here in the 9C by the Slavonic tribe known as the Pšovs. A Pšov princess called Ludmila married into the Přemyslid family who ruled from Prague, but it was at Mělník that she tutored her grandson, Prince (and later Saint) Wenceslas in the ways of Christianity. She herself was later canonised as one of Bohemia's patron saints, while the castle at Mělník became a kind of dower house of the country's royal widows. Vines had been grown on the sheltered slopes below the castle at an early date, but it was **Emperor Charles IV** who imported new and better varieties from Burgundy in the mid 14C, giving instructions for them to be packed in honey to preserve them during their long journey.

Mělník's castle passed through several ownerships and rebuildings before becoming the property of the princely **Lobkowicz** family in 1753, who however preferred to reside in Prague, and left the castle much as they found it. Dispossessed at the beginning of the Communist regime, the family returned in the 1990s and are vigorously developing the attractions of the property.

★ **Zámek (Castle)** ⊘ – *Guided tour*. Approached through a gateway, the three wings of the castle are arranged around a courtyard and though some of the structure is medieval, present a Renaissance-cum-Baroque appearance, with arcades and bold sgraffito decoration. A number of interiors have been restored and filled with Lobkowicz furniture and other items, some of them recovered from various ministries in Prague. There are fine paintings and a Map Hall. Mělník served as the centre for the Lobkowicz vineyards, and a separate tour takes in the castle's wine cellars.

From the castle itself and from the public terrace just below there are magnificent **views** over the confluence of the two rivers and over the vast plain towards the Central Bohemian Highlands.

Sv. Petra a Pavla (Church of St Peter and St Paul) ⊘ – Originally Romanesque, the church was rebuilt in Gothic style in the 14C and 15C. Its landmark tower dates from this time, though it topped by a Baroque cap. The crypt houses an extensive **ossuary**.

Náměstí míru (Peace Square) – Partly arcaded, Mělník's market square has much of the charm of the typical Bohemian provincial town, and seems infinitely far away from the metropolitan bustle of Prague. The medieval **Town Hall** on the north side with twin gables and a clock tower gained its present appearance from an 18C rebuilding. A short distance to the east is the town's only surviving gateway, the **Pražská brána** (Prague Gate).

NELAHOZEVES★★

27km north Population 1240

Famous as the rustic birthplace of the composer Antonín Dvořák, this little village on the Vltava is dominated by its splendid Renaissance castle, its interiors a magnificent setting for one of the country's finest private art collections.

★★ **Zámek (Castle)** – The castle stands four-square on a bluff overlooking both river and village. It was begun in 1552 by Florián Griespek of Griespach. As the court official in charge of all royal building work in Bohemia, Griespek was able to call on the services of some of the best architects and craftsmen, and among those who contributed to the construction of his castle was the royal builder **Bonifác Wohlmut**. Though conceived of as a kind of great country house, Nelahozeves has the formidable outward appearance of a North Italian *castello*, with corner bastions and massive rustication relieved by elaborate sgraffito work. A bridge across a dry moat leads through an archway into a partly arcaded courtyard, of altogether lighter appearance. A south wing was never built; in its place stands a low wall. The east wing boasts a unsophisticated Renaissance portal with coats of arms, but it is the north wing which is architecturally outstanding, with a first floor which was originally an open loggia.

In 1623 Nelahozeves came into the possession of the princely **Lobkowicz** family, though they never used it as their main residence. By the time it was confiscated by the State after the Second World War it was in very poor shape and the restoration process stretched over decades. The castle was restituted to the Roudnice branch of the family after 1989.

★★ Collections – *Guided tour*. Successive generations of Lobkowicz were great patrons of the arts. Their collections comprise more than a thousand paintings as well as an array of **glass** and **porcelain**, superb items of **furniture** and **sacred objects** such as a **16C altarpiece★** of gold and silver thread and precious stones.

The tour takes visitors though the tastefully arranged rooms of the north and east wings of the castle. The two most striking interiors are the **Arkádové haly** (Arcade Hall) and the **Rytířský sál (Knights Hall★)**, the latter a superb Renaissance space two storeys high with a contemporary fireplace, rich stucco work and remains of wall-paintings.

Spaniards feature strongly among the fascinating portraits on show. There are two likenesses of **Polyxena of Lobkowicz**, one showing this noble woman of Spanish origin attending to the injuries suffered by the Catholic Governors defenestrated from Prague Castle in 1618. An exquisite **Velasquez** depicts the infant *Margareta Theresa of Spain★*. Hapsburgs appear in number, among them Rudolf II as a young man and his sister, Anne of Austria. Rudolf's famous Cabinet of Curiosities is shown in great detail in another picture.

There are two **Canalettos** of about 1747, *View of the River Thames with Westminster Abbey and Bridge★*, and *River Thames with St Paul's Cathedral on Lord Mayor's Day★*. Among the Dutch and Flemish pictures is a charming trio in which monkeys and cats play out an allegory of aristocratic life, while a village scene by Jan Breughel celebrates a more rustic way of life. The undoubted masterpiece among these masterpieces however is **Peter Brueghel's Haymaking★★★**, one of the series of his Months of the Year, and the only one in private ownership. Beyond the peasants at work in the front of the picture and the villages and rock outcrops in the middle ground, a city spreads itself enticingly on both banks of a broad river, its outline very much like that of Prague.

Other great works include Cranach the Elder's *Virgin and Child with St Barbara and St Catherine★*, *Hygieia Nourishing the Sacred Serpent★* by Rubens, and Veronese's *David with the Head of Goliath★*.

The most impressive display of glass and porcelain is in the **Dining Room**, where the table is set for 24 guests. Many members of the Lobkowicz family were musically inclined; their court orchestra was famous and they supported numerous composers, among them Beethoven, who dedicated several works to his friend Josef Franz Maximilian (1772-1816), an accomplished musician himself. Instruments, original scores and many other items in the **Music Room** recall these connections. In the early 19C the topographer Carl Robert Croll recorded the Lobkowicz possessions in a series of charming landscapes and townscapes, and many of these are on show.

> ## A gift to visitors
>
> Suitable souvenirs can be hard to find when off the beaten track in the Czech Republic, but the museum shop (☎ *0205 785 331*) at Nelahozeves Castle is an exception, with an array of tasteful objects and even a children's corner.

Rodiště Antonína Dvořáka

(Dvořák's Birthplace) – Almost in the shadow of the castle stands the substantial house where Dvořák was born in 1841. It is now a small museum devoted to his memory. Music was all around the young Dvořák, sacred music in the church, folk music in the village; soon he was playing with his butcher father in a local band and enjoying violin lessons from his teacher Mr Spitz.

MICHELIN GREEN GUIDES
Art and architecture; ancient monuments; history;
landscape; scenic routes touring programmes; local maps; town plans; site plans;
A selection of guides for holidays at home and abroad.

ORLÍK ★

75km south

Perched on a crag high above the raftsmen negotiating the wooded gorge of the Vltava the medieval stronghold of Orlík must have presented an impossibly Romantic sight. In the 19C however, the castle was tamed, given a bland, mock-Gothic appearance, and in the 20C its setting suffered a not dissimilar fate; the river was dammed and its level rose by 60 m to lap tamely at the castle walls.

Orlík was the seat of one of the two branches of the princely **Schwarzenberg** family, faithful servants of the Hapsburg Emperor and at the same time staunch Bohemian patriots. **Karl Phillip Schwarzenberg** (1771-1820) crowned his military career by defeating Napoleon at the Battle of Leipzig in 1812, while his descendant Karl VI (1911-86), by leading the aristocratic defence of the Czechoslovak Republic in the late 1930s incurred the wrath of the Nazis. In 1940 they confiscated Orlík, as did the postwar regime of reconstituted Czechoslovakia. The family went into Austrian exile, but after 1989 Karl VII returned, becoming President Havel's Chancellor.

Visit ⊙ – Orlík is approached through an attractive landscaped park which contains a family vault. The interior of the castle is furnished in a combination of Empire and neo-Gothic styles, with fine displays of weaponry and hunting trophies.

PLZEŇ ★

Pilsen

88km west Population 110700

The busy regional capital of western Bohemia, Pilsen owed its early prosperity on its strategic location on the ancient highway between Prague and the great cities of Bavaria like Nuremberg. In the 19C and early 20C it became the industrial power-house of the Austro-Hungarian Empire, then of Czechoslovakia, turning out armaments and heavy machinery from the world-famous Škoda works. But more than anything else the city is identified throughout the world with Pilsner, the lager beer first brewed here in the 1840s, and universally imitated but never excelled.

SIGHTS

★**Náměstí Republiky (Republic Square)** – **Pilsen's** central square is the biggest in Bohemia, spacious enough to accommodate the city's splendid Gothic parish church. Now lined with buildings from many periods of the city's long history, the square occupies two blocks of the regular chequerboard pattern of streets laid out by King Wenceslas II's surveyor in 1295, when it was decided to found a town to control the trade route westward from Prague. The city's pride in itself is expressed most forcefully in the flamboyant Renaissance **Town Hall**★ on the north side of the square; completed 1559, its boldly rusticated and sgraffito'd façade is topped by

Brewery entrance, Pilsen

an array of gables, finials, chimneys, and a little cupola. In the winter of 1633/34, General Wallenstein stayed in house *no 12/105* on the east side of the square, and it was here that the over-ambitious warlord betrayed his Emperor by extracting an oath of personal loyalty from his officers. The streets leading off the square have many fine examples of turn-of-the-century houses.

★**Chrám sv. Bartoloměje (St Bartholomew's Cathedral)** ⊙ – The great Gothic church has the country's highest (103m) tower, a lofty reticulated vault, an early 16C chapel founded by the Sternbergs, and, adorning the High Altar, the late-14C **Pilsen Madonna**, a fine example of the "Beautiful Style". The **plague column** close to the church's western entrance dates from 1681.

The Blessings of Beer

Despite Pilsen's many and varied points of interest, it is to pay homage to the city's most celebrated product that most visitors from abroad pause here. Beer was brewed in the city from the very earliest days; many of its citizens had the right to brew beer on their own premises, a privilege they guarded with great tenacity, although the quality of the product seems to have been variable to say the least. In 1842 a group of citizens founded the Burgher Brewery (*Bürgerbräu* in German, *Měštánský pivovar* in Czech), bringing in an experienced Bavarian brewer to supervise the operation. Almost by accident, he created the bottom-fermented beer which has delighted serious drinkers ever since. Its character owes something to the quality of Bohemian hops from Žatec, to the water from the inexhaustible local springs, and to the caves carved into the sandstone underlying the site of the brewery, which provided ideal conditions for storage. The beer was given the name *Prazdroj* (*Urquell* in German), meaning "original source", to distinguish it from its many imitators.

Pilsner can be found all around the world, but to drink it in its place of origin is a special thrill. However, before indulging your thirst you should visit the prizewinning museum which celebrates the city's longstanding connection with beer.

★**Pivovarské muzeum (Museum of Brewing)** ⊙ – *Veleslavínova 6*. Appropriately enough, the museum is housed in one of the buildings whose owner enjoyed brewing privileges, and although it has been much rebuilt since medieval times, it is full of atmosphere, and makes an ideal setting for a fascinating array of equipment and items connected with beer and brewing.

★**Plzeňský Prazdroj** ⊙ – *U Prazdroje 7. Guided tour*. The renowned establishment where Prazdroj has been brewed for a century and a half stands just to the east of the city centre, guarded by a triumphal arch built to mark the brewery's 50th anniversary in 1892.

Masné krámy (Meat Market) – *Pražská 16*. The medieval building which once housed the butchers' stalls forms part of the **Art Gallery of Western Bohemia** *(under reconstruction)* whose collections include wonderful **Gothic statuary** and a representative collection of **modern Czech art**. The gallery also has exhibition space in the restored medieval building opposite.

Beer on tap

Pilsner beer can be enjoyed in the brewery itself or in any number of establishments around the town, notably at the wood-panelled U Salzmannů beer hall *(Pražská 8)*.

Františkánský klášter (Franciscan Monastery) ⊙ – *Františkánská*. Beyond the Baroque facade are Gothic cloisters which make a fine setting for an exhibition of **medieval, Renaissance and Baroque sculpture**. The **Kaple sv. Barbory (Chapel of St Barbara)** has 15C wall-paintings.

Západočeské muzeum (West Bohemian Museum) ⊙ – *Kopeckého sady 2*. The museum documents the history of the region, but besides its fine collection of glass and porcelain its outstanding attraction is the **municipal armoury**★, a splendidly presented array of blunderbusses, muskets and other weaponry.

Velká synagoga (Great Synagogue) ⊙ – *sady Pětatřicátníků 11*. The size and prosperity of the city's late-19C Jewish community is reflected in the grandeur of this splendid twin-towered building in neo-Moorish style. Completed in 1893 and the second largest synagogue in Europe after Budapest's, it is undergoing restoration after years of serious neglect.

> ### Thank you, America!
>
> The Communist regime discouraged memories of the American liberation of much of western Bohemia at the end of the Second World War, preferring rather to celebrate the glorious role of the Red Army. Pilsen was the largest Czechoslovak city to be freed by the US Army; units commanded by General Patton arrived here on 6 May 1945 and were only prevented from driving on to Prague by General Eisenhower's insistence that the Allied agreement assigning the occupation of the capital to the Soviet forces be respected.
> In 1995 the 50th anniversary of the liberation was marked by the unveiling of a memorial at the upper end of Americká Street with the inscription *Díky, Ameriko!* "Thank You, America!".

EXCURSION

★**Klášter Kladruby (Kladruby Monastery)** ⊘ – *29km west.* "A dream made stone" (Brian Knox) is an apt description of the abbey church which metamorphosed into a Baroque-cum-Gothic fantasy under the inspired direction of **J. B. Santini-Aichel**, (1667-1723) whose masterpiece it is.

The Benedictine abbey was founded in 1115 but suffered grievously in the Hussite troubles of the early 14C. Around 1712, Abbot Finzguth ordered the patched-up church to be rebuilt, choosing an architect he knew would be capable of reinterpreting medieval glories in the language of the Baroque. Beneath Santini's **cupola** and his extraordinarily complex **vaulting** are panel **paintings** by the **Asam** brothers and an array of furniture designed by Santini himself; the altar has sculpture by **Matthias Bernard Braun**. From inside, the cupola appears conventionally Baroque; from outside, with a ring of ogee windows gripping a swelling spiked dome, it seems to stem from the overstretched imagination of a Hieronymus Bosch.

Like the church, the monastery buildings (by K. I. Dientzenhofer) underwent decades of neglect. Parts have been restored and house a library, mementoes of the Windischgrätz family, and a superb gallery of Braun sculptures brought here from the castle park at Valeč near Carlsbad.

PRŮHONICE
16km southeast Population 1 780

Almost within sight of the city, and easily accessible just off the Brno motorway, the village and park at Průhonice are a popular excursion for people from Prague. Weekend leisure here seems to have a certain cachet; the country's first motel was built here in the 1960s, there is a golf course, and an air of developing prosperity.

The 200 ha **park** threaded by 40km of pathways was the creation of Count Ernst Silva-Taroucca (1858-1936), Austria-Hungary's last Minister of Agriculture. The park spreads out from Průhonice **castle**, rebuilt by the count in a Gothic-cum-Renaissance style while retaining its Romanesque **chapel** with its wall-paintings. The castle houses the botanical department of the Academy of Sciences and is not open to the public. The luxuriant grounds have alpine gardens and lakes, but the main attraction is the **arboretum★**, an English-style park planted with more than 1 000 native and exotic tree species, one of the finest of its kind in Central Europe.

SLAVKOV U BRNA★
Austerlitz
20km east of Brno/220km southeast of Prague Population 5 920

The Battle of the Three Emperors was won by Napoleon Bonaparte on 2 December 1805, the first anniversary of his coronation as Emperor of the French. That evening he proclaimed to his troops: "Only say: I was at Austerlitz, and they will know what sort of man you are". In the course of the day his Grande Armée had crushed a force of 15 000 Austrians and 75 000 Russians led by Tsar Alexander I and Austrian Emperor Francis I.

After crossing the Rhine and winning the Battle of Ulm, Napoleon led his army into Austria and occupied Vienna. His Russian and Austrian opponents retreated northwards into Moravia, avoiding any engagement. Realising that further pursuit would weaken his forces by obliging him to detach a rearguard, Napoleon decided to engage the enemy east of Brno, close to Austerlitz (now Slavkov). He succeeded in concealing the real disposition of his 75 000 men and even appeared to be preparing to retreat.

Napoleon at the Battle of Austerlitz, by L. Lejeune

together with his commander, General Kutuzov, the Tsar decided to block the French army's line of retreat towards Vienna by outflanking its right wing. Deliberately weakening this wing in order to draw the enemy on, Napoleon planned to direct his attack at the Prace plateau, where the bulk of his opponents' forces were stationed, thereby cutting them off from the road leading towards Olomouc.

The Sun of Austerlitz" – At 7 o'clock on the morning of 2 December, in a dense fog concealing the true whereabouts of the French, the allied right wing under the command of Buxhövden engaged the French right wing led by General Davout. Bitter fighting soon developed around the villages of Telnice and Sokolnice. At around 8am, the rising sun began to disperse the fog; observing Kolowrat's Austrian troops moving down from the Prace plateau towards Sokolnice, Napoleon ordered Soult to attack the Allied centre. By 11am the summit was in French hands, the Russian artillery had been captured, and Marshals Lannes and Murat had pushed General Bagration northward and taken Santon Hill. This was the moment at which the cavalry of the French Imperial Guard made its celebrated charge, routing the Russian Imperial Guard near Slavkov itself. With the collapse of the allied centre, the French were able to push the Russians back towards the Žatčany fishponds; the dams of the ponds came under constant artillery fire, forcing the Russian troops to attempt escape across the frozen surface, but the ice was thin and many drowned.

The Austrians and Russians lost 26 000 men killed or captured, the French 9 000. The brilliant victory won beneath a brilliant winter sun enabled Napoleon to dictate terms to his opponents. Francis I signed an armistice at Slavkov Castle on 4 December, then concluded the Treaty of Preßburg (Bratislava) on 26 December, bringing about peace between Austria and France and the return of the Russian forces to their homeland.

THE BATTLEFIELD

The battlefield extends over an area of some 110Km^2 between Slavkov and the eastern outskirts of Brno. Nearly two centuries after the battle the villages have grown, the highway linking Brno and Olomouc has become a motorway, and most of the fateful fishponds have been drained. An array of monuments and memorials recall the battle so vividly described by Tolstoy in *War and Peace*.

Křenovice – *3km west of Slavkov.* General Kutuzov, commander-in-chief of the allied armies, stayed in one of the village's farmhouses *(no 65/222)*. The church was used as a hospital for Russian casualties.

Zbýšov – *3km west of Křenovice.* The church tower is pockmarked with cannon-balls.

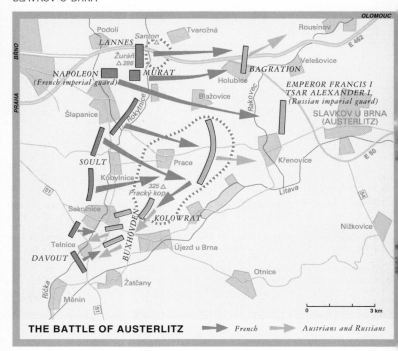

THE BATTLE OF AUSTERLITZ ➡ *French* ➡ *Austrians and Russians*

★ **Pracký kopec (Prace Heights)** – *5km west of Zbyšov.* The great memorial crownin the hilltop is dedicated neither to victory nor defeat but to peace. Designed by th Secession architect Josef Fanta and called the **Mohyla míru** (Mound of Peace), it wa built between 1910-12, largely as a result of the efforts of a Brno priest, Alo Slovák. Its base serves as an ossuary and a small **museum** ⊘ tells the story of th battle. The site offers a fine prospect of the battlefield. On the left of the road t Sokolnice, a chapel dedicated to St Anthony of Padua marks the spot from whic the Austrian artillery bombarded Telnice, the starting signal for the battle.

Sokolnice – *5km southwest of Pracký kopec.* The mansion house (*No access*) an its surrounding parkland was the scene of fierce fighting on the morning of December. French artillery emplacements in the wall surrounding the park can b seen from the road. The little River Řička – once better known by its German nam Goldbach – served as a highly effective base of operations for the French.

Žuráň Hill – *12km north of Sokolnice.* This hill with its burial mounds from th period of the Great Migrations was where Napoleon set up his field HQ. A ston block is carved with a relief map and the words addressed by the Emperor to h troops before the battle. A small area of ground is French territory. There is a fin view over this crucial part of the battlefield.

Santon Hill – *2.5km east of Žuráň Hill.* The hill was given its name by veterans wh had seen Mount Santon during Bonaparte's Palestinian campaign. A replica cannon installed on the summit which the French engineers levelled in order to make gu emplacements. Because of its steppe vegetation the area is now a nature reserve.

Stará pošta (Old Post Office) – *5km east.* The posthorn over the door is a remind that the house where Napoleon spent the night of 28 November was once a po office. During the battle itself the house served as Bagration's headquarters, an it was here that the Austrian envoy Prince Liechtenstein met Napoleon in order t discuss the terms of an armistice.

★ **Zámek Slavkov (Slavkov Castle)** ⊘ – In 1509, the commandery built by the Teuton knights in the 13C at Austerlitz (a Germanisation of Novosedlice, the name of th nearby hamlet) came into the hands of the **Kaunitz** family. The family's wealth an influence increased following the Battle of the White Mountain in 1620, and the played a leading role at the Hapsburg court in Vienna. At the end of the 17C th diplomat Dominik Andreas Kaunitz rebuilt his residence in Baroque style to a desig by Martinelli. In 1756 another Kaunitz, Wenzel Anton, Empress Maria Theresa Chancellor, succeeded in engineering an allliance between Austria and her trad tional enemy, France.
The castle has a fine collection of **17C and 18C paintings** as well as an **Battle of Austerli exhibition**. Outside, the 15 ha park has sculptures by Matthias Bernard Braun.

TÁBOR ★

87km south Population 36 820

On the easily defended promontory between the River Lužnice and one of its tributaries, the site of Tábor seems to have been first occupied by the Celts in prehistoric times. It certainly provided an excellent location in the 13C for a royal fortress, which was however destroyed by the Přemyslid monarchs' bitter rivals, the Vítek lords of southern Bohemia. But Tábor's days of fame belong to a later period. In 1420, the hilltop served as a refuge for the radical followers of the martyred John Huss when they fled Prague following the defenestration of the Catholics from the windows of the New Town Hall *(see p. 130)*. Under their fierce general, one-eyed **Jan Žižka of Trocnov** (c 1376-1424), they gave their stronghold the name of the biblical mountain which was the scene of Christ's Transfiguration, sallying forth to spread their creed and crush their ideological opponents wherever they could find them. The layout of the town, unusually for the Czech lands, is confusingly irregular, perhaps deliberately so in order to disorientate any attacker who managed to penetrate what used to be a famously impregnable set of town walls, perhaps because the houses still stand where the first Taborites pitched their tents at random in 1420.

★ **Žižkovo náměstí (Žižka Square)** – From the modern town **Pražská** (Prague Street) leads past many a gabled and sgraffitoe'd façade to the focal point of historic Tábor, the sloping square bearing the name of the redoubtable general, who continued to dismay his many enemies even after the loss of his remaining eye. His **statue** dates from 1884. The square has a further fine display of Renaissance gables. It is overlooked from the north by the tall tower of the **Děkanský kostel** (Deanery Church); inside, the church has fascinating examples of the diamond vaulting peculiar to Bohemia and Saxony. Also with a fine tower, the triple-gabled **Town Hall** dates from about 1521, though its present appearance is partly due to a 19C neo-Gothic rebuilding. It houses the **Husitské muzeum** (Hussite Museum) ⊙, which as well as displaying a definitive selection of Hussite memorabilia, also gives access to the **Podzemí** (Tábor Underground), an intriguing labyrinth of interconnecting cellars.

Bechyňská brána (Bechyně Gate) ⊙ – Incorporating the round tower of the castle, this is the town's only remaining gateway, dating from the mid 15C. It houses an exhibition on medieval life.

★ **Poutní místo Klokoty (Klokoty pilgrimage church and monastery)** – *1km west.* As if to defy Tábor's traditions of protest and asceticism, this delightful place of pilgrimage was built in exuberant Baroque style at the very beginning of the 18C. Enclosed by walls with chapels at their corners, it presents an extraordinary silhouette with an array of bulbous cupolas surmounted by lanterns.

*The current **Michelin Red Guide Europe** offers a selection of pleasant hotels in convenient locations.*
Each entry specifies the facilities available (gardens, tennis courts, swimming pool, beach facilities) and the annual opening and closing dates.
There is also a selection of establishments recommended for their cuisine – well prepared meals at moderate prices; stars for good cooking.

TELČ★★★

Dreaming away in the quiet countryside of southern Moravia, this tiny town has hardly changed since it was rebuilt after a great fire in 1530. Great fishponds hem it in to north and south and the Renaissance residence of the Lords of Hradec dominates the town's western end, but it is the perfection of the arcaded and gabled houses lining its square that gives Telč its special allure. Often described as the most beautiful town in the Czech Republic, it was added to UNESCO's World Heritage List in 1992.

★★★ Náměstí Zachariáše z Hradce (Zacharias of Hradec Square)

– Named after the 16C lord who rebuilt the castle, Telč's square owes its elongated funnel shape to the forking of two ancient routeways. It was first laid out on a spit of dry land among the surrounding marshlands, which medieval settlers transformed into the productive fishponds which still give the town its characteristic and highly attractive setting. The settlers' houses were built of timber, and were consumed by the fire of 1530, though many of the present buildings retain a Gothic core as well as their original cellars. Following the fire, the houses were rebuilt and linked by a continuous **arcade** running along the north and south sides of the square. Above the arcades, each house has a **Renaissance** or **Baroque façade** of great individuality, with murals and wonderful sgraffito work and **gables** of extraordinary variety; some are battlemented, some arched, other stepped, while **house no 61** on the north side is a delight of half pillars and swallow tails. But somehow the rules of good neighbourliness are never flouted and the result is an enchanting townscape of unusual harmony, further enhanced by the exclusion of through traffic. Standing out among the lesser houses on the south side is the Renaissance **Town Hall** of four bays.

A **fountain** and a **plague column** are sited where the square broadens towards its eastern end of the square; beyond is the **Kostel sv. Ducha** (Church of the Holy Ghost), its tall (nearly 50m) Romanesque **tower** a reminder of the town's 13C origins. At the western end of the square, a number of houses were demolished in the 17C to make way for the Baroque **Jesuit College** and its twin-towered church. Squeezed into the space between college and castle is **Sv. Jakuba** (St James' Church), the twin-aisled Gothic parish church.

★★ Zámek (Castle)

– *Guided tour.* The **castle** was one of the residences of the Lords of Hradec, members of the powerful Vítkov family whose principal seat was at Jindřichův Hradec in southern Bohemia. Its present appearance is largely due to the major rebuilding and refurnishing which took place in the second half of the 16C under the reign of **Zachariáš of Hradec** (1526-89), a scholar and able administrator. His travels in Italy had familiarised him with Renaissance ideas in design and architecture, and he employed Italian builders to convert his medieval castle into a splendid Renaissance residence. The core of the castle is the **central courtyard** with its arcades and loggias.

The tour takes visitors through some of the finest interiors in the Czech lands. They include: the **Armoury**, with richly ornamented stellar vaults; the **Treasury★**, with elaborate architectural *trompe l'oeil* sgraffito work; the **Theatre Hall★**, its entrance covered in paintings of mythological subjects; the **African Hall** with an array of safari

Fine facades line the square in Telč

trophies; the **Golden Hall★★** with a coffer ceiling with carving of great richness and virtuosity and a musicians gallery with a parapet painted with allegories of the senses, and the **Marble Hall** with a fine collection of arms and armour. Other rooms are furnished in comfortable 19C style.

The **kaple Všech svatých (All Saints Chapel★)** is richly decorated in gilt and stucco and houses a marble tomb with effigies of Zachariáš and his wife, Catherine of Wallenstein; it is surrounded by a wrought-iron grille of exceptional virtuosity.

To the east, the intimate castle **garden** is closed off from the town by arcaded walls and a squat tower, while to the west the **park** with its neo-Classical greenhouse is shaded by exotic trees.

★**Galerie Jana Zrzavého (Jan Zrzavý Gallery)** – Part of the castle, the gallery celebrates the work of the painter **Jan Zrzavý** (1890-1977). Influenced at first by Impressionism, Fauvism and the Cubism of his fellow-countryman Bohumil Kubišta, Zrzavý then pursued his highly individual, sometimes rather melancholy vision, in which spiritual depths are revealed in subjects as varied as lonely women, the landscapes of Brittany, and the industrial waste tips of Ostrava. The gallery houses numerous examples of the work of this fascinating artist, undeservedly unfamiliar outside his native country.

TEREZÍN

THERESIENSTADT
65km north Population 2 900

In 1941 the Nazis emptied this grim fortress town of its inhabitants and turned it into a Jewish ghetto. Czech Jews formed the majority, joined later by Jews from Germany and other countries. Deceitful propaganda portrayed Theresienstadt (Terezín's German name) as a "harsh but civilised" community, but it reality it was a staging post on the way to the Final Solution, its population held here while awaiting transport to the death camps.

Terezín has never really recovered from this terrible time. Its barrack-like buildings have been scantily repopulated, but the building of a motorway bypass has diverted the Prague-Dresden traffic which brought with it at least some of the currents of normal life, and the army which once garrisoned the place has been reduced to a symbolic presence. Tourists come here to ponder on the town's terrible past and to visit the Muzeum Ghetta (Ghetto Museum). On the far bank of the River Ohře is the Malá pevnost (Small Fortress), used as a prison by the Austrians, then by the Gestapo.

THERESA'S TOWN

Frightened by the growing power of Prussia to the north, Emperor Josef II ordered the construction of a series of great strongholds which would block any attempt by his aggressive neighbour to advance on Prague and the Austrian heartland. He laid the foundation stone of the fortress town named after his mother Maria Theresa on 10 October 1780, but despite being built in line with the most up-to-date ideas of Baroque fortification, Theresienstadt never fulfilled its intended function. When in 1866 Prussia finally decided to smash for ever Austria's ability to interfere in German affairs, the fortress, like its equivalent at Hradec Králové, was simply ignored.

Terezín is laid out on a conventional chequerboard pattern, protected by brick walls and bastions and by the moats once fed by the diverted river. The dour streets are dominated by a monumental neo-Classical church.

THE GHETTO

The first Jews arrived here in November 1941. In mid-1942 Terezín's Czech citizens were expelled and the whole town became a prison, incarcerating not only Jews from the Czech lands but others whom the Nazis decided to spare such as war veterans from Germany and prominent Jews from other countries.

By the time of liberation in May 1945 some 140 000 people had passed through; many of them died here, though most were destined to perish in extermination camps like Auschwitz. Under Nazi supervision, the ghetto was self-governing and a semblance of normal life was upheld. Because of the presence of many members of

The fate of the Archduke's assassin

Though found guilty of the capital crimes of treason and murder, Gavrilo Princip escaped execution because he was under age, receiving instead the maximum sentence of 20 years imprisonment. Brought to Terezín, he perished nevertheless, in 1918 suffering a slow and painful death from tuberculosis.

the country's intellectual elite, culture thrived; there were lectures, seminars, music and drama, drawing and painting. The children's opera *Brundibar* was performed more than 50 times, though Viktor Ullmann's opera, *The Emperor of Atlantis*, was suppressed when the SS censors realised it was a satire on the Hitler state.

When a visit from the International Red Cross became imminent, the Nazis embarked on a campaign of "beautification", and forced the famous German director Kurt Gerron to make a mendacious film entitled *The Führer Gives the Jews a Town*. The Red Cross were fooled and gave Terezín a satisfactory report.

In the chaotic conditions at the end of the war typhus raged through the ghetto, claiming an additional swathe of victims.

What happened in Terezín, and why, are the themes of the excellent **Muzeum Ghetta** (Ghetto Museum ⊙).

THE FORTRESS

Malá pevnost (Small Fortress) – To the south of the avenue of trees linking town and fortress is the bleak expanse of the **National Cemetery**, the resting place of thousands of victims from both the Terezín ghetto and the prison set up by the Gestapo in the Small Fortress in 1940.

Under Austrian rule the **Small Fortress** held many of the Empire's political opponents, among them Gavrilo Princip, the Serbian student who fired the fatal shot at Archduke Franz Ferdinand in June 1914. Austrian rule was harsh, Nazi rule unspeakable, a fact amply documented in the cells and other installations of this sombre place. Most of those imprisoned here during the Occupation were Czechs involved in resistance activities, but they were accompanied by representatives of more than a dozen Allied nations. Some 2 500 died here, many more in the concentration camps and other places of execution to which they were sent.

Between 1945 and 1948 some 4 000 Germans, many of them arrested arbitrarily, were interned in the Small Fortress and around 600 of them failed to survive the experience.

TŘEBOŇ★★

136km south   Population 9 230

In an enchanting setting of forests and great fishponds and protected by a ring of walls and gates, this quiet and well-preserved little place is one of the most attractive of all the southern Bohemian towns. It was founded in the 12C, when settlers moved into the otherwise uninhabited border area between Bohemia and Austria and began to clear the dense woodlands and drain the extensive marshlands. Třeboň's overlords were the mighty Vítek family, rich and confident enough to defy the power of the Bohemian kings on more than one occasion. They are recalled in the town's German name, Wittingau. Their line ran out with the death of bachelor **Petr Vok of Rožmberk** (†1611), whose court here rivalled that of Emperor Rudolf II for its patronage of the arts, its learning, its interest in the esoteric and its often eccentric lifestyle.

Třeboň is famous for its beer, brewed here since 1379, though the fine buildings of the present brewery, on the site of the Rožmberk arsenal, date mostly from the 19C. The town also has a modest spa, where the curative properties of the local peat are exploited.

★**Masarykovo náměstí (Masaryk Square)** – The subtly curving, subtly sloping square is lined with attractive Renaissance and Baroque town houses, though none of them matches the sheer exuberance and originality of the **Bílý koníček** (Little White Horse Hotel), with its wonderful battlemented and turreted gable. Opposite is the **Town Hall** built in 1562, though much altered since. It has a fine tower, 31 m high, with gallery, clock and cupola. **House no 89** dating from the middle of the 16C bears the name of Josef Štěpánek Netolický, a famous fishpond builder. In the centre of the square stand a plague column of 1780 and a Renaissance fountain whose side panels are adorned with circular reliefs, while to the east is the early 16C **Hradecká brána** (Hradec Gate), one of the town's surviving gateways.

★**Zámek (Castle)** ⊙ – *Guided tour*. The original medieval stronghold was transformed into an expansive Renaissance residence by Vilém of Rožmberk from the middle of the 16C, using the services of the architect **Domenico Cometa**. After the Rožmberks had died out with Petr Vok, the **castle** passed through various hands. The Swedes sacked it in the Thirty Years War, carrying off Petr Vok's magnificent library to Stockholm. In 1658 Třeboň was acquired by the

---

A stay in southern Bohemia

The peace and quiet visitors hope for in southern Bohemia can probably best be found in Třeboň, and the town is well located for a tour of the area. The **Bílý koníček** (Little White Horse Hotel) is a characterful choice, but even more appealing and with more facilities is the Renaissance Hotel Zlatá Hvězda (Golden Star) *(Masarykovo náměstí 107, ☎ 0333 757200)* on the other side of the square.

The Bohemian rybník – the carp pond

Ever since the Middle Ages, human use of the countryside around Třeboň has enhanced, rather than diminished its ecological richness and diversity. Farmland coexists with near-natural landscapes ranging from woodlands to sand dunes and peat bogs and many kinds of wetland. In 1977 the exceptional quality of this landscape acquired international recognition when an area of about 700km² was declared a UNESCO Biosphere Reserve. About a tenth of this consists of water bodies; there are thousands of ponds, almost all of them artificial, created from late medieval times onwards to provide this landlocked part of Europe with a fishy supplement to its daily diet. Among the fish farmed are catfish and tench, but the king of the ponds is the **carp**, the Christmas dinner of every Czech. Look out for portrayals of this noble fish in and around Třeboň; he features in murals, on the facade of a bank, and as a statue.

The great age of pond building came in the 16C, when specialists like Josef Štepánek Netolický worked on a grand scale, not only making ponds but linking them with an artificial waterway, the 45km long **Zlatá stoka** (Golden Canal). Pond is perhaps too humble a word to describe great expanses of water like the **Svět (World pond)** just south of Třeboň, or the **Rožmberský rybník (Rožmberk fishpond)** to the north; more than 7km² in area, it is the largest in the country, its waters held back by a 2.5 km dam 12 m high.

Schwarzenbergs, who subsequently became the greatest landowners in the whole of southern Bohemia. Their ownership came to an end as a result of the land reforms of the early 1920s when many of the Czechoslovakia's great aristocratic estates were broken up.

Occupying much of the southwestern corner of the town, the castle is arranged around an outer, irregularly shaped and well-tree'd courtyard and an inner courtyard. The outer courtyard is graced by a fine fountain of 1712 by Pl Bayer, incorporating the Schwarzenberg emblem of a crow pecking out the eyes of a Turk. Cometa's treatment of the white walls gives the whole complex a homogenous appearance, relieved by the archway into the inner courtyard by a lively painted portico. Tours of the interior concentrate on the rooms refurnished in Renaissance style or alternatively on the apartments evoking the way of life of the last Schwarzenberg owners from the 19C onwards.

★**Sv. Jiljí (St Giles' Church)** – Dominating the northern part of the town, this fine **Gothic church** belonged to the Augustinian monastery which for centuries was one of the main centres of culture in Southern Bohemia, producing amongst much else the sublime paintings of the Master of the Třeboň Altarpiece, now in the National Gallery in Prague. Still here is a lovely mid-15C **Madonna sculpture**, and there are wall-paintings in the presbytery as well as in the cloister.

EXCURSION

★**Jindřichův Hradec** – *31km northeast*. Population 23 030. Like Třeboň, the busy district town of Jindřichův Hradec is built on the banks of one of southern Bohemia's great fishponds.

Town life revolves around the gently sloping square with its unusually ornate plague column, but most visitors come here to see the splendid **zámek (Castle★★ ⊙)**, once the chief residence of the powerful Lords of Hradec. A grim-looking round tower, a hall and a chapel are reminders of the castle's medieval origin, but the dominant character was given by the rebuilding undertaken at the peak of the family's fortunes in the 16C. The principal courtyard is closed by a superb three-storey arcade, there are fine Renaissance interiors, some with original decor as well as paintings by Brandl, Škréta and Salvator Rosa, and the complex is perfectly rounded off by the **Rondel★**, a wonderfully light-hearted pleasure pavilion set in a formal garden.

VELTRUSY★

25km north

The star-shaped summer residence built by the Chotek family in the early 18C and set in a great landscape park by the banks of the Vltava is one of the most fascinating country houses in Bohemia.

★**Exterior** – *600m on foot from camp site car park*. The four wings of the house converge on a rotunda pierced by a **sala terrena** and topped by a dome. The walls and vaults of the *sala terrena* are decorated with paintings of hunting scenes and vignettes from the *commedia dell'arte*. A monumental **stairway** on the northern side with sculpture by Franz Anton Kuen looks out on to a **formal garden** separated from

The Choteks' country house at Veltrusy

the park beyond by a wall with more fine sculpture by Kuen depicting the seasons. On the southern side the informal parkland sweeps right up to the house.
The array of **park structures★** includes Maria Theresa's Pavilion, an Egyptian Bridge, a Gothic Mill, and the Temple of the Friends of Nature, the last possibly inspired by a building in London's Kew Gardens.

★**Interior** ⊘ – *Guided tour*. The first floor rooms are richly furnished in Baroque and Rococo style, with much chinoiserie. The splendid Main Hall beneath the cupola has allegorical frescoes by the Viennese painter Josef Pichler.

The Choteks of Chotkov and Vojnín

The Choteks were one of the country's most distinguished old families. Veltrusy's builder was Wenzel Anton Chotek (1674-1754), who rescued the family's fortunes after they had suffered the consequences of being on the wrong side in the Thirty Years War and became Governor of Bohemia. His architect was probably Giovanni Alliprandi. His son Rudolf (1706-71) served Empress Maria Theresa in various capacities, and in 1754 was the initiator of the world's first trade fair, held at Veltrusy and entitled The *Grand Fair of Goods Manufactured in the Kingdom of Bohemia*. His nephew, Johann Rudolf (1748-1824) was responsible for re-landscaping the park in English style and giving it an extraordinary collection of garden buildings and follies. As Burgrave of Prague Castle, he was responsible for opening the Royal Hunting Park, the Stromovka, to the public. Karel Chotek (1783-1863) was an indefatigable "Improver", promoting roads and bridges, parks and green spaces, and beautifying Prague's riverside. His grand-daughter, Sophie, married Hapsburg Archduke Franz Ferdinand, and was assassinated with him at Sarajevo in 1914.

ZBRASLAV★★

12km south Population 7 700

Part of Prague even though separated from the main built-up area of the city by a sliver of countryside, Zbraslav still has something of the atmosphere of a country town. In the past it was a popular destination for weekend trippers, ferried in large numbers up the Vltava by paddlesteamer and disgorged at the town's quayside. The main visitor attraction nowadays is the former monastery which makes a fine setting for the National Gallery's superb collection of Asian art.

★★**Zámek Zbraslav (Zbraslav Castle)** ⊘ – **Sbírka asijského umění (Collection of Asian Art)** – In store for most of the Communist period, the national collection of Asian art is one of the finest in Europe. It has finally found a worthy home in the stately buildings

What A Shame About Love, Rosamunde, Roll Out The Barrel!

These are the Czech, German and English titles of one of the great hit songs of the 20C, which polka'd its way around the world in the 1930s and 40s. You can probably whistle or hum it, but you may not know that it was a Zbraslav man, Jaromir Vejvoda (1902-88), who wrote it. Born to a family whose members manned many of the local brass bands, Vejvoda turned out catchy polkas and waltzes all his life, though none matched the popularity of *Škoda lásky – What A Shame About Love*. The best place to take a break in Zbraslav is on the main square, in the family restaurant also called Škoda lásky, decorated with much Vejvoda memorabilia.

designed in the early 18C by J. B. Santini-Aichl and F. M. Kaňka for Zbraslav's Cistercian monastery, originally founded in 1292 and subsequently destroyed by the Hussites. For much of the postwar period the monastery and its grounds were the setting for an array of **19C and 20C sculpture**, most of which has been transferred to the National Gallery's Veletržní palác (Trade Fair Palace) in Prague, though a number of fine pieces still grace the well-treed park.

The emphasis of the beautifully displayed collections is on Japan and China, though there are also items from South and South East Asia, Tibet, and the Islamic world. Labelling is in Czech and English with much useful contextual information, drawing attention particularly to the links between Oriental and European art.

Ground floor – **Japanese art** occupies most of the ground floor rooms, with a wonderful array of lacquer-work, religious objects, sword-fittings, enamels, fans, screens, and ceramics. Because of their fragility, painting and graphic works are shown in rotation, but there are usually examples of the work of Hiroshige, Hokusai and other masters.

Japanese items make up the majority of the exhibits in the richly endowed Rainer Kreissl Collection displayed separately.

Upper floor – The outstanding collection of **Chinese art** demonstrates the existence of that country's extraordinary variety of artistic traditions from the earliest times onwards. Thus there are ritual vessels and funerary objects from the Neolithic period as well as Tang horses, Song and Qing porcelain, everyday items from the Ming period, and an array, regularly rotated, of paintings and calligraphy. The Buddhist statuary is particularly striking, with a wonderful 12C-13C polychrome Guanyin Goddess of Mercy and an array of Buddhas of similar date presented as if in a cave temple.

The gallery's holdings of art from the other regions of Asia is less comprehensive, but includes many fine pieces, among them 10C-13C Indian temple sculpture, Buddhist sculpture from Indo-China, Indonesia, and religious objects from Tibet. Prayer mats, metal and ceramic vessels and calligraphy are the mainstay of the Islamic collection.

ZVÍKOV★

94km south

Strung out along the rocky promontory above the confluence of the Vltava and Otava rivers, the royal stronghold of Zvíkov has been less subjected to rebuilding than many other Bohemian castles and has kept much of the atmosphere of its medieval heyday. The cliffs which once rose sheer from the riverside made the site of Zvíkov easily defensible, and people lived here in prehistoric times, among them the Bohemian Celts, who built an oppidum, one of their town-like settlements. Sometime in the early 13C work was begun on a royal fortress. Under the reign of King Otakar II (c 1230-78) the castle was extended, becoming a prestigious residence as well as an imposing stronghold, with a series of luxuriously appointed interiors arranged around an elegant arcaded courtyard. Some beautification was carried out in Renaissance times, but then the castle fell into decay until its **Schwarzenberg** owners began to restore it in the 19C. As at Orlík, the damming of the Vltava has turned the valley below the castle into a lake, but the deep forest still extends all around, and the approach to Zvíkov along the narrow neck of land remains an exciting experience.

★ **Hrad (Castle)** ⊘ – The **castle** is guarded by the Písek Gateway and a tall defensive tower with a conical cap. Beyond, the smooth Renaissance walls of the royal palace belie the inner courtyard which is a gem of Bohemian Gothic, two storeys of arcades, linking a series of splendid state rooms and the lofty castle chapel, with its sedilia, wall-paintings and a fine altarpiece of around 1500.

Admission times and charges

The visiting times marked in the text with the clock symbol ⊘ indicate the normal hours of opening and closing. These are listed here in the same order as they appear in the main text. Admission times are liable to alteration without prior notice and so the information given here should serve merely as a guide-line. Museums, churches etc may refuse admission during private functions, religious services, filming, or special occasions, and may stop issuing tickets up to an hour before closing time. Almost all visitor attractions are closed on Mondays and many close on national holidays.

Some establishments, particularly castles in country areas, may only be visited as part of a guided tour. As there may only be a restricted number of such tours on any given day it is advisable to check their times in advance. The commentary is sometimes only in Czech, but leaflets and other material are usually available in English and German and sometimes in other languages.

The admission prices indicated are the full rate for a single adult; reductions for children, students and young adults, senior citizens and groups should be requested on site and be supported by proof of ID. In some cases admission is free on certain days of the month. Czech citizens are sometimes admitted at a lower rate than foreign visitors, though this practice is less common than at one time.

Many churches and chapels are kept locked, and are only opened for services or concerts. While it is not acceptable to wander at will around a place of worship during a service, there may be a chance to sightsee briefly once the service is over and before the building is locked. For a longer visit, telephone or apply at the Farní úřad (parish office). There is normally no charge for admission, but a voluntary contribution to the upkeep of the building will be welcome.

Facilities for disabled visitors are improving, though older establishments may lack even a basic level of provision. (Disabled facilities are indicated by &.)

PRAGUE

Anežský klášter

Klášter sv. Anežky České – Open 10am to 6pm. Closed Monday. Kč70. Guided tour available. ☎ 2481 0628.

Belveder

Palace – & Open only for special exhibitions, then daily except Monday, 10am to 6pm. Charge varies. ☎ 2437 3368.

Bertramka

Visit – Open April to October, daily 9am to 6pm; November to March, daily 9am to 5pm. Kč50. Guided tour available. ☎ 54 38 93.

Betlémské náměstí

Betlémská kaple – & Open April to October, daily 9am to 6pm; November to March, daily 9am to 5pm. Kč30. Guided tour available – apply to Prague Information Service ☎ 2448 2562.

Náprstkovo muzeum – & Open daily except Monday, 9am to noon and 12.45pm to 5.30pm. Kč30. Free admission first Friday in the month. ☎ 2222 1416.

Břevnovský klášter

Abbey Churh and Monastic buildings – Guided tours of abbey church and monastic buildings: 10 April to 10 October, Saturday 9am, 10.30am, 1pm, 2.30pm, 4pm, Sunday 10.30am, 1pm, 2.30pm, 4pm; 11 October to 9 April, Saturday and Sunday 10am, 2pm. Kč50. ☎ 3335 1565.

Celetná ulice

Prašná brána – Open April to October, daily 10am to 6pm; closed November to March. Kč30. Guided tour available – apply to Prague Information Service ☎ 2448 2562.

Czech Cubist Art Exhibition (in the Black Madonna House) – & Open daily except Monday 10am to 6pm. Kč35. Guided tour available. ☎ 2421 1732.

Muzeum Antonína Dvořáka (Vila Amerika)

Open daily except Monday, 10am to 5pm. Kč30. Guided tour available. ☎ 29 82 14.

Muzeum hlavního města Prahy

History of Prague Exhibition – Open daily except Monday, 9am to 5pm. Kč30; first Thursday in the month, 9am to 8pm, admission free. Guided tour available. ☎ 2481 6772.

Hradčanské náměstí

Vojenské historické muzeum (Schwarzenberský palác) – May to October, daily except Monday, 10am to 6pm. Kč40. Free admission Tuesday. Guided tour available. ☎ 2020 2023.

Jiřský klášter

Bazilika – ♿ Open April to October, daily except Monday, 9am to 5pm; November to March, daily except Monday 9am to 4pm. Kč100 (Prague Castle collective ticket, see Pražský hrad below). Guided tour available. ☎ 2437 3368.

Klášter: Medieval, Renaissance and Baroque Art Collection of National Gallery – ♿ Open daily except Monday 10am to 6pm. Kč70. Guided tour available. ☎ 2051 5457.

Josefov

With the exception of the Staronová synagoga, all the synagogues in the Josefov as well as the Starý židovský hřbitov are administered by the State Jewish Museum and admission to them is by collective ticket (Kč250) obtainable from any of the Museum's ticket offices. Opening hours are identical: daily except Saturday, April to October, 9am to 6pm; November to March, 9am to 4.30pm. Guided tour available.

Klausova synagoga – ☎ 2310 302.

Maiselova synagoga – ♿ ☎ 2481 0099.

Pinkasova synagoga – ☎ 232 6660.

Španielská synagoga – ♿ Kč40 (or by collective ticket). ☎ 2481 9464.

Starý židovský hřbitov – No telephone.

Staronová synagoga – Open daily except Saturday, April to October, 9am to 6pm (5pm Friday); November to March 9am to 4.30pm (2pm Friday). Kč200. No telephone.

Karlova

Dům pánů z Kunštátu a Poděbrad – Open daily May to September, 10am to 6pm. Kč20. Guided tour available.

Sv. Klimenta – Open on application. ☎ 2222 0364.

Vlašská kaple – Open on application to Italian Embassy. ☎ 5732 0011.

Karlovo náměstí

Novoměstská radnice – Tower open daily except Monday, May to September 10am to 6pm; halls open during exhibitions, daily except Monday 10am to 6pm. Kč20. ☎ 2491 2810.

Sv. Ignáce – Open daily 6am to noon and 3.30pm to 6.30pm. ☎ 2492 1254.

Sv. Jana na Skalce – Open on application. ☎ 2491 5371.

Kostel Sv.Cyrila a Metoděje: Národní památník obětí heydrichiády – ♿ Open daily except Monday May to September 10am to 5pm; October to April 10am to 4pm. Kč30. Guided tour available. ☎ 29 55 95.

Karlův most

Staroměstská mostecká věž – Open daily August to September, 10am to 10pm; March, October, 10am to 6pm; November to February, 10am to 5pm. Kč30. Guided tours available – apply to Prague Information Service ☎ 2448 2562.

Malostranské mostecké věže – Open daily April to October, 10am to 6pm. Kč30. Guided tours available – apply to Prague Information Service ☎ 2448 2562.

Klementinum

Sv. Salvatora – Open on application ☎ 2222 0295.

Křižovnické náměstí

Sv. Františka – Open daily 7am to 8am or on application. ☎ 2110 8200.

Galerie Křižovnícků – Open daily except Monday and Friday, May to October, 10am to 6pm; February to May and November to December, 10am to 5pm. Kč40. Guided tour available. ☎ 2110 8226.

Letecké muzeum

♿ Open daily except Monday, June to October, 10am to 6pm. Kč40. Admission free Tuesday. Guided tour available. ☎ 2020 7511.

Letohrádek Hvězda

Museum – Closed for reconstruction.

Loreta

Interior – Open daily except Monday, 9am to 12.15pm and 1pm to 4.30pm. Kč80. Guided tour available. ☎ 2051 6740.

Malá Strana

Sv. Tomáše – ♿ Open daily 11am to 1pm and 2.30pm to 5pm. ☎ 53 02 18.

Sv. Josefa – Open daily 10am to 5pm. ☎ 5731 5242.

Vojanovy sady – Open daily in summer, 8am to 7pm; in winter 8am to 5pm. ☎ 53 67 91.

Zahrady pod Pràžským hradem (Ledeburská zahrada, Malá a Velká Pálffyovská zahrada) – ♿ Open daily July and August 10am to 8pm; April to June and September to October, 10am to 6pm. Kč40. Guided tour available. ☎ 5701 0401.

Panny Marie ustavičné pomoci u Kajetánky – Open on application. ☎ 53 02 18.

Lékárna Dittrich U zlatého lva – Open April to October, Tuesday to Friday noon to 6pm, Saturday and Sunday 10am to 6pm; November to March, Tuesday to Friday 11am to 5pm, Saturday and Sunday, 10am to 5pm. Kč20. ☎ 5731 0961.

Vrtbovská zahrada – Open daily April to October 10am to 6pm. Kč30. ☎ 5753 1480.

Panny Marie Vitězné – Open Monday to Friday, 8.30am to 6.30pm, Saturday and Sunday 8.30am to 8pm. ☎ 5731 6780.

Tyršovo muzeum tělesné výchovy a sportu – Open Thursday, Saturday and Sunday 9am to 5pm. Kč15. Guided tour available. ☎ 5700 7111

Panny Marie pod řetězem – Open on application. ☎ 53 72 22.

Muchovo muzeum

♿ Open daily 10am to 6pm. Kč120. Guided tour available. ☎ 2421 5408.

Na Příkopě

Sv. Kříže – Open Monday to Friday 8am to 6pm. ☎ 2421 0962.

Národní muzeum

♿ Open daily May to September, 10am to 6pm; October to April, 9am to 5pm. Closed first Tuesday in the month. Admission free first Monday in the month. Kč70. ☎ 2449 7111.

Národní Technické Muzeum

♿ Open daily except Monday, 9am to 5pm. Kč50. Guided tour available. ☎ 2039 9111.

Narodní třída

Panny Marie Sněžné – ♿ Open daily 9am to 6pm. ☎ 2422 5731.

Nový Svět

Sv. Jana Nepomuckého – Open on application. ☎ 2039 2111.

Obecní dům

Ceremonial rooms – Guided tour only. Kč150. Enquire at Obecní dům Information Centre, ground floor, open 10am to 6pm.

Olšanské hřbitovy

Open daily May to September, 8am to 7pm; March, April and October, 8am to 6pm; November to February, 9am to 4pm. ☎ 6731 0652.

Nový židovský hřbitov – Open April to September, Monday to Thursday and Sunday, 9am to 4.30pm, Friday 9am to 1.30pm; October to March, Monday to Thursday and Sunday, 9am to 4.30pm, Friday 9am to 12.30pm. ☎ 73 30 22.

Petřín

Rozhledna – Open daily April to August, 10am to 7pm; September and October, 10am to 6pm; November to March, Saturday and Sunday, 10am to 5pm. Kč30. ☎ 53 17 86. Guided tour available – apply Prague Information Service ☎ 2448 2562.

Bludiště – ♿ Open daily April to August, 10am to 7pm; September and October, 10am to 6pm; November to March, Saturday and Sunday, 10am to 5pm. Kč30. ☎ 53 13 62. For guided tour apply Prague Information Service ☎ 2448 2562.

Sv. Vavřince – Monday to Friday in summer, 10am to 4pm; in winter by application. ☎ 3335 3547.

Štefánikova hvězdárna – Open April to August, Tuesday to Friday 2pm to 7pm and 9pm to 11pm, Saturday and Sunday 10am to noon, 2pm to 7pm and 9pm to 11pm; September, Tuesday to Friday 2pm to 6pm and 8pm to 10pm, Saturday and Sunday, 10am to noon, 2pm to 6pm and 8pm to 10pm; October, Tuesday to Friday 7pm to 9pm, Saturday and Sunday 10am to noon, 2pm to 6pm and 7pm to 9pm; November and December, Tuesday to Friday, 6pm to 8pm, Saturday and Sunday 10am to noon and 2pm to 8pm; January and February, Tuesday to Friday, 6pm to 8pm, Saturday and Sunday, 10am to noon and 2pm to 8pm; March, Tuesday to Friday 7pm to 8pm, Saturday and Sunday 10am to noon, 2pm to 6pm and 7pm to 9pm. Kč15. ☎ 5732 0540.

Muzeum Policie ČR

Muzeum Policie – ♿ Open daily except Monday, 10am to 5pm. Kč10. Guided tour available. ☎ 29 89 40.

Panny Marie a sv. Karla Velikého na Karlově – ♿ Open Sunday, 2pm to 5.15pm. ☎ 29 51 98.

Poštovní muzeum

Open daily except Monday, 9am to 11.30am and 2pm to 5pm. Kč25. Guided tour available. ☎ 231 2006.

Pražský hrad

Castle courtyards and interiors – ♿ Courtyards open daily April to October, 5am to midnight; November to March, 5am to 11pm. Interiors (Old Royal Palace, crypt of St Vitus' Cathedral, St George's Basilica, Mihulka Powder Tower) open daily, April to October, 9am to 5pm; November to March, 9am to 4pm. Kč120 (valid for 3 days). Guided tour available. Ceremonial interiors open twice yearly, normally in April and October. ☎ 2437 3368.

Obrazárna Pražského hradu – ♿ Open daily, 10am to 6pm. Kč100. ☎ 2437 3531.

Lobkovický palác (Narodní muzeum) – ♿ Open daily 10am to 6pm. Kč40. Guided tour available. ☎ 53 73 06.

Muzeum hraček (Nejvyšší purkrabství) – Open daily 9.30am to 5.30pm. Kč40. Guided tour available. ☎ 2437 2294.

Jižní zahrady – Open daily, April to September, 10am to 6pm. ☎ 2437 3368.

Staroměstské náměstí

Staroměstská radnice – Interior open daily, April to October, Monday 11am to 6pm, Tuesday to Sunday 9am to 6pm; November to March, Monday 11am to 5pm, Tuesday to Sunday 9am to 5pm. Kč30. Guided tour available. ☎ 2448 2629.

Sv. Mikuláše – Open Tuesday, Thursday and Friday 10am to noon; Wednesday 10am to noon and 2pm to 4pm; Sunday 9.30am to 10.30am and 11.30am to noon. ☎ 232 25 89.

Expozice Franze Kafky – Open Tuesday to Friday, 10am to 6pm, Saturday 10am to 5pm. Kč20. ☎ 232 16 75.

Matky Boží před Týnem – ♿ Open only for services. Under partial reconstruction. ☎ 231 81 86.

Stavovské divadlo

Theatre – Open for drama, opera and ballet performances. ☎ 2490 1448. Guided tour available, Kč30, apply Prague Information Service. ☎ 2311127 or 2481 6184.

Sv. Havla – Open on application. ☎ 2318186.

Šternberský palác

Národní galerie – Open daily except Monday 10am to 6pm. Kč70. Guided tour available. ☎ 2051 5457.

Strahovský klášter

Strahovská knihovna – Open daily 9am to noon and 1pm to 5pm. Kč40. Guided tour available. ☎ 2051 6671.

Strahovská obrazárna – Open daily except Monday 9am to noon and 12.30pm to 5pm. Kč35. Guided tour available. ☎ 2051 7278.

Sv. Mikuláše (Malá Strana)

Church – Open daily April to September, 9am to 5pm; October to March 9am to 4.30pm. Kč35. Guided tour available. ☎ 0602 22 35 80.

Bell tower – Open daily except Monday April to September, 10am to 6pm. Kč30. Guided tour available. ☎ 0602 22 35 80.

Sv. Víta

(See under Pražský hrad above).

Tower – Open daily, April to October, 9am to 5pm depending on weather conditions. Kč20. ☎ 2437 3368.

Troja

Trojský zámek – Open daily except Monday, April to October 10am to 6pm; November to March, Saturday and Sunday 10am to 5pm. Kč100. Admission free first Tuesday of month. ☎ 689 07 61. Guided tour available.

Zoo – ♿ Open daily except Monday; June to August 9am to 7pm; April, May, September and October 9am to 6pm; March 9am to 5pm; November to February 9am to 4pm. Kč50. Guided tour available. ☎ 688 1800.

Uměleckoprůmyslové muzeum

♿ Open daily except Monday 10am to 6pm. Kč50. Guided tour available. ☎ 5109 3111.

Ungelt

Dům U zlatého prstenu – Open daily except Monday 10am to 6pm. Kč60. Admission free first Tuesday in the month. ☎ 2482 8004.

Sv. Jakuba – ♿ Open daily 9.30am to 4pm (closed for lunch).☎ 23265 77.

Václavské náměstí

Františkánská zahrada – ♿ Open daily in summer 7am to 10pm; winter 8am to 7pm. ☎ 2109 7490.

Valdštejnský palác

Palace – Seat of the Senate of the Czech Republic. May be open on application. ☎ 5707 2713.

Valdštejnská zahrada – Closed for reconstruction.

Veletržní palác

Muzeum moderního a současného umění – ♿ Open daily except Monday 10am to 6pm, Thursday to 9pm. Kč120. Guided tour available. ☎ 2430 1024.

Vinohrady

Sv. Ludmily – Open on application. ☎ 2252 1558.

Chrám Nejsvětějšího jšího Srdce Páně – Normally open 5pm to 6pm or on application. ☎ 6275749.

Vyšehrad

Nové děkanství (New Deanery) – Exhibition – Open daily April to October 9.30am to 5.30pm; November to March 9.30am to 4.30pm. Kč20. Guided tour available. ☎ 296651.

Sv. Petra a Pavla – Open in summer Monday, Wednesday, Thursday, Saturday and Sunday 9am to noon and 1pm to 5pm; Friday 9am to noon or by request; in winter only on application. Guided tour available. Kč30. ☎ 295237.

Vyšehradský hřbitov – Open daily May to September 8am to 7pm; March, April and September 8am to 7pm; rest of year 9am to 4pm. ☎ 298574.

Výstaviště

Lapidárium – ♿ Open Tuesday to Friday noon to 6pm, Saturday and Sunday 10am to 6pm. Kč20. Guided tour available. ☎ 373198.

Maroldovo panorama – Open Tuesday to Friday 2pm to 5pm, Saturday and Sunday 10am to 5pm. Kč15. ☎ 20103301.

Žižkov

Armádní muzeum – Open May to October daily except Monday and Friday 10am to 6pm; November to April, Monday to Friday 9am to 5pm. Kč40. Admission free Tuesday. Guided tour available. ☎ 20204926.

Televizní vysílač – ♿ Open daily 10am to 11pm. Kč60. ☎ 6273497.

DAY EXCURSIONS

BRNO
🛈 Radnická 8. ☎ (05) 4221 1090

Moravská galerie – Decorative Arts – ☎ (05) 4221 6104, 4232 1250. Closed for reconstruction.

Moravská galerie – 20C Czech Art – ♿ Open Wednesday and Friday to Sunday, 10am to 6pm, Thursday 10am to 7pm. ☎ (05) 4221 5753.

Moravské zemské muzeum – ♿ Open daily except Monday 9am to 5pm. ☎ (05) 4232 1205.

Stará radnice – Open daily 9am to 5pm. ☎ (05) 4221 2665.

Vila Tugendhat – Open Wednesday to Sunday 10am to 6pm. ☎ (05) 4521 2118.

Punkevní jeskyně (Moravský kras) – Open April to September 8.20am to 3.50pm; October to March 8.20am to 2pm. ☎ (0506) 41 8602; http://www.cavemk.cz Reserve tickets in advance for guided tour in high season.

ČESKÉ BUDĚJOVICE
🛈 STET Náměstí Přemysla Otakara II 2.– ☎ (038) 680 24 40.

Černá věž – Open March to June daily except Monday 10am to 6pm; June and July daily 10am to 7pm; September to November daily except Monday 9am to 5pm. Kč10. ☎ (038) 635 25 08.

ČESKÝ KRUMLOV
🛈 Náměstí Svornosti 1. ☎ (0337) 71 11 83

Hrad – Open daily except Monday, April and October 9am to noon and 1pm to 3pm; May and September 9am to noon and 1pm to 4pm; June to August 9am to noon and 1pm to 5pm. Kč110. Guided tour only (except tower). ☎ (0337) 71 14 65. http://www.ckrumlov.cz/

Muzeum – Open daily May to September 10am to 12.30pm and 1pm to 5pm; March and April and October to December, Tuesday to Friday 9am to noon. Closed 24 December. Kč20-30. ☎ (0337) 71 16 74.

Mezinárodní centrum Egona Schieleho – Open daily 10am to 6pm. Guided tour available. Kč130. ☎ (0337) 71 12 24.

ČESKÝ ŠTERNBERK

Hrad – Open November to March only on application, daily except Friday, 9am to 4pm; April and October, Saturday and Sunday 9am to 4pm; May and September daily except Monday 9am to 5pm; June to August daily except Monday 9am to 6pm. Kč100. Guided tour only. ☎ (0303) 85 51 01.

CHEB

Chebské muzeum – Open daily except Monday 9am to noon and 1pm to 5pm Kč50. Guided tour available. ☎ (0166) 42 22 46.

Hrad – Open daily except Monday, April and October 9am to noon and 1pm to 4pm; May and September 9am to noon and 1pm to 5pm; June to August 9am to noon and 1pm to 6pm. Kč40. Guided tour available. ☎ (0166) 42 29 42.

FRANTIŠKOVY LÁZNĚ

Muzeum – Open February to December Tuesday to Friday 10am to noon and 1pm to 5pm, Saturday and Sunday 10am to 4pm. Guided tour available. Kč15 ☎ (0166) 54 23 44.

HLUBOKÁ NAD VLTAVOU

Alšova jihočeská galerie – Open October to March daily 9am to 11.30am and noon to 4pm; April to September daily 9am to 11.30am and noon to 6pm. Closed 24 and 31 December. Kč30. No charge last Sunday in the month. ☎ (038) 796 70 41, 796 71 20.

Lovecký zámek – Open April and October Monday to Friday 9am to 3pm, Saturday and Sunday 9am to 5pm; May and September daily 9am to 5.30pm; June to August 9am to 6.30pm; in winter by application only. Kč30. ☎ (038) 96 53 40 or 96 57 91.

Zámek – Open April to May and September to October daily except Monday, 9am to noon and 12.30pm to 4.30pm; June daily except Monday, 9am to noon and 12.30pm to 5pm; July and August daily, 9am to noon and 12.30pm to 5pm. Guided tour only. Kč130. Groups must reserve in advance. ☎ (038) 796 70 45.

HRADEC KRÁLOVÉ   🄱 Gočárova 1225, ☎ (049) 340 21, 321 33.

Galerie moderního umění – Open daily except Monday 9am to noon and 1pm to 6pm. Kč12. ☎ (049) 551 48 93.

Muzeum východních Čech – Closed for reconstruction. ☎ (049) 551 46 24/6.

CHLUM

Muzeum – Open April to October daily except Monday, 9am to noon and 1pm to 5pm. In winter by application. Kč10. ☎ (049) 595 10 58.

KARLOVY VARY   🄱 Vřídelní kolonáda. ☎ (017) 322 40 97, 322 93 12.

Sv. Petra a Pavla – Open daily 9am to 5pm.

Sv. Máří Magdaleny – Main part of the church only open only for Mass.

Hrad Loket – Open November to March daily except Monday, 9am to 4pm; April to September daily except Monday, 9am to midday and 1pm to 5pm. Guided tour available. Kč100. ☎ (0168) 68 41 05, 68 41 55.

Hrad KARLŠTEJN

Open November to March daily except Monday 9am to noon and 1pm to 4pm; April and October daily except Monday 9am to noon and 1pm to 5pm; May, June and September daily except Monday 9am to noon and 12.30 to 6pm; July and August daily except Monday 9am to noon and 12.30 to 7pm. Guided tour only. Kč200. ☎ (0311) 68 16 17, 68 16 95.

Zámek KONOPIŠTĚ

Open November to March daily except Monday 9am to noon and 1pm to 3pm; May to August 9am to noon and 1pm to 6pm; September 9am to noon and 1pm to 4pm. Guided tours only (choice of two). Kč110 and Kč240. ☎ (0301) 213 66, 242 71.

Hrad KŘIVOKLÁT

Oen November to March on application, Monday to Friday 9am to 3pm; November, December and March also Saturday and Sunday 9am to 3pm; April daily except Monday 9am to 4pm; May and June daily except Monday 9am to 5pm; July to September daily 9am to 5pm; October daily except Monday 9am to 3pm. Guided tours only (choice of two). Kč60 and Kč110.

KUTNÁ HORA   🄱 Palackého 377. ☎ (0327) 51 23 78, 51 55 56.

Chrám sv. Barbory – Open May to September daily except Monday 9am to 6pm; November to March daily except Monday 9am to noon and 2pm to 4pm; April and October daily except Monday 9am to noon and 2pm to 4pm. Guided tour available. Kč30. ☎ (0327) 51 21 15.

Hrádek – Open April and October daily except Monday 9am to 5pm; May, June and September daily except Monday 9am to 6pm; July and August daily except Monday 10am to 6pm. Guided tour. Kč90. ☎ (0327) 51 21 59.

Vlašský dvůr – Open daily November to February 10am to 4pm; March and October 10am to 5pm; April to September 9am to 6pm. Closed 24 December. Guided tour. Kč50. ☎ (0327) 51 28 73.

Voršilský klášter – Open May to October daily except Monday 9am to 5pm; in winter by appointment only. Guided tour. Kč30. ☎ (0327) 51 29 80.

Chrám Nanebevzetí Panny Marie – Closed for reconstruction

Kostnice – Open daily April to September 8am to noon and 1pm to 6pm; October and March 8am to noon and 1pm to 5pm; November to February 9am to noon and 1pm to 4pm. Guided tour available. Kč30. ☎ (0327) 76 11 43.

LEDNICKO-VALTICKÝ AREÁL

Zámek Lednice – Open April and October Saturday and Sunday 9am to noon and 1pm to 3.15pm; May to September daily except Monday 9am to noon and 1pm to 5.15pm. Guided tour only (except Národní zemědělské muzeum). Kč105. ☎ (0627) 34 01 28.

Zámek Valtice – Open April, September and October daily except Monday, 9am to noon and 1pm to 5pm; May to August daily except Monday 8am to noon and 1pm to 5pm. Guided tour only. Kč70. ☎ (0627) 35 24 23.

LIDICE

Muzeum – November to March daily 9am to 3pm; April to October daily 8am to 5pm. Closed 24 December to 1 January. Guided tour available. Kč60. ☎ (0312) 25 30 63. 25 30 88.

MARIÁNSKÉ LÁZNĚ   **B** Hlavní 47. ☎ (0165) 58 92. 62 24 74

Goethův dům – Open daily except Monday 9am to 4pm. ☎ 27 40.

Klášter premonstrátů/Teplá – Open daily November to December and February to April, 9am to 11am and noon to 3pm; May to October 9am to 11am and noon to 4.30pm. Closed 24 December. Guided tour. Kč90. ☎ (0169) 39 22 64, 39 26 34.

MĚLNÍK

Zámek – Open daily March to December 10am to 6pm. Guided tour only. Kč60. ☎ (0206) 62 21 21, 62 21 27. http://www.lobkovicz-melnik.cz

Sv. Petra a Pavla – Open March, November and December daily except Monday 9.30am to noon and 12.30pm to 3.330pm; April to October daily except Monday 9.30am to noon and 12.30pm to 5.30pm. Guided tour available. Kč30. ☎ (0206) 62 23 37.

NELAHOZEVES

Zámek – Open daily except Monday 9am to noon and 1pm to 6pm. Guided tour only. Kč350. ☎ (0205) 78 53 31.

Památník Antonína Dvořáka – Open daily except Monday 9am to noon and 2pm to 5pm; Friday 9am to noon. Kč30. ☎ (0205) 78 50 99.

Zámek Orlík – Open daily except Monday April and October 9am to 4pm; May and September 9am to 5pm; June to August 9am to 6pm. Guided tour only. Kč120. ☎ (0362) 84 11 01.

PLZEŇ   **B** Náměstí Republiky 41. ☎ (019) 70 32 750

Chrám sv. Bartoloměje (tower) – Open daily 10am to 6pm (closed in bad weather).

Františkánský klášter – Closed for reconstruction.

Pivovarské muzeum – Open daily 10am to 6pm. Guided tour available. Kč60. ☎ (019) 72 35 574, 722 49 55.

Plzeňský Prazdroj – Open by appointment, Monday to Friday 8am to 4pm, Saturday and Sunday 8am to 1pm. Guided tour only Kč20 – 100 (5 different tours). ☎ (019) 706 11 11, http://www.Pilsner-Urquell.com

Velká synagoga – Open May to October, Monday to Friday and Sunday 11am to 5pm; rest of year Sunday or by prior appointment. Kč40. ☎ (019) 72 35 7 49.

Západočeské muzeum – Open daily except Monday 9am to 5pm. Guided tour available. Kč20. ☎ (019) 22 40 28, 72 36 0 54.

Klášter Kladruby – Open March and November, Saturday and Sunday 10am to 2pm; April, May and October, Saturday and Sunday 10am to noon and 1pm to 3pm; June and September, Saturday and Sunday 10am to noon and 1pm to 4pm; July and August daily except Monday 9am to noon and 1pm to 5pm; rest of year by appointment only. Guided tour only Kč80. ☎ (0183) 63 17 73.

SLAVKOV U BRNA

Mohyla míru – Museum open November to April daily except Monday 9am to 12.30pm and 1pm to 3.30pm; May and September daily except Monday 8.30am to 12.30pm and 1pm to 5pm; June to August daily 8.30am to 12.30pm and 1pm to 7pm. Guided tour available. Kč30. ☎ (05) 4424 4724. http://muzeum-brno-venkov.cz

Zámek (historické muzeum) – Open April to May and September to November daily except Monday, 9am to noon and 1pm to 4pm; June to August daily 9am to 5pm; rest of year by appointment. Guided tour available. Kč60. ☎ (05) 4422 0988 or 4422 1685. http://www.austerlitz.cz

TÁBOR
🆔 Žižkovo náměstí 2. ☎ (0361) 48 62 30

Husitské muzeum – Open November to March Monday to Friday 8.30am to 5pm; April to October daily 8.30am to 5pm. Guided tour available. Kč40. ☎ (0361) 25 42 86.

Bechyňská brána – Open May to October, Tuesday to Sunday 9.30am to 5pm.

TELČ

Zámek – Open daily except Monday, April and October 9am to noon and 1pm to 4pm; May to September 9am to noon and 1pm to 5pm. Guided tour only. Kč100. ☎ (066) 96 29 43.

TEREZÍN
🆔 Památník Terezín – ☎ (0416) 78 22 25. 78 24 42
http://www.siscr.cz/terezin/

Malá pevnost – Open May to September daily 8am to 6pm; October to April daily 8am to 4.30pm. Closed 24-26 December and 1 January. Guided tour available. Kč100. ☎ (0416) 782 225, 782 442, 782 131.

Muzeum Ghetta – Open May to September daily 9am to 6pm; October to April daily 9am to 5.30pm. Closed 24-26 December and 1 January. Guided tour available. Kč100. ☎ (0416) 782 577.

TŘEBOŇ
🆔 Masarykovo náměstí 103/II. ☎ (0333) 72 11 69

Zámek – Open daily except Monday, April, May, September and October 9am to 4pm; June to August daily except Monday 9am to 5pm; rest of year by appointment. Guided tour only. Kč70 (choice of two). ☎ (038) 635 69 21.

Jindřichův Hradec: zámek – Open April to October daily except Monday 9am to noon and 1pm to 3.15pm; May to September daily except Monday 9am to noon and 1pm to 4.15pm; rest of year by appointment. Guided tour only (choice of three). Kč120. ☎ (0331) 32 12 79.

VELTRUSY

Zámek – Open January and February by appointment; March, April and October to December, Saturday and Sunday 9am to 4pm; May to September daily except Monday 8am to 5pm. Guided tour only. Kč120. ☎ (0205) 78 11 44, 78 11 46.

ZBRASLAV

Zámek: Sbírka asijského umění – Open daily except Monday 10am to 6pm. Guided tour available. Kč70. ☎ (02) 5792 1638/9.

ZVÍKOV

Hrad – Open April and October Saturday and Sunday 9.30am to 4.30pm; May and September daily except Monday 9.30am to 4pm; June to August daily except Monday 9am to 5pm. Guided tour available. Kč70. ☎ (0362) 89 96 76.

Glossary

With its array of accents and long chains of consonants, Czech looks a formidable language, and learning it does indeed present special difficulties for native English-speakers, unless they happen to know any one of the family of Slavonic languages of which Czech is a member. Like them, it has a complex grammar, with nouns and adjectives declining in no fewer than seven cases and verbs with perfective and imperfective aspects. On the plus side, it uses the Latin rather the Cyrillic alphabet, is spoken almost exactly as it is written, and always has the stress on the first syllable of the word. Any attempt to use Czech will endear you to local people, and as in any country it's worth while memorising a few stock phrases and learning to recognise key signs.

In places frequented by foreign visitors English and German are likely to be spoken. For many years German was one of the country's languages, and many members of the older generation are fluent in it. Younger people seem more attracted to English, the global language of business and popular culture.

Pronunciation

Vowels		Consonants	
a	as in gap	c	as in its
á	as in southern English bath	č	as in church
e	as in yes	ch	as in Scottish loch
é	as in air	j	as in yes
i, y	as in city	ň	as in onion
í, ý	as in meet	r	like a trilled Scottish r
o	as in top	š	as in shine
ó	as in door	ž	as in pleasure
u	as in book	ř	the unique Czech consonant, a combination of trilled r and a z sound as in pleasure.
ů, ú	as in school		

Basic vocabulary

Hello!	Ahoj (informal greeting, can also mean Goodbye!)	Help!	Pomoc !
Good morning	Dobrý den	What?	Co ?
Good evening	Dobrý večer	Where?	Kde ?
Good night	Dobrou noc	Where is/are?	Kde je/jsou ?
Goodbye	Na shledanou	When?	Kdy ?
Yes	Ano	How?	Jak ?
No	Ne	How much?	Kolik ?
Please	Prosím	How much does it cost?	Kolik stojí ?
Thank you	Děkuji	I don't speak Czech	Nemluvím česky
Sorry	Pardon	Do you speak English/German?	Mluvíte anglicky/ německy ?

Numerals

1	jeden (jedna f. jedno n)	16	šestnáct
2	dva (dvě f, n)	17	sedmnáct
3	tři	18	osmnáct
4	čtyři	19	devatenáct
5	pět	20	dvacet
6	šest	30	třicet

7	sedm	40	čtyřicet
8	osm	50	padesát
9	devět	60	šedesát
10	deset	70	sedmdesát
11	jedenáct	80	osmdesát
12	dvanáct	90	devadesát
13	třináct	100	sto
14	čtrnáct	1000	tisíc
15	patnáct		

Days of the week

Monday	pondělí
Tuesday	úterý
Wednesday	středa
Thursday	čtvrtek
Friday	pátek
Saturday	sobota
Sunday	neděle

Months of the year

January	leden	July	červenec
February	únor	August	srpen
March	březen	September	září
April	duben	October	říjen
May	květen	November	listopad
June	červen	December	prosinec

In town

Město	Town	Kaple	Chapel
Dům	House, building	Klášter	Monastery
Vila	Villa, detached house	Synagoga	Synagogue
Dvůr	Courtyard	Hrad	Castle (fortified)
Věž	Tower	Zámek	Castle (country house/chateau)
Divadlo	Theatre	Brána	Gate
Ulice	Street	Palác	Palace
Ulička	Alley, lane	Radnice	Town hall
Třída	Avenue	Pošta	Post office
Náměstí	Square	Nemocnice	Hospital
Schody	Steps	Muzeum	Museum
Most	Bridge	Galerie	Gallery
Ostrov	Island	Výstava	Exhibition
Nábřeží	Embankment	Zahrada, sady	Garden(s)
Trh/tržiště	Market, market place	Koupaliště	Swimming pool
Kostel	Church	Hřbitov	Cemetery
Katedrála/chrám	Cathedral, large church		

Ukončete výstup a nástup!

The recorded voice on the Prague Metro first warns you to stop entering or leaving the train: Ukončíte prosím výstup a nástup! as the doors are about to close: Dveře se zavirají and then goes on to announce the name of the next station: Příští zastávka - Malostranská!

On the road and in the country

Silnice	Road	**Potok**	Stream
Cesta	Path, track	**Nádrž, přehrada**	Dam, reservoir
Dálnice	Motorway	**Les**	Wood, forest
Parkoviště	Car park	**Kopec**	Hill
Benzina	Petrol	**Hora**	Mountain
Objížd'ka	Diversion	**Pomník, památník**	Monument
Jezero	Lake	**Bojiště**	Battlefield
Rybník	Lake, fishpond	**Pramen**	Spring
Řeka	River		

Signs and shops

Tam	Push	**Směnárna**	Bureau de change
Sem	Pull	**Pokladna**	Booking office, cash desk
Pozor	Danger	**Šatna**	cloakroom
Vstup/vchod	Entrance	**Občerstvení**	Refreshments
Výstup/východ	Exit	**Knihkupectví**	Bookshop
Otevřeno	Open	**Lahůdky**	Delicatessen
Zavřeno	Closed	**Cukrárna**	Patisserie
Zakázáno	Forbidden	**Lékárna**	Pharmacy
Záchod	Toilets	**Potraviny**	Grocery, small supermarket
Muži, páni	Men, gentlemen	**Nádraží**	Railway station
Ženy, dámy	Women, ladies	**Autobusové nádraží**	Bus station
Col	Customs	**Zastávka**	Bus, tram stop

Restaurant terms can be found in Useful Addresses *p. 29*

Index

Wenceslas Square . . . . .Sights, monuments and places more often mentioned
(Václavské náměstí)in English and sometime.
followed by their written form in Czech.

Wallenstein, Albrecht von . . . . . .People, historical events or terms subjected to ar
explanatory note.

The names of the sites described under excursions from Prague are given in Czech
only and, as whole index, classified according to Czech alphabetical order.

A

Aachen, Hans von 77
Adalbert, Bishop
of Prague 54
Adam Pharmacy
(Adamova Lékárna) 210
Adria Palace 163
Agnes of Bohemia,
Saint 54, 104
Ambassador (hotel) 211
Amerika (villa) 112
Archbishop's Palace 114
Arcimboldo, Giuseppe 77
Arco (café) 170
Army Museum (Armádní
muzeum) 225
Astronomical Clock 188
Austerlitz 260
Aviation Museum 139

B

Břevnov Monastery 109
Ball Game Hall 137
Bank of the Legions
(Legio banka) 170
Bank of Moravia
(Moravská banka) 212
Bartolomíjská 108
Bat'a 210
Battle of the White
Mountain 57, 142
Beethoven, Ludwig van
91
Belvedere 106
Bendl, Johann Georg 79
Beneš, Edvard 60
Bernhardt, Sarah 157
Bertramka 107
Bethlehem Square
(Betlémské náměstí) 107
Bezalel, Rabbi Judah
Loew ben 86
Bíla hora 141
Bílek (villa) 109
Black Madonna House
111
Black Rose House 159
Boii 53
Brahe, Tycho 86, 167
Brandl, Peter 79

Braun, Mathias Bernard
79
Bretfeld Palace 153
Brick Gate (Cíhelná
brána) 222
Bridge of the Legions
(Most Legií) 219
Brixi, František Xaver 91
Brno 231
Brod, Max 87
Brokoff, Ferdinand
Maximilian 79
Brožík, Václav 81
Buquoy Palace 157

C

Capuchin Monastery 145
Carlsbad 244
Carolinum 193
Castle Steps (Zámecké
schody) 152
Celetná ulice 111
Charles Bridge 132
Charles IV, Emperor 55,
175
Children's Island
(Dětsky ostrov) 219
Church see proper noun
City Library 137
Clam-Gallas Palace 128
Colloredo-Mansfeld
Palace 129
Comenius 87
Commercial Bank
(Komerční banka) 159
Cyril, Saint 53
Czech National Library
136
Czechoslovak Trading
Bank (Československá
obchodní banka) 159
Czernin Palace 116

Č

Čapek, Josef and Karel
88
Čech Bridge
(Čechùv most) 220
Čech 53

Černá Pole 233
Černínská 167
Černohorsky, Bohuslav
Matěj 91
České Budějovice 234
Česky Šternberk 238
Česky Krumlov 236

D

Decorative Arts Museum
(Uměleckoprùmyslové
Muzeum) 206
Descartes, René 142
Devětsil 84
Dientzenhofer, Christoph
78
Dientzenhofer, Kilian
Ignaz 78
Display on Franz Kafka
190
Dubček, Alexander 62
Dušek, František Xaver
91
Dvořák, Antonin 92,
112, 257
Dvořak Museum 112

E

Emauzy (monastery) 130
Estates Theatre 192
Exhibition Park
(Vystaviště) 222

F

Faust house 130
Ferdinand I of Hapsburg,
Emperor 56
Forman, Miloč 94
Franciscans' Garden 211
Frantíškovy Lázně 239
Franz Ferdinand,
Archduke of Hapsburg
247
Fundamental Articles 59
Funicular 172
Fürstenberg Garden 152

G

Gallery of the Knights
of the Cross 139
Gardens below the Castle
149
*George of Poděbrady,
King of Bohemia* 128
Giovanni, Francesco 206
*Goethe, Johann Wolfgang
von* 239, 255
Golden Lane
(Zlatá Ulička) 181
Golden Ring House 208
Golden Stag (house) 152
Golem 126
Goltz-Kinsky Palace 189
Grand Hotel Evropa 212
Grand Prior's Palace 156
Granovsky Palace 207
Group 42 85, 216

H

Hanava Pavilion 141
Havel, Václav 63, 88
Heydrich, Reinhard 131
High Synagogue 123
Hlávka Bridge (Hlávkùv
most) 220
Hluboká nad Vltavou 240
Holy Cross (chapel of the)
109
Holy Rood (church of the)
159
Home for Distressed
Gentlewomen 181
House of the Lords of
Kuntát and Poděbrady
128
Hradčanské náměstí 114
Hradčany 116
Hradec Králové 241
Husova 128
Huss, John 56, 108
Huss Memorial 187
Hybernská 170

CH

Cheb 242
Chotek family 268
Chotek Gardens 141

I - J

Infant Jesus of Prague
155
Investment Bank
(Živnostenká banka) 158
Italian Chapel 129
Italian Quarter 154
Jalta (hotel) 212
Janáček, Leoš 92
Jewish Town Hall 123
Jindřišská 211
Jindřichùv Hradec 267
Jirásek Bridge
(Jiráskùv most) 219
Jiřské náměstí 181
*John of Luxembourg,
King of Bohemia* 54
*John of Nepomuk,
Saint* 58, 134

Josefov 121
Jubilee Synagogue 127
Jungmann, Josef 87,
163
Jungmannovo náměstí
163

K

Kafka, Franz 87, 171,
190
Kaiserstein Palace 148
Kampa 155
Karlova 127
Karlovo Náměstí 130
Karlovy Vary 244
Karlštejn Castle 246
Karmelitská 155
Kaunitz Palace 148
Kepler, Johannes 86,
129, 167
Kinsky Palace 170
Kinsky (villa) 172
Kish, Egon Erwin 87
Kladruby Monastery 260
Klárov 149
Klausen Synagogue 123
Klementinum 136
Kolowrat Garden 152
Konopiště Castle 247
Koruna Palace 210
Kovařovič (villa) 222
Kraus, Karl 87
Křenovice 261
Křiřík Fountain 223
Křivoklát Castle 249
Křížovnické náměstí 138
Kubišta, Bohumil 83,
215
Kupecky, Jan 79
Kupka, František 83
Kutná Hora 249

L

Lapidarium 222
Ledebour Garden 152
Lednice-Valtice Complex
251
Leopold Gate
(Leopoldova brána) 221
Letná 140
Lidice 253
Liechtenstein family 251
Lobkowicz family 256,
257
Lobkowicz Palace 154,
182
Loket 246
Loretánská 117
Loretánské náměstí 116
Loretto Shrine 143
Lucerna Palace 212
Lusatian Seminary 148

M

Magistrála 166
Main Station (Hlavní
nádraží) 166
Maisel Synagogue 124
Malá Strana 146
Malá Strana Bridge
Towers 135

Malé náměstí 127
Malostranské náměstí
147
Maltézské náměstí 156
Mánes Bridge (Mánesùv
most) 220
Marchetti, Francesco 206
Mariánské Lázně 254
Mariánské náměstí 137
Marienbad 254
Marold Panorama 224
Martinic Palace 115, 117
Masaryk, Jan 116
*Masaryk, Thomáš
Garrigue* 60, 88, 176
Masaryk Station
(Masarykovo nadráží 170
Masaryk Embankment
(Masarykovo nábřeží
219
Master Theodoric 75
Mathey, Jean-Baptiste
78
Matthew of Arras 75,
201
Matthias, Emperor 57
Melantrichová 193
Mělník 256
Meran (hotel) 212
Methodius, Saint 53
Michna Palace 155
Mirror Maze (Bludiště)
172
Mocker, Josef 201
Moravian Karst 234
Most Sacred Heart of
Our Lord
(church of the) 218
Morzin Palace 153
Mostecká 148
*Mozart, Wolfgang
Amadeus* 91
Mozarteum 163
Mucha, Alfons 83, 157
Mucha Museum 157
Munich Agreement 60
Municipal House
(Obecní Dùm) 168
Museum of Modern
and Contemporary Art
(Muzeum moderního
a současného umění)
215
Museum of Torture 129
Myslbek, Josef Václav 81
Myslbek 159

N

Na Kampě 157
Na Poříčí 170
Na Příkopě 158
Náměstí Jana Palacha
184
Náměstí Jiřího z
Poděbrad 217
Náměstí mirù 217
Náměstí Republiky 170
Nàprstek Museum
of Ethnography
(Náprstkovo muzeum)
108
Narodní Galerie
(St George's Convent)
118

Národní Galerie
(Sternberg Palace) 193
Národní Třída (National
Avenue) 163
National Gallery of Czech
19C Painting 105
National History
Exhibition of the
National Museum 182
National Memorial 225
National Museum
(Národní Muzéum) 160
National Technical
Museum (Národní
Tecnickě Muzéum) 161
National Theatre
(Národní Divadlo) 159
Nelahozeves 256
Neruda, Jan 153
Nerudova 153
New Deanery 221
New Town 166
Nostiz Palace 156
Nové Město 166
Novotny Jetty
(Novotného lávka) 220
Novy Svět 167

O

Old Deanery 179
Old Jewish Cemetery
125
Old-New Synagogue 123
Old Royal Palace 179
Old Town 185
Old Town Bridge Tower
134
Olšany Cemeteries 170
Orlík 258
Otakar II, King of
Bohemia 54
Our Lady and
Charlemagne
(church of) 173
Our Lady beneath the
Chain (church of) 156
Our Lady of Perpetual
Succor (church of) 153
Our Lady of the Snows
(church of) 163
Our Lady of Tyn
(church of)
Our Lady Victorious
(church of) 155

P

Pacassi, Nicola 176
Palace of Industry
(Prùmyslovy palác) 223
Palacky, František 59,
87
Palacky Bridge
(Palackého most) 219
Pálffy Garden 152
Parler, Peter 75, 201
Pařížská třída 122
Pešánek, Zdeněk 85
Peterka Building
(Peterkův dúm) 210
Petřín 171
Pilsen 258
Pinkas Synagogue 125

Planetarium 224
Plzeň 258
Poděbrady, George of,
King of Bohemia 56
Pohořelec 116
Police Museum of the
Czech Republic
(Muzeum Policie ČR)
173
Porges z Portheimu
Palace 164
Postal Museum (Poštovní
Muzeum) 173
Powder Tower 111
Prace Heights 262
Pracky Kopec 262
Prague Castle 174
Prague Castle Galler
178
Prague City Museum
(Muzeum Hlavníha
Město Prahy) 113
Prague Congress Centre
(Kongresové centrum
Praha) 221
Prague Defenestration
56
Prague Defenestration
(Second) 180
Prague Spring 62
Prague Uprising 61
Princess Libuše 53
Prokop, Saint 54
Průhonice 260
Punkva Caves
(Punkevní jeskyně 234

Q - R

Rieger Park (Riegrovy
sady) 217
Rudolph II, Emperor 57,
175
Rondocubism 84
Royal Gardens 137
Royal Riding School 183
Rozhledna 172
Rudolfinum 183

S

Sadowa (battle of) 242
St Agnes of Bohemia
(convent) (Anežky
Kláster) 104
St Bartholomew (church)
109
St Clement (church)
New Town 173
St Clement (church)
Old Town 129
St Cyril and St Metho-
dius (orthodox
cathedral) 131
St Francis (church) 138
St George (convent)
(Jiřsky Kláster) 117
St Giles (church) 128
St Havel (church) 193
St Ignatius (church) 130
St James (church) 208
St John at the
Wash-house (church)
155
St John Nepomuk
(church) 167

St John on the Rock
(church) 130
St Joseph (church) 148
St Lauwrence (church)
172
St Ludmila (church) 217
St Martin(rotunda) 221
St Michael (church) 172
St Nicholas (church)
Old Town 189
St Nicholas (church)
Malá Strana 198
St Peter and St Paul
(church) 222
St Saviour (church) 137
St Thomas (church) 148
St Ursula (church) 164
St Vitus (cathedral) 200
Salm Palace 114
Samo 53
Savery, Roelant 77
Schönborn Palace 154
School of Prague 76
Schwarzenberg family
236, 240, 258
Schwarzenberg Palace
114
Sedlec 251
Sepolkras 90
Shooters' Island
(Střelecky ostrov) 219
Síma, Josef 85
Slavonic Island
(Slovansky ostrov) 219
Slavia (café) 165
Slavín 222
Slavkov u Brna 260
Smetana, Bedřich 91
Smetana Embankment
(Smetanovo nábřeži 220
Smetana Museum
(Muzeum Bedřicha
Smetany) 184
Sněmovní 152
Sokolnice 262
South Gardens 182
Spálená Street 131
Spanish Synagogue 127
Spranger, Bartholomaeus
77
Star Castle 141
Staré Město 185
Staroměstské náměstí
186
Sternberg family 238
Sternberg, Count Kaspar
Maria von 148
Sternberg Palace 148,
193
Stifter, Adalbert 238
Strahov Abbey 195
Stromovka 224
Sweets-Sporck Palace
170
Sylva-Taroucca Palace
159

Š

Šaloun, Ladislav Jan 83
Škréta, Karel 79, 120
Štavnice Island
(Ostrov Štavnice) 220
Štefánik Observatory 172
Šverma Bridge
(Švermův most) 220

ábor Gate (Táborská
  brána) 221
ábor 263
anêcní dûm 131
elč 264
elevision Tower
  (Televizní vysilač) 225
eplá Abbey 256
erezín 265
heresienstadt 265
hirty Years War 57
hree Ostriches House
  148
hun Palace 152
hun-Hohenstein Palace
  153
hunovskà Street 152
omášek, František,
  Archbishop of Prague
  200
omášek, Vacláv Jan 91
own Hall of the New
  Town 130
own Hall of the Old
  Town 187
oy Museum (Muzeum
  hraček) 182
rade Fair Palace
  (Veletržní Palác) 214
rnka, Jiři 93
roja Palace 205

Třeboň 266
Turba Palace 156
Tuscan Palace 115
Tyn Court 207
Tyršovo muzeum 155

U

U Flekù (tavern) 131
U Nováků 212
Újezd 155
Ungelt 207
Úvoz 116, 153

V

Vejvoda, Jaromir 269
Velkopřevorské náměstí
  156
Veltrusy Castle 267
Velvet Revolution 63
Vernier Palace 158
Vinohrady 217
Vltava 218
Vodičkova 211
Voyan Gardens 149
Vries, Adrien de 77
Vrtba Garden 154
Vyšehrad Cemetery 222
Vytoň 219

W

Wallenstein, Albrecht von
  213
Wallenstein Palace 212
Wallenstein Riding
  School 149
Wenceslas, Saint 54
Wenceslas Square 209
Wiehl Building
  (Wiehlhùv dùm) 212
Willmann, Michael 79

Z

Zbraslav 268
Zbyšov 261
Zelenka, Jan Dismas 91
Zlatá husa 211
Zoo 206
Zvíkov 269

Ž

Ženíšek, František 80
Žižka of Trocnov, Jan
  56, 224, 263
Žižkov 224